EXPERIMENTAL METHODS IN PSYCHOLOGY

EXPERIMENTAL METHODS IN PSYCHOLOGY

ROBERT C. CALFEE

Stanford University

HOLT, RINEHART AND WINSTON

New York Chicago San Francisco Philadelphia

Montreal Toronto London Sydney

Tokyo Mexico City Rio de Janeiro Madrid

Acknowledgment for permission to reproduce excerpts from previously published material is made to:

American Psychological Association. From Biederman et al. (1973) and Collingwood et al. (1978), papers published in the *Journal of Experimental Psychology* and the *Journal of Educational Psychology*, respectively. From Ethical principles in the conduct of research with human participants (1973). Copyright © 1973, 1978 by American Psychological Association, Washington, D.C.

Psychonomic Society Inc., Austin, Texas. From Klatsky et al. (1982), paper published in *Memory & Cognition*.

V. H. Winston & Sons, Silver Spring, Maryland. From Kulka and Kessler (1978), paper published in *Applied Social Psychology*.

Library of Congress Cataloging in Publication Data

Calfee, Robert C.
  Experimental methods in psychology.

  Includes index.
  1. Psychology, Experimental—Methodology.
2. Psychology—Research.   I. Title.

BF181.C245   1985   150′.72   84–9100

ISBN 0-03-018851-2

Address correspondence to

383 Madison Avenue
New York, NY 10017

5 6 7 8 9   039   9 8 7 6 5 4 3 2 1

CBS COLLEGE PUBLISHING

  Holt, Rinehart and Winston
  The Dryden Press
  Saunders College Publishing

Cover illustration: Fred Otnes / Bill Erlacher Artists Associates

Composition by York Graphic Services, Inc., York, Pennsylvania
Printing and binding by R. R. Donnelley & Sons Co., Chicago

To the memory of W. G. Chase

Preface

Ten years ago I wrote *Human Experimental Psychology*. That text combined methodology with content, and broke new ground by focusing on studies of human cognition as the basis for the undergraduate course in experimental psychology.

The tendency today is to concentrate once more on experimental methods: it is almost taken for granted in many places that the examples will be largely from studies of human cognition.

The goal of this book is to introduce the student to the work of the experimental psychologist, to the reasoning that underlies the development of a research question, the planning of an investigation, and the analysis and interpretation of the findings. Theory, measurement, design—these are central themes in this text. In addition, and consistent with the concentration on human cognition, there is detailed consideration of the "human" side of the experiment. Finally, separate chapters deal with the tasks of reviewing the literature, reading a research study, and writing an investigation.

This is not a text on statistics. Some students will have had an introduction to psychological statistics prior to the course; for them, the appendix should provide adequate review of basic statistical concepts and procedures. For the student who has not had statistics, the appendix will need instructional support.

After Chapter 1, most of the chapters are designed to stand alone. The order of presentation suits my purposes and style, but a different sequence should be quite feasible. The text is relatively lean, but has sufficient examples to flesh out the concepts. It is not a compendium; I have been relatively sparing of references. These decisions are consistent with the emphasis on method rather than content.

Several people have from time to time labored with me on this work; reviewers and editors contributed substantially to a clearer and more accurate final version of the book. I wish particularly to acknowledge James Anderson, Troy State University; Edwin Brainerd, Clemson University; Thomas Mehle, University of Nebraska/Lincoln; Terry Pettijohn, Ohio State University/Marion; Lanna Ruddy, SUNY/Geneseo; and Philip Young, Towson State University. The ideas and the techniques communicated spring from many other sources as well—instruction, guidance, and examples have come from many teachers, colleagues, students, and friends over the past twenty years. Finally, Jay Thorp has been the constant companion who kept all the pieces together, corrected my stylistic faux pas, asked good questions, and handled other tasks too numerous to list. I am especially grateful for her help.

R. C. C.

CONTENTS

Preface vii

1 The Structure of Psychological Experiments   1

What's the Question?   2
What's the Answer?   3
Psychological Theories   5
One Good Question Leads to Another   7
Factors, Levels, and Response Measures   8
Experimental Designs   11
What Does the Answer Mean?   15
Summary   17

2 Reviewing the Literature   19

Before You Begin   20
Varieties of Research Literature   21
The Research Report   26
Summary   38

3 The Psychological Experiment as a Social Situation   40

The Subject   40
The Experimenter   45
Interactions Between Experimenter and Subject   47
Experimenter Expectancy   47
The Ethical Responsibilities of the Experimenter   51
Summary   61

4 Collecting Psychological Data   63

The Ethnographic Method   64
Simple Data   68
Complex Data   77
The Interpretation of Psychological Data   88
Summary   95

5 Psychological Measurement   98
Detection, Discrimination, and Decision   99
Psychological Magnitudes   115
Integration of Information   126
Summary   135

6 Experimental Control   138
Variability   139
Confounding   151
Interaction   158
Experimental Procedures   162
Control in Subject Selection and Assignment   164
Summary   170

7 Between-subjects Designs   173
One-way Designs   173
Factorial Between-subjects Designs   187
Summary   203

8 Within-subjects and Mixed Designs   205
One-way and Factorial Within-subjects Designs   205
Mixed Designs   217
Choice of Between- or Within-subjects Variation in a Factor   223
Visual and Memory Search: A Laboratory Experiment   228
Enhancing Recall Through Novelty: A Field Study of Memory for Television News   236
Summary   241

9 How to Study a Research Report   244
The Contents of the Research Report   245
Two Examples   252
A Postscript   264
Summary   265

10 Writing a Research Report   266
Preparing to Write a Report   267
The First Draft   270
Revising the Final Report   271
An Example of Editing and Revision   276
Summary   297

Appendix: Statistical Analysis   299
Glossary   329
References   339
Index   347

EXPERIMENTAL METHODS IN PSYCHOLOGY

1

The Structure of Psychological Experiments

This book is about experimental psychology. More particularly, it is about the *methods* of experimental psychology, because it is these methods that distinguish the field. While we might define experimental psychology as "whatever experimental psychologists do," many researchers besides experimental psychologists use the same techniques: social and clinical psychologists, educational and developmental psychologists, linguists, anthropologists, sociologists, and even a few computer scientists now employ experimental methods in behavioral research.

In studying the various aspects of the experimental method of research you will recognize some overlap with other research methods. For instance, description is the foundation for virtually all scientific research; the naturalist depends on careful description as much as the anthropologist does. Hence, this book covers the descriptive techniques needed for experimental investigations. Issues of measurement—what it means to measure something, how one establishes the validity and reliability of a measure, and so on—are common to all science, and so this topic is also addressed.

Our primary aim is to explore the experimental method; to set forth the principles underlying it; and to describe the manner in which experiments are planned, observations taken, and data analyzed and interpreted. Several experimental techniques will be described, followed by a couple of examples, one from research in the laboratory and a second from reports of a more practical character. You will see how the behavioral researcher plans an investigation and carries it out, and how he or she makes sense of the findings and communicates them to others. You will learn about the importance of theory in formulating a research question and how theory aids in interpreting the results of an investigation.

This book emphasizes the study of cognition or thought processes in human beings. Such an emphasis does not mean that the experimental method is limited to these domains; a good deal of research in experimental psychology uses animal subjects, and many psychologists restrict themselves to the investigation of regularities in observable behavior without any particular concern for the underlying processes. The decision to concentrate on human psychology is based largely on the need for simplicity; the concepts and techniques for the study of animal behavior differ significantly from those for research on human beings. The focus on cognitive processes reflects the growing importance of this area within the field of experimental psychology.

This introductory chapter presents an overview of the reasoning behind the experimental method in psychology. The task of formulating a research question is discussed, as is the job of reaching a meaningful answer to the question. Research is by its nature a risky enterprise, with a lot of stumbling around in the dark; if the researcher already understood the phenomenon under investigation, experiments would be unnecessary. The challenge is to formulate the right question, after which follow-up studies may be relatively straightforward. Even in the best of circumstances, however, breakthroughs are less common than confusion and failure. In doing research it helps to have a certain amount of persistence and drive, as well as a dash of optimism and humor.

In this chapter you will also find a list of the major "building blocks" used in experimental research. As you have probably discovered in other science courses, one of the hurdles in any field of study is the vocabulary. Many of the terms in this chapter will be new to you; others will be familiar words with new meanings. These words will be used again and again in later chapters, and this first pass is intended to alert you to the importance of certain concepts and their labels.

WHAT'S THE QUESTION?

Psychological research serves two primary purposes. First, it helps us discover the variables that determine human behavior and the circumstances under which these influences hold sway. Second, it leads to the creation of theories that help us understand how people think and act. In achieving these ends the researcher's first step is the formulation of a scientific question, one that is clear and precise and that can be answered by objective evidence.

"Does noise slow a person's reactions?" This question is more complex than might appear at first glance but, suitably phrased, it can provide the starting point for a scientific investigation. Certain points require further elaboration. How is noise to be defined? Noise is not the same as loudness; it is characterized by a quality of obnoxiousness. Kryter (1966), noting that "there is a basic 'unwantedness' or 'noisiness' to sound beyond that due solely to its measurable loudness" (p. 1346), identified three features that appear critical to noise: high pitch, complexity, and length (more than a quarter-second). This analysis of basic issues is essential to formulating a research question. Notice that the definition offered by Kryter begins to identify the variables of potential relevance. The researcher would also have to answer a number of other questions: What reactions? What kinds of people? What kinds of situations? But all these questions are answerable. The question that begins this paragraph thus provides a reasonable basis for a scientific inquiry.

Not all questions are scientifically answerable. "Is noise bad for you?" cannot be answered scientifically because the answer depends on a value-laden judgment; one must resort to something other than the scientific method to decide the meaning of *bad*. Nor is "Do loud noises frighten away ghosts?" a valid scientific question, because it is impossible to obtain objective evidence about ghostly behavior. Until we develop more trustworthy methods for recording the activity of spirits, this question and others like it must remain outside the sphere of experimental inquiry.

Although personal experiences, thoughts, and feelings cannot be studied directly, people's reports of their experiences can serve as data for scientific inquiry. "Does noise really make people feel more irritable?" The word *really* is the problem here. We can certainly ask people to describe their feelings and experiences: "Tell me how you feel when you are exposed to various kinds of noise." The responses to such a question comprise objective data, which may demonstrate that people experience increased irritation in noisy environments. We define certain types of behavior as indicators of irritation and then show that these behavioral indicators increase with an intensification of noise. For instance, the subject may shout "I can't take this racket any more!" and leave the experimental room. Even this dramatic response is not a sure sign of what is *really* happening in the subject's mind. Nor is it essential to wrestle with this issue; for practical purposes we can go a long way by relying on observable behavior and verbal reports.

WHAT'S THE ANSWER?

An experiment is typically designed to test one or more hypotheses. The researcher may suspect that noise slows down a person's reactions and plans a study to investigate this proposition. The primary focus is on the effect of *noise* versus *no noise* on some performance measure. Other variables, many of which are not of immediate interest, may also influence performance. Noise may slow down the reactions of naturally calm people but speed up those of nervous people. The sound of jet planes near an airport may slow the work rate in nearby factories while rock music may increase it.

Suppose that, cognizant of such complexities, the researcher decides nonetheless to ignore all factors except the one or two of immediate concern. The "answer" yielded by such an experiment, whether or not it supports the investigator's hypothesis, will almost certainly be of limited applicability and may in fact be misleading. The findings of any given study depend on the context in which the study is carried out. In the present example, the effect of noise on people's reactions is likely to depend on the type of noise, its duration and intensity, the subject's ability to tolerate (or appreciate) the noise, the reactions being measured, the length of the study, and so on. For the results to be meaningful the investigator must identify these secondary sources of variation and must find a way to *control* them.

Research on behavioral and social questions is a challenge. Many factors may affect the outcome of any given study, and we lack trustworthy theories to guide our thinking about these complexities. As a consequence the researcher faces some tough decisions in planning an experiment. Which variables are most relevant to the outcome of the study? What kinds of subjects should be tested, and how many? A multifaceted experiment with many variables built into the design constitutes a rich source of information, but it is also difficult to plan and to manage. A simple design with one or two variables is easier to carry out, but the results are likely to be ambiguous and untrustworthy.

In a study of the effects of noise, for instance, should the subjects be male, or female, or both? If only one person is tested, the effects may depend in some unknown way on the characteristics of the particular individual.

	Ability?
Subject 1	Motivation?
	Gender?
	Age?
	Et cetera?

If two people are tested, then the investigator has at least a peek at individual differences. For instance, if gender is thought to be related to the effects of noise, then the experimenter can test one male and one female.

	Ability?
Subject 1	Motivation?
Male	Age?
	Et cetera?

	Ability?
Subject 2	Motivation?
Female	Age?
	Et cetera?

If resources permit the testing of four subjects, two subject variables can then be included in the design. For instance, suppose the researcher has a hunch that both gender and age are important determinants of the influence of noise on performance. With four subjects in the design, two college students and two middle-aged subjects—a male and a female from each age level—can be selected. This plan allows the experimenter to separate the effects of gender and age.

	Ability?
Subject 1	Ability?
Male	Motivation?
College	Et cetera?

Subject 2	Ability?
Male	Motivation?
Middle-aged	Et cetera?

Subject 3	Ability?
Female	Motivation?
College	Et cetera?

Subject 4	Ability?
Female	Motivation?
Middle-aged	Et cetera?

If the two middle-aged subjects both find noise objectionable compared with quiet while the college students report no difference, age may be an important factor in considering the effects of noise. If males and females both find noise equally objectionable (or rewarding), then gender can be eliminated as a control factor.

Now we can put together the "question" and the "answer." The researcher formulates a psychological question, in part by identifying a set of variables that are hypothesized to contribute substantially to variation in a performance measure. The choice of variables represents the investigator's "best guess" about the state of the world. The "answer"—the results of the experiment—depends greatly on the soundness of these initial decisions. The findings will be inconclusive if the primary variables are weak or if the researcher ignores secondary variables that produce large and unpredictable fluctuations in performance. Sometimes the answer is clear-cut but quite different from the experimenter's original hypothesis. If the original decisions are sound, the experimenter can learn something even from unexpected findings, which will help in planning a follow-up study. Surprises are not uncommon in behavioral research, and virtually never is a question answered with any certainty from the results of a single study.

PSYCHOLOGICAL THEORIES

A considerable amount of psychological research is generated by the psychologist's curiosity about the effects of particular variables on observable behavior. Empirically based experiments answer straightforward questions of the form "What will happen to X if I vary Y?"

- What is the effect on worker productivity when noise level is varied?

- What is the recall rate for strings of numbers ranging in length from six to twelve?

- If the goal is to ensure that people wear seat belts when driving , what is the relative effectiveness of (a) buzzers, (b) interlocks (the car will not start until the belts are fastened), (c) laws (the police arrest anyone whose belt appears not to be fastened), and so on?

- What is the relation between the number of people in a small group and the time taken to solve various types of problems?

Theoretical questions are generated by a different kind of curiosity, in which the psychologist puzzles about the events that underlie observable behavior. The researcher faces the same decisions in planning a theoretical study as in designing an empirical investigation. One must still select a set of factors and plan a design that will provide trustworthy and interpretable data. The model aids in selecting the variables and in interpreting the outcome of the research.

The most active theoretical arena in psychology at the present time falls under the heading of **information-processing theory**. The focus of this theoretical approach is on mental processes. The mind is seen as a kind of processor of information, which takes various inputs from the "outside world," transforms and translates them, and then produces behavioral responses as outputs.

Suppose you are a researcher interested in how a student adds two numbers. You select several addition problems and present them to a sample of students. You record the answer given by each student to each problem and the length of time taken to produce the answer. The observable measures are correctness and speed, both of which might be expected to vary with the difficulty of the problem ($50 + 20 = ?$ is likely to be easier than $47 + 26 = ?$). The observed relations between performance and difficulty do not tell you how the student is thinking, however. For this you must construct a model describing the thought processes in which difficulty can be related to performance in some clear-cut way. The predictions of the model can then be compared with the experimental findings.

To illustrate, consider two theoretical models for describing the mental processes that underlie the addition of a pair of single-digit numbers. One possibility is that the student computes the sum by mentally "counting on the fingers." In this case the larger the sum, the longer it should take to count up to the answer ($7 + 9 = ?$ should take longer than $3 + 2 = ?$). A second possibility is that the student looks up the numbers in a table in memory. Since the student must search the table for the answer no matter what the value of the two digits, the amount of time it takes to find the answer should be the same for any pair of digits.

How might we evaluate the two models? Both predict that the student will give the correct answer, and so data on accuracy are irrelevant to the comparison. The two models do differ in their predictions about the time required to add a pair of numbers. The counting model predicts that the response time will increase as the sum of the two numbers goes up. We therefore need to arrange all the sums in order of increasing value: $0 + 0 = 0$ is lowest; $0 + 1 = 1$ and $1 + 0 = 1$ are next; then $0 + 2 = 2$, $1 + 1 = 2$, and $2 + 0 = 2$; and so on. The counting model predicts

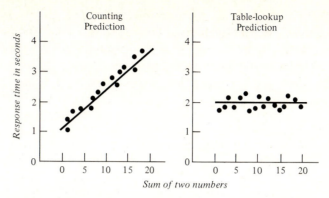

Figure 1–1 Hypothetical results based on counting models and table-lookup models of mental arithmetic

a steady increase in response time as the sum increases (Figure 1–1). The table-lookup model predicts that response time should be the same for all sums, as illustrated by the flat line in the right-hand panel of the figure. The scattering of dots in the two panels shows the kind of data that would be consistent with each of the models; we expect some variability or "noise" in the observations, but the general pattern of results is quite different for each.

As for any other kind of research, a theoretically oriented experiment must include attention to the fundamental question: What variables besides those of primary interest might influence performance? In the present case these variables might affect not only the trends in the data but the appropriateness of one or the other model. For instance, we might expect that the way the student has been taught to add might be important. Some mathematics programs emphasize rote memorization while others stress the concept of counting. Students in the first program might be expected to operate according to the table-lookup model, while students in a concept-oriented program would be more likely to perform in the manner of the counting model. The amount of practice a student has had may also matter. Younger students often find fingers a convenient device in calculating sums, but with practice the older student becomes quite fast with all sums. The researcher's instructions can make a difference, too. An emphasis on speed may cause a student to resort to a table-lookup strategy, while stress on accuracy may lead a youngster to cross-check by counting.

ONE GOOD QUESTION LEADS TO ANOTHER

Experimentation is a dynamic process. In planning an experiment the researcher makes many decisions on which the outcome of the study depends. The results may confirm some predictions, but there are likely to be surprises. These can lead to additional analyses, an altered set of decisions, and even a new experiment.

For instance, suppose that an experiment shows that exposure to noise slows the reactions of middle-aged people but has no effect on, or actually reduces, the reaction time of younger subjects. For a follow-up experiment the researcher might decide to investigate the underlying processes, the previous experiences, or the attitudes and preferences that could have produced the variation due to age.

As a second example, suppose that the experimenter has evaluated the two models of mental addition proposed earlier and that for second graders *neither* model describes the data adequately. Instead, the response time increases with the value of the smaller of the two numbers, so that $3 + 2 = ?$, $2 + 9 = ?$, and $6 + 2 = ?$ all take about the same time. Based on this pattern, the experimenter might then propose a model in which the student starts with the larger of the two numbers and then adds the second number by counting. This model predicts that the size of the larger number is not relevant, so that $13 + 2 = ?$, $2 + 17 = ?$, and $21 + 2 = ?$ should take the same response time, as should any other sum involving 2. This analysis can help the researcher plan the follow-up experiment.

A point made earlier deserves reemphasis here. Suppose that an experiment has been well planned and carefully implemented, but the findings show that the data contradict the hypothesis under test or that the critical variable has no effect. Such outcomes do not mean that the experiment is a failure. Psychological research is not a matter of setting up a batch of hypotheses like so many bowling pins and then trying to knock down as many as possible. Rather, the process is one of continual exploration. The researcher formulates a question based on practical need, intellectual curiosity, or theoretical analysis. The first study reveals something about the nature of the answer but is also likely to be incomplete or uninformative in some respects and to raise some new questions. The next study sheds additional light on the topic but also turns up new issues and puzzles. Sometimes the researcher makes a major breakthrough, and fireworks light the sky (or at least the pages of a journal). More often, research is a slow and painstaking activity, a matter of tracing a path through a complex maze, with many false turns and dead ends— and without any real assurance that the maze even has a solution.

FACTORS, LEVELS, AND RESPONSE MEASURES

The set of arrangements for carrying out an experiment is called the **experimental design**. This section of the chapter defines and illustrates the basic elements for constructing a design: factors, levels, and response measures.

Factors

A *factor* is a variable that the experimenter defines and controls in such a fashion that its effects can be evaluated. A factor is also referred to as an *independent variable*. In the experiment on noise, the factors might include the presence or absence of noise, the type of noise, its level and intensity, and the age and gender of the subjects. In the experiment on mental addition, the factors might be the sum of the two numbers, the method used to teach addition, the amount of practice, the experience of the students, and the instructions for the task.

It is helpful to distinguish three categories of factor: treatment, subject-classification, and nuisance factors. A **treatment factor** is an aspect of the environment that is directly manipulated by the experimenter; we generally think of these factors as variations in "experimental" treatments. For instance, suppose the researcher is interested in the effect of the amount of reward on performance in a learning task. Variation in the reward factor might entail paying one group of subjects ten cents for every correct answer while paying subjects in another group one dollar.

A **subject-classification factor** is a characteristic of the subject that is intrinsic and hence not easily modified but one that can be taken into account by the experimenter when selecting the sample of subjects. If the researcher includes both nine- and twelve-year-old students in a study, then age is a subject-classification factor. Gender, ability, and family background are other examples of subject-classification factors. Variables in this category allow the researcher to assess the extent of differences between individuals.

Nuisance factors are variables the experimenter builds into the design, not because of intrinsic interest in the effects but because the results are likely to be difficult to interpret if these factors are not included. Such factors are defined by their function in the design of the study and may be either treatment or subject-classification factors. While nuisance factors may be of no particular interest, the researcher cannot afford to ignore them. For instance, if the subject is tested several times during an experiment, then time should be included as a nuisance factor in the design. A person's performance may change over test trials, either because of learning or boredom or both. If the experimenter disregards the time factor, then changes in performance from one treatment condition to another may reflect variation due to the treatment conditions, the passage of time, or any combination of these two factors.

One point in the preceding paragraph deserves emphasis because of its importance: the designation of a variable in the study. A variable may be a nuisance factor in one design and a treatment or subject-classification factor in another. For instance, the researcher interested in the effects of payoff on learning rate is advised to include equal numbers of male and female subjects in each of the reward conditions. Even though the investigator may not be especially interested in the influence of the gender factor, only by including this variable in the design will there by any assurance that the findings are applicable to both sexes. A second researcher, with primary interest in the investigation of individual differences due to gender, may consider the male–female factor of primary interest as a subject-classification factor and variation in payoff a secondary or nuisance variable.

When deciding which nuisance factors to build into a design, the researcher is wrestling with the issue of **control.** The concept of control is dealt with more fully in Chapter 6; for the present you may simply imagine that an experiment is poorly controlled to the extent that one or more of its facets are not well designed. Control techniques consist of a set of procedures for designing, carrying out, and analyzing an experiment so as to ensure that the data provide a clear and convincing answer to the experimental question.

Levels

Each specific variation in a factor is called a **level** of the factor. In this book I will also on occasion use **condition** to refer to a level of factor, especially for treatment factors.

For some factors the number of levels is small. Male and female, for instance, are the only two levels for gender. Eye color and blood type are other examples of subject-classification factors with a small number of levels. Levels are often defined in a binary, "yes–no" fashion: *noise* versus *no noise* or *reward* versus *no reward*, for instance. Whenever the number of levels is restricted, the researcher faces a relatively simple decision; if the factor is to be incorporated in the design, then all levels will be included.

More often, the number of potential levels of a factor is very large, and so the choice of levels for the design is a major consideration in planning it. For instance, a factor may have many levels because it is quantitative; the subject's age, the duration or volume of a tone, or the amount of practice on a task can all be measured on a numerical scale, and so the experimenter has a virtually infinite number of choices. To be sure, some choices make more sense than others. Suppose the researcher is interested in the effects of the duration of a noisy tone on perceived discomfort. The experimenter might select 2.837 and 5.369 seconds as the levels of the tone-duration factor, but these levels would strike most people as rather bizarre.

A factor may also have many levels because it is inherently complex. For instance, the set of all brief verbal reinforcements is rather large: "That's fine!"; "Right!"; "Gee, I couldn't agree more!"; "That's the best idea I've heard yet!"; among others. While the experimenter's first inclination might be to consider every variation as a separate level, it would be more reasonable to attempt to categorize the various responses into a relatively small number of levels.

Response Measures

The researcher evaluates a subject's performance by means of one or more **response measures,** which are also referred to as *dependent variables.* Behavior in any given situation can generally be measured in a wide variety of ways, some quantitative and some qualitative. The researcher can record what is said or done, how long it takes to start or to finish an action, what the subject thinks about the situation, and so on. The experimenter may construct a test instrument to fit one particular study or select an "off the shelf" instrument with previously established standards and "norms." In most investigations, and especially when new ground is being broken, it is a good idea to assess performance in a variety of ways rather than to rely on a single index.

As mentioned above, measures may be quantitative and numerical or qualitative and descriptive. Examples of the first type include the number of correct answers on a reading test or the amount of time taken to complete the test. A more qualitative index might be a characterization of the mistakes on the test: failure on a more literal point, misinterpretation of an inference, or inability to comprehend the main point of the passage. Verbal responses to the Rorschach test are an instance of an especially complex descriptive measure.

EXPERIMENTAL DESIGNS

An experimental design is best thought of as the overall research plan. It spells out the arrangement of the treatment factors: what are the various conditions that have to be set up for assessment of the experimental question? It specifies the subject-classification factors: what kinds of individuals need to be selected for the sample? It defines the assignment of subjects to treatments: how does the researcher decide which subjects are to be placed in each of the treatment conditions?

Although the techniques of experimental design are commonsensical, it is important to make the underlying principles explicit so that common sense does not desert us when dealing with complex problems. Experimental design has a special vocabulary for these principles, and the remainder of this section lists some of the most important vocabulary terms in the area of design. These terms will be used again and again in the rest of the book, so you should think of this section as an overview.

One-way Designs. The simplest design entails variation in a single treatment factor. The sole purpose in such designs is to discover how performance is affected by the manipulation of one critical factor. Three research questions are listed below, each accompanied by a sketch of the design. S is an abbreviation for "subject," and the number after S indicates a particular subject; S1 is subject 1, S2 is subject 2, and so on. For these examples we will assume that the researcher has the resources to test five subjects in each treatment condition:

What is the difference in learning rate for rote associations when the subject has been administered a "memory" drug compared with subjects who are given a sugar tablet of similar appearance?

Memory Drug	Sugar Tablet
S1	S6
S2	S7
S3	S8
S4	S9
S5	S10

What happens to problem-solving skill as problem difficulty increases?

Easy Problem	Medium Problem	Difficult Problem
S1	S6	S11
S2	S7	S12
S3	S8	S13
S4	S9	S14
S5	S10	S15

What is the effect on feelings of stress as the number of hours without sleep is increased?

Number of Hours Without Sleep

24	36	48	60
S1	S6	S11	S16
S2	S7	S12	S17
S3	S8	S13	S18
S4	S9	S14	S19
S5	S10	S15	S20

One-way designs, as these plans are known, are quite simple. Unfortunately, they are also of limited usefulness in behavioral research since most problems are too complex to be understood by variation in a single factor. Nonetheless, these simple designs provide a useful foundation for learning the basic concepts of design and analysis, and so one-way designs will be our starting point later in the text when we go into the details of experimental design techniques.

Factorial Designs. Most problems investigated by psychologists and other behavioral scientists are sufficiently complex to require that several factors be included in the research plan to achieve adequate control. Consequently present-day studies are most likely to employ what are known as **factorial designs,** in which the researcher uses combinations of two or more factors to investigate a question.

Let us reexamine the research questions presented earlier and see how each one-way design might be recast as a factorial problem.

Some subjects are better than others at remembering nonsense materials (as we shall see later in the text, the reason for these differences may depend on the strategies used by individuals). The experimenter will gain a clearer picture of what is going on if each subject is pretested for "rote-memory skill" so that both high- and low-ability groups can be assigned to each treatment. One prediction is that the drug will have little effect on high-ability groups because they are already making full use of their mental capacity.

	Memory Drug	Sugar Tablet
High Ability	S1	S11
	S2	S12
	S3	S13
	S4	S14
	S5	S15
Low Ability	S6	S16
	S7	S17
	S8	S18
	S9	S19
	S10	S20

The effect of problem difficulty on problem-solving skill may depend on the impulsiveness of the problem solver. The researcher can investigate this possibility by selecting people who are either impulsive or reflective, giving to each group problems that range from easy to difficult.

	Easy Problem	Medium Problem	Difficult Problem
Impulsive	S1	S11	S21
	S2	S12	S22
	S3	S13	S23
	S4	S14	S24
	S5	S15	S25
Reflective	S6	S16	S26
	S7	S17	S27
	S8	S18	S28
	S9	S19	S29
	S10	S20	S30

The effects of sleep deprivation on stress may depend on the kind of task confronting the subject under this condition. A design to evaluate this possibility could assign groups of people to go without sleep for 24, 36, 48, or 60 hours and then ask them to undertake a simple and well-known chore or a complex and unfamiliar task.

Number of Hours Without Sleep

	24	36	48	60
Simple, Well-known	S1	S11	S21	S31
	S2	S12	S22	S32
	S3	S13	S23	S33
	S4	S14	S24	S34
	S5	S15	S25	S35
Complex, Unfamiliar	S6	S16	S26	S36
	S7	S17	S27	S37
	S8	S18	S28	S38
	S9	S19	S29	S39
	S10	S20	S30	S40

Each of these plans is a factorial design. While more complex to manage than a one-way design, factorial designs have a number of advantages. In particular, they provide improved control over the experiment, and (though it is not obvious from the examples) they are more efficient. The advantages and disadvantages of both plans are discussed in greater detail in later chapters.

Between- and Within-subjects Variations. Another important decision in planning a design is whether to assign different subjects to each level of a factor or to administer all levels of the factor to each subject. Random assignment of subjects to levels of a factor is referred to as a **between-subjects variation.** All of the examples presented above were of this type, with different subjects in each of the treatment conditions. When each person is tested on all levels of a factor, this is called a **within-subjects variation.** Sometimes this type of variation is referred to as the "subject serving as his or her own control." When the subject is tested under two or more treatment conditions, the researcher can determine the differential response of the individual. For instance, if a within-subjects plan were to be used for the memory-drug experiment, it would be possible to measure for each individual the difference in performance with the sugar tablet (the "control" condition) and with the memory drug. If a between-subjects plan is used, then the researcher must rely on averages over different groups of subjects to decide whether the memory drug is effective.

The decision about between- versus within-subjects variation depends on several considerations. Sometimes the researcher has little or no choice; subject-classification factors like gender or personality dictate a between-subjects plan. Convenience can also determine the decision. If each treatment takes only a minute or two to administer and the subject is available for an hour, it makes sense to use a within-subjects plan in which each individual is tested under a large number of conditions, if this is practical.

In many instances the experimenter confronts a genuine choice in arranging conditions for between- or within-subjects variation. Within-subjects designs tend to be more efficient and to provide a clearer picture of the treatment effects. But repeated testing of a subject can lead to problems: learning, fatigue, and interaction of one treatment with another, to name a few. To the extent that these problems can be resolved for a particular factor, the within-subjects plan is preferable, otherwise a between-subjects arrangement should be employed.

In most situations the result of such considerations is a **mixed design,** in which some of the factors are between-subjects and others are within-subjects. Details of how to make decisions about the design—frequently the most important step in planning an experiment—are discussed more fully in later chapters.

WHAT DOES THE ANSWER MEAN?

The researcher's ultimate goal is to reach some reasonably clear-cut conclusions from the evidence produced by an experiment. Problems arise when the general questions in the researcher's mind are not well matched by the specific questions that the experiment, as actually designed, can answer. Mismatches can occur when the researcher is not completely clear about the purposes of the experiment and hence lacks direction when planning it. They can also occur because choices must be made in designing an experiment, and choices entail compromises. These choices may seem straightforward and justifiable at the outset, but they take on a different perspective after the data have been collected and the researcher begins to interpret the findings.

The results of any particular experiment are of little interest in and of themselves; their value lies in what they tell us about a broader range of situations. The experimenter's decisions in planning an investigation are crucial in determining how far one can "go beyond the information given," to use Bruner's (1957) phrase. If the experiment has been thoughtfully planned and carefully executed, the researcher can be relatively confident in making generalizations.

The researcher is well advised during the planning of an experiment to keep two "bottom-line" questions in mind. Neither presents a pleasant prospect, but better to worry about them early in the game, when remedies are possible, than wait until it is too late:

> If the results do turn out as expected, what *alternative* interpretations might make as much sense as the one proposed? That is, are the findings crucial evidence in support of a particular hypothesis, or can they be explained in some other way?
>
> If the results do *not* turn out as expected, how will this outcome be explained? It may be difficult to consider the possibility that your predictions will fail, but such failures do occur, and not uncommonly. The researcher needs to put personal convictions aside from time to time and reflect on the possibility that he or she may need to rethink the question.

Reflecting on unpleasant situations is difficult and frustrating. It is not easy for a person to consider the possibility that an enterprise will not turn out as desired or that someone else's interpretation of an event may make better sense than one's own. Only by adopting this frame of mind, however, can the researcher sustain the critical and analytic perspective that leads to continual refinements in the design. If plausible alternatives to the original explanation can be found, the researcher should seek ways to improve the plan so that the findings permit a clear choice between the competing explanations. This style of thought is the foundation for establishing what has been referred to previously as *experimental control*.

For instance, suppose the researcher has hypothesized that subjects exposed to loud and intermittent noise will make more errors on a proofreading task than subjects in a quiet surrounding. Here is a simple one-way design for testing this hypothesis:

Quiet	*Noisy*
S1	S6
S2	S7
S3	S8
S4	S9
S5	S10

Let us assume that the results are as predicted. This finding may mean that intense noise interferes with attention to the task. Another interpretation, however, is that the subject's performance is disrupted because of stress due to unpredictable interruptions of a difficult task. An extension of the noise versus no-noise design allows an evaluation of these two hypotheses, both of which might be influencing performance to some degree. The revised design includes combinations of the two factors, one related to the effects of intensity and the other to the influence of predictability:

	Soft Noise	*Loud Noise*
	S1	S11
Predictable	S2	S12
	S3	S13
	S4	S14
	S5	S15
	S6	S16
Not	S7	S17
Predictable	S8	S18
	S9	S19
	S10	S20

This new design is more complex than the original, and as laid out it requires twice the number of subjects. However, the results are more meaningful because the alternate interpretation can be evaluated.

Hindsight always comes easier than foresight, but the more a researcher considers problems and ambiguities before an investigation, the greater the likelihood that the data will be conclusive. While little can be done to improve a design after the results are in, a certain amount of common sense is also warranted. Any proposal can be subjected to questions and criticisms without end, and the researcher may agonize over innumerable theoretical and practical matters, but finally decisions must be made. With reasonable planning the results should shed new light on the experimental question. The answer will not be complete, nor will it be certain, but a handful of good data is better than none.

Scientific knowledge accumulates gradually, and advances come at a frustratingly slow pace. Research is not for those who prefer quick, simple, and final answers to complex questions. Patience and endurance are needed. As in working a jigsaw puzzle, with each additional investigation the researcher adds a piece to the overall picture and learns something about the pieces to look for next. This book describes some of the procedures and strategies for tackling the puzzles of behavioral research and presents examples of some relatively successful "solutions." The landscape of behavioral research is by no means a rose garden, but neither is it entirely bleak. The methods of experimental psychology have taught us far more about how to improve the conditions of life than we have the political and economic means to accomplish.

SUMMARY

The goals of psychological research are to investigate the factors that influence observable behavior and to construct theories of the processes that underlie it. The researcher typically begins with a general question, which is then elaborated and refined until the foundation is laid for an experiment. An important part of the planning process is the identification of the factors that are viewed as the most significant determinants of a given behavior. Behavior is determined by many factors, and so the results of any one experiment can provide only a partial picture of the complete situation.

A psychological theory is a description of the processes underlying observable behavior. In planning a theoretical study the researcher makes many of the same decisions as are made for an empirical investigation. The data from an experiment can reveal the adequacy (or shortcomings) of a theoretical model and can suggest the conditions under which the theory is applicable. In turn, a good theory can help guide the planning of an experiment, aid in the interpretation of the findings, and provide direction for further research on a problem.

Several technical terms were introduced in this introductory chapter. A *factor* is a variable that is under the control of the experimenter. A *level* is a specific variation or condition for a particular factor. The levels of a factor may be restricted to a small number of categories: male versus female or the presence versus the absence of a particular treatment. In other instances a factor may have a large number of levels, as in the case of a quantitatively defined factor or one that is inherently complex.

Most factors fall into one of three categories. A *treatment* factor entails manipulation of environmental conditions by the experimenter. For instance, in a study of driving performance, the treatment factors might include the driving conditions ("daytime with dry roads" and "rainy night" are two levels of this complex factor), number of lanes on the highway, number of hours without sleep, amount of alcohol consumed during the hour preceding the test, and so on. A *subject-classification* factor is a preexisting characteristic of the subject. In the driving study, subject-classification factors might include age, driving experience, gender, personality profile, and so on. A *nuisance* factor refers to variations that are controlled by the investigator to ensure that the results can be interpreted without ambiguity. Nuisance factors may be either treatment or subject-classification factors under other circumstances. The researcher does not have a special interest in nuisance factors, but to ignore them is to jeopardize the clarity of the findings. For instance, the researcher may not be interested in the effects of the make, style, size, and horsepower of the automobile on driving performance, but when these factors are included in the design, information about the applicability of the findings to a wide range of vehicle types is obtained.

A *response measure* is an index of the subject's performance under the conditions of the experiment. The measure may be quantitative and numerical, such as the number of driving errors during a thirty-minute driving simulation or the proportion of the total driving time during which the driver is at risk; or it may be qualitative and descriptive, such as a written evaluation by an observer during the driving task. The researcher is well advised to record a variety of measures during an experiment, especially when the problem is relatively unexplored.

Finally, the interpretation of the experimental findings is the researcher's effort to show how the findings shed light on the original question. The interpretation necessarily goes beyond the data, extending to situations that were not included in the design of the experiment. The experimenter can have more confidence in these generalizations when he or she considers alternative explanations *before* rather than *after* the experiment is conducted. Are there explanations of the predicted findings that differ from those that the experimenter has in mind? What will be the explanation if the results are not as expected? If nothing is found? If the findings contradict the predictions? The researcher should keep these questions continually in mind during the planning of an experiment. By reflecting on these sometimes distressing possibilities, the researcher is often led to improvements in the design of the investigation.

2

Reviewing the Literature

When I entered graduate school to study psychology, I subscribed to several research journals and made a resolution to read the preceding ten years' research in order to acquire an adequate knowledge of studies already undertaken. Now, many years later, I still find it hard to keep up with the research reports that pile up on my desk each month, and my knowledge of previous research is highly selective, to say the least. This mountain of research journals, reports, books, and so on, some in my office, some at home, shelf after shelf in the library, and now even spools of computer records—this is the *literature*. Somewhere in this array lies the answer to the question "What is already known about a research question?" Here is the challenge when the professor says "Your assignment is to review the literature. . . ."

You as a student coming new into the field of behavioral science face a frustrating task: how to become familiar with past research. At first you may feel that you know too little, but you may quickly come to sense that you know too much. How can you most efficiently achieve a reasonable level of understanding of a particular topic? This chapter presents a strategy for attaining that goal.

The method described here is based on two distinctions. First, you need to distinguish among the various kinds of reports found in the research literature: reviews, summaries, abstracts, and research papers. Second, you must learn to know when to select and skim and when to immerse yourself in detailed study of a paper. This chapter begins with a description of the different sources of information and the uses of each. Next it discusses how to select one or two critical research papers so you can gain a first-hand acquaintance with actual research on a topic, a process that requires intelligent skimming. (Discussion of how to study a research paper will be postponed until Chapter 9.) The chapter ends with a concrete example of how to use a carefully selected research paper for "getting into the literature."

BEFORE YOU BEGIN

What to Look for. The next section of the chapter introduces you to the various sources of research literature, but first a few words about what to look for and what to expect. Before undertaking a review it may be important for you to reflect on your notions of the topic, including why it has captured your interest. In addition, these general questions, which might not have occurred to you initially, can provide a useful perspective:

- What are the recurring themes, issues, and theoretical questions?

- What variables are most commonly the focus of the investigations?

- Which researchers seem to be most frequently mentioned in the reports?

- What journals and other publications are typically referenced by the authors?

- What review sources are mentioned, if any?

The Writing Style. If yours has been a sheltered life you may need to prepare yourself for the kind of writing that is typical of research papers. The organization and style of scientific articles differs substantially from that of the literature with which you are most familiar: writing intended to inform, to persuade, or to amuse. The chief aim of scientific writing is to present the facts as concisely as possible, with only those interpretations and comments that are supported by the facts. As Kerlinger (1973) puts it:

> It is not the function of the investigator to *convince* the reader of the virtue of the research. Rather, it is to *report* as expeditiously and clearly as possible, what was done, why it was done, the outcome of the doing, and the investigator's conclusions. The report should be written so that the reader can reach his [or her] own conclusions as to the adequacy of the research and the validity of the reported results and conclusions. (p. 694)

The consequence is that the scientific style of writing is compact, often dry, and sometimes given to jargon. Some writers manage in spite of these constraints to achieve a degree of sparkle and humor, and many attain such clarity and precision that reading their papers is a genuine pleasure. On the other hand, writing skill is not strongly correlated with scientific creativity, and on occasion you may find yourself struggling to understand a topflight piece of research couched in turgid and muddled prose. A report may be so poorly crafted, with sentences that are overly long and words that are poorly chosen, that you must virtually translate the piece.

Not much can be done to change works already in print. (I have taken some liberties with a few of the examples presented in this book, and those scholars who excel in review of the research literature sometimes work miracles in interpreting papers that might otherwise go unnoticed because they are so difficult to understand.) Fortunately, recent trends encourage writing that is clear and readable, that avoids jargon when possible, and that even permits writers to express their own personality and character on occasion:

> Absolute insistence on the third person and the passive voice has been a strong tradition in scientific writing. Authorities on style and readability have clearly shown that this practice results in the deadliness and pomposity that they call "scientificese." . . . Now, reputable journals are breaking the tradition with notable success, and writing manuals are recommending a more personal style. . . . If any discipline should appreciate the value of personal communication, it should be psychology. (APA, 1974, p. 28)

To be sure, there is little new under the sun. You might enjoy skimming a few psychology journals from the 1930s and 1940s for examples of a rich and personal style that contrasts noticeably with present practice.

VARIETIES OF RESEARCH LITERATURE

When you first set forth to learn about a problem area, it is best to search through a variety of sources so that you gain a perspective on the kinds of coverage available. A valuable lead, and one that should not be overlooked, is your introductory textbook. Assuming that you found it readable and stimulating, look up the relevant topics in the index or chapter headings and examine the references provided there. Other gateways to the research literature include abstracts, reviews and theoretical papers, and primary research reports.

Abstracts and Indices

Several services provide behavioral and social scientists with an abbreviated but up-to-date list of current articles organized by topic and author. Some of the services list reports according to author, title, key word, and source. These are typically referred to as indices. Others provide a brief summary of the major points in a research report along with other information. These are called abstracts.

Among the most important services available to the behavioral sciences are *Psychological Abstracts, Child Development Abstracts, Current Index to Journals in Education (CIJE), Dissertation Abstracts, Science Citation Index,* and *Social Science Citation Index.* Associated with these services are computer search systems. PASAR (Psychological Abstracts Search and Retrieval) and ERIC (Educational Resources Information Center) are available on many campuses, and for a modest fee anyone can conduct a "key word" search through these compilations.

The sources are listed above in the approximate order of their usefulness to undergraduate students. *Psychological Abstracts* covers the broad array of topics investigated by scholars in the field (at last count, more than 750 journals from the

United States and other countries); *Child Development Abstracts* ranges more widely than you might think from the title, as does *CIJE*; the citation indices are enormous, and relatively few of the references contained in them are from psychology, although there are cross-references to related papers.

Figure 2–1, which shows segments from *Psychological Abstracts*, gives an idea of how the system works. Typically, you will enter the abstracts either through the Subject Index (in case you know the topic in which you are interested), or the Author Index (in case you want to follow the work of a particular individual). Each entry is tagged with one or more code numbers, which provide the cross-reference to the actual abstract. To the left in Figure 2–1 is a segment from the Author section; the entry of interest to us is the one by Richard Kulka, which has the code number 11969. In the center panel is a segment from the Subject section; the main topic is adjudication, which includes as a specific entry an article on "Litigant physical attractiveness," and so on, with the same code number.

The abstract itself, which appears on the right side of Figure 2–1, contains several chunks of information. First is the code number, which is used only by the abstracting service and does not appear anywhere on the published article. Next is the name and institution of the author or authors and the title of the paper, both in boldface type. The complete citation or reference follows: the name of the journal, the year of publication, the volume and issue number, and the pages. Then there is the actual abstract, usually taken directly from the paper. Finally, there is a count of the number of references in the article. This particular piece contains quite a few references, far more than the average for a research paper.

Once you have located a few critical researchers on a topic, *Science Citation Index* and *Social Science Citation Index* provide a tool for tracking down other current research in this area, because researchers doing related work generally cite the works of these individuals. The citation indices list current articles according to the authors referenced by each article. Since indices operate in reverse of abstracts, an example may help. Figure 2–2 presents a few of the articles from the 1983 *Social Science Citation Index* that referenced papers that I have written. The information is dense and must be unpacked with care. The list is headed by the name of the author being cited. The next heading, which is indented, is the reference information for the article being cited in a particular instance. The first listing under my name is a 1970 paper that I published in *Perceptual and Motor Skills*, volume 31, page 895. This paper was referenced by D. von Winte in *Psychological Bulletin*, volume 91, page 609, in 1982. From this listing I cannot tell anything about the topic or the substance of the report; for that information I would have to look up the article by von Winte. But it is a lead, and that is the purpose of the citation indices. If you decode the other two entries, you will discover that Rebecca Barr, a colleague at Chicago, referenced a paper of mine in the *Journal of Teacher Education* on page 75 of a book, and that Gerry Duffy mentioned a paper I published in the 1981 *Reading Research Quarterly* in his 1982 article in the same journal (the abbreviations can be found in the citation index). An interesting approach, somewhat reminiscent of a detective novel.

AUTHOR

Kunn, Deanna, 7316
Kuhn, Donald M., 4548
Kiihne, D., 9886
Kuhnert, Karl W., 8520
Kuiper, A., 11158
Kuipers, Benjamin, 2566
Kulczycki, J., 3560
Kuleck, Walter J., 6493
Kulhavy, Raymond W., 4276, 12904
Kulich, Ronald J., 5498
Kulikowski, J. J., 8808
Kulka, Richard A., [11969]
Kulkosky, Paul J., 11574
Kulzer, Erwin, 4773
Kumar, Pramod, 9518
Kumar, R., 7208, 9753, 11893
Kumar, R. Ravi, 6475
Kumar, Shailendra, 3563
Kumari Bachan, 5509
Kumar Khattri, Pradeep, 3234
Kumea (Shorter, D. L.), 11894
Kummer, Hans, 9001
Kun, Anna, 5450
Kunce, Joseph T., 5539, 5631, 10956
Kundi, M., 10730
Kundu, Gorachand, 5298
Kunimoto, Savuri, 7327

(p. 32 of Index)

SUBJECT

Adjudication
age & type of crime & mental disorder & ability to stand trial & pretrial treatment, comparative review of forensic psychiatry caseloads, 3175
assessing probabilities of compound vs component events in judicial context, law students, 221
authoritarianism, individual & group judgments about guilt & punishment & verdict change following deliberation, college students, 9624
California Supreme Court case decision, therapist liability to nonpatient victim, 906

— — —

legal & mental health collaboration, development of social policy for child custody, 11892
legal vs psychiatric criteria & community & institutionally based evaluation, determination of competency to stand trial, defendants, 5339
litigant physical attractiveness, simulated juridical judgment, college students, implications for judicial process, [11969]
model for use of psychological evaluation services, referral process & adequacy of evaluation in courts & correctional organizations, 7506
offender reaction & admission of involvement, likelihood of being recommended for probation, sex offenders, 9560
outcome of treatment following recommendations & hospitalization & discharge with resultant changes in mental status, men remanded into custody for medical reports, 8216
parent characteristics & behavior patterns & impact on child & treatment considerations, father-daughter incest, legal implications, 7780

(p. 75 of Index)

ABSTRACT

[11969] Kulka, Richard A. & Kessler, Joan B. (U Michigan Inst for Social Research, Ann Arbor) Is justice really blind? The influence of litigant physical attractiveness on juridical judgment. *Journal of Applied Social Psychology*, 1978 (Oct–Dec); Vol 8(4), 366–381. —Examined the influence of litigant physical attractiveness on the decisions of 91 undergraduates playing the role of nondeliberating jurors in an automobile negligence trial. Seeking to achieve a more realistic simulation of actual courtroom practice than that produced in prior studies, which have relied exclusively on short written synopses as their method of trial presentation, this experiment tested the hypothesis that physical attractiveness would have a significant impact on juridic judgments even though an audiovisual presentation of the trial permitted the introduction of a variety of other important stimuli typically present at a jury trial. This prediction received empirical support: Ss exposed to an attractive plaintiff and an unattractive defendant more often found in favor of the plaintiff and awarded more money in damages than Ss viewing an unattractive plaintiff and an attractive defendant. However, in contrast to findings from general studies of interpersonal evaluation, analyses of Ss' perceptions of the 2 litigants provided only limited evidence for a global (positive) physical attractiveness stereotype within the context of a simulated trial. Instead, the observed effect of physical attractiveness on Ss' decisions was apparently mediated by differential perceptions of the seriousness of the accident itself. Implications for the judicial process are mentioned. (66 ref)
—*Journal abstract.*

(p. 1333 of Abstracts)

Figure 2–1 Excerpts from *Psychological Abstracts*, showing entry 11969, "Is justice really blind?" (*Psychological Abstracts*, 1980 [Jan–Jun], 63[2], pages indicated.)

cited author

CALFEE R . . .

cited reference yr, journal, vol, page

70 PERCEPT MOTOR SKILL 31 895

citation source author, journal, volume, page, year

VON WINTE D PSYCHOL B 91 609 82

76 J TEACHER ED 27 323

BARR BK# 26572   75 82

81 READING RES Q 16 346

DUFFY GG READ RES Q   17 4388 82

Figure 2–2 Excerpt from *Social Science Citation Index*, showing selected citations for R. CALFEE. (*Social Science Citation Index*, 1983, column 863.)

Abstract, index, and citation sources contain a great deal of information packed into a small space. No effort is made to evaluate the articles; because all of the articles are from "refereed" journals (i.e., the journal editor relies on a panel of experts in the field to referee each paper and decide whether it is suitable for publication), it is assumed that each paper is of reasonable quality.

While these sources are invaluable to the experienced researcher, the novice needs guidance in learning to use them. The information is so compact, the terminology so specialized, and the prior knowledge required so extensive that before you launch out on a search, you should be sure that you have a fairly clear idea of what to look for and of how to manage the mass of information that you may quickly accumulate. It is often better to gain some familiarity with a problem through some of the resources described below and then, based on that knowledge, to venture forth into abstracts and the like.

Reviews and Theoretical Papers

A large number of useful sources are covered by this heading. There are journals like *Psychological Review* and *Psychological Bulletin* and volumes like *Annual Review of Psychology*. The *Review* and the *Bulletin* are published several times a year and contain articles on a wide variety of topics from many areas of psychology, as indicated by this sampling of titles:

Group versus individual performance: Are N + 1 heads better than one? (G. W. Hill, *Psychological Bulletin*, May 1982)

Influential companions: Effects of one strategy on another in within-subjects designs of cognitive psychology (E. C. Poulton, *Psychological Bulletin*, May 1982)

Phonetic trading relations and context effects: New experimental evidence for a speech mode of perception (B. H. Repp, *Psychological Bulletin*, July 1982)

The problems of flexibility, fluency, and speed-accuracy trade-off in skilled behavior (D. G. MacKay, *Psychological Review*, September 1982)

A cognitive-social learning model of social-skill training (G. W. Ladd and J. Mize, *Psychological Review*, April 1983)

This list suggests the variety of topics covered in these journals—along with the predilection for colons, hyphens, and occasional jargon. The reader needs background and time to make full use of these sources.

Annual Review provides a relatively systematic source of summary information; certain topics are covered every year (physiological psychology, developmental psychology, educational and counseling psychology, cognition and learning, motivation, perception and sensory psychology, personality, personnel and organizational psychology, psychopathology, and social psychology), while others are included every two or three years (comparative psychology, psychology and the law, and the history of psychology). Less formal articles of a review character can be found in *Psychology Today* and occasionally in *Scientific American*. More focused but generally excellent summaries appear in series like *The Psychology of Learning and Motivation, Attention and Performance, Advances in Child Development and Behavior, Progress in Experimental Personality Research, Nebraska Symposium on Motivation, Advances in Experimental Social Psychology,* and *Progress in Behavior Modification,* among others; and this list could be extended.

American Psychologist, a journal designed to serve the needs of all psychologists, publishes many of the "invited addresses" by leaders in the field. At the national and regional conventions of psychologists, outstanding members of the association are asked to report on their research activities, and these speeches, when printed in *American Psychologist,* provide a wide range of information, as exemplified by these titles from the February 1983 issue of the journal:

Profile analysis: A different view of auditory intensity discrimination (D. M. Green)

The role of social support in adherence to stressful decisions (I. L. Janis)

The journal, which is published once a month, also lists the journals published by the American Psychological Association (APA); articles of general interest, including reviews of topical issues; and advertisements for recent books and journals. More than half of all psychological research is reported in journals that are *not* published by APA. *American Psychologist* also contains professional notes and letters from individual psychologists expressing their opinion about "hot topics."

A number of general handbooks have been published over the past few years, including Carterette and Friedman (1973–1978), Estes (1975–1978), Kling and Riggs (1971), Lindzey and Aronson (1968), and Mussen (1970), among others. They are quite systematic and are generally compendious—they attempt to bring together and present in concise form *everything* that is known on a topic—but they run the danger of becoming dated. Still they can be a useful starting point if you do not try to understand every detail provided. They are often excellent reference sources and are worth looking into when you have gathered the basic information and need to evaluate your own analysis of the topic.

All of these sources have certain features in common. A review paper aims to bring together and integrate the available research and theory on a particular topic or in a particular domain. Reviews vary in their emphasis on comprehensiveness versus integration. In some instances the aim seems mainly to accumulate a complete and extensive bibliography, with relatively little effort to criticize and integrate the information available. In other instances the writer is more selective, focusing on fewer papers but subjecting each to a careful critique, with attention to both strengths and weaknesses. Finally, you will occasionally encounter a paper that succeeds in the difficult task of tying together an entire body of research, achieving a coherent understanding of the problem as a whole. The integration may be achieved through an empirical scheme, through analogy, or through a formal theory. The result may not be the final word—the chances of this are always slight—but at least the reader is able to grasp the existing state of affairs. Such reviews are especially helpful when you are the "new person on the block."

As noted above, theory provides one approach to integrating a body of research. Most psychological theories tend to be heuristic rather than formalistic; that is, they tend to justify rather than to predict. There are exceptions to this generalization, and you are increasingly likely to encounter papers built on a solid theoretical foundation in which the author begins with a statement of the model—of the assumptions and consequences—after which relevant data are presented. The theoretician may recount studies from his or her own laboratory or may rely in part or in whole on the research of others. In any event the emphasis in such papers is on the development and exposition of a particular theoretical position, and less attention is likely to be given to the experimental procedures. Papers of this genre have some limitations, but for the beginner they have the advantage of focusing attention on a coherent set of ideas and findings. *Psychological Bulletin* and *Psychological Review* publish theoretical papers, as do a number of relatively new journals, primarily those in the field of cognitive psychology (*Cognitive Psychology*, *Cognitive Science*, *Discourse Processes*, and *Journal of Mathematical Psychology*, among others).

THE RESEARCH REPORT

The research report, most usually a journal article, is the keystone of the literature on a topic. Each report describes one or more experiments in detail, with a presentation of the problem under investigation, the methods used in the research, an analysis of the findings, and an interpretation of the results. A well-written research report provides all the information needed by another psychologist to replicate the study; that is, to redo the original investigation more or less exactly.

One of the best ways of "getting into the literature" is to discover a few research reports that are reasonably up to date and are critically related to the topic in which you are interested. Once you have succeeded in identifying some promising candidates, the Introduction, Discussion, and Reference sections of these papers can serve as a starting point for locating other promising sources. The task is not only to study the experiments presented in the body of the report, though you will probably want to do so, and detailed advice on how to proceed will be presented in Chapter 9. In addition you can take advantage of the author's expertise as a sort of mini-review (for that is what a good introduction is) of the most pertinent issues and the most informative references to other work.

The more general surveys found in the sources described previously have the advantage of framing the issues in a broad perspective. This can be quite useful once you have some understanding of the area but can be overwhelming when you are a newcomer. It usually makes more sense to bite off a small piece of the problem and work on that until you are satisfied that you have a reasonably good understanding of research procedures, methods of analysis, and patterns of results. The research paper is ideal for this purpose; matters that can be fuzzy and ill defined in the abstract take on a clearer image when seen in a specific context. I am *not* suggesting that you base your review of the literature solely on the introductions from one or two research papers. Balance is essential, and you need to establish linkages between the specifics found in the research report and the broader perspectives to be gained from major reviews.

The Process of Selection

The strategy of using the research report as the starting point for a literature review has many advantages, but the success of this approach depends on the process of selection. A procedure I have found effective on many occasions is based on the assumption that one of the most important considerations in the choice of key papers is that they be up to date. You may not always be led to the very best research, but you are likely to discover the most recent thinking about the topic, and this will usually direct you to a solid foundation.

To begin, you must find out which journals publish reports on the topic in which you are interested. Your introductory textbook should provide some clues; scanning through the list of periodicals (or serials) in your library will also help. Don't forget to check in *American Psychologist* for the listing of APA journals. Finally, Figure 2–3 (page 28) lists several behavioral science journals organized according to major domains in psychology.

Once you have identified the most promising journals, scan the table of contents of the most recent issue, looking for promising titles. Whenever an inter-

General Research
  American Journal of Psychology
  Behavioral Science
  British Journal of Psychology
  Bulletin of the Psychonomic Society
  Canadian Journal of Psychology
  Journal of Experimental Analysis of Behavior
  Journal of Experimental Psychology: General
  Journal of General Psychology
  Journal of Mathematical Psychology
  Psychological Reports
  Quarterly Journal of Experimental Psychology
  Scandinavian Journal of Psychology
Learning and Thinking
  Cognitive Psychology
  Journal of Experimental Psychology: Human Learning and Memory
  Journal of Verbal Learning and Verbal Behavior
  Memory and Cognition
Perception and Performance
  Journal of Applied Psychology
  Journal of Experimental Psychology: Human Perception and Performance
  Perception and Psychophysics
  Perceptual and Motor Skills
Educational Psychology
  American Educational Research Journal
  British Journal of Educational Psychology
  Educational and Psychological Measurement
  Journal of Educational Measurement
  Journal of Educational Psychology
  Review of Educational Research
Developmental Psychology
  Child Development
  Developmental Psychology
  Journal of Experimental Child Psychology
Social and Personality
  Journal of Applied Social Psychology
  Journal of Experimental Research in Personality
  Journal of Experimental Social Psychology
  Journal of Personality and Social Psychology
    [formerly *Journal of Abnormal and Social Psychology*]
Animal Behavior
  Journal of Comparative and Physiological Psychology
  Journal of Experimental Psychology: Animal Behavior

Figure 2–3 Journals publishing experimental research in psychology, organized according to primary focus (partial listing)

esting lead turns up, skim the Abstract and the Introduction to see whether you are on the right track (titles can be misleading). The Abstract is generally printed in small type, and as noted earlier the writing tends to be very compact and technical. Nonetheless, with patience and care you can make your way through this telegraphic message and with practice it will become easier to "read an abstract."

Looking at the Discussion, which is located at the end of the research report, can also provide useful clues. You may find it difficult to comprehend this material in some instances; after all, you will not have read the main body of the report and so you won't have all of the context. Nonetheless, a few items may leap out from the page, telling you that you are on the right track. Finally, read the list of references at the end of the report. Which authors are mentioned? Which journals are listed? What are the dates of the articles? Are any review papers among the references?

After you have gone through the most recent issue of each of the journals on your list, work backward through successively earlier issues in similar fashion until you have enough material for serious study. Don't spend a great deal of time on a journal if you are not striking pay dirt and stop the search as soon as you have located a reasonable number of prospects: three to five key articles should suffice to keep you busy at the task of thoroughly understanding them and of following up the cross-references.

Here is a summary of how to select a set of research reports:

1. Skim quickly through one or more *convenient* overview sources: your introductory text, the card catalogue, reviews, or the like. You are looking for names and for journals.

2. Identify one or two journals that appear to be good sources for the research topic in which you are interested.

3. Beginning with the most recent issues of these journals, search through the table of contents for titles that seem relevant to your topic. Work backward through successively earlier issues until you have located some good candidates. If you have to go back more than ten years, you are looking in the wrong place, you do not have a well-defined topic, or there is no literature to be found.

4. For each of the promising candidates, look through the Introduction, the Discussion, and the Reference sections to learn what the authors have to say about your topic and to locate any other promising leads.

This strategy has served me well through the years, but it does have some limitations that should be mentioned. If your aim is to carry out a *comprehensive* review of the literature, this approach can easily lead you to focus on too narrow a set of issues, researchers, and paradigms. To achieve breadth you are better advised to begin with the abstracts and indices listed earlier or with review sources. These are technically more demanding and often require a modicum of experience. They provide a much richer source of information, however.

The tradeoff is between detailed and concrete knowledge of an issue versus broad but relatively superficial knowledge. It is usually impossible to satisfy both criteria when you are new to a field, and so you must decide what is important for your immediate purposes and proceed accordingly. Scientific psychology has become an increasingly technical field during the past quarter-century, and my experience leads me to advise students who are new to the area to master one or two specific domains and then undertake the task of more comprehensive summary and integration.

Two Examples. This section presents the Introduction and Reference sections of two research reports. The first, which discusses the role of pictorial and verbal cues in memory for faces, is a laboratory experiment. The introduction is a good example of how to present a problem, review the issues, and present contrasting hypotheses, all laying the groundwork for the series of experiments reported in the article. The introduction is sharply focused on the issues of central importance, and many of the references are drawn from the primary author's previous studies.

In the second report, the problem is of a more practical nature: does an individual's appearance influence a jury's decision to convict or acquit him or her of a crime? The researchers, while stressing the importance of realism, are nonetheless able to create a well-controlled experimental design for the investigation. The introduction is quite extensive in the number of issues discussed and references listed. Previous work on decision making by juries as well as on the more general effects of personal appearance on rated attractiveness leads to the identification of a number of potentially relevant factors. In addition, the investigators are able to pose a rather interesting hypothesis about the expected outcome of the study, a hypothesis that is likely to surprise and amuse you.

The introduction to each article has been annotated to highlight how the review of previous work is organized and to show how this review leads to the postulation of specific hypotheses. These two papers differ considerably in content and style, but they both illustrate the value of a well-crafted introduction in providing a coherent background to a problem in a few pages. Moreover, you will discover that, although the two papers are listed under different topical headings in *Psychological Abstracts* and although they have no references in common, the underlying issues overlap considerably. In combination they provide a solid foundation for identifying the issues and the previous work done on the effects of pictorial and verbal information in perception, memory, and judgments based on facial appearance.

Memory & Cognition
1982, Vol. *10*, 195–206

Semantic interpretation effects on memory for faces

ROBERTA L. KLATZKY, GALE L. MARTIN, and ROBBIE A. KANE
University of California, Santa Barbara

The margin notes read:

> The first sentence is a good summary of the entire paper.

> The next section of the paragraph relates this paper to a larger problem of the relation between verbal and pictorial memory.

> The key issue being debated at present in the literature is in the contrast between *semantic* and *physical* codes.

> In memory for faces both of these codes may be operative.

> The literature suggests that memory for faces is based largely on physical codes. (Notice that the evidence presented on this point is skimpy.)

The present experiments address the question of whether memory for faces is enhanced when the faces are interpreted in terms of occupational categories. As such, the experiments are part of a larger research effort exploring the effects of semantic interpretation on memory for visual stimuli. This research has adopted a general distinction between two kinds of memorial information about visual stimuli: information about their physical detail (Bartlett, Till, & Levy, 1980; Klatzky & Stoy, 1978; Mandler & Ritchey, 1977; Nelson, Reed, & Walling, 1976; Rafnel & Klatzky, 1978). The first type of information has been called semantic, conceptual, meaningful, or verbal; the second has been called physical, structural, schematic, sensory, pictoliteral (Klatzky, in press), or simply "visual." They will be called here the semantic and physical codes.

Put in these terms, the present studies address whether the act of semantically interpreting a face, or, more specifically, relating it to a category whose stereotype it matches, affects memory, and whether it does so by influencing a semantic code or a physical code. Although these codes cannot be specified precisely, the physical code of a face is assumed to include concrete visual attributes and to be achieved with minimal influence from "top-down" processing, and the semantic code is assumed to represent the face as a meaningful concept. The semantic code might include information about visual appearance, such as "looks clean-cut" or "has moustache," but this visual information would be more abstract than that of the physical code. The semantic code could also include the information not directly related to vision, for example, regarding the probable income or the beliefs of the person whose face is being viewed. . . .

The question of whether and how semantically interpreting a visual stimulus affects memory is of particular interest regarding faces, because there is a substantial literature suggesting that face recognition is mediated predominantly by physical codes. For example, extensive training in the verbal description of facial features fails to improve recognition (Baddeley, 1979; Malpass, Lavigueur, & Weldon, 1973). . . .

Notwithstanding the importance of the physical code to face memory, semantic interpretation could still play an important role. Rafnel and Klatzky (1978) reviewed the evidence for two types of semantic interpretation effects on memory for visual patterns; these same effects could also apply to face memory. One type of effect, which is consistent with the idea that the physical code is of primary importance in remembering faces, would be for semantic interpretation of a face to enhance its physical code. . . . Several studies (Bower & Karlin, 1974; Patterson & Baddeley, 1977) have shown that making semantic judgments about faces at encoding (e.g., judging personality traits) leads to better recognition than making physical judgments (e.g., judging thickness of lips). Investigating the basis for this effect, Winograd (1981) found evidence that semantic judgments are effective because they lead to scanning a face as a whole, which in turn increases the probability of encoding a distinctive feature. . . .

The second means by which semantic interpretation might enhance memory for faces is by providing a distinct semantic code, which, when associated with the physical code in memory would increase the amount of information stored about the face. . . .

In the present studies, semantic interpretation of a face was induced by presenting, along with the face, a category label that the face had previously been judged to match. The semantic categories that were used were common occupations. These were chosen because there is evidence that the memorial representations of at least some occupations include substantial information about facial appearance. This evidence stems from psychological studies of facial stereotyping by occupation (Klatzky, Martin, & Kane, in press; Litterer, 1933; Shoemaker, South, & Lowe, 1973), and it is also indicated by everyday stereotyping of faces (e.g., in advertising). At the same time, occupations are not so obvious that faces are unambiguously classifiable without a category label, as other facially relevant categories (e.g., race, sex) would be. Thus, it should be possible to direct interpretation of a face by category labeling. (pp. 195, 196)

Memory for faces might still be affected by semantic cues. For instance, such cues might support the physical codes; the subject pays more attention to the physical image because of the verbal cues.

Semantic cues might be added to the physical cues; the subject can use both a physical image and a list of semantic features as a basis for memory.

In the present studies the person's occupation was used as a verbal cue to support the pictorial stimulus in various ways. (The remainder of the introduction provides an overview of five experiments, designed to explore the general hypothesis, and to distinguish between the two roles of semantic cues sketched above.)

Baddeley, A. Applied cognitive and cognitive applied psychology: The case of face recognition. In L.-G. Nilsson (Ed.), *Perspectives on memory research*. Hillsdale, N. J.: Erlbaum, 1979.

Bartlett, J. C., Till, R. E., & Levy, J. C. Retrieval characteristics of complex pictures: Effects of verbal encoding. *Journal of Verbal Learning and Verbal Behavior*, 1980, *19*, 430–449.

Bower, G. H., & Karlin, M. B. Depth of processing pictures of faces and recognition memory. *Journal of Experimental Psychology*, 1974, *103*, 751–757.

Klatzky, R. L. Visual memory: Definitions and functions. In R. Wyer, T. Srull, & J. Hartwick (Eds.), *Handbook of social cognition*. Hillsdale, N. J.: Erlbaum, in press.

Klatzky, R. L., Martin, G. L., & Kane, R. A. Influence of social-category activation on processing of visual information. *Social Cognition*, in press.

Klatzky, R. L., & Stoy, A. M. Semantic information and visual information processing. In J. W. Cotton & R. L. Klatzky (Eds.), *Semantic factors in cognition*. Hillsdale, N. J.: Erlbaum, 1978.

Litterer, O. Stereotypes. *Journal of Social Psychology*, 1933, *4*, 59–68.

Malpass, R. S., Lavigueur, H., & Weldon, D. E. Verbal and visual training in face recognition. *Perception & Psychophysics*, 1973, 14, 285–292.

Mandler, J. M., & Ritchey, G. H. Long-term memory for pictures. *Journal of Experimental Psychology: Human Learning and Memory*, 1977, 3, 386–396.

Nelson, D. L., Reed, V. S., & Walling, J. R. Pictorial superiority effect. *Journal of Experimental Psychology: Human Learning and Memory*, 1976, 2, 523–538.

Patterson, K. E., & Baddeley, A. D. When face recognition fails. *Journal of Experimental Psychology: Human Learning and Memory*, 1977, 3, 406–417.

Rafnel, K. J., & Klatzky, R. L. Meaningful-interpretation effects on codes of nonsense pictures. *Journal of Experimental Psychology: Human Learning and Memory*, 1978, 4, 631–646.

Shoemaker, D., South, D., & Lowe, J. Facial stereotypes of deviants and judgments of guilt or innocence. *Social Forces*, 1973, 51, 427–433.

Winograd, E. Elaboration and distinctiveness in memory for faces. *Journal of Experimental Psychology: Human Learning and Memory*, 1981, 7, 181–190.

Journal of Applied Social Psychology, 1978, 8, 4, pp. 366–381

Is Justice Really Blind?—The Influence of Litigant Physical Attractiveness on Juridical Judgment

RICHARD A. KULKA
University of Michigan

JOAN B. KESSLER
California State University, Northridge

The introductory sentence in this paper establishes only the general context.

The social consequences of the problem are sketched.

The foundation study is mentioned—probably worth reading.

Legal practitioners have assumed for some time that a wide variety of psychological factors known to effect nonjudicial decisions or evaluations are also operative in the courtroom. In particular, it is a common belief that jurors in a trial are often influenced by the personal and social characteristics of a defendant or plaintiff, being more lenient in their decisions when a litigant has certain positive characteristics and more severe when he or she possesses certain negative ones, even when such characteristics appear unrelated or irrelevant to the particular offense or circumstances (e.g., Bloomstein, 1968; McCart, 1964; Monahan, 1941).

However, in spite of an abundance of rich anecdotal evidence circulating among members and observers of the legal profession, only recently have systematic and controlled investigations of evaluative influences on the juridic decision process been undertaken, typified by the widely cited pioneering study of jury decisions conducted by Kalven and Zeisel (1966). To date analyses of data from actual jury trials and experimental data from simulated juries suggest that selective characteristics of defendants and plaintiffs such as sex (McGlynn, Megas, & Benson, 1976; Nagel & Weitzman, 1971; Rose & Prell, 1955: Stephan, 1974), age (Reynolds & Sanders, 1975), race (Bullock, 1961; Hindelang, 1969; Kaplan, 1972; McGlynn et al., 1976; Gleason & Harris, Note 1), ethnicity (Goldberg, 1971), socioeconomic status (Allison, 1964; Reed, 1965; Silverstein, 1965; Gleason & Harris, Note 1), family status (Broeder, 1965), social or moral character (e.g., Landy & Aronson, 1969; Nemeth & Sosis, 1973; Rumsey, 1976; Sigall & Landy, 1972), and defendant attitudes (Griffitt & Jackson, 1973; Mitchell & Byrne, 1973) may have a significant influence on the verdicts jurors render and the punishments or awards which they recommend (see also reviews by Nagel, 1969; Stephan, 1975, pp. 95–117).

In an attempt to extend this promising line of research, the study reported here sought to examine the impact of physical attractiveness on juridic judgments. From a rapidly accumulating literature describing the effects of physical attractiveness on social evaluation and behavior in a variety of other contexts (e.g., Byrne, London, & Reeves, 1968; Cavior & Dokecki, 1973; Chaikin, Derlega, Yoder, & Phillips, 1974; Clifford & Walster, 1973; Dion, 1972; Dipboye, Fromkin & Wiback, 1975; Horai, Nacarri, & Fatoullah, 1974; Landy & Sigall, 1974: Mills & Aronson, 1965), there is now ample evidence to suggest that this variable may have a significant influence on the perceptions and decisions of jurors in a courtroom. (For an excellent review of this literature, see Berscheid & Walster, 1974.) Moreover, some other litigant characteristics known to influence juror decisions (e.g., social or moral character, socio-economic status) are apparently often inferred on the basis of a person's physical appearance (Dion, Berscheid, & Walster, 1972; Miller, 1970).

Several recent investigations in which college students assumed the role of nondeliberating jurors suggest that physical attractiveness of litigants may indeed influence the product of juror decision-making. For example, Stephan and Tully (1977) reported that physically attractive plaintiffs in a personal injury suit involving a nondisfiguring injury more often won judgments in their favor and were awarded more money in damages than were physically unattractive plaintiffs. In a student-faculty court simulation of a cheating case, Efran (1974) found that defendant physical attractiveness was negatively correlated with certainty of guilt and severity of recommended punishment and positively related to interpersonal attraction toward the defendant. A significant negative relationship between physical attractiveness and assigned length of sentencing was also found in a study by Leventhal and Krate (1977), in which the nature of crime and economic status of the defendant were controlled.

Similarly, Sigall and Ostrove (1975) reported an interaction between physical attractiveness of the defendant and the relationship of

Next follows a veritable gold mine of factors and associated references.

The phenomenon is not unique to jury decisions; these references establish a broader framework.

And now to the focus of this study: the factor of physical appearance.

Next, the suggestion that the effects of physical appearance are rather complex; the concept of *interaction* between two factors will be discussed later in the text, as will the notion of *confounding*.

attractiveness to the crime committed. When the offense was unrelated to attractiveness (burglary), an attractive defendant received a more lenient sentence than an unattractive defendant. However, when the crime was attractiveness-related (swindle), an attractive defendant was more severely punished. Although the design of their study confounded *written* descriptions of physical, moral, and social attractiveness by simultaneously varying these characteristics in two experimental conditions, Friend and Vinson (1974) also found a significant interaction involving defendant attractiveness in a negligent homicide case. . . .

On the whole, then, evidence from these studies suggests that physical attractiveness of litigants may produce significant variation in juror verdicts. However, a few important compromises in the design of these experiments—notably the use of written materials and photographs—may undermine the generalizability of their results to the way in which actual juries decide real cases. In each of these investigations, participants are presented with a short written account or synopsis of testimony describing the basic facts of a particular case. Although a number of other studies have also used this inexpensive and convenient method of trial presentation, a few methodological investigations suggest that having subjects read a short vignette may not provide a very realistic simulation of actual courtroom practice (e.g., Bermant, McGuire, McKinley, & Salo, 1974; Miller, Bender, Florence, & Nicholson, 1974). (pp. 366–369)

Aha! Here is the question of semantic and physical cues appearing in a different situation.

And finally, the bottom line: the setting for the study has been established. (The results are quite intriguing!)

Allison, J. L. Poverty and the administration of justice in the criminal courts. *Journal of Criminal Law, Criminology, and Police Science*, 1964, 55, 241–245.

Bermant, G., McGuire, M., McKinley, W., & Salo, C. The logic of simulation in jury research. *Criminal Justice and Behavior*, 1974, 1, 224–233.

Berscheid, E., & Walster, E. Physical attractiveness. In L. Berkowitz (Ed.), *Advances in experimental social psychology* (Vol. 7). New York: Academic Press, 1974.

Bloomstein, M. J. *Verdict: The jury system.* New York: Dodd, Mead, 1968.

Broeder, D. W. Plaintiff's family status as affecting juror behavior: Some tentative insights. *Journal of Public Law*, 1965, 14, 131–143.

Bullock, R. Significance of the racial factor in the length of prison sentences. *Journal of Criminal Law*, 1961, 52, 411–415.

Byrne, D., London, O., & Reeves, K. The effects of physical attractiveness, sex, and attitude similarity on interpersonal attraction. *Journal of Personality*, 1968, 36, 259–271.

Cavior, N. N., & Dokecki, P. R. Physical attractiveness, perceived attitude similarity, and academic achievement as contributors to interpersonal attraction among adolescents. *Developmental Psychology*, 1973, 9, 44–54.

Chaikin, A. L., Derlega, V. J., Yoder, J., & Phillips, D. The effects of appearance on compliance. *Journal of Social Psychology*, 1974, 92, 199–200.

Clifford, M. M., & Walster, E. The effect of physical attractiveness on teacher expectation. *Sociology of Education*, 1973, 46, 248–258.

Dion, K. K., Berscheid, E., & Walster, E. What is beautiful is good. *Journal of Personality and Social Psychology*, 1972, 24, 285–290.

Dipboye, R. L., Fromkin, H. L., & Wiback, K. Relative importance of applicant sex, attractiveness, and scholastic standing in evaluation of job applicant resumes. *Journal of Applied Psychology*, 1975, 60, 39–43.

Efran, M. G. The effect of physical appearance on the judgment of guilt, interpersonal attraction, and severity of recommended punishment in a simulated jury task. *Journal of Research in Personality*, 1974, 8, 45–54.

Friend, R. M., & Vinson, M. Leaning over backwards: Jurors' responses to defendants' attractiveness. *Journal of Communication*, 1974, 24, 124–129.

Goldberg, A. D. The ethnic factor in criminal sentencing. *Western Political Quarterly*, 1971, 24, 425–437.

Griffitt, W., & Jackson, T. Simulated jury decisions: The influence of jury-defendant attitude similarity-dissimilarity. *Social Behavior and Personality*, 1973, 1, 1–7.

Hindelang, M. J. Equality under the law. *Journal of Criminal Law, Criminology, and Policy Science*, 1969, 60, 306–313.

Horai, J., Nacarri, N., & Fatoullah, E. The effects of expertise and physical attractiveness upon opinion agreement and liking. *Sociometry*, 1974, 37, 601–606.

Kalven, H., Jr., & Zeisel, H. *The American jury*. Boston: Little, Brown, 1966.

Kaplan, K. J. Latitude and severity of sentencing options, race of victim and decisons of simulated jurors: Some issues arising from the "Algiers Motel" trial. *Law and Society Review*, 1972, 7, 87–98.

Landy, D., & Aronson, E. The influence of the character of the criminal and victim on the decisions of simulated jurors. *Journal of Experimental Social Psychology*, 1969, 5, 141–152.

Landy, D., & Sigall, H. Beauty is talent: Task evaluation as a function of the performer's physical attractiveness. *Journal of Personality and Social Psychology*, 1974, 29(3), 299–304.

Leventhal, G., & Krate, R. Physical attractiveness and severity of sentencing. *Psychological Reports*, 1977, 40, 315–318.

McCart, S. W. *Trial by jury*. New York: Chilton, 1964.

McGlynn, R. P., Megas, J. C., & Benson, D. H. Sex and race as factors affecting the attribution of insanity in a murder trial. *Journal of Psychology*, 1976, 93, 93–99.

Miller, A. G. Role of physical attractiveness in impression formation. *Psychonomic Science*, 1970, 19, 241–243.

Miller, G., Bender, D., Florence, T., & Nicholson, H. Real versus reel: What's the verdict? *Journal of Communication*, 1974, *24*, 99–111.

Mills, J., & Aronson, E. Opinion change as a function of the communicator's attractiveness and desire to influence. *Journal of Personality and Social Psychology*, 1965, *1*, 173–177.

Mitchell, H. E., & Byrne, D. The defendant's dilemma: Effect of jurors' attitudes and authoritarianism on judicial decisions. *Journal of Personality and Social Psychology*, 1973, *25*, 123–129.

Monahan, F. *Women in crime*. New York: Washburn, 1941.

Nagel, S. S. *The legal process from a behavioral perspective*. Homewood, IL: Dorsey Press, 1969.

Nagel, S. S., & Weitzman, L. J. Women as litigants. *Hastings Law Journal*, 1971, *23*, 171–198.

Nemeth, C., & Sosis, R. H. A simulated jury study: Characteristics of the defendant and the jurors. *Journal of Social Psychology*, 1973, *90*, 221–229.

Reed, J. P. Jury deliberations, voting and verdict trends. *Southwestern Social Science Quarterly*, 1965, *65*, 361–374.

Reynolds, D. E., & Sanders, M. S. Effect of defendant attractiveness, age, and injury on severity of sentence given by simulated jurors. *Journal of Social Psychology*, 1975, *96*, 149–150.

Rose, A. M., & Prell, A. E. Does the punishment fit the crime? A study in social valuation. *American Journal of Sociology*, 1955, *61*, 247–259.

Rumsey, M. G. Effects of defendant background and remorse on sentencing judgments. *Journal of Applied Social Psychology*, 1976, *6*, 64–68.

Sigall H., & Landy, D. Effects of the defendant's character and suffering on juridic judgment: A replication and clarification. *Journal of Social Psychology*, 1972, *88*, 149–150.

Sigall, H., & Ostrove, N. Beautiful but dangerous: Effects of offender attractiveness and nature of the crime on juridic judgment. *Journal of Personality and Social Psychology*, 1975, *31*, 410–414.

Silverstein, L. *Defense of the poor in criminal cases in American state courts*. Chicago: American Bar Foundation, 1965.

Stephan, C. Sex prejudice in jury simulation. *Journal of Psychology*, 1974, *88*, 305–312.

Stephan, C. Selective characteristics of jurors and litigants: Their influence on juries' verdicts. In R. J. Simon (Ed.), *The jury system in America: A critical overview*. Beverly Hills, CA: Sage Publications, 1975.

Stephan, C., & Tully, J. C. The influence of physical attractiveness of a plaintiff on the decisions of simulated jurors. *Journal of Social Psychology*, 1977, *101*, 149–150.

Walster, E. Assignment of responsibility for an accident. *Journal of Personality and Social Psychology*, 1966, *3*, 73–79.

Reference Note

1. Gleason, J., & Harris, V. the effects of race, socio-economic status and perceived similarity to defendant on decisions by simulated jurors. Paper presented at the meeting of the Eastern Psychological Association, New York, 1975.

SUMMARY

Science depends on accumulated knowledge. Not every piece of research is a gem, but the results of well-designed failures can be as important as the rare but exciting breakthrough. For the newcomer to the field, a major hurdle is gaining knowledge of previous work through review of the literature. The goals of such a review are (a) to identify the recurring themes and questions, (b) to discover the factors that seem to be most salient, (c) to learn the names of the prominent researchers doing work on the topic, and (d) to find the journals and other sources in which pertinent research is typically published. A secondary hurdle is the scientific writing style, which tends to be compact, dry, impersonal, and packed with unfamiliar vocabulary. The person new to a field will find that reading scientific reports is a slow and arduous task at the beginning, but with practice it does become easier.

A variety of sources are available to the student who wants to gain familiarity with a particular topic. Besides the knowledge learned from previous courses (and the textbooks from those courses), the three major sources for review are (a) abstracts and indices, (b) reviews and theoretical papers, and (c) journal articles and other research reports.

Several abstracting services exist to aid psychologists and other behavioral scientists in locating research papers on a given topic. *Psychological Abstracts* is one of the most valuable of these services. In it, papers from a large number of sources are indexed by topic and by author; the index number allows the reader to locate the abstract, along with other pertinent information. Abstracts and indices are an important source of information, but to use them effectively it helps to be fairly clear about what you need to know. Some of these services are available in computerized form, and a computer search can be initiated if the appropriate facilities are available.

Reviews and theoretical papers are prepared by scholars to integrate existing research and clarify the direction for future investigations. If the student is fortunate, he or she will be able to find a recent review that provides a good starting point for more detailed work. *Psychological Review*, *Psychological Bulletin*, and *Annual Review of Psychology* all publish review papers. Handbooks and edited volumes (some published annually) can also be consulted for integrative summaries.

Finally, the introduction to a journal article often provides an excellent mini-review, and if the student can locate a few good articles, the information in the introduction often provides an excellent analysis of existing knowledge on a topic. In addition, the references at the end of the papers can be used to search for other relevant studies.

The problem is how to locate the first few reports and how to analyze them once found. The search strategy outlined in the chapter suggests that you (a) skim some general sources for journal titles and authors' names (try your introductory text, the abstracts, the card catalogue, and so on), (b) select one or two journals that seem most likely to publish research on the topic, (c) start with recent issues of the journals and work backward through title pages until you locate some good leads, and (d) for each promising paper examine the Introduction, Discussion, and Reference sections for ideas and for other leads. The two examples at the end of the chapter illustrate how to carry out this last step.

3

The Psychological Experiment as a Social Situation

The psychological experiment is an interaction between experimenter and one or more subjects. The experiment is therefore a social situation, an interaction among people. This chapter focuses on the social conditions of the experiment; that is, the roles played by experimenter and subject, and the interactions between the two can influence the outcome of a study. The ethical responsibilities of the researcher for ensuring the safety and well-being of the subjects are also emphasized.

THE SUBJECT

Research reports typically give only passing attention to the individuals who comprise the sample of subjects:

> The subjects were 77 college students enrolled in an introductory educational psychology course. They participated as part of a class requirement and also received $2 each. (Reynolds and Anderson, 1982, p. 625)

The description is sometimes more informative than the preceding example:

> The sample consisted of 77 students in Grades 7 and 8. The students came from two above-average general mathematics classes at a junior high school in the Los Angeles metropolitan area. Approximately 43% of the students were female, and approximately 26% were minority (Black, Asian American). Because the mathematics classes at this school were tracked by ability rather than by grade, each class had both grades. Both classes were taught by the same teacher. (Webb, 1982, p. 644)

In yet other instances, the description of the subjects and the setting of the experiment may be quite extensive. For example, in the same issue of *Journal of Educational Psychology* from which the two preceding excerpts were drawn, another article (Schofield and Francis, 1982) takes almost a full page to describe the school in which the research was conducted and how classes, students, and a specific lesson were chosen for observation.

For the most part, however, research papers say relatively little about the subjects' role. This section of the chapter attempts to fill that gap by providing answers to two questions:

- Where do subjects come from?

- What are they like?

Where Do Subjects Come From?

If you skim through the Subjects section of several psychology journals, you will quickly discover that the college undergraduate is the prototypical subject. Not too long ago you may have had the opportunity yourself to serve as a subject in a psychological research study. Jung (1971) reports that 75 percent to 90 percent of all research on humans is based on this population, most often "volunteers" who are required to participate in one or more experiments as part of their introductory psychology course. The requirement is partly justified as a means of teaching students what psychology is all about. But as a matter of convenience college professors naturally turn to the nearest available human beings when setting up experiments.

Subjects from other populations are, however, required for certain types of research problems: educational or developmental studies, for instance, or investigations of special populations (the mentally retarded, the academically gifted, the emotionally disturbed, and so on). Experiments in naturalistic or field-based settings also require the researcher to deal with people (and situations) that differ markedly from the undergraduate performing under the well-controlled conditions of the psychological laboratory.

More will be said later about the unique circumstances of research on special populations, but first let us look more carefully at the typical undergraduate subject. The process usually begins with a sign-up sheet. The researcher posts an announcement of a project, describing the study, listing any hazards or incentives, and asking for interested volunteers to write their names on the sheet. This procedure seems relatively innocuous, but the style with which it is carried out can significantly influence the types of people who decide to sign up. Sometimes a fee is paid for participation, and though the amount is usually quite small, for the student who is living close to the margin even a few bucks makes a difference. Some projects are intrinsically more interesting than others, and quite aside from the reality, the way a project is described can glamorize it or make it sound dull. As a result of such factors, different kinds of people can be expected to sign up for the project.

The data on the effects of variation in subject selection procedures are scarce, but one study describes the characteristics of that small proportion of students who *really* volunteer; that is, those who sign up for psychological experiments even though they do not have to and will not be paid. Rosenthal and Rosnow (1975) found that these individuals, compared with nonvolunteer students, tend to be higher in socioeconomic status, better educated, more intelligent, more social, and more in need of social approval. They are typically joiners, and while they comprise an interesting group, they are hardly what one would call a representative sample of people in general or psychological subjects in particular.

What Are the Subjects Like?

The College Undergraduate. Knowing that subjects are typically college undergraduates tells us a great deal about them. Compared with the general population of the United States, they are relatively young, from families with above average income, white, intelligent, and at least moderately ambitious (Atkinson and Feather, 1965). Because they are enrolled in introductory psychology courses, they are not representative of college students in general; students who plan to major in the "hard" sciences and in fields like engineering and mathematics seldom study psychology unless it is a general university requirement.

This account of the undergraduate subject may project an image of uniformity that is quite misleading. It is true that because college students have gone through a selection process they tend to be less variable in some areas than the population at large. Within these limits, however, one finds considerable variability. Researchers may disregard the individual differences among their subjects, but these differences exist and can affect performance substantially even in the well-controlled environment of the psychological laboratory (Hunt and Lansman, 1975; Carroll, 1976). Among the variables that are known to influence performance significantly are gender, reading ability, and response style (reflective or impulsive, holistic or analytic), and the list could be easily extended.

One characteristic of subjects that has been shown to influence performance, though it is typically disregarded, is the reaction of the individual to the experimental situation. Several styles can be identified from the research literature; most subjects probably represent a combination of these reactions. Orne (1962) portrays most subjects as cooperative and eager to do a good job, partly because of their desire to help advance the science. A variation on this theme is the "faithful" subject (Fillenbaum, 1966; Weber and Cook, 1972). These subjects aim not so much to cooperate as to project their most honest and unbiased reactions to the experimental setting as they perceive it. This response may be construed as the path of least resistance taken by a passive and unmotivated individual, but it may also indicate that the subject wants to behave as a "true witness."

This portrait of the subject may be a bit too rosy; it is based on reports that date back quite a way and so is perhaps truer of students of the fifties than those of later decades. This conjecture is supported by Argyris' (1968) findings, in which introductory psychology students expressed strong hostility toward the requirement that they participate as subjects. In some instances they recounted their efforts to "screw up" the results as a way of expressing resentment (Masling, 1966).

Then there is the "worried" subject, whose attitude Rosenberg (1969) describes as *evaluation apprehension*. This syndrome threatens the trustworthiness of a study because the subjects' concerns can influence their behavior. Some investigators (Weber and Cook, 1972; but also cf. Jung, 1971) have concluded that while certain subjects fit this category, for most the attitude is more often "Let's get it over." If this conclusion is valid, then the matter merits attention by researchers. The subject is not a "stupid automaton" (Pierce, 1908), and so the researcher should consider how to arrange the experimental environment so that the subjects understand as clearly as possible what is happening, why, and what is likely to be the final outcome. To leave the subject in the dark may jeopardize the experiment; it may also be ethically irresponsible, as we shall see later.

To return to the question that began this section—what are subjects like?—we can now say that the college students who comprise the sample for many experiments differ in several respects from a random selection of the general population. Nonetheless, the researcher will discover that undergraduate subjects differ considerably from one another in ability, in aptitude, in interests, and in their approach to the experimental task. To ignore these differences is to weaken the control over the experiment. Though it is not possible to take into account every dimension of human difference, the experimenter should consider which dimensions are most likely to influence the problem under investigation and then take steps to include these dimensions as factors in the design.

Subjects from the "Real World." Certain kinds of people are rarely seen on college campuses: children, working adults, and young adults who lack the interest, ability, or money to attend college, among others. The researcher who wants to study visual perception in infants, short-term memory in first-graders, typing skills in experienced secretaries, or social interactions in army tank crews, must go beyond the readily available population of undergraduates to locate the special group in question. If the college undergraduate is accessible and docile (though one might challenge these traits), other populations are certainly not. Gaining access to special populations, persuading them to serve as experimental subjects, ensuring that they understand the task, and maintaining their motivation throughout the study—small wonder that, faced with these tasks, psychologists so frequently turn to a "handy random sample" of college students.

In reviewing research projects with off-campus populations and in undertaking such projects on your own, there are several considerations to keep in mind. First, no matter how you may have characterized a particular population, remember that within that population individuals are still likely to vary a great deal. Five-year-olds are not all alike, nor are secretaries, airplane pilots, or any other group. Undergraduate samples are relatively homogeneous, and so the investigator can often prepare a fixed set of procedures for an experiment with the assurance that they will work for most subjects who walk through the door. Such is not the case with more specialized populations. Instructions that work with five-year-olds may be mystifying to three-year-olds but insulting to ten-year-olds. A thirty-minute task may be within the tolerance of a youngster of normal intelligence but impossible for a child who is mentally retarded—and it may prove intolerable when the subject has a behavior problem or is emotionally disturbed.

Second, the constraints on selecting people from the "real world" are often greater than those that pertain to selecting undergraduates. The latter have flexible schedules and a considerable amount of free time, a life-style that is conducive to serving as an experimental subject. Moreover, college students are accustomed to carrying out tasks assigned to them by someone else, including tasks that do not always make a great deal of sense to them. Nonstudents are different. Their time is often not their own. When not working, however, they tend to decide what they will and will not do. Accordingly the researcher must take special care in approaching nonstudent populations.

Having identified a sample of subjects from some special population, next comes the question of how to arrange the experiment. The researcher can transport the subjects to the laboratory or bring the laboratory to the subjects (trailers can be towed to remote locations, or a spare room can be fixed up). In many instances the research problem dictates that the study be done in the "real world." Applied research often has this character: not only the subjects but also the environments must be sought out as they naturally occur.

The real-world setting can also influence the social conditions of the study. For instance, the laboratory researcher generally deals with subjects as individuals or as groups artificially constituted for the purposes of the experiment. The field researcher, in contrast, must deal with people as members of social organizations. In the "real world" individuals tend to arrange themselves into groups—hierarchies, networks, overlapping webs—that must be considered in planning the investigation.

Suppose you are interested in carrying out an educational research project. You will quickly discover that you cannot simply search for a sample of students, for students come in classes and classes come in schools. Accordingly, you must first locate a principal who will let you talk with teachers. Once you have managed to obtain permission from the principal, you must approach the teachers, whose approval to work with youngsters is usually a separate matter. The goal in sight, you then discover that students are members of another group—families—and that you need to obtain the approval of the parents and sometimes of the students as well. At this point in your odyssey, you again appreciate why so much research is conducted in university laboratories with undergraduates as subjects.

Finally, just as individuals differ within categories, so groups differ, and each level of a social hierarchy carries its own sources of variation. Elementary school children differ, but so do the teachers and classes within which the children spend many of their waking hours, the schools within which the classes are located, the neighborhoods and communities within which the schools are located, and so on. Elements at lower levels may be affected by higher-level conditions. You are unlikely to find a freewheeling, arts-oriented classroom in a school directed by an authoritarian principal who emphasizes the basic skills of reading, writing and 'rithmetic! On the other hand, what factors are relevant may be quite different at different levels of an organization. The neighborhood income level may be high or low, but whether the principal relies on an authoritarian or democratic style of leadership is a separate issue, and within these combinations of factors a particular teacher may chose to emphasize reading over mathematics or vice versa. These complexities are not endless, but they do require attention.

THE EXPERIMENTER

The influence of experimenter variables on the outcome of psychological research has a long history. Boring (1950) tells that in 1796 the chief astronomer at the Greenwich Observatory in England fired his assistant because the assistant's recordings of star motions were not in perfect agreement with his own. Twenty years passed before other researchers began to realize that such differences were the rule rather than the exception and that it was not simply a matter of individuals "making up their minds" to be accurate and unbiased. People are different, and these differences affect virtually everything they do.

The potential for experimenter bias in psychological research is so great at so many stages of any study that one would think that psychology would have focused on this problem almost immediately. But even after astronomers identified the "observer effect," its implications were not fully realized by experimental psychologists. A century ago psychologists relied a great deal on the introspective method, which viewed the experimenter and the subject as one and the same. Psychology fell on hard times for a while because the researchers could not agree on the basic data; the results of one investigator could not be repeated by other scientists. The "experimenter effect" outweighed all other variables! Then came behaviorism and an emphasis on "objective" methods of research, and the experimenter effect was forgotten.

Recently, the topic has come back into vogue, with interesting consequences. In one of the more unusual tales about the experimenter effect, an experimenter relying on "friendly persuasion" persuaded seventeen out of twenty army recruits to taste grasshoppers, whereas an experimenter who relied on "pulling rank" could only get ten "tasters" from a sample of twenty recruits (Smith, 1961). Obviously, the experimenter effect has important consequences for psychological experiments. What, then, is the nature of this variable, and how can it be brought under control?

Who Is the Experimenter?

What kinds of people carry out psychological research? The stereotype is the white-robed professor, slightly weird, pursuing incomprehensible questions about irrelevant or bizarre aspects of human behavior. In fact, a good deal of the research is carried out by graduate or undergraduate research assistants—people quite like yourself.

Experimenters vary considerably in their background, experience, training, and style, all of which affect the experimenter's behavior and hence the subject's performance. While the literature on experimenter effects is growing, descriptions of the experimenter are still rarely encountered in research reports, and experimenter variables are seldom included in the design of a study *unless* the study is primarily concerned with such factors. Research reports must have a section (however brief) on subjects; there is no corresponding requirement for a section on experimenters.

How Do Experimenters Behave?

While comparatively little is known about variations in experimenters, we do know something about how such variations influence the conduct of an experiment. For instance, there is evidence that the gender of the experimenter is important (Binder, McConnell, and Sjoholm, 1957), especially for younger children (Stevenson, 1961). Interaction between experimenter and subject gender is also apparent; though the data are weak and gender is mixed up with several other variables, one suspects that the matter deserves attention.

Rosenthal (1976), whose work on experimenter bias we will examine shortly, summarizes the smattering of data on gender effects: men and women vary in predictable ways when approaching the task of being an experimenter. Women smile more, exchange glances with the subject more often, and tend to follow the experimental procedures more carefully. Some of these tendencies may reflect cultural styles and may be undergoing change. Nonetheless, at present female experimenters are treated with more consideration and attention, especially by male subjects. Children, interestingly enough, behave better and work harder when the experimenter is a man.

Though the anecdotal evidence is hard to summarize, it does appear that subjects are influenced by the experimenter's personality. Johnson (1976) has done a good job of bringing together a number of the relevant studies, along with an incisive critique and a couple of practical suggestions for handling the problem. One recommendation is that the experimenter alter the approach to each subject as a factor in the design. Thus, the experimenter may act warmly toward some subjects while remaining more aloof toward others. Johnson also points out that experimenter effects tend to be strongest when the experimenter factor is related to the experimental task. If the research focuses on judgments of warmth, then the experimenter's affective attitude will influence performance; if the study concerns smoking, then whether the experimenter appears to be a smoker may be an important variable; and so on.

INTERACTIONS BETWEEN EXPERIMENTER AND SUBJECT

Certain effects may be associated with the experimenter qua experimenter and the subject qua subject, but some of the strongest influences on the experimental procedure arise from the interaction between the two. The psychological experiment is a social relationship, and certain assumptions are made about the status of each party. The experimenter is the "boss" or expert and is in command of the situation; the subject is the "worker" and tends to do what he or she is told (Argyris, 1968; Runkel and McGrath, 1972). As Orne (1962) has noted, besides boss–worker, parent–child, and doctor–patient, relatively few situations allow one person to assume control over another. The subject is likely to do almost anything within fairly broad bounds if the researcher utters the magic words, "This is an experiment."

While the experimenter may appear authoritative on the surface and the subject subservient, it seems likely that both vary in how comfortable they feel in these roles. Some experimenters assume an inscrutable mien, while others adopt a more companionable approach. As noted earlier, subjects also vary in their approach (cooperative, negative, "faithful," or worried). Whether they do so in response to the experimenter's style is not known, though this seems likely.

The experimental situation is a strange environment. Subjects are naturally curious about what is really going on, and they seek reassurance from the researcher that all will be well, that they are succeeding and not making fools of themselves. Within the limits allowed by the experimenter, they will want to look around, ask questions, examine the apparatus, and so on. Undergraduates often express a desire to "get to know the experimenter as a person" (Rosenthal, 1976, p. 190ff).

From the initial greeting to the final debriefing, the experimenter and the subject interact in a variety of ways. Complications from this interaction can arise at any time during the actual conduct of the experiment, more so in some areas of psychology than in others. It is therefore important that you understand the chronology of the experimental situation so that you can learn to anticipate such complications. In the next two sections we examine the ways in which experimenters can introduce error and bias into a study.

EXPERIMENTER EXPECTANCY

The experimenter is seldom a neutral participant in a research project. He or she is likely to have some expectations about the outcome of the study and often has a strongly vested interest in the satisfaction of these expectations. It is therefore natural to wonder whether the experimenter will somehow behave in a way that biases the results. Anyone can make mistakes through sloppiness, and such mistakes lead to random errors in the measurements. Bias takes place when mistakes are systematic, which introduces measurement errors of a more serious character.

On rare occasions researchers have intentionally biased the outcome of a study, but such instances of misconduct are not the issue here. Rather, we are concerned with the unconscious pressure to make the data "come out right." In science the method is more critical than the outcome. If the designated procedures meet the canons of scientific rigor and objectivity, then the results must speak for themselves. Can the profession of experimental psychology be assured that this principle is respected in carrying out research where human interactions are so prominent?

Sources of Experimenter Bias

Rosenthal (1976) has actively investigated the issue of bias. Before reviewing his conclusions let us look briefly at those critical points during a study where the experimenter's expectations are most likely to influence performance. The experimenter is responsible for *greeting the subject* and for *familiarizing him or her with the laboratory situation*. It is most often the experimenter who *administers the experimental treatments*. The experimenter often has the tasks of *observing, judging, and recording* the subject's responses to the situation. The experimenter is likely to have responsibility for *calculating the results*; computers now handle much of this work, but judgment is required to solve some problems, as we will see in later chapters. Finally, it is up to the experimenter to *interpret the results*, including decisions about which findings to highlight and which to downplay. Experimenters in all areas of science have similar responsibilities, though some of the responsibilities just mentioned are unique to the behavioral sciences; they are all points at which the experimenter's expectations can influence the data.

In *Experimenter Effects in Behavioral Research*, Rosenthal (1976) provides a careful analysis of each of these sources of error and bias and then presents the results of a large number of studies designed to measure the magnitude of unconscious experimenter effects. First, an example of a study designed to demonstrate that expectations can affect the outcome of an experiment. In this study subjects were shown several photographs of people and asked to rate each as a success (with + 10 the highest rating) or a failure (with − 10 the lowest rating). Some of the experimenters (all of whom were undergraduates with little research experience) were led to believe that the subjects would rate most of the people as successes (a mean rating of +5 was expected), while other experimenters were told that the photographs were of "losers" and that the mean rating would be low (− 5). The experimental results supported the expectancy hypothesis. Subjects rated the photographs as more or less successful depending on what the experimenters had been led to believe, even though standard instructions and procedures were followed throughout.

In 1976 Rosenthal was able to compile more than 300 such experiments, a third of which provided statistically trustworthy evidence of expectancy effects. What is the mechanism producing these effects? Several plausible hypotheses have been evaluated and discarded; obvious efforts to influence the subjects, cheating, and systematic errors in recording and analyzing the data appear *not* to be the source of the effect. Rosenthal suggests that nonverbal communication of some sort is responsible, but as he admits, "After hundreds of hours of careful observation, no well-specifiable system of unintentional signalling has been uncovered" (1976, p. 301). Interestingly, the expectancy effects are as noticeable in animal studies as in human experiments, a result that is hard to reconcile with our usual concepts of communication.

As you might expect, these findings have been questioned and criticized. Barber (1976), for instance, has argued that in spite of Rosenthal's reassurances, the standardization of instructions and procedures was not adequately controlled, partly because the experimental task was so judgmental and ambiguous for both experimenter and researcher. This debate is likely to go on for some time. Researchers are naturally prone to arrange conditions that favor their particular hypothesis (there's nothing wrong with this strategy as long as the methodology is precise and public), and so we may expect a spate of experiments in which the "believers" produce data supporting the expectancy hypothesis and the "doubters" counter with evidence contrary to the hypothesis.

In addition to reviewing experimental studies on the expectancy effect, Rosenthal (1976, p. 20ff) also presents a cogent and informative analysis of potential sources of experimenter bias, and attention to these sources can be quite helpful in planning and evaluating a study. His analysis is based on sequence of events that constitute an experiment, from the experimenter's greeting of the subject to the final debriefing. Some of these events are mentioned here; others are treated in the following section on ethics.

The observing and judging roles appear to be especially susceptible to influence by expectation and general attitudes toward people. Rosenthal describes studies in which observers watching nursery school children at play noted more or less activity depending on whether the individual observer thought a particular child was above or below par; anthropologists portrayed the identical Mexican village in turn as happy, cooperative, placid, and depressed; a Russian city appeared less drab to sociologists the longer they stayed there. While such accounts are surely cause for concern, it is hard to know how far they can be generalized; documentation of the actual conditions and of the experimenter's expressed expectations was virtually nonexistent in these examples.

Errors in recording data and in analyzing results can also be caused by experimenter expectations. That such errors occur is certain, and in a few celebrated instances, scholars of greater or lesser rank have been accused of inaccurate, biased, or even dishonest reporting of data. For instance, there has been a rather heated debate about the trustworthiness of the studies of the noted English psychometrician Sir Cyril Burt on the relative importance of genetic and environmental factors in the intelligence of twins (Hearnshaw, 1979; also Gould, 1981). By and large it appears that most scholars are honest, and modern procedures for recording and analyzing data tend to reduce the "human element" at this stage of a research project. Nonetheless, there is still room for bias. For instance, a researcher is far less likely to take a closer look at the details of the data when the analysis supports the hypothesis than when it does not.

Reducing Experimenter Bias

What can be done to handle problems like the ones just described? Rosenthal (1976) has several recommendations. First, more than one experimenter should be included in the design of the study. The approach can be as simple as repeating the basic study with two or more investigators chosen at random. Silverman (1974) did just this in a study of altruism. The experimenter made phone calls to randomly selected subjects, explaining to whoever answered that his car had broken down and he had used his last coin for this emergency call; would the person please phone a garage and ask them to rescue him? The rate of altruism varied substantially when the study was replicated, showing that the experimenter was an important factor. Had further studies been done the researcher would have had to identify the "caller" factors of potential importance: the tone of voice, the approach (it is pretty hard to tell the caller exactly what to say in this situation), gender (does the stereotype of the helpless female evoke a higher rate of altruistic responses?), and so on. If the researcher had already had some ideas about relevant experimenter factors, these factors could have been included in the design from the beginning, yielding results more accessible to interpretation.

Rosenthal's second recommendation is the standardization of the experimenter's behavior in subject–experimenter interactions. Consistency can be achieved through attention to the instructions and in the maintenance of a constant environmental setting. The experimenter should become experienced in all procedures, not just the typical, "planned" events but the unusual and the unexpected ones as well. It is also worthwhile to test the procedures on a few "pilot" subjects selected to represent the range of variation in subjects. Their data will not be included in the analysis since the purpose in testing them is to evaluate the procedures. Several experimenters have also recommended that an end-of-session checklist be used by both experimenter and subject to document their perceptions of the session (Adair, 1973; Orne, 1969), a relatively cheap approach unless the checklist is too long and complicated.

Third, it may be desirable to keep the experimenter in the dark about the expected outcome, assuming that the experimenter who collects the data and the researcher are different individuals. Psychological experiments are frequently single-blind studies: the subject is not fully informed of either the nature of the study or the conditions under which he or she is participating. This approach reduces the effect of subject expectations. A double-blind procedure can serve to minimize bias due to experimenter expectations: both subject and experimenter are kept in the dark. For instance, the investigator in a drug study gives an assistant two packages of pills, one labeled A and the other B. The assistant is given no information about the predicted results of either medication. The assistant then selects subjects at random to whom either A or B are administered and records the results. If the double-blind approach works as planned, the assistant cannot in any way favor one drug over the other. You can imagine some of the difficulties that are likely to be encountered in implementing a parallel procedure in a behavioral study. In psychological experiments the treatment condition often cannot be administered unless the experimenter is thoroughly knowledgeable about the procedures and the rationale behind them, so that a double-blind is impossible.

The fourth recommendation is to automate the procedures, treatments, and all other aspects of the experiment insofar as is feasible. Automation generally entails apparatus and machinery, and indeed computers are seeing increased application in psychological laboratories. Machinery brings both advantages and disadvantages. Uniformity is a clear plus, but it can turn into inflexibility. Laboratory assistants are probably less likely to "break down." One of my professors once warned me, "If you need more apparatus than a pencil and paper, you will have equipment problems." I have recalled that advice more than once in my career.

These cautions notwithstanding, automation can bring many benefits in the right situation. But what if you have neither the equipment nor the money to obtain it? The impoverished behavioral scientist can gain many of the advantages of automation by dint of a little imagination and forethought. The fewer times the data have to be rewritten, for instance, the less chance for errors of any sort—bias or otherwise—and the less work to do. And even when the basic procedures of a study are handled by a computer, a human touch is still both necessary and desirable.

These recommendations, though discussed here in terms of error and bias, all help the researcher to obtain clean data and interpretable results. Vigilance is the key. No matter how automated the process Murphy's law holds: "If anything can go wrong, it will!" Just because procedures have worked well once does not mean that they will work well always, under all variations in treatments, and for all kinds of subjects. Machines go haywire. Assistants become tired or jaded. The researcher who begins a project with a totally objective attitude becomes excited by the first few observations, which can easily color his or her attitudes and expectations (Rosenthal, 1976, Ch. 12; Tversky and Kahneman, 1971; Kahneman, Slovic, and Tversky, 1982).

The bottom line, for better or worse, is that an experiment is a lot of work. The researcher cannot take anything for granted. No matter how detailed and thoughtful the original plans, a behavioral study requires continuing attention from beginning to end. This is the burden that rests on that group of people who serve collectively as the experimenter.

THE ETHICAL RESPONSIBILITIES OF THE EXPERIMENTER

The ultimate purpose of scientific research is to improve the human condition by increasing our understanding of the world. Most people view science with hope and trust. They realize that science requires a long-term investment and do not demand immediate payoffs, but they do expect scientists to repay the public trust.

Science is just one part of the complex social contract that governs those of us who live in the modern world. This contract is seldom made fully explicit, and it changes over the years. Sometimes the public grows disenchanted with the ability of researchers to solve the pressing problems that confront us; other times scientists are honored with our highest accolades. The strength and security of the contract varies from one discipline to another. Thus, the "hard" sciences like physics and chemistry have a longer history and can show greater payoffs than the "soft" sciences like psychology and sociology; the activities of engineers have more obvious impact on daily life than the work of educational researchers.

Science is more frequently the work of an individual than a group, and it is to these individuals that society grants the right to conduct research. This grant is given with the understanding that the individual will fulfill it in an ethically responsible fashion. As society has grown more complex and interdependent, total reliance on the individual's personal sense of responsibility has become too risky, and so various constraints, including professional guidelines and governmental regulations, have been placed on scientists. We now discuss the fundamental principles underlying the ethical responsibilities of the researcher, the major elements of the ethical codes that govern psychological researchers, and the pragmatics of ethical behavior.

Ethical Principles in Behavioral and Social Science Research

Ethics, according to the dictionary, is "the discipline dealing with what is good and bad, and with moral duty and obligation" (Webster's). It is virtually impossible to promote ethical behavior by setting forth an absolute code of conduct, for people vary in what they consider to be good and bad in different situations. Moreover, it is the spirit rather than the letter of the law that is paramount in ethics.

In our society the key to ethical behavior is a sensitivity to the consequences of one's actions as an individual and a respect for the rights and well-being of others. Even this generalization, though it would probably seem reasonable to many American citizens, reflects a set of assumptions about what is right and what is wrong. The point is, in the United States (and many other Western nations), the individual ultimately bears the responsibility for conducting himself or herself in an ethical manner, and all ethical codes eventually turn to the individual not only for compliance but for sensitivity to the moral imperatives of the culture.

Codes of Ethics

Behavioral scientists are traditionally given a certain authority over other human beings. They must use this power ethically. Not too many years ago, the ethical responsibilities of the behavioral scientist rested on an implicit understanding about the appropriateness of various practices for handling subjects; bad practices were handled on a case-by-case basis and were sometimes swept under the rug. In 1953 the American Psychological Association adopted a code of ethics, the first professional organization to do so and still one of the few to have such a code. This code has been revised about every ten years since 1953, most recently in 1973, when a new set of ten principles was set forth. (There are also standards for the protection of animals when used as subjects [APA, 1971] and for the professional activities of psychologists [APA, 1977a].)

In the early 1960s the federal government entered the picture. Concerned more with problems in medical research than in behavioral research, Congress passed a law protecting the rights of human subjects, and federal regulations now require the researcher to take certain steps to ensure that subjects are well treated. If the researcher works for an institution (like a university), then the institution has the responsibility of reviewing all investigations in which human beings serve as subjects to ensure that their rights are protected.

The fundamental concept underlying both the APA guidelines and the federal regulations reflects the consensus of the profession and of the public regarding what is acceptable.

> Behavioral research is ethical when the benefits and relevance of the research balance the costs in time and risks of harm to the subjects, when their interests and well-being are respected, and when they are properly informed about the nature of the research and the voluntary nature of their participation.

This general concept is spelled out in detail in professional and governmental documents. Its most pertinent aspects are summarized in Figure 3–1 under four major headings: personal responsibility, consent and participation, protection from harm, and confidentiality. The professional guidelines and federal regulations differ slightly in their emphasis, but for present purposes it makes sense to highlight the similarities.

Personal Responsibility. Appropriately enough, the first two principles in the APA guidelines elaborate the point made at the beginning of this section: ethical behavior is a personal responsibility. Federal regulations place little stress on this point and in fact give the institution (the university or college) the burden of monitoring the behavior of individual researchers. While it is quite reasonable to require the institution to review the practices of its members, the burden on the individual is not thereby lessened. Incidentally, in case you plan to undertake a project of your own, you should be aware that most universities require that all behavioral science research projects be approved by a Human Subjects Review Board.

Informed Consent and Voluntary Participation. Human beings should know what they are getting into, and why, and should have a chance to say "no":

Personal Responsibility

In planning a study the investigator has the personal responsibility to make a careful evaluation of its ethical acceptability. . . .

Responsibility for the establishment and maintenance of acceptable ethical practice in research always remains with the individual investigator. The investigator is also responsible for the ethical treatment of research participants by collaborators, assistants, students, and employees, all of whom, however, incur parallel obligations. [Principles 1 and 2]

Informed Consent and Willing Participation

Ethical practice requires the investigator to inform the participant of all features of the research that reasonably might be expected to influence willingness to participate, and to explain all other aspects of the research about which the participant inquires. . . .

. . . When the methodological requirements of a study necessitate concealment or deception, the investigator is required to ensure the participant's understanding of the reasons for this action. . . .

Ethical research practice requires the investigator to respect the individual's freedom to decline to participate in research or to discontinue participation at any time. . . . [Principles 3, 4, and 5]

Protection from Harm

The ethical investigator protects participants from physical and mental discomfort, harm, and danger. . . . the investigator is required to inform the participant of [any risk, and] secure consent before proceeding. . . .

After the data are collected, ethical practice requires the investigator to provide the participant with a full clarification of the study and to remove any misconceptions that may have arisen. . . .

. . . the investigator has the responsibility to detect and remove or correct [any undesirable] consequences, including, where relevant, long-term aftereffects. [Principles 7, 8, and 9]

Confidentiality

Information obtained about the research participants during the course of an investigation is confidential. [Principle 10]

Figure 3–1 Ethical principles in the conduct of research with human participants. (Excerpts from APA [1973], pp. 21, 29, 42, 54, 61, 77, 83, 89.)

such is the thrust of informed consent and voluntary participation. The idea is clear enough, but as we shall see in a later section, some interesting difficulties arise when one tries to put the idea into practice.

Protection from Harm. Protection from harm was a major concern of the legislators who wrote the original laws for protection of human subjects. In some instances subjects have been severely mistreated, sometimes without being aware of the fact, and were then denied any remedy. In one case that provoked outrage when it became public knowledge, black males were inoculated with syphilis bacteria in the 1930s and were then left to suffer as the disease progressed so that scientists could study the effects. In psychological research the harm is sometimes more difficult to evaluate: what is the harm suffered by a high-strung seven-year-old who bursts into tears or becomes angry when given a task that is virtually impossible to solve?

To cover this dilemma the concept of minimal risk has been introduced. The notion is that a normal person is not unreasonably harmed by everyday stresses and strains. Administering a mathematics achievement test to an elementary school student may make the student unhappy, but it falls within the limits of minimal risk. More problematic for behavioral researchers are situations in which the subjects are deceived or embarrassed, or are subjected to undue pressure or harassment. To be sure some commercial enterprises charge people to undergo just such "harm," sometimes without their being fully aware of what they are getting into. Whether such actions are ethical is an interesting question but not directly germane to the ethics of research. Experimental subjects are not generally "asking for trouble."

Confidentiality. Finally there is the matter of confidentiality. Subjects should know when any personal information or behavior will be made public knowledge. The usual assumption is that subjects will be told who is "looking on" during an experiment and that the results for individuals will be confidential.

Putting the Principles into Practice

The preceding principles are viewed by most researchers and their clients as quite reasonable. The difficulties come in deciding how to apply them in specific situations. In this section we will "walk" the subject through the steps of an experiment, commenting along the way about the various ethical considerations. Before the subject is even a glint in the researcher's eye, however, an important ethical decision will have to be considered: is the study as conceived a worthwhile venture? Some projects are difficult to justify, no matter how careful the experimenter may be in protecting the subjects. Badly designed studies fall into this category; the waste of time and energy cannot be justified. Trivial or irrelevant projects are likewise questionable, though here it must be determined what is trivial or irrelevant.

But let us assume that the ethical decision to carry out the research has been made. The study is about to begin.

Recruiting Subjects

The major ethical consideration in recruiting subjects for an experiment is obtaining informed consent. What techniques are used to gain it, and are the subjects fully informed about what they are getting into? As a rule of thumb the researcher should avoid whenever possible recruiting subjects who are under his or her influence, including friends, family, associates, and students. Unfortunately, they are often the subjects most readily available. If you ask them to lend a hand, they will feel obliged to say "yes," regardless of what you tell them about the situation or their real feelings about it. In fact, researchers commonly recruit such subjects and will continue to do so. The point is, each such request must be viewed as an ethical matter, one that requires the experimenter to weigh the implicit pressures of the request against the value of the study, both to the individual and to the discipline.

What should the subject be told about the study? In some instances the researcher may consciously mislead or deceive candidates because of the nature of the research; this matter will be considered shortly. But researchers often fail to think seriously about what information is reasonable to provide. In general, a policy of full disclosure is best: how long the study will take; why it is being done; what will happen; of what value is it to the subject (often the most honest answer is "none"); what feedback will be given at the end of the study. When student volunteers serve as subjects, the experimenter should think about ways to make the experience serve a useful educational purpose.

When research is carried out with special populations (i.e., those who are not undergraduates), the researcher should keep in mind who the real subjects are. Although considerable time and energy may have to be devoted to contacting whoever is responsible for granting consent for the research—administrators, teachers, and parents, for instance—the students (or other subjects) still deserve an explanation of what is going to happen to them, why, and so on.

Running the Experiment

Ethical misconduct can occur at any time during the experiment, but three major categories warrant particular mention: maltreatment, involuntary constraint, and deception. While the three sometimes overlap, it is possible to deal with them as separate problems.

Maltreatment. The misbehavior of some researchers has been so extreme that virtually all professionals would declare them unethical:

> [A study in a military setting] . . . involved taking untrained soldiers, disorienting them, placing them in an isolated situation, giving them false instructions and leading them, as individuals, to believe that they had caused artillery to fire on their own troops and that heavy casualties had occurred. The subjects ran, cried, and behaved in what they could only consider an unsoldierly way, and no amount of debriefing could remove the knowledge that they had done so. (APA, 1973, p. 74)

This example and others like it are obviously intolerable, but what about situations that are less clear-cut? Two considerations are of primary importance in determining the extent of maltreatment in any particular situation: how severe is the harm, and how permanent is it?

Some psychologists believe that research entailing *any* stress whatsoever is unjustified. This position seems unnecessarily extreme to me, and more than a little naïve. Mild embarrassment, the strain of mental activity, the shock produced by plunging your foot into a basin of ice water—all of these stressors have been employed by experimental psychologists in research on human behavior. None strikes me as especially inhumane, nor do they seem to have irreversible consequences.

The primary apparatus set up by psychologists is seldom a torture chamber, but maltreatment can arise through neglect as well as through malice. Procedures that are innocuous to some individuals may cause more strain for others, and the researcher needs to remain sensitive to this. The stress and strain of an hour in the laboratory is "no big deal" for most undergraduates, but it may matter to the individual who is facing a final exam the next day or who is fighting a bad cold or a raging headache. A routine check for special circumstances affecting the individual is usually a good idea, both as a way of showing respect for the person and of maintaining better control over the experiment.

One of the most serious threats of maltreatment occurs when the psychologist gives inadequate attention to the long-term effects of a laboratory experience. College students are highly motivated to do well. Consequently, they are upset when they experience failure, as well they might during an experiment, for laboratory studies often present tasks that are novel and that are designed to challenge the individual to go beyond his or her limits. Furthermore, deception, intentional or not, can leave the subject with concerns that have no basis in fact. We should not overdramatize the extent of lasting effects due to laboratory experiences; most undergraduates (and others) take such events in stride. Nonetheless, as a matter of courtesy and to obviate the occasional bad reaction, the researcher should as a matter of course take steps to ensure that the subject never leaves the laboratory with unresolved worries, concerns, or misunderstandings. The importance of debriefing will be discussed below; for now, it is important to note that maltreatment includes future as well as present effects.

Involuntary Constraint. Both professional guidelines and federal regulations give the subject the right to discontinue the experiment at any time. This principle would seem easy to observe but it is not. On the one hand, subjects may sometimes feel coerced to endure experimental conditions that they find intolerable. If a study entails undue strain or discomfort, the experimenter has a special responsibility to ensure that subjects feel totally free to request discontinuance of the experiment whenever they near the limits of tolerance. A violation of this assurance is found in a study of pain (APA, 1973, p. 67) in which medical students submitted to wearing headbands that could be tightened by thumbscrews to create pressure on the head. The subjects, who had been selected from the researcher's classes, were instructed to endure as much pain as they could (legitimate, perhaps, though near the threshold of ethical behavior) and were then pressured to continue further when they said they had reached that limit (clearly unethical behavior, and contrary to contemporary regulations).

At the other extreme, consider the researcher who is administering writing tests to a class of elementary school students, a task that would seem to fall into the minimal risk category. Should individual students be allowed to terminate the exercise if they feel that they do not want to participate, assuming that the principal, teachers, and parents have given their consent? You can imagine the "ripple" effect that would result if one student asked to be excused on the grounds of the "voluntary participation" principle. The nonrandom "deselection" of students would render the data of little value.

Deception. Finally, there is the matter of deceiving the subject during the course of an experiment (Rubin, 1970):

- The subject is told that the study has one purpose when another is actually intended. For instance, the experimenter says "This research is to discover how quickly you can solve a problem" when in fact the problem is impossible to solve and the purpose of the study is to investigate the responses of competent people caught in frustrating situations.

- The subject is given false or misleading information or feedback. For instance, the researcher might note, "You are taking a lot longer to memorize these nonsense syllables" when the subject is actually doing better than average. In an educational experiment, classroom teachers serving as subjects might be told, "These five students in your class have fairly low IQs and will probably do worse than average," when the students are actually a random sample from the class.

- The subject believes that other members in a group experiment are genuine participants when they are actually "shills," confederates of the experimenter who have been assigned a role. Thus, the subject might be told, "Sam, you and these other two people have been randomly selected to judge the artistic merit of several samples of abstract art" when, in fact, the other two "subjects" are under instructions to give high ratings to outrageously bad paintings to see how Sam's judgments are affected by group pressure.

Planned deception is fairly commonplace in certain fields of psychological research (one researcher [Carlson, 1971] estimated that studies in personality and social psychology misinformed subjects about three-quarters of the time) and fairly rare in others (less than 5 percent of the studies reported in the *Journal of Experimental Psychology* employ deception, according to Menges [1973]). Deception through omission may be a commonplace occurrence, but there is no documentation of this state of affairs.

Opinions differ markedly and often heatedly about the ethics of deception. On the one hand, some researchers feel that deception is *never* justified (e.g., Runkel and McGrath, 1972, p. 238). By this criterion relatively few experiments are ethical, because subjects are seldom told everything. On the other hand, there are scholars who think that deception can usually be employed (except in the most extreme cases) as long as the subject is debriefed at the end of the experiment. Yet another point of view holds that subjects should be told everything but then be asked to play a role as if they believed a particular state of affairs were true (Kelman, 1972; also cf. Holmes and Bennett, 1974). This approach was used by Zimbardo (1975) in his research on prisoner–guard relations. The subjects were Stanford undergraduates, who spent a weekend "locked up" as though they were in a prison; some pretended to be prisoners, and others acted as guards. The subjects all knew that they were in a simulation, but the stresses and strains nonetheless were quite intense. Playing a role can entail some of the same reactions as the "real thing."

What should be done about deception? Honesty is a good policy, perhaps the best. To the fullest extent possible, subjects should eventually be completely informed about the purposes and the nature of a study. This assurance is the foundation principle of informed consent. If the researcher thinks that an initial deception is critical to the conduct of an experiment, then as with all forms of maltreatment, its negative features must be weighed against the benefits derived from the research, alternative approaches carefully considered, and the likelihood of long-term effects contemplated. Some situations go beyond ethical bounds because of the likelihood of lasting harm to the subject:

> An experimenter interested in creating realism in an experiment convinced subjects that they were being hired for a quasi-permanent job. At the end of one day of "employment," they were told that it was merely [*sic!*] an experiment. One subject complained that he had turned down other employment opportunities on the strength of this offer (APA, 1973, pp. 37–38).

The procedures would have been unethical, in my opinion, even if no one had complained of harm, or if the subject in question was overstating the case—the experimenter should have foreseen the possibility of long-term consequences, and altered the procedures accordingly.

Ethics is not a matter of the damage actually done but of the harm that might ensue.

The End of the Experiment

Before subjects leave the experimental situation, it is the responsibility of the experimenter to undo any adverse effects of deception and misinformation by ensuring that all questions are answered and all stress alleviated insofar as possible. At this point the experimenter has the opportunity to make the subject "feel good" about the experience (Mills, 1976). Subjects should also be thanked for their participation before they leave.

Debriefing the subject is almost always a good idea, even when the investigation seems completely straightforward, with no tricks. The experimenter should leave enough time for the debriefing and should plan the procedures in advance. What did the subject think was going on? How did he or she feel about it? Were there any problems, concerns, questions? The researcher may be able to give the subject some feedback about performance and may also want to dissuade the subject from "spilling the beans" by telling other potential subjects about the experiment. The communication links among students in introductory psychology classes are often extensive, virtually ensuring that within a short time after the first subject is tested, everyone else will know what happened.

For the subject the experiment should be finished when he or she leaves the laboratory. If the researcher has done a good job of debriefing, all that remains are memories and (one hopes) good feelings. Proof of the ethical character of the experiment is furnished when this condition is met. In the military example described earlier, in which the soldiers were absolute panicked because they thought they had killed some of their fellows, it is unlikely that any amount of debriefing could have relieved their anxiety and embarrassment. The experiment was thus unethical in its roots.

The federal regulations mandate confidentiality: the experiment should not entail unnecessary intrusion into the subject's private and personal affairs and the reporting of the results should not make public the identity of the individual participants. Invasion of privacy and lapses of confidentiality are fairly rare in psychological research, but these lapses stand out. Vigilance is essential. Even though public attitudes about personal matters have become more liberal over the past few decades, not every individual chooses to go along with the trend. Thus, questions about sexual behavior, family background, personal income, and other sensitive areas should be respected by the researcher. Privacy has been invaded when the person is forced to say "That's none of your business!"

The reliance on statistics and the technical format for reporting psychological research tends to ensure the confidentiality of data. Some fields of psychological research have traditionally relied on case-study material, and qualitative investigations are becoming more commonplace in other areas of research. The more extensive the data base on the individual subject, the more the researcher must guard against revealing individual identities when reporting the results. Another serious problem, and one that is hard to guard against, is the discussion of individual cases outside of the laboratory by researchers. Such conversations are likely to be repeated only locally; it is not a matter of national publicity. But the individual's reputation is equally important whether locally or nationally, whether in print or voiced in a hallway.

What Do Subjects Think?

Psychologists have become increasingly sensitive to the need for establishing and maintaining ethical standards for the protection and well-being of human subjects in research settings. The accounts of questionable practice documented in the

1973 guidelines support the need for standards, and one hopes that the mistreatment of subjects is now largely a thing of the past.

On the other hand, instances of unethical behavior appear to have been fairly rare in the past, and there is reason to believe that psychologists may be overly sensitive about the stress produced by their procedures. Sullivan and Deiker (1973) surveyed both college undergraduates and research psychologists on the ethics of several experimental situations and found that in eighteen out of twenty categories, psychologists were much more troubled by the potential for harm than were students. When presented with experimental procedures that entailed stress, pain, loss of self-esteem, and even experimentally induced unethical behavior, students thought the deceptive practices ethical and justified by the experimental question 66 percent of the time, compared with the psychologists' rating of 33 percent. Students were most concerned about the induction of unethical behavior (experiments in which subjects were led to do things that they thought were wrong); both students and psychologists were most concerned about linking a course grade to participation in the subject "pool." This finding does not mean that the psychologists' perceptions and judgments were wrong; indeed one would hope that an experienced behavioral scientist *would* be more aware of the potential for harm than would an inexperienced undergraduate.

There is also the possibility that psychologists may be mistaken about the relative discomfort associated with various procedures. For instance, Farr and Seaver (1975) asked students to rate the unpleasantness of several experimental situations that appeared to threaten physical or psychological well-being. They were surprised to find that students considered giving a five-minute speech more disagreeable than suddenly discovering that electrodes attached to their scalps were beginning to smoke! To be sure, the ratings might have been different had the subjects actually undergone the various experiences, but the fact remains that what is perceived as undesirable by one person may not trouble another, and vice versa.

SUMMARY

Psychological research generally involves a set of highly stylized social interactions. Experimenter and subject both have roles that are partly established by the conditions of the experiment and partly implicit in being an experimenter and being a subject.

The journal descriptions of the sample of subjects are often rather abbreviated, but the subject is typically a college undergraduate enrolled in an introductory psychology course who undertakes the research as part of a course requirement. Variations on this theme do exist: clinical and educational research often require the investigator to conduct research in the "real world" with "real people." Even among the undergraduate students who make up the typical sample of subjects, there is considerable variation in ability, background, and attitudes toward the experimental setting.

If journal articles have little to say about the subjects, they have virtually nothing to say about the experimenter. The white-robed professor is a stereotype; more often, research is conducted by a graduate student, with or without the white robe. The few studies on how the experimenter's characteristics affect subjects' performance suggest that further research on this topic might be enlightening.

The interaction between experimenter and subject has been investigated to some extent. Though some of these studies have methodological shortcomings, it appears that the experimenter's expectations about the outcome of an investigation may influence the results of the study substantially, although the mechanisms have yet to be fully understood. Given this state of affairs, it is prudent to consider potential sources of experimenter bias in the design and conduct of an experiment. Including experimenter factors in the design, standardizing procedures and instructions, adopting single- or double-blind techniques, and automating the procedures are all ways to reduce the potential influences of experimenter bias.

Because psychological research is a social situation sanctioned by society the experimenter, as the person in charge of the research, has certain ethical responsibilities. These responsibilities ultimately fall on the shoulders of the individual researcher, but guidelines for the ethical conduct of research have been promulgated by the American Psychological Association and the federal government. The basic principles underlying these guidelines are the personal responsibility of the researcher and, for the subject, the assurance of informed consent and voluntary participation, protection from harm, and the confidentiality of information obtained during the experiment.

Ensuring that a study respects the ethical guidelines requires the researcher to provide for the subjects' well-being at *all* phases of the study. Though attention tends to be focused on the experiment proper, it is equally important that the subject be treated properly before and after. The subject should be informed as completely as possible about the nature and purposes of the study at the outset, and a complete debriefing (with special care given when deception or stress have been part of the experimental procedures) should be carried out at the conclusion of the study.

Subjects generally contribute their time to the cause of advancing psychological knowledge at no cost, and most subjects feel good about this contribution. It therefore behooves the researcher to respond with concern for the subject's well-being. This consideration is the foundation for ethical research.

4

Collecting Psychological Data

People gather data all the time, generally without thinking too much about it. Sometimes the data are from the physical world: while walking I realize that the daylight is fading, glance at my watch, and am surprised by the lateness of the hour. Sometimes the data are from the psychological world: my son's report card shows a C in mathematics, and he informs me that the math teacher doesn't like him. Both kinds of data lead me to inferences and hypotheses, which may suggest the need for more data. I ask my son to show me his homework assignments, and upon examining them I quickly conclude that less time watching television and more time working on math assignments will improve his grades, the teacher's attitude notwithstanding.

Perhaps because collecting data is so commonplace, one easily takes the process for granted. When the researcher records the number of correct answers given during a learning task, notes how long the subject takes to perform a job, or rates the attentiveness of students in a classroom, the data collection operations seem natural and obvious. Yet in each instance the researcher has made important assumptions about the nature of performance and the relations between performance and knowledge.

A piece of data is called an **observation.** It is seldom interesting in its own right but only in that it informs us about broader aspects of the person's capabilities. It is therefore essential for the researcher to consider carefully how observable performance, which furnishes the data, is linked to underlying competence.

Collecting data involves a general principle: *observation is the foundation of all research.* Later in this book you will learn a variety of sophisticated techniques for designing well-controlled experiments. These techniques serve a vital role in advancing knowledge in psychology. Still, the value of an experiment depends not only on its being well designed but also on the quality of the data collection procedures. Here the best models do not come from experimental designs but from the careful efforts of astronomers, naturalists, clinicians, and ethnographers.

In this chapter we examine data collection procedures that are both simple and complex. Then our discussion turns to issues of interpretability and validity. To begin we explore one of the most intensive methods of data collection now used in the behavioral sciences: ethnographic description.

THE ETHNOGRAPHIC METHOD

When the research project requires a detailed account of performance or when the researcher is uncertain about the critical features of the behavior being examined and needs to know "everything," ethnography may be the most appropriate method. It can also be the best choice when the researcher is a novice or when a novel problem is being investigated.

The ethnographic approach is *descriptive*, *introspective*, and *participatory*. It is descriptive in that the ethnographic record resembles a novel. It is introspective in that the ethnographer typically relies on internal cues and reactions as a guide for recording observations. It is participatory in that the ethnographer becomes actively engaged with the people and the situations being observed. While it is possible to create a design for ethnographic observation, the ethnographic approach is also workable when the background knowledge is insufficient to create such a plan. Spradley (1979), perhaps overstating the point, says, "Ethnography starts with a conscious attitude of almost complete ignorance" (p. 4).

The ethnographic method, which has its origins in cultural anthropology, emphasizes the cultural and contextual determiners of behavior. "Foreign" situations are favored, not because of a fascination with the esoteric but because of the hazards of trying to be a true witness in a familiar situation. When you try to observe what is "really" happening in a situation that you already know, the inclination is to overlook features that may be obvious to you but that may be critical to understanding the phenomenon. The difficulty works in both directions. When you ask a question of someone who knows that you already know the answer, the response is likely to be different from the one you would receive if the respondent thinks that you are a stranger to the situation.

Suppose you decide to conduct an ethnographic observation at the meat counter of a supermarket (I am assuming that you are familiar with this situation and that you look like you have been shopping before). What questions, if any, would you ask of the shoppers? Suppose you ask someone, "What are you doing?" I suspect that in response most people would look at you cautiously and give you wide berth. A more detailed inquiry—"I noticed you looked first at the chicken, then the rump roast, and finally put some liver in your shopping basket. Could you tell me what you were thinking about?"—might elicit a rather direct response: "None of your business!" What should you record, and how should you interpret this exchange?

How then can a researcher conduct ethnographic research on problems with which he or she is already familiar—is the task impossible? The answer is that such research is possible, but continuous assessment of perceptions and assumptions is essential.

The ethnographic method entails three distinctive phases. First is the selection of a situation for study. The question under study, along with your judgment about the range of variation and the typicality of the situations available, will determine the situation selected. Next is the actual process of data collection, which generally takes the shape of detailed field notes. Finally comes analysis and interpretation: what concepts can be employed to make sense of the observations; what are the similarities and differences between events; and what are significant episodic and structural themes?

Field notes are the core of the ethnographic method. Spradley (1979) identifies three essential elements that must be recorded for each facet of a situation: a *place*, a set of *actors*, and a series of *activities*. In the field notes, then, one expects to find a detailed account of events as they occur in time, with clear descriptions of where, who, and what happened. In short, the notes should resemble careful newspaper reporting.

The Courtroom. The approach is illustrated by Spradley's (1980) field notes from his experiences during the convening of a grand jury. Most of the participants, including Spradley himself, were strangers to the situation:

> I followed the hallway until I saw a sign over two large doors: CRIMINAL COURT. I decided to go in even though there were still five minutes before the appointed hour of 9:00 A.M. I pushed open one of the swinging doors and found myself in a large courtroom.
>
> There were rows of spectator benches, all made of heavy dark wood, oak or walnut, to match the paneled walls. The rows of benches went for more than twenty-five feet until they met a railing that seemed to neatly mark off a large area for "official business." I went in, sat down in the last row of spectators' benches, and looked around at a few other people seated at various places in the courtroom. The high ceiling and heavy dark wood made me feel as if I were in a sacred, almost religious place. Two people sitting in front of me were talking in hushed tones and I could not hear what they said. As newcomers came in, they would stop, look around, and then move very slowly to find a place to sit. At the right of the area behind the railing were twelve high-back leather chairs behind another railing. A large oak table with massive chairs all faced toward a high lectern which I took to be the judge's bench. All this area was empty. I waited.
>
> A few minutes after nine a man walked in with a brisk manner. He looked at the people scattered around the large courtroom, all of us in the spectators' area, and said, "Hello. I assume you are all here for the prospective grand jury. Judge Fred Adams is going to be on the bench and it would be

better if you all sat in the jury box." Slowly people got up and I joined them as we moved together toward the front. How easy for some unknown man to give orders and we all obey. I took a seat in the front row and soon all twelve chairs were filled. Several people sat in the first row of the spectators' area; three men sat in chairs inside the area of "official business." . . . I was conscious of standing out in my casual clothes and beard. All the others were dressed neatly; the men in suits and ties, some in sportcoats. Many dark business suits. They all looked professional. The women were well dressed in suits, dresses, high heels, makeup. All looked older than myself. It was as if they had all dressed for some formal occasion. I felt a little out of place, but decided it didn't matter. . . .

The man who had called us to the jury box . . . was joined by a sheriff's officer in full uniform, gun mounted on his left hip. He walked across the courtroom and stood near a door near the high judge's bench. The man and the police officer kept looking at each other; one glanced at his watch; there was an air of expectancy in the jury box also. You could feel something important was about to happen, but I'm not sure how we knew.

"Will everyone rise!" The officer shouted his command at the exact instant that the door opened. "The court of Fred Adams, honorable judge of Marshall County, is now in session." (That is an approximation since I couldn't write while standing and I couldn't remember exactly what he said.) I stood at attention and felt my heart beating faster than usual. A tall, gray-haired man in full black robe walked slowly in, turned toward the bench, and went up and sat down. Everyone was completely attentive. The moment had arrived. . . . (pp. 74–75)

This record, which covers portions of a fifteen-minute episode, is fairly typical of ethnographic field notes: detailed description, attention to time, interwoven interpretive comments, and so on. The situation, rather than being selected for a particular purpose, was instead an instance of applying ethnographic skills to a situation in which the writer was an actual participant. The writer was new to the situation in some respects but was familiar with the culture in other ways. The record is mostly a matter of writing down the "facts," but also includes occasional interpretive remarks ("How easy for an unknown man to give orders . . . "). The author also inserts his personal reactions in the record; these insertions are not only appropriate but are viewed by many ethnographers as essential for an accurate description.

An adequate interpretation of these notes could turn on any of several pieces of evidence offered. From the complete notes it appears that people differ in their response to the unfamiliar courtroom setting. Some are excited, others are obviously nervous. Some move to assume leadership while others try to fade into the background. These interpretations generate hypotheses that may be checked for internal consistency and that may be confirmed by additional observations. Spradley (1980) has described in some detail the process of analysis; the task is rather complex, and a full exposition would take us far afield, but you might be interested in reading his recommendations on your own.

We have examined the ethnographic method of observation first because it provides a contrast with the more standard techniques employed by experimental psychologists. Ethnography entails prolonged interaction with the "informant": the observer must be willing to engage in extended contact with the subject, who in turn must on occasion be willing to answer rather stupid questions. The interaction is in most respects natural and nonmanipulative. The informant is in charge of the situation and can decide how to handle any questions posed by the interviewer. The data are complex, allowing considerable leeway in interpretation.

In contrast, the subject in the typical laboratory experiment is expected to do what he or she is told. The experimental procedures constrain the responses and the interactions. The data are relatively simple to record and appear easy to interpret.

Concept Learning in the Laboratory. These contrasts between ethnographic and standard techniques may be more apparent than real. I recall observing an experiment several years ago in which the subjects (college sophomores) had to solve a concept identification problem. A series of cards was presented, each card displaying a geometric shape that varied along several dimensions; one card might have a large red circle with vertical stripes, while the next would be a small blue square with horizontal bars, and so on. The subject's task was to figure out which combinations were instances of the "concept," as designated by the experimenter. For instance, the experimenter might have chosen red circles as the concept to be identified. The testing continued until the subject made ten correct responses in succession.

One particular subject, after listening to the intentionally vague instructions, said to the experimenter, "This sounds like a simple problem. I might just have to push the "+" button whenever the card is red, right?" The experimenter, flustered by the question, responded that he could not give any more details. The subject wrinkled his brow as the first card was presented. After the first dozen cards he appeared to have figured out the concept: all blue figures. He responded correctly to cards 7 through 12. When card 13, a blue figure, was presented, he glanced at the experimenter, wrinkled his brow, and pushed the "−" button—an error. Several more correct responses followed, again a puzzled look at the experimenter, and again an error—never quite enough successes to meet the criterion for ending the test. The session continued in this fashion for the better part of an hour, until the experimenter said that time was up. The subject was then told the correct answer; he shook his head and left. When I asked the experimenter about the subject's data, I was told "He did not meet the criterion, and we discard the data for any subject who fails to learn the problem."

You might consider the possibility that my ethnographic account of the situation provides a better basis for interpreting the subject's responses than was revealed by the "quantitative" data in the official record. . . .

SIMPLE DATA

As the example just given suggests, all psychological data are complicated in some sense: though the record may show only that the subject succeeded or made an error, the actual event is probably much more intricate. Nonetheless, the recorded outcome of some data collection procedures is fairly simple (a checkmark or the recording of a number, for instance), whereas other data collection procedures entail fairly complex records. In this section we discuss procedures that yield fairly simple observations, that is, either categorical or numerical values; in the next section we will discuss procedures that yield more complicated data.

Simple data generally reflect a straightforward recording of the subject's response:

- Sam said he preferred Johnson for president.

- In a sample of 100 college students, 33 preferred Johnson for president.

- Sam took ten seconds to say that he preferred Johnson for president.

For each example the basic datum can be recorded without ambiguity. Multiple events are easy to *aggregate*; that is, it is possible to calculate averages and to graph them.

Whether data are simple depends on how easily and directly they can be recorded and handled, not necessarily on how easily they can be interpreted. Data are easy to interpret to the extent that we possess a theory for linking observable performance (of any kind, simple or complex) to underlying mental events. An example of the role of theory in psychological research will be presented in the next chapter; for now we will focus on the practical ramifications of data collection.

Discrete, Categorical Data

Some measures can be easily classified into a small number of discrete, categorical "bins":

- The answer was right or wrong.

- The subject judged the task as easy, so-so, or difficult.

- The subject pushed button A, B, C, or D.

- The kindergartner labeled a *snark* as animal, vegetable, or mineral.

Such data have two distinguishing features: (a) the number of different responses is small, and (b) it is easy to determine the subject's response on any given occasion.

Yet the actual responses may be quite complex. For instance, the answers on a multiple-choice test are categorical responses, but the nature of the task can be and often is quite complicated.

The apparent simplicity of collecting categorical data is sometimes misleading. The task may be straightforward, but the creation of a meaningful response set can pose quite a challenge. In fact, developing a response set is similar to designing an experiment. You must decide on the goals of the study, then identify the factors that will influence the category chosen in a particular situation, and finally think about how the design might be adequate to support a particular interpretation.

As a concrete example, suppose you are planning an experiment on the variables that influence a person's preferences for automobiles of various sizes. Age, gender, income, and a variety of other factors might determine the preference. You make plans to include these variables in the design, along with a training program that helps people sort out the reasons for their preferences. What kind of data should you collect to assess the influence of these factors? Always start with the most direct approach:

What Size Automobile Do You Prefer?

a. Large

b. Mid-sized

c. Compact

d. Subcompact

A reasonable starting point, but you can probably see some problems with this design. Will all subjects interpret the choices similarly? What if a subject doesn't care for any of the choices? What about the subject who wants to complicate the issue: "My preference in car size depends on my transportation needs." We will return to this example shortly.

Perhaps the most common type of categorical data is the two-choice response, or so-called binary data. Typical answers are "yes" or "no," "right" or "wrong," "true" or "false," "large" or "small," "would you rather be a bartender or a banana rancher," and so on. While such data are easy to collect, they can be difficult to interpret. "Do you prefer a large car?" is hard to answer with a simple "yes" or "no": the most accurate response is likely to entail shades of meaning. "Have you stopped beating your spouse?" is a tough one; you are damned whether you say "yes" or "no." Scoring a person's answer on a multiple-choice test as "right" or "wrong" is convenient, but some errors are more plausible than others. "Right–wrong" scoring gives no insight into the reasoning behind the answer. These cautionary remarks are not meant to argue against the use of binary responses; they are quite useful for many purposes. On the other hand, such data provide only a peek into the nature of a phenomenon, and more complex data are necessary for understanding the underlying processes.

Multiple-choice responses are common in modern life. With three or four alternatives to work with, the clever data collector may actually be able to design a system that reveals the thought underlying the subject's decision. The guidelines in Figure 4–1 provide commonsense suggestions for evaluating multiple-choice questions. They also contain some implicit advice for subjects about how to approach such tests! The important lesson in Figure 4–1 is that multiple-choice questions, like other questions designed to elicit categorical responses, are most effective when constructed according to a design framework. If the data are to be interpretable, more is required than simply writing a question with four answers.

The usual assumption is that once a researcher has created a set of response categories the subject's task is to select the single response that comprises the "best

A. In general
    1. Write in clear, concise, and readable language.
    2. Eliminate irrelevant information.
    3. Use technical terms only when essential.
    4. Avoid negatives.
B. The stem
    1. Include the essence of the problem.
    2. Put as much of the material in the stem as possible.
    3. Place the "slot" for the alternatives at the end of the stem.
C. The alternatives
    1. Create three to five alternatives.
    2. Each alternative should be reasonably plausible, and all alternatives should be fairly similar.
    3. One and only one of the alternatives should be the best answer. Avoid "all of the above" and "none of the above" as alternatives.
    4. Arrange the alternatives randomly, unless they form a natural list.

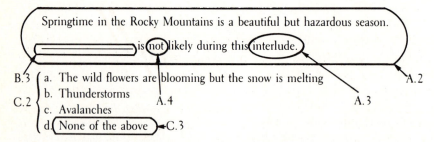

Figure 4–1 Guidelines for the construction of multiple-choice questions and an example of a poorly written test item with some problems highlighted

answer." Sometimes a more informative approach is to ask the subject to rate each of the alternatives. Consider the following test item:

> Amy studied the telephone system in her business class. The teacher told the students to remember that 411 was the number for local information in most cities. This fact was practical for office workers, and it would be on the test.

> **a.** Amy knows the telephone number for local information.

> **b.** Amy knows the telephone number for the White House.

> **c.** Amy knows the telephone number for finding a long distance number for a city with area code 415.

> **d.** Amy knows the telephone number for George Washington, the first president.

The typical instruction would be to "pick the right answer." The student might reasonably argue that none of the answers is clearly correct, though you probably know which is meant to be the "correct" answer.

Another approach would be to ask the person being tested to judge each answer as "true" or "false." Even more interesting would be to ask, "How certain are you about the answer you gave to each question?" This inquiry is likely to reveal that subjects are quite certain that Amy does *not* know George Washington's phone number. What makes someone so certain about something that they have not been taught?

Finally, you might provide the subject with a list of justifications and ask him or her to indicate which one determined the response to each alternative:

- The answer was stated in the paragraph.

- The answer can be inferred from the paragraph.

- The answer is common knowledge.

- The answer is a guess.

One last illustration of the role of design in planning categorical choices in data collection is seen in Figure 4–2, which shows materials for testing word perception skills in kindergartners (Calfee, 1977). In the early stages of learning to read, the child must learn to discriminate letters and to handle strings of letters. The test in Figure 4–2 employed artificial letters to assess these skills. The children were instructed to look at the target, the "word" in the circle at the top, and then mark any of the "words" beneath it that were "exactly the same as the word in the circle." The children practiced on several examples to clarify the meaning of "exactly the same" and to ensure that they knew that they could mark more than one alternative.

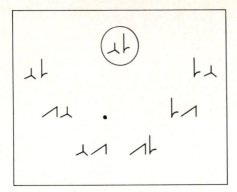

Figure 4–2 Sample of stimulus display in "word" matching test. The kindergartner is told to study the word in the circle and mark any words below the circle that look exactly the same. (After Calfee, 1977)

Children frequently make mistakes on readiness tests of this sort. The question is, What do the mistakes mean? The alternatives in Figure 4–2 were designed to help clarify this issue. If you examine these alternatives carefully, you will discover that they are designed according to the plan presented in Figure 4–3. One factor in the plan calls for both letters in the target to be repeated in the alternative, or for the first or the second letter to be replaced by another letter. The second factor requires the letters in the alternative to appear in the same order as the target, or to be reversed. Twelve test items were constructed with artificial letters according to this plan, and the arrangement of the alternatives below the target was scrambled.

Figure 4–3 also shows how often each of the alternatives was marked by the kindergartners. As you can see, the correct match (both letters present and in the same order) was marked by the students most of the time, whereas any alternative with a changed letter was unlikely to be marked. The "reversed" alternative (both letters present, but in reverse order, as in *was* for *saw*), was marked about one-third of the time. These errors appeared to be conceptual rather than perceptual, however; about one out of three students marked both this alternative *and* the correct match on every one of the twelve items. Based on this interpretation the study was repeated with a second group of students who were given explicit instructions, reinforced by examples, that "same" meant that the letters had to be in the same order. The results were virtually identical to the data in Figure 4–3, except that the reversal errors dropped to 15 percent, the level one might expect to have resulted through inattention or unfamiliarity with the task. In this study the design of the alternatives played a critical role for ensuring interpretable results and learning how to improve student performance.

Letters in Alternative

	Both	A only	B only
Same Order	AB 83%	AX 14%	YB 14%
Changed Order	BA 31%	XA 10%	BY 10%

Figure 4–3 Design of "word" matching test in Figure 4–2. AB is the target "word." The alternative for each cell of the design is shown at the top of the cell and the percentage of times kindergarten children marked each alternative is shown at the bottom. (Data of Calfee, 1977)

Continuous, Numerical Data

Some data collection procedures lead naturally to the recording of numbers:

- How long did the subject take to hit the brake in a simulated driving emergency after two martinis?

- What was the subject's galvanic skin response while working arithmetic problems of varying difficulty?

- How far off the target was the subject in a dart-throwing task performed under various levels of perceptual distortion?

- How many correct answers did the subject make on a 100-item spelling test?

In each example the most natural datum to record is the number generated by some sort of measuring device. In the next chapter we will discuss situations in which people are asked to generate numbers themselves, either by rating something or by estimating magnitudes. In the present discussion the numbers are generated by the mechanics of the data collection process.

Data of this sort appear to be relatively simple: all the researcher has to do is record the "meter reading." But as you may now suspect, nothing can be taken for granted in research. Three kinds of issues must be considered in collecting numerical data: *precision*, *extreme values*, and *the scale of measurement*.

Precision. As noted previously, categorical data entail a small set of response categories, and so there is little problem in deciding what response to record in any particular instance. For numerical data, however, the precision of the measuring instrument can be an important consideration. Some mental processes operate at extremely rapid rates, often in the millisecond ($\frac{1}{1000}$ of a second) range. Timing such events calls for relatively high accuracy. On the other hand, accuracy can be overdone; recording the distance between a dart and the bull's-eye to the nearest .0001 inch is rather foolish.

Precision can be achieved in a variety of ways. Suppose your goal is to collect data on the amount of time it takes a subject to decide whether or not a string of letters is a word. This task may take only a fraction of a second—250 to 350 milliseconds. The effect of an experimental factor on the reaction time may be only a few tens of milliseconds. Without special equipment you will probably not be able to measure these events with adequate precision. For instance, most of the variability that results from using a stopwatch may be your own reaction time. One way to solve the problem without special equipment is to have the subject scan a list of letter strings, thus repeating the task several times in succession.

Figure 4–4 illustrates this latter approach. The experimental question is the effect of reading upside down on reading speed. Shown in the figure are two sets of twenty-four four-letter strings; half the strings in each set are real words, and the remaining are pronounceable nonwords. The subject's task is to look at each letter string, rightside up or upside down, and decide whether or not it is a word. It takes most college students about a second to respond in the rightside up orientation; turning the letter string upside down adds about a third of a second to the response time—an amount hard to detect without specialized equipment. The measurement problem can be solved by having the subject go through an entire list in one or the other orientation, indicating which letter strings are words and which are not (be sure to emphasize accuracy). If you carry out this experiment, you should find that the typical college subject takes about 24 seconds to perform the task under the normal orientation and about 32 seconds with an inverted list. The difference of 8 seconds, when divided by 24 (the number of strings in the list), allows you to estimate the effect of inversion on each word: $\frac{8}{24} = \frac{1}{3}$, or about a third of a second per string. If you are interested in a factor with smaller effects than the example, you can simply add more items to the list.

Extreme Values. Strange things can happen when measuring responses on a numerical scale. With categorical data the set of possible responses is constrained, and the most unusual event is likely to be a failure to respond. When the experimenter is timing the subject's response, when physical movement is being measured, or when physiological reactions are being recorded, there may be no upper or lower limits to the measure. For instance, a subject may normally take between 15

DRAD	FOWL
LENS	ONEN
OCEN	NORM
LOWF	SPUD
BUNK	KRET
FOLT	PWAS
CLIP	TRIM
NIER	REIN
ACTS	REPY
HUSK	WAIL
NOHR	SACT
DUPS	PELT

Figure 4–4 Illustration of word lists that might be used in a serial task to measure effect of inverted printing

and 30 seconds to scan the word list in Figure 4–4; an incipient sneeze may double or triple this value. The driver in a simulated emergency task may take his or her eyes off the road at the critical moment, adding 50 to 100 feet to the normal braking distance. The student taking a multiple-choice test may skip an item early in the test; past that point the responses on the answer sheet will appear random.

Unusual deviations from the norm, generally referred to as **outliers,** pose special problems in the collection of numerical data. It takes only a few such deviations to alter the average value in a particular condition; even worse, extreme values can greatly increase the random variability in a data set. As we shall see later in the book, variability is the critical index against which the significance of treatment effects is assessed in behavioral research. Accordingly, a scattering of outliers can seriously jeopardize the interpretation of an experiment.

What can be done to reduce the impact of extreme scores? First, the researcher must become aware of the problem, of the conditions under which it is likely to occur, and of the impact of extreme deviations on the interpretability of the findings. Second, it is important to be alert for the occurrence of outliers during the conduct of a study. If the subject's response is unusual in any respect, the researcher should inquire into the reasons for the deviation. The subject may tell you, "I had to sneeze." Unless the experiment is concerned with the effects of sneezing upon reaction times, the researcher has reasonable cause to discard the measurement and repeat the trial. Third, the researcher should be alert during data analysis for the presence of outliers. This step entails care in the descriptive analysis of the data; the frequency distributions (Chapter 6) must be examined for unusual numbers. The human eye is a pretty good tool for this purpose, which requires judgment: the goal is to detect observations that are exceptional, not to eliminate those data that conflict with the researcher's predispositions.

The Scale of Measurement. A major difficulty in interpreting numerical data is deciding what the numbers mean. To put the matter more precisely, what is the appropriate scale of measurement? We encounter this question again in the next chapter, and so the present discussion is rather brief, sketching issues that are dealt with in more detail later.

Suppose that a group of subjects takes 10 seconds to solve problems of type A, 20 seconds to solve problems of type B, and 30 seconds to solve problems of type C. From these results one might conclude that the difference in difficulty between type A and type B problems is about the same as the difference in difficulty between type B and type C. Now let us measure the same results according to the rate of problem solution. Type A problems are solved at a rate of 6 per minute, type B at a rate of 3 per minute, and type C at a rate of 2 per minute. Now it appears that the gap between A and B is greater than the gap between B and C. Which is the proper interpretation?

Here is a second example. Two groups of subjects, freshmen and seniors, are pretested on a reading exam. The freshmen get a score of 90 percent correct while the seniors get only 10 percent correct. After a special training session, both groups show a gain of 10 points on the posttest. At first glance the treatment may appear to have had the same effect for both groups. On further reflection, however, notice that the improvement for the freshmen amounts to 100 percent of the possible room for improvement (they were only 10 percentage points below perfect performance), whereas in this regard the improvement for the seniors is only 11 percent: they have achieved 10 percentage points out of the 90 that they had to go. Once again, which is the more meaningful analysis?

A number is a number is a number. . . We tend to think of numbers as solid, objective quantities. Yet the trustworthiness of the number system in any particular instance depends on the measurement operations that generate the numbers. If you have a quarterback with the number 11, and a tailback with the number 22, you cannot add the two to obtain a fullback with the number 33. Quantitative measurement is the assignment of numbers to objects or events according to a particular rule, and the nature of the rule determines what numerical operations are appropriate. The assignment rule determines the characteristics of the scale of measurement. Sometimes the numbers serve only to identify objects, as in the football-player example; sometimes the numbers indicate whether one object is greater, smaller, or equal to another (the two earlier examples fit this description);

sometimes adding and subtracting is meaningful (differences can then be evaluated); and sometimes multiplying and dividing are appropriate.

None of these common operations should be taken for granted. The key to the meaningful interpretation of data, whether numerical or categorical, is the construction of a theoretical framework within which observations can be related to a scale of measurement. The next chapter shows how theory can be applied to resolve problems like the ones posed above.

COMPLEX DATA

Neither categorical descriptions nor the assignment of numbers is adequate to summarize some kinds of observations. Complexity arises either because a phenomenon is truly complicated or because we lack the concepts to translate it into a simple form. In either event observations in some psychological investigations are likely to be relatively complicated; these are the focus of the present section. Three types of complex data are discussed: language data, questionnaires and interviews, and observations.

Language Data

Language seems inherently complicated to most observers. As simple a task as reading a single word (a language act) can produce multifaceted outcomes. One youngster reads *yacht* as "yak," another says "yasht," and a third comes up with "sailboat." The researcher may count all these responses as errors, but doing so obscures significant differences in the character of the three answers.

The situation becomes even more intriguing with larger units of language: sentences, paragraphs, and discussions. To describe adequately the principles needed to record and analyze such observations requires an understanding of the structure of language, which could take us far beyond the goals of this book. Suffice it to say that principles from linguistics and psycholinguistics provide the researcher with tools to simplify considerably the task of language analysis. From the several excellent works on this topic (Clark and Clark, 1977; Dale, 1972), a few of these principles have been selected for mention.

First, there are natural divisions common to virtually all languages at virtually all stages of development. The divisions correspond more or less to the concepts of sound (phoneme), word (morpheme), sentence (syntax), and larger segments of discourse (linguistics is a little fuzzy in this area). You may associate these divisions with the conventions of written language (a word is a string of letters set off by blank spaces, for instance), but you need to look beneath the surface to really comprehend these divisions. For instance, the child who has not yet learned to read may treat the phrase *in the house* as a single unit, akin to a word. In some languages prepositions and articles are written as part of the noun, and so the child's intuitions are not far off the mark. Similarly, the college student may say that *neuropsychological* is one word, while recognizing that it combines four distinct elements that can be isolated to get at the underlying meaning. The same remarks can be made about language at all levels: the surface structure does not always correspond to the underlying structure.

Take a simple sentence like "The car in the driveway is not the one with the broken window." You probably have little difficulty in understanding this message and may think of it as a single "chunk" of information. Yet consider all the detailed propositions that are intertwined in this statement:

- There is a car.

- It is in the driveway.

- There is a car with a broken window.

- The first-mentioned car could be the same as the second-mentioned car.

- The previous statement is not true.

Such detailed analysis may seem to complicate unnecessarily the collection and interpretation of language data. In fact, the main task for the language researcher is to decide on the level of language performance that is most suitable to the goals of a particular project and to find the most appropriate way of extracting from the flow of language the pieces of information to represent that level.

It is a mistake, for example, to count words when your major interest is in ideas. To be sure, the number of words in an utterance (something said by a person) provides a rough index of the individual's linguistic productivity. A more precise measure may be derived by counting the number of *content words* (nouns and most verbs and adjectives) and disregarding the *function words* (articles, pronouns, and some verbs and adjectives). One person may say, "My two weeks this summer plunging through the churning rapids of the Colorado was one of the most thrilling experiences of my life!" while another describes the same event this way: "Going down the river—it was the Colorado—was really exciting—I did it this summer for two weeks—and the water was really almost like boiling when you went into the rapids—I've never done anything like that before in my life!" The first utterance contains twenty-three words and the second forty-four, yet the two messages contain more or less the same number of ideas. The point is not that one style is better or more comprehensible than the other—that is another matter—but rather that a simple count of total words can be a misleading measure of the two utterances.

Psychologists have given increasing attention during the past few years to describing language according to its structural features. A complete account of a language event may begin with an audio recording (a video recording is even more appropriate; speakers often provide visual and gestural support for what they say: a raised eyebrow, a serious look, or a clenched fist). While raw data of this sort serve the purpose of illustration and anecdote, they are unwieldy. Some type of simplification is generally necessary to generate the actual observations.

Methods of structural analysis now exist for the several levels of language usage. As noted above, the distinction between content and function words can help at the word level. In handling connected prose (a paragraph or so), a technique known as propositional analysis is now in widespread use. Figure 4–5 illustrates the application of this technique to a relatively simple passage.

In recent years psychologists have become increasingly interested in how people handle complexity: how word problems in mathematics are understood, what strategies are used by chess masters, what is entailed by the process of reading comprehension, and so on. In all of these examples the key to progress in research has been the creation of a structural framework—a theoretical model of the situation—that can be used to grapple with complex data. For instance, several researchers have investigated the comprehension of stories by young children (Mandler and Johnson, 1977; Stein and Glenn, 1979). It turns out that many stories, whether told by the young or the old, can be described by what is referred to as a *story grammar*. Just as a complex sentence can be divided into parts (clauses, phrases, subject, and object), so a story can be separated into chunks. Moreover, the nature of these segments is amazingly consistent over a wide range of stories found in Western culture. Figure 4–6 (page 81) illustrates how the story grammar concept can be used to parse a third-grade story, and how it then serves as a guide for evaluating a student's retelling of the story. The student's language behavior in this situation is certainly complex on the surface, but with the story grammar as a guide, it is possible to "measure" the response in an objective and meaningful fashion.

Questionnaires and Interviews

The most direct way to collect data on what a person knows or feels about something is to ask questions and allow the person to discuss the topic. Questionnaires provide a limited opportunity for response, but when properly designed they allow the researcher to survey a wide range of populations efficiently. The interview is a more open-ended situation, but as we shall see, the researcher can structure the situation so as to have some cake and eat it, too.

Questionnaires. Whether by mail or phone, the questionnaire has become commonplace for most of us. From political polls to finding out how you liked your motel room, checklists of various sorts are a cheap method of acquiring data from relatively large samples of people. The method is more frequently used by applied psychologists than by laboratory scientists, but the technique has broad applicability.

In constructing a questionnaire the researcher needs to consider both the content and the form. While the content is of primary interest to the researcher, creating a workable and effective layout is often the key to obtaining valid informa-

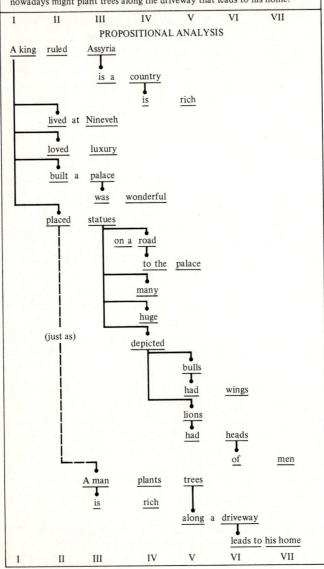

THE KING OF ASSYRIA

The rich country of Assyria was ruled by a king who lived at Nineveh. This king loved luxury and he built a wonderful palace. On the roadway that led to the palace he placed many huge and fantastic statues depicting bulls with wings and lions with the heads of men, just as a rich man nowadays might plant trees along the driveway that leads to his home.

I	II	III	IV	V	VI	VII

PROPOSITIONAL ANALYSIS

A king — ruled — Assyria

is a — country

is — rich

lived at — Nineveh

loved — luxury

built a — palace

was — wonderful

placed — statues

on a — road

to the — palace

many

huge

(just as)

depicted

bulls

had — wings

lions

had — heads

of — men

A man — plants — trees

is — rich

along a — driveway

leads to — his home

I	II	III	IV	V	VI	VII

Figure 4-5 Example of propositional analysis

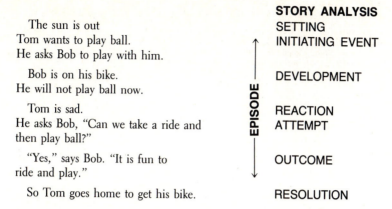

The sun is out

STORY ANALYSIS
SETTING

Tom wants to play ball.
He asks Bob to play with him.

INITIATING EVENT

Bob is on his bike.
He will not play ball now.

DEVELOPMENT

EPISODE

Tom is sad.
He asks Bob, "Can we take a ride and
then play ball?"

REACTION
ATTEMPT

"Yes," says Bob. "It is fun to
ride and play."

OUTCOME

So Tom goes home to get his bike.

RESOLUTION

Figure 4–6 Structural analysis of a simple one-episode story

tion. The researcher needs to consider in turn the introduction, the instructions, the sequencing of the questions, the layout of the questions, and the format of the answers (Williamson, Karp, Dalphin, and Gray, 1982).

The introduction and the instructions tell the respondent the purpose of the questionnaire and the nature of the task. They are critical to the questionnaire's success; it is here that the respondent's attention is captured (or not) and he or she convinced that filling out the form is a reasonable chore that will not take much time. The respondent must also be convinced that the information yielded by the questionnaire serves an important purpose. In general, the likelihood that a respondent will complete a form depends on its length; the greater the number of pages, the lower the response rate. If you want a high return rate, restrict the questionnaire to one page, with six to ten questions and a few lines for written comments. The introduction and the instructions provide no information to the researcher, so they should convey in as few words as possible a sharp, clear message about why the data are needed and what the respondent needs to do.

The person designing a questionnaire generally begins with a concept of the information that is needed. Specific questions then tumble out, often in a jumbled disarray. The final editing of the questionnaire should ensure that (a) the sequence follows a discernible and rational order, (b) questions on a similar theme are blocked together, (c) the most important and straightforward questions appear at the beginning and the least important and most ambiguous at the end, and (d) redundant questions are eliminated. Any of these guidelines may be disregarded on occasion, but the researcher should have a good reason for doing so. Respondents become irritated when they are asked to wend their way through an apparently unorganized and repetitive list of items that seems to lack rationale.

The layout of the questions and the format of the responses tends to be specific to a particular questionnaire, and it would take us far afield to discuss these issues in detail here. In general, it is a good idea to provide adequate space (don't cramp the questions), to give clues about the end of one topic and the beginning of the next, to make the response choices as simple as possible, and, where a complex response is required by the question, to give an example. Layout and response format is an art form, so before administering a questionnaire to a large sample, it is always a good idea to ask a few colleagues to take the questionnaire and to then discuss any difficulties with them. Listen to criticisms carefully, and don't be defensive; they are trying to help.

Format and layout are often linked with content. Questionnaire items generally fall into four categories: they examine the respondent's (a) background, (b) behavior, (c) knowledge, or (d) attitudes. Each of these categories poses particular problems, but as listed here they generally progress from simple to more difficult: asking a respondent's gender and educational background is relatively more straight-forward than probing attitudes. The key is often asking a question or series of questions at the right level of generality. Williamson, Karp, Dalphin, and Gray (1982, pp. 134–135) illustrate the point with the following two questions:

How often do you vote in national elections?

1. Always

2. Often

3. Seldom

4. Never

Did you vote in the last national election?

1. Yes

2. No

3. Not sure

The lack of specificity in the first question—the response categories are ambiguous— invites the respondent to overestimate his or her voting record. The second question is quite clear-cut.

Because questionnaires represent an intrusion on the respondent's time, the researcher should figure out ways to make it easier to give valid information than to "cop out." For instance, consider the following two items (paraphrased from Williamson et al., 1982, pp. 135–136):

How do you feel about the Supreme Court decision regarding prayer in the public schools?

1. Oppose it

2. Favor it

3. Don't know about it

The Supreme Court has ruled that no state or local government can require the reading of the Bible or other religious documents in the public schools. How do you feel about this decision?

1. Strongly oppose it

2. Oppose it

3. No opinion

4. Favor it

5. Strongly favor it

The second version provides all respondents with the same minimal information, increasing the likelihood that the responses spring from a similar base of knowledge and eliminating the "I don't know" category.

The wording of questions and of responses can easily reflect the prejudices of the item writer. Loaded questions come naturally to the fore when a person feels strongly about a matter—and researchers have feelings like anyone else:

Do you think Congress should vote a freeze on nuclear war and all its horrors?

1. Yes

2. No

3. Not sure

While not all respondents may answer "Yes," the question puts pressure on the individual who might otherwise give a more complex response to the issue.

Yes–no questions and answers are often troublesome. In a state survey conducted a few years ago, teachers were asked to respond to the following question with regard to several categories in reading and mathematics (e.g., vocabulary, comprehension, basic computation, and so on): "Do you teach this topic—yes or no?" Imagine yourself in the teacher's place. What does it mean to "teach vocabulary?" Both terms are incredibly complex and not easily encompassed by a simple "yes" or "no." The question leads to a biased and uncertain response.

Yes–no questions are also used as "filters" in some questionnaires:

Do study guides help you learn more?   Yes ﹘﹘﹘   No ﹘﹘﹘

    If you marked yes, please explain how ﹘﹘﹘﹘﹘﹘﹘﹘

﹘﹘﹘﹘﹘﹘﹘﹘﹘﹘﹘﹘﹘﹘﹘﹘﹘﹘﹘﹘﹘﹘﹘

﹘﹘﹘﹘﹘﹘﹘﹘﹘﹘﹘﹘﹘﹘﹘﹘﹘﹘﹘﹘﹘﹘﹘

If you think about it for a moment, you will understand why the respondents to this question tended to mark "Yes" and then change the answer to "No." Open-ended, unstructured questions are often a good idea when the answers are likely to be complex or when the designer is not quite sure what to expect. Because they clearly demand more of the respondent, they should be used in moderation. Furthermore, they should not be voluntary (or semivoluntary, as in the example above) if the information is important.

Interviews. The interview as a method of data collection has some obvious shortcomings (Kerlinger, 1973, Ch. 28; Williamson et al., 1982, Ch. 7). The procedure takes a lot of time, and the data can be difficult to interpret. If the interview schedule is totally unstructured, the interviewee comes closest to expressing his or her own point of view but may never get around to discussing the main point and may neglect to mention facts and ideas of great personal significance. If the interview schedule is tightly structured, the interviewer may discover a great deal about the researcher's point of view but little about the thoughts of the interviewee. The interviewer must be skilled in interpersonal interactions and must be aware of his or her internal responses during the interview. Interviewer bias is always a concern; leading questions, the tone of voice, even a slight hesitation in writing down a response may all influence the interviewee's decisions about what to say and how to say it.

Despite these problems the interview can be an exceptionally effective method of data collection. Once again, the key to success is in the planning of the situation. A vague and apparently pointless question, a series of unrelated inquiries with no clear purpose, a set of highly focused questions that can elicit only one- or two-word answers are all unlikely to engage the interviewee or generate useful data for the researcher. Planning an interview schedule requires the researcher to lay out the structure of the answers that may be forthcoming. This statement may appear puzzling because it seems to call for the researcher to be a mind reader. In fact, this is exactly what has to happen for the researcher to construct an effective interview schedule. Seldom does the researcher begin a project completely in the dark. Most research questions have a history of some sort; there is a literature. And the researcher usually has a set of hypotheses about the nature of the phenomenon. Both of these sources can be used in thinking through a set of scenarios or possible responses to the interview.

Given that the researcher does have some notion of what to expect, one of the most efficient techniques for designing an interview is the so-called funnel technique (Cannell and Kahn, 1968; Kerlinger, 1973, pp. 481ff). The basic idea behind this technique is to begin the interview with a broad question that specifies the purpose of the discussion and then to follow with a set of increasingly detailed and constrained questions. The opening question gives the interviewee free rein to formulate an answer that reflects most accurately his or her point of view. It also reveals whether the interviewee has a coherent point of view and provides information about the specific items that are most salient at that point in time. The follow-up questions help the interviewee recall items that escaped mention at first and provide an organized framework for expressing ideas that might otherwise come out completely muddled. The interviewee who is completely confused is unlikely to be helped very much no matter how well designed the follow-up questions, but the individual who gets off the track at the beginning is likely to find such guidance helpful and may even remark on this point.

Writing good questions is a difficult task, even when you have some idea of the form of the answers. The substance of the questions depends on the nature of the topic, but a few guiding principles are worth taking into account. The opening statement should give the interviewee a clear idea of the goal of the interview: "I'm interested in what you think (or how you feel, etc.) about X." The first question should be open-ended, but it must also meet several other criteria (Kerlinger, 1973, pp. 485ff). *Open-ended* is not the same as *vague*; the question should give the interviewee a clear sense of where to begin and what direction to take. It should also place reasonable demands on the interviewee without putting him or her in an impossible situation. So that the individual can start talking in a free and confident manner, the question should be designed to draw on the interviewee's prior knowledge. The researcher should try to avoid leading questions, questions that call for a socially desirable answer, or questions that are likely to lead to matters that are delicate or embarrassing (unless these happen to be the focus of the interview—an ethical concern in most instances). Questions should be designed to yield an answer more complex than "yes" or "no." Follow-up questions must meet many of the same criteria, though the major aim of such questions is to lead the interviewee to focus more precisely and specifically on particular topics.

The funnel technique was employed to measure story comprehension in the example presented earlier in the chapter. Here is the structure of the questions for the student after the story was read:

Tell me whatever you can
remember from the story.   (*Opening question*)

What happened next? (if necessary)   (*Nonspecific probe*)

Why did Sue's father, Joe, want
to find another place to fish?

       * * * * *

Why did Sue run into the lake?
What did she do then?   (*Specific probes*)
How did the story end?

In this simple example the content of the questions is determined by the framework of the story. The structure—general to specific—is used to bring the subject's attention increasingly to bear on the framework. The first questions give free rein, and finally (as necessary) the subject is presented with highly detailed questions. If the researcher has no conceptual framework for formulating the questions at the most detailed level, then there will be difficulty in creating the specific questions. As noted at the beginning of this section, it is a good idea to begin the construction of an interview schedule by thinking about the structure of the answers.

The funnel technique can be designed to combine the advantages of both the open-ended approach and the detailed questionnaire. The interviewee is able to express a perspective in any form desired but is also required to cover those topics considered critical by the researcher. The probes make certain that reluctant subjects are not underestimated; some people tend to be more verbose than others, but the follow-up questions provide both direction and encouragement. Finally, the structure of the interview—and the fact that the interviewer has already considered the probable organization of the various types of answers—makes it relatively easy for the interviewer to document the main themes and supporting details of the interview in a readily interpreted format. A major disadvantage of the completely free-form interview is that much more time may be required to transcribe and interpret the interview than is required by the interview itself. The researcher should always beware of data that are too complicated!

Observational Data

Actions can be as important as words in describing human behavior. How can we portray the social dynamics on the children's playground? How can we characterize the blooming, buzzing confusion of a first-grade classroom? A team of skilled craftsmen works together with speed and precision to service a racing car during a pit stop. How can we record their activity? A father, mother, and two young children crowd the kitchen area during the preparation of the evening meal. How can we capture their moves and interactions?

In each instance the alert and trained observer is able to record an informative, accurate, and interpretable account of events that appear incomprehensible to the person unfamiliar with the situation. The observer's capability is like that of the skilled naturalist or woodsman who walks through a patch of forest, spotting all manner of flora and fauna, along with activities that completely escape the untrained eye. The method may be ethnographic, a checklist of critical events, or a minute-by-minute tally of behaviors. The goal is to capture a slice of life for closer examination.

There is a commonsense basis for observation, but the use of observation for scientific data collection goes beyond reliance on untutored experience and intuitive analysis:

> Everyone observes the actions of others. We look at other persons and listen to them talk. We infer what others mean when they say something, and we infer the characteristics, motivations, feelings, and intentions of others on the basis of these observations. We say, "He is a shrewd judge of people,"

meaning that his observations are keen and that we think his inferences of what lies behind the behavior are valid.

This day-by-day kind of observation of most people, however, is unsatisfactory for science. The social scientist must also observe human behavior, but he must be dissatisfied with the inadequacy of uncontrolled observations. He seeks reliable and objective observations from which he can draw valid inferences. (Kerlinger, 1973, p. 537)

An observation is adequate for scientific purposes if two different observers agree reasonably closely on what events transpired. One key to the successful observation of complex situations is for the researcher to be clear about what the observer is to focus on. The capabilities of the human observer are incredible—we can see a great deal and can detect subtle patterns in the most complicated backgrounds. Still, like other human beings, observers in a psychological experiment have limited attention spans; since they cannot see everything that happens, researchers must define clearly what are the most essential things to look for.

Because human beings are not video cameras, total objectivity is impossible. The observer continually makes perceptual and subjective interpretations of the available data; there is a natural tendency to "go beyond the information given" (Bruner, 1957) and to read into a set of events what you expect to see. The study of eyewitness behavior (e.g., Loftus, 1974, 1975) suggests that most untrained observers are far from being "true witnesses." The researcher therefore needs to inform and train the observers carefully, to calibrate observers against one another until they have learned how to resolve ambiguous situations. Clear guidelines, careful instructions, plenty of examples, and lots of practice are the ingredients for obtaining trustworthy observational data.

Observational schemes come in a great variety of styles: rating scales, counting techniques, anecdotal descriptions, categorical checklists, and so on (Kerlinger, 1973, Ch. 31; Webb, 1981). A complete account of the different methods would go beyond the purposes of this book. However, the point can be illustrated by considering various approaches to the grand jury episode presented at the beginning of the chapter. Spradley's description gives a flavor of the ethnographic method: lots of descriptive detail along with personal asides and reactions. Another approach would be to construct a type of "sociogram" by recording the number of contacts made between the various participants while they were waiting for the judge to arrive. Because of his unusual appearance (he had a beard) and dress, one suspects that Spradley might be treated as an outcast; men might be more likely to talk to other men and women to other women in this strange situation; and so on. A checklist based on various aspects of the appearance and behavior of each individual (formally or casually dressed, quiet or animated, nervous or calm, and so on) could be constructed. All these methods might be improved by adding the dimension of time. Spradley mentioned that he arrived at 8:55 and that "a man" (presumably the bailiff) arrived a few minutes after nine, but otherwise he did not keep track of time.

Recording the time of each critical event can increase the value of an observation. Another approach is to divide time into "slices" and record the state of affairs during each slice.

The observational system provides a means of recording a miniature history of a situation. The format of the observational record should allow the researcher to calculate a number of summary measures directly from it: the amount of time spent by each person on a given activity, the number of events of different sorts, the amount of interaction between people, the link between one kind of activity and another, and so on. An observational record generates a rich data set, even though it entails a considerable simplification of "reality." Is the simplification too great? Should one measure be preferred over another? These and similar questions depend upon the goals of the research. The main point is that it is possible to design observation schemes that make good use of human observational capabilities, that provide a substantial amount of information about a situation, and that permit a relatively straightforward summarization of potentially significant features of the events.

THE INTERPRETATION OF PSYCHOLOGICAL DATA

The researcher has made an observation—simple, complex, or somewhere in between. What does the information mean? The natural tendency is to think that the datum means what it says, that it can be taken at face value. In fact, for psychological data (as for data in the other areas of science), observation is only the first step in a demanding process of analysis and interpretation. The task of interpretation has come up again and again throughout this chapter. In this section we consider three hurdles to interpretation that must be considered in all research:

- The relation of the data to underlying psychological constructs. How can any one set of observations be linked to other sources of information?

- The validity of the observations. What evidence and reasoning support the conclusion that the data can be interpreted in a particular manner with some degree of confidence?

- The reliability of the observations. Are the observations sufficiently stable and consistent to guarantee reproducibility of the data?

Psychological Constructs

A young boy cocks his slingshot and lets fly a pellet at a pigeon. The damaged bird flutters to earth a few houses away. There another young boy picks it up with care and takes it into his house to clean it and bind its wounds. A week later he releases the creature to fly off to freedom. Our perspective focuses again on the first youngster, who has just inadvertently struck a little girl on the playground. As the boy turns away from her, whether embarrassed or uncaring is hard to tell, the second youngster comes over and speaks comfortingly to the girl until she stops crying. The anecdote could be spun out further, but the point is probably clear. Complex though these data may be, most people would probably reach fairly similar judgments about the character of each boy, and would view the evidence as supportive of their judgment.

What is it that allows people to interpret complex observations like those sketched above? How is it that we handle the question "What do the data mean?" This problem has been posed in a commonsense framework, but the same question is essential for interpreting the most sophisticated psychological experiment. A behaviorally oriented psychologist might say that the data simply mean what they mean; the observations should be taken at face value. If the activities of the first youngster are viewed as undesirable, such a psychologist might be satisfied to count the rate of such activities and attempt to design a reinforcement schedule that would decrease the rate. The child would be rewarded for behavior that was respectful of other people and things and punished for actions that were harmful. The psychologist taking this approach would argue that there is little need to look beneath the surface for a deeper meaning, and the behaviorist tradition has indeed demonstrated that this point of view can have immediate and practical value for many kinds of research and development projects (Bandura, 1969; Goldstein and Foa, 1980).

Other psychologists are more inclined to search for a deeper meaning in behavioral observations. They look for patterns that appear in a variety of situations and attempt to formulate hypotheses about the reasons for these patterns. Such generalizations, referred to as **psychological constructs,** are the basic building blocks for psychological theories.

As is true in many other sciences, constructs in psychology often have their origins in commonsense notions. Many people would say that the first boy lacked empathy or sensitivity compared with the second boy. As our understanding of the causes of behavior becomes clearer, constructs become defined in different, often counterintuitive ways, reflecting a more complete understanding of a given behavior. In modern physics, terms like *weight, mass, energy,* and so on have meanings that are related in a precise and coherent fashion to the tenets of physical theory. These meanings differ in significant ways from commonsense ideas. Indeed, one of the major functions of physics instruction is to help the student redefine these terms based on a new perception of how the physical world operates.

Definitions of the sort just described are referred to as **constitutive definitions;** they describe the substantive nature of the construct and show how it is related to other constructs (Torgerson, 1958, Ch. 1). Gravity is the tendency for two planetary objects to attract each other; without it the earth would go spinning into the galactic voids and we would be flung into the stratosphere and beyond. Where our understanding permits, constitutive definitions may be precise and highly formalized. In other instances the constitutive definition of a construct may be rather vague and fuzzy; lots of examples may be the best we can manage for such fuzzy constructs.

Another approach to characterizing a construct is to rely on an **operational definition:** the researcher spells out one or more **operations** that describe how one can proceed to collect evidence about the existence and nature of the construct. The operational method can be used as an adjunct to the constitutive definition. For instance, the researcher may choose to define the amount of tension felt by subjects in a particular situation by means of a questionnaire, by measuring the galvanic skin response, or by counting the number of jerks and other signs of discomfort. Which measure is chosen might be an important consideration in interpreting the data, but the choice is often a matter of convenience. The researcher's goal is the measurement of tension as constitutively defined; the questionnaire responses and the like are important only insofar as they lead to this goal.

In some instances operational definitions seem to have taken over the task of constitutive definition, most often when the construct of interest is either difficult to think through or when there are conflicting points of view about the phenomenon. For instance, you may have heard the statement, "Intelligence is what an intelligence test measures." Such a definition may strike you as deeply unsatisfying—and it is. Simply placing the label *intelligence* on a paper and pencil test is no explanation of anything. The untangling of the construct of intelligence is a tough task, and one that has led to considerable disagreement and even political uproar. Nonetheless, this task must be tackled if we are to arrive at an adequate definition of the construct.

Operational definitions can play a useful role in the birthing of new constructs, but operations are most properly viewed as the servants of constitutive definitions, not as substitutes. As the theoretical framework that makes sense of a particular set of constructs is refined, we begin to reach a nontrivial understanding of the adequacy of different operations as representatives of a particular construct. Fluency in reading might be defined operationally as the number of words a person can pronounce per minute. Does it matter whether the words are correctly pronounced? Is it important for the person to understand the meaning of the passage? Should the reader be able to handle nonsense material as well as meaningful text? All these questions are concerned with the operationalization of the construct of "reading fluency." Answers to these questions will come not from examining the operations but from thinking through what we want to mean by the construct.

Validity

Does a given data collection procedure actually measure what we want it to measure or what we think it measures? This is the question of validity. The answers to this question depend in part on the constructs that we have in mind—in fact, one type of validity is referred to as **construct validity.** Two other types of validity, criterion validity and content validity, which are also used in behavioral research, will be discussed first. Then these will be tied to the concept of construct validity.

Criterion Validity. Suppose that you have developed a new test and you want to validate it. Assume further that there already exists a *criterion measure*, a trustworthy measure of the construct that your test is designed to assess, though your instrument might have certain advantages in ease of administration, cost, or time. The criterion validity of the new test can be established by showing that it is closely related to performance on the criterion measure; thus, it is possible to predict performance on the criterion by the scores on the new test. This method is also referred to as **predictive validity.**

To illustrate, suppose there is a test of clerical ability that is trustworthy and that experts in the field agree is an appropriate index of this skill. Unfortunately, it takes a week to administer, and an experienced professional is required to collect the information and interpret it. You have developed a "screening" test that takes only a hour; it has a multiple-choice format and can be administered to groups and computer-scored. To establish the criterion validity of the new test, you would administer it to a representative group of potential clients, also assessing their performance on the criterion measure. You would determine the strength of the relationship between the two indices (the correlation coefficient, to be described later in the text, could be used for this task). If the relationship was satisfactorily close, this would be evidence for the criterion validity of the new procedure.

Criterion validity is a useful technique in many instances. Its appropriateness depends strongly on the existence of a well-defined construct and on the availability of trustworthy criterion measures. Unfortunately, many of the phenomena of greatest importance and interest in psychological research are still poorly defined, and dependable criteria for evaluation are lacking. Thus, criterion validity is all too often a matter of the blind leading the blind. In addition, the relation between a derivative test and its criterion is not always a stable property of the test. A multiple-choice test of mathematics achievement at first may be highly correlated with the ability to solve mathematics problems. But what will happen to this relation if mathematics instructors, because of the importance of test scores, change their teaching to emphasize the skills necessary to do well on multiple-choice tests but neglect the development of the concepts and skills that are not needed on such tests? Then the criterion validity will be jeopardized, a fact that may not become apparent unless the test is validated on a regular basis and in a variety of settings. For instance, it would probably be important to cross-check the multiple-choice scores with the students' ability to explain how they figured the answers when choices were not provided.

Content Validity. A thorough and systematic review of the substance of what is being assessed is the foundation for establishing content validity. For instance, suppose you have been given the job of designing a system for evaluating college courses. Content validation might be established by asking both students and professors what distinguishes good from poor courses and what techniques are appropriate for course evaluation. My own experience in this area suggests three dimensions that might show up in an examination of the content of this problem. The first dimension covers the various facets of the course per se:

- Is the instructor well organized?

- Is the syllabus understandable and easy to follow?

- Is the textbook readable?

- Are the assignments and examinations appropriate and fair?

You might think of additional entries for this list, though neither complexity nor exhaustiveness is essential to the point being made.

The second dimension covers the different methods students might use to express their ideas about the course:

- A rating sheet or survey could be checked.

- Individual students could be interviewed.

- Independent judges (or peers) might be asked to observe the course.

The third dimension is time. It is typical for courses to be evaluated just once during a semester or quarter, usually at the end. Yet many of the important clues about teaching quality (and many of the ideas about how to improve teaching) come from observing the process of instruction, not just the final product. Moreover, one would want to gather such information more than once, ideally in a representative sample of situations, thereby avoiding the possibility that the data reflect a particularly good or bad day. Collecting additional information from students some time after the course was over might also be advisable. Full appreciation of the benefits or shortcomings of a particular course may come about only after a semester or two, when the student has had a chance to apply what was learned in other situations.

Construct Validity. Analyzing the content domain for validation of a data collection procedure can be quite a task; it is not always seen as the tough intellectual challenge that it actually is. In fact, when properly designed the plan for content validation flows naturally into the task of establishing construct validity. Psychological constructs—intelligence, sensitivity, empathy, authoritarianism— are often hard to pin down. These and other such constructs are difficult to bring under the microscope.

Construct validity is established to the extent that the researcher can present **convergent evidence;** that is, evidence showing that data from many sources point consistently and coherently to the reality of the construct under investigation. If data from a variety of perspectives all lead to the same interpretation, then we can be fairly confident that the construct exists and that it behaves according to our conception of it. We may not be able to see, hear, taste, or smell the construct, but we know it is there, and we know how to trace its path by our data collection system. Scientists of all sorts have to solve this type of problem; it was a long time before physicists could see molecules, atoms, and subatomic particles, but that did not stop them from formulating these constructs and using them to interpret data.

Suppose, for example, that the researcher has hypothesized the existence of a construct of teaching effectiveness such that individual instructors can be placed on a scale from "very effective" to "very ineffective." If the data from the variety of sources listed earlier converge, allowing each instructor to be assigned a single value on the scale, then we have support for the construct. Further research could be based on this construct to uncover evidence of the correlates of effective teaching. We could then be on our way to formulating a theory of teaching and might be in a good position to develop programs for training instructors to be more effective.

The data might lead to substantial modification of the original hypothesis and still be useful in framing a description of the construct. For instance, professors judged initially to be ineffective on the basis of student ratings might receive much higher ratings by the same students a year later; the "tough" teacher may not at first be popular but may gain respect over time. Such findings would undercut the simplest notion of teaching effectiveness but would point the way toward refining a more adequate set of interrelated constructs.

Construct validation, as you can now see, is at the heart of the scientific enterprise. We begin with commonsense notions based on everyday experience. Through critical analysis, through the use of design techniques, and from data itself, we accumulate evidence that allows us to refine our original notions. Content validation can be thought of as the early phases of hypothesis formulation and design. As the data begin to shape our understanding, the outline of the construct (or constructs) becomes clearer, and we gain more confidence in our understanding of the system of relations.

Reliability

Kerlinger's (1973) definition of reliability seems to me one of the clearest that has been written:

> Synonyms for reliability are: dependability, stability, consistency, predictability, accuracy. A reliable man, for instance, is a man whose behavior is consistent, dependable, predictable—what he will do tomorrow and next week will be consistent with what he does today and what he has done last week. We say he is stable. An unreliable man, on the other hand, is one whose behavior is much more variable. Sometimes he does this, sometimes that. He lacks stability. We say he is inconsistent.

So it is with psychological and educational measurements: they are more or less variable from occasion to occasion. They are stable and relatively predictable or they are unstable and relatively unpredictable; they are consistent or not consistent. If they are reliable, we can depend on them. If they are unreliable, we cannot depend on them. (pp. 442–443)

One reason I like this definition is that it does not say anything about statistical procedures. It stresses the *construct* of reliability rather than the operations that have grown up around it. We will see how to compute reliability indices, but for now the emphasis will be on the meaning of the concept.

You may have sensed a close relation between validity and reliability, and your perception is correct. In some textbooks it is said that a data collection procedure cannot yield valid results unless the measures are reliable. The reverse is also true in that a measure may have a high index of statistical reliability, but if it is of questionable validity, then its dependability is undercut.

For instance, suppose a reading test consists entirely of arithmetic problems— addition, subtraction, and so on. This test will probably be quite reliable and may even correlate highly with other measures of reading performance. The problem is that reliability has been defined in too limited a fashion: the focus is on the internal consistency of the set of items and not on the question of how consistently these items relate to other indices of reading performance. It is often more desirable to have a trustworthy measure with modest reliability than to employ a highly reliable index of questionable validity.

Reliability is partly a matter of precision. Is your bathroom scale reliable for measuring weight? It depends on what is being weighed. If you need to know how the battle of your bulge is going, the bathroom scale is adequate. This same device is a poor instrument for determining the carat value of the family diamonds. People's weights cover a wide range, from children weighing less than 30 pounds to adults weighing more than 200 pounds. The measurements of the bathroom scale may be off by a few ounces, but over this range of variability the need is for consistent measurement to the nearest pound. Diamonds, by contrast, vary over fractions of an ounce, and so in weighing them the error of measurement from a bathroom scale (or for that matter, a postage scale) is intolerable—even if the instrument gives an accurate reading "on the average."

The same principle applies in behavioral research. Can a relatively untrained interviewer reliably assign people to job categories based on a five-minute interview? The answer depends on the amount of variability in the people's characteristics and the tolerance for error. Suppose the interviewer is processing recruits at a military induction center, and the task is to decide whether each inductee is to receive a preliminary assignment as a mechanic, cook, military policeman, or the like. Given the amount of variability in the abilities and interests of the population of recruits, the interviewer can probably make gross decisions with a fair degree of reliability. On the other hand, the same interviewer will probably be inconsistent if asked to make fine-grained decisions: should a particular person assigned as a mechanic be given small-equipment repair, vehicle maintenance, or helicopter work?

The small amount of variability within this category and the need for detailed technical knowledge of specific job demands will in this case tax the interviewer's skills. The judgments are likely to reflect little more than chance decisions.

What steps can the researcher take to enhance the reliability of the data collection process? This question has three answers. The first solution takes relatively little thought, but it can be expensive: *collect more data*. If a test is unreliable, make up more questions. If a panel of judges cannot agree on a rating task, get more judges. If an interviewer has trouble classifying a person after a ten-minute interview, try a fifteen-minute interview. If there is a real construct "out there," increasing the amount of information should reduce the margin of error in the observation. The random errors and sloppiness that lead to unreliability in one or two observations quickly average out when six to ten observations are available.

Second, *sharpen your focus and refine your ideas*. Inconsistent data may result from the researcher's being confused. This uncertainty shows up in the procedures, and it is left to the subjects to resolve the ambiguity—and it will probably be resolved in a variety of idiosyncratic ways. A clearer formulation of the constructs you are assessing will often increase the reliability of the data.

Third, *be careful*. Unclear instructions, failure to standardize the procedures, and sloppy recording techniques all increase the error of measurement and thereby jeopardize the reliability of the data collection method.

The common theme that runs through this entire chapter deserves reemphasis. The researcher, in collecting data, is trying to cut through the fuzziness of the real world to observe the simple regularities that are the foundation of the *real* "real world." Data collection procedures are for this reason critical to the entire scientific enterprise. It is always a good idea to consider a number of alternative methods of data collection; plan these so that they vary substantially in objectivity, in reliability and validity, in efficiency, and in appropriateness. What brings the approaches together into a coherent framework is the search for order and parsimony:

> Now this is the peculiarity of scientific method, that when once it has become a habit of mind, that mind converts all facts whatsoever into science. The field of science is unlimited; its material is endless. Every group of natural phenomena, every phase of social life, every stage of past or present development is material for science. The unity of science consists alone in its method, not in its material. The man who classifies facts of any kind whatever, who sees their mutual relation and describes their sequences, is applying the scientific method and is a man of science. . . . It is not the facts themselves which form science, but the methods by which they are dealt with. (Pearson, 1892)

SUMMARY

Careful and controlled observation is at the core of all data collection in science. Sometimes the observation requires sophisticated equipment; sometimes the unaided eye is sufficient. The discussion of data collection for psychological research begins with the ethnographic approach, the most naturalistic method now in use. This approach is descriptive, introspective, and participatory.

Though the records from an ethnographic observation are complicated, many of the data collected in psychological investigations are relatively simple, at least on the surface. Simple data arise from a fairly straightforward recording of behavioral events, where the measurement is generally a single index, either categorical or numerical. The subject's response on a multiple-choice test is a typical instance of a simple categorical observation. This response may be actually rather difficult to interpret, but if the researcher gives careful attention to the design of the task and to the set of response alternatives, multiple-choice data can be quite meaningful.

Numerical data are frequently reported in psychological research. Whenever the data are in the form of numbers, three issues need to be considered: precision, extreme values, and the scale of measurement. Precision refers to the accuracy of the measurement. The tendency is to overdo precision, measuring performance to several decimal places when one decimal place is more appropriate. On the other hand, some behavioral processes take place in hundredths or thousandths of a second, and some cleverness may be required to obtain measures that are sensitive to these effects. Extreme values (or outliers) are not uncommon when performance is measured on a numerical scale; the subject may, for instance, miss the cue in a timed task and take several seconds to make a reaction, where the usual time might be a half-second. Extreme values make it difficult to identify patterns in the data, and the researcher is well advised to be alert to such events. Finally, just because a number has been assigned to a behavioral event does not ensure the "numericality" of the event. Just as quarterbacks and tailbacks cannot be added to produce a fullback, so the researcher needs to be cautious about carrying out numerical operations on behavioral measurements unless these operations are justified by the procedures.

Complex data are less straightforward; they cannot be summarized by a single index. Three common types of complex data in psychological research are language measures, questionnaires and interviews, and observations. In each of these three categories, the key to planning data collection and laying the foundation for analysis is the development of a structural model that can be used to make sense of the data.

Scientific measurements are seldom interesting in themselves but only insofar as they provide enlightenment about the processes that underlie a phenomenon. The interpretation of psychological data depends on the answers to three questions:

- What is the psychological construct that is the foundation for the measurement, and how is the particular measurement linked to other indices of performance?

- What is the validity of the measurement, and how can we be assured that the index is measuring the construct that it intends to measure?

- What is the reliability of the measurement, and is the index sufficiently stable and consistent so that we can expect a similar measure to be obtained under similar circumstances?

While each question raises distinctive issues, all three come to a single focus. Data are useful, for the most part, insofar as they help us to understand how the world "works." Without a theoretical framework for making sense of a set of observations, the researcher is likely to be in a state of confusion, unable to formulate a reasonable interpretation of the data, and without a clear idea of either the validity or reliability of the measures. In contrast, given a theoretical framework, the investigator is likely to be able to understand the meaning of the data, in spite of the "bumps and warts" that are so common in social science investigations. The essence of the scientific method is to formulate a conceptual framework for a problem and to use that framework to develop trustworthy procedures for collecting data that are interpretable within that framework.

5

Psychological Measurement

The preceding chapter focused on techniques for collecting data in psychological research. It contained frequent reference to **measurement,** a concept so much a part of the modern experience that we take it for granted. The process of measurement seems completely straightforward in most psychological experiments. The researcher counts the number of correct responses on a list of test questions or times with a stopwatch how long a subject takes to press a response button or reads a dial that shows the force with which a driver has pressed a brake pedal. In such instances the techniques of data collection lead naturally and directly to the assignment of numbers to the observations; the researcher does not need to give the matter much thought.

The task of assigning numbers to objects and events so that the results are meaningful and valid is actually quite a conceptual challenge. In the *measurement of physical events*, like timing an event or measuring the force of a response, we rely on theories from the physical sciences. Translating numbers into concepts that are meaningful for the *measurement of psychological processes* is a different matter, because here we lack trustworthy theories. Some progress has been made toward solving this problem in recent decades, but considerable work remains to be done.

The present chapter focuses on a problem even different from that of the measurement of psychological responses. In *psychological measurement*, researchers study how the human being performs as a measuring instrument. Examples include situations in which the subject is asked such questions as

- Do you hear a tone in the earphones?
- Which of these two patches of light is brighter?
- How heavy does this brick feel? How many pounds would you say it weighs?

- How good does pizza taste compared with fried chicken? With a sirloin steak? With stewed okra?

- Rank each of these people according to their contributions to world peace:
  Martin Luther King
  Mahatma Gandhi
  Eleanor Roosevelt
  Henry Kissinger

While not all of these tasks may strike you as "numerical," they all entail measurement of some sort; in each instance people have the job of assigning quantitative relations to objects or events.

The chapter begins with a discussion of people's ability to detect a stimulus and to discriminate among similar stimuli. Deciding whether or not a stimulus is present (the absolute threshold), and deciding whether two stimuli are the same or different (the difference threshold) are the most fundamental types of psychological measurement. We examine the basic principles of such measurement and see how they apply to the design of detection and discrimination tasks. Next we examine situations in which the subjects actually respond with numbers or with relational judgments. We delve more deeply into the nature of measurement as a conceptual system and then study several situations that illustrate how humans use numbers.

DETECTION, DISCRIMINATION, AND DECISION

The Zero Point and the Unit of Measurement

As already noted, physical measurement is so engrained in modern life that we take it for granted. Scientists and philosophers have given considerable attention to the foundations of measurement and to the theoretical and practical consequences of different approaches to the concept (Campbell, 1957). As used by physical scientists, measurement is the assignment of numbers to an object or event according to a specified operation or rule. For instance, to measure the length of a rope you can determine its number of "feet" by starting at one end and marching heel-to-toe to the other while counting the number of steps. The length of the rope *as measured by this operation* is the number of steps that you count off.

The process described above is an excellent example of operational definition (Ch. 4), but it does not tell us very much about the constitutive definition of length. Any number of other operations could be used to measure length; you could count the number of strides or use a foot rule or yardstick, for instance. You might even employ a surveyor's transit to measure an extremely long rope. The choice of one operation over others depends on purpose and convenience. We generally rely on a standardized operation as the basis for calibrating all other operations, using something like the English foot or the international meter (the National Bureau of Standards keeps models of such units as the basis for comparison). Counting repeated events is the basis for measurement in many physical domains. Time is measured by counting, as is weight, the frequency of electromagnetic waves, and so on.

Although counting with a standardized unit is the basis for many types of measurements, we often rely on less direct methods as valid and practical alternatives. We trust these indirect operations because we have a theoretical basis for relating them in a simple way to the more fundamental operation of counting. Sometimes the relations are quite simple. For instance, if you measure with a yardstick instead of a foot rule, you know that you must multiply the length in yards by three in order to find the number of feet; choice of the unit of measurement means that you have to multiply or divide by the appropriate constant to change from one scale to another. In other instances the relations between operations are more complex. Thus, relying on a surveyor's transit to measure length entails a knowledge of trigonometry and an understanding of how to put this knowledge to use. The data from the transit (distances and angles) must undergo some fairly complex transformations before the measure of length is obtained.

For situations in which measurement is determined by a counting process, two matters are essential to interpreting the numbers. The first is the **unit of measurement.** The unit chosen is generally a preset standard; using a foot rule is clearly preferable to using your own foot because variation in foot size will lead to unreliable measurements when several people use their feet for this purpose. As a matter of convenience you can actually do a reasonably good job of measuring moderate distances by using your foot if a ruler is not available. The standard gives you more confidence when you compare your measurements with those made by other observers.

The choice of a particular unit depends on the nature of the objects being measured. As noted in the preceding chapter, the unit of measurement often depends on the precision required. Distances between atoms are measured in angstroms (an angstrom is one ten-billionth of a meter), while interstellar distances are measured in light years (a light year is approximately 10 quadrillion meters). The same set of measurement concepts can be employed over this incredible range of absolute magnitude, but different standards of measurement may be required to handle different situations. If the meter were used as a standard for measuring both interatomic and interstellar distances, the numbers would get out of hand.

The second requirement for measurement by counting is the establishment of the **zero point** on the scale. In physical measurement finding zero is often quite simple: start counting exactly at the end of the board that you are measuring for a bookshelf; be sure that the measuring cup has nothing in it before pouring in the milk to make a custard; remember to reset the stopwatch before the race begins. In other instances finding zero is more difficult, for either theoretical or practical reasons.

For example, you may recall from your science courses that converting from one temperature scale to another requires more complicated arithmetic than conversion for scales of length, weight, volume, and so on. The reason for the additional complexity is that neither the Fahrenheit nor the Centigrade scales of temperature start from a true zero; it is as though you always began measuring the length of a board a yard from one end and then counted the number of additional feet to the other end. A strange procedure, but strange things can happen when you are not entirely sure of what you are doing, which is exactly what occurred when the temperature scales were developed. The Fahrenheit and Centigrade scales were both established before scientists knew how to cool something down to what is truly zero on the temperature scale (the point where molecular motion stops). In fact, the concept of absolute zero did not evolve until some time after the Fahrenheit and Centigrade scales were in use. There is a temperature scale based on absolute zero, incidentally; it is known as the Kelvin scale.

Measuring the Zero Point and the Unit for the Human Senses

In 1860 Gustav Fechner published his theoretical and experimental investigations on psychophysics, the relation between the physical and psychological domains. His paper was a landmark in the history of scientific psychology, establishing the transition from "armchair" research to reliance on empirical and quantitative experiments.

Fechner had developed and evaluated several methods for measuring human sensitivity to visual, acoustic, and tactile stimuli. His methodological work would have been important in its own right, as would his empirical findings about the human sensory apparatus. Fechner went beyond the methods and the data, however, to explore the theoretical meaning of the research. Many of his theoretical ideas have not stood the test of time, but the concept of a **threshold** still plays an important role in discussions of psychophysical performance.

Fechner defined the threshold as the point of noticeable change in the person's experience of a stimulus. The **absolute threshold** (*detection*) is that level of a stimulus that can just barely be detected; the **difference threshold** (*discrimination*) is the amount by which two stimuli have to differ for a person to discriminate between the two. Essentially, Fechner's theory proposed that the absolute threshold was the zero point of a person's sensitivity in a given sensory domain and the difference threshold was the unit of measurement on the psychophysical scale. To the extent that the theory was workable, the results of psychophysical experiments would allow the researcher to measure psychophysical phenomena using the same basic counting procedure that provides the foundation for most physical measurement.

A variety of procedures have been devised to measure the thresholds. Some were originated by Fechner; others are more recent developments. The procedures vary in the way stimuli are presented, in the subject's task, in the method of data analysis, and in the approach to interpreting the results. It is important to realize that there is no "true" threshold. This construct is of considerable importance in thinking about human sensitivity, but like many psychological constructs, it is not amenable to direct measurement, at least not at the present time. "True" or not, however, the threshold can be measured by a set of operations—the psychophysical methods to be described in the next two sections—whose results are consistent when compared with one another.

We now present two of the most useful methods for measuring sensitivity (for a comprehensive and reasonably up-to-date review of other methods, see Engen [1971]). First we look at the continuous adjustment method, a technique akin to a doctor's pressing harder and harder at a sore spot, asking each time "Does it hurt?" The patient will eventually say "Yes!" Then we discuss the random presentation method, which is something like watching for shooting stars. From time to time a critical event occurs, sometimes brief and dim, sometimes long and bright. After each event the subject is asked "Did you see anything?" Sometimes the answer will be "yes" and sometimes "no." From the relation between the stimulus intensity and the pattern of answers, the researcher can measure the subject's discrimination performance.

The Continuous Adjustment Method

In the **continuous adjustment method,** the stimulus is increased or decreased in small steps until the subject detects a change. You are familiar with this technique if you have ever had your hearing tested. In measuring the absolute threshold the tester usually begins with a subliminal stimulus and slowly increases the intensity until the subject reports that he or she has detected the stimulus. In measuring the difference threshold, a standard stimulus is presented along with a comparison stimulus that is clearly different from the standard; the comparison is then changed in small steps until the subject can no longer tell a difference ("the two are equal") or decides that the comparison has moved to the opposite side of the scale.

Figure 5–1 illustrates the method for assessing the difference threshold in the judgment of line length. The subject views a vertical line 5 centimeters long (about 2 inches) on the left side of a television screen. This, the **standard stimulus,** remains constant during the entire test. On the right side of the screen is a second vertical line, the **comparison stimulus.** As the first trial begins, the comparison stimulus is 40 millimeters long, clearly shorter than the standard.

The subject is told that the comparison stimulus will be gradually lengthened. When the observer can no longer distinguish between the standard and the comparison, he or she is to announce that they are equal; when the comparison appears longer than the standard, this change is also to be reported. At the beginning of the second trial the comparison stimulus is set to a value clearly larger than the standard stimulus and is gradually shortened until it appears equal and then shorter than the standard.

Comparison Stimulus (in millimeters)	Alternate Ascending and Descending Test Series (L = Longer; E = Equal; S = Shorter)					
	I	I	III	IV	V	VI
60						
59						
58		start				
57		L				start
56		L		start		L
55		L		L		L
54	L	L		L		L
53	L	L		L	L	L
52	E	L	L	L	L	L
51	E	L	L	L	E	E
Standard Stimulus → 50	E	E	E	L	E	E
(5 centimeters) 49	E	E	E	E	E	E
48	E	E	S	E	E	E
47	E	E	S	E	E	E
46	S	E	S	S	S	E
45	S	S	start	S	S	S
44	S	S			S	S
43	S				S	
42	S				S	
41	S				S	
40	start				start	
upper threshold	52.5	50.5	50.5	49.5	51.5	51.5
lower threshold	46.5	45.5	48.5	46.5	46.5	45.5

(1) Upper threshold (average) = 51.0

(2) Lower threshold (average) = 46.5

(3) Point of subjective equality = $\dfrac{\text{upper threshold} + \text{lower threshold}}{2}$ = 48.75

(4) Interval of uncertainty = upper threshold − lower threshold = 4.5

(5) Difference threshold = $\dfrac{\text{interval of uncertainty}}{2}$ = 2.25

Figure 5–1 Measurement of difference threshold for 5-centimeter stick (standard stimulus) using continuous adjustment method (comparison stimuli varied at 1-millimeter increments)

The sequence of events for the remaining trials is laid out in the figure. At the end of each trial, the tester resets the comparison stimulus to a new starting point at the opposite end of the stimulus dimension, alternating the back-and-forth series until the data are sufficient to provide a stable estimate of the subject's performance.

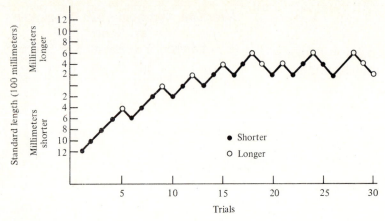

Figure 5–2 Fictitious data from an ascending series of the staircase method. The subject judged whether a comparison line was longer or shorter than a 100-millimeter standard.

Figure 5–1 also presents the descriptive measures that summarize the results of the procedure. The upper and lower thresholds give the stimulus values that pertain when the judgment changes on each trial, and an average is given for each. The *point of subjective equality* is the average of the two thresholds; it lies halfway between the upper and lower points. The *interval of uncertainty* is the difference between the upper and lower thresholds, and the *difference threshold* is one-half this range; that is, the distance from the point of subjective equality up to the upper threshold and down to the lower threshold.

The point of subjective equality is interpreted as the value of the comparison stimulus that is perceptually equivalent to the standard stimulus. The interval of uncertainty estimates the range of variation over which the subject is uncertain about whether the comparison is shorter or longer than the standard. This index measures the subject's sensitivity to the variations in the stimulus; the greater the interval of uncertainty, the less sensitive the subject is to differences between the standard and the comparison. The difference threshold is an estimate of the amount by which the comparison stimulus must be changed from the standard for a difference to be detected.

The continuous adjustment method illustrated in Figure 5–1 is somewhat inefficient and time-consuming, and psychophysicists often prefer a variation called the *staircase method,* which is shown in Figure 5–2. In this illustration the comparison line is initially set to be much shorter than the standard. The subject's first four responses are "shorter," and after each of these judgments the tester increases the length of the comparison line. The fifth stimulus in the series is judged "longer," and so the sixth stimulus is shortened by the tester. Since the next three stimuli are rated "shorter," the tester continues to shorten the comparison line until the subject says "longer," and so on. As you can see, the "staircase" stabilizes in this example

Bodily Region	Absolute Threshold (gm/sq mm)
Tip of tongue	2
Tip of finger	3
Back of finger	5
Front of forearm	8
Back of hand	12
Calf of leg	16
Abdomen	26
Back of forearm	33
Loin	48
Thick parts of sole	250

Figure 5–3 Absolute thresholds for pressure in various regions of the body. (Data of von Frey, 1906)

after about fifteen test stimuli. (If you rotate the figure clockwise, you can see the stairs.) The average of the responses from trial 15 to the end of the series yields a point of subjective equality that is roughly 3 millimeters longer than the standard; the range of variation between upper and lower thresholds is about 4 millimeters, for a difference threshold of 2 millimeters.

The staircase method saves a lot of time because the series does not have to be restarted on each trial. The efficiency of the technique is improved further by using larger steps at the beginning of the test and then making the steps smaller as the subject begins to home in on the threshold. A caution: the results can be influenced by the subject's expectation that the stimulus is going to be changed. This problem can be handled by warning the subject to attend carefully and report his or her "actual" perceptions as accurately as possible or by varying the procedure slightly so that sometimes the comparison stimulus is not shifted in the opposite direction when the subject changes the response.

The adjustment methods are most appropriate for measuring the sensitivity of stable processes like the senses of sight, sound, and touch. The relative sensitivity of the senses is the same from one methodology to another, even though the absolute numbers may change somewhat. Figure 5–3 shows threshold estimates of sensitivity to touch in various regions of the body. These data were collected more than seventy-five years ago (von Frey, 1906, reported in Woodworth, 1938) using the continuous adjustment method. The equipment was very crude: a set of bristles of varying diameter fastened to the ends of wooden rods. The stimuli ranged from fine human hairs to tough hog bristles. The pressure exerted by each stimulus was calibrated by pressing it against a sensitive balance weight. The absolute threshold for a particular skin region was measured by determining the weakest hair in the series that could be detected by the subject. These thresholds vary widely, more than two orders of magnitude from one region of the body to another. The same results can be replicated with today's far more sophisticated technology, a tribute to the trustworthiness of the method and the stability of the phenomenon.

The Random Presentation Method

In the **random presentation method** the experimenter selects a graded series of stimulus values over the range of the dimension being studied. The sample stimuli are then presented in random order to the subject, who makes a judgment after each stimulus presentation.

Figure 5–4 illustrates the method for assessment of length threshold for judgments of a 50-millimeter line, the same problem presented in the preceding sec-

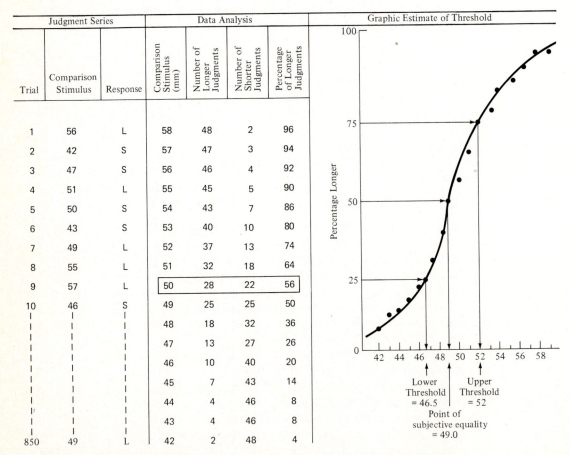

Judgment Series			Data Analysis				Graphic Estimate of Threshold
Trial	Comparison Stimulus	Response	Comparison Stimulus (mm)	Number of Longer Judgments	Number of Shorter Judgments	Percentage of Longer Judgments	
1	56	L	58	48	2	96	
2	42	S	57	47	3	94	
3	47	S	56	46	4	92	
4	51	L	55	45	5	90	
5	50	S	54	43	7	86	
6	43	S	53	40	10	80	
7	49	L	52	37	13	74	
8	55	L	51	32	18	64	
9	57	L	50	28	22	56	
10	46	S	49	25	25	50	
			48	18	32	36	
			47	13	27	26	
			46	10	40	20	
			45	7	43	14	
			44	4	46	8	
			43	4	46	8	
850	49	L	42	2	48	4	

Lower Threshold = 46.5 Upper Threshold = 52

Point of subjective equality = 49.0

Figure 5–4 Measurement of difference threshold for 5 centimeter stick (standard stimulus) using random presentation method, 50 presentations of each comparison stimulus from 4.2 to 5.8 centimeters in 1-millimeter increments

tion. The basic judgment task differs in a number of ways from the adjustment procedure described earlier. On each stimulus presentation the subject sees the standard stimulus on the left and a comparison stimulus on the right and judges whether the latter is longer or shorter; the equal judgment is seldom used in this procedure because that would provide an easy out for the subject. After the subject responds the next value of the comparison stimulus is presented for judgment. Testing continues in this fashion until the experimenter has enough data for stable estimates of the thresholds. In the example given in Figure 5-4, the subject receives 850 test trials—a large number, but each may last for only a few seconds.

Data collected by this procedure can be analyzed by a variety of more or less sophisticated techniques. The graphic approach in Figure 5–4 is simple and yields estimates comparable to those obtained with more complicated techniques. The first step in the analysis is to count the number of longer and shorter responses for each value. The percentage of longer judgments is then plotted for each value of the comparison stimulus, and a smooth curve is drawn through the data points. A line dropped from the 50-percent point on the curve to the comparison stimulus axis can be used to estimate the point of subjective equality. This is the value of the comparison stimulus where the subject is equally likely to say "longer" or "shorter," thereby providing a reasonable estimate of the comparison stimulus judged most similar to the standard. The upper and lower thresholds are typically defined as the values on the comparison axis that correspond to the 75th and 25th percent levels of performance. The interval of uncertainty is estimated by the difference between these two thresholds, just as in the continuous adjustment method.

Let us now see how this method served for the investigation of a practical problem of national concern. Breast cancer is a disease that endangers many women; in the United States tens of thousands are afflicted with this disease each year. Early detection is vital to effective treatment and self-examination is a cheap method of detection. The effectiveness of this approach, however, depends upon a person's tactile sensitivity, which leads to a number of important questions. What is the absolute threshold for detection of a breast lump; how much do individuals differ in this threshold; how can sensitivity be increased?

Adams, Hall, Pennypacker, Goldstein, Hench, Madden, Stein, and Catania (1976) sought answers to the first two questions. With the technical assistance of the Playtex and General Electric corporations, artificial breasts were designed with embedded "lumps" (steel spheres) that ranged in size from 1.6 to 6.9 millimeters ($\frac{1}{16}$ to $\frac{1}{4}$ inch). Sixteen subjects, fifteen women and one man, ranging in age from twelve to fifty-eight, participated in the study.

Data are shown in Figure 5–5 for twelve of the subjects; four subjects performed so poorly or so well that their thresholds could not be estimated (important data in their own right.) The absolute threshold is approximately 3 millimeters on the average, with a range from 1.5 to 5 millimeters. Even more important than the average is the amount of variability, which for these untrained people ranged from almost total insensitivity to a remarkable ability to detect miniscule particles. An important question, unanswered by this project, is the extent to which training programs can improve an individual's sensitivity in this task.

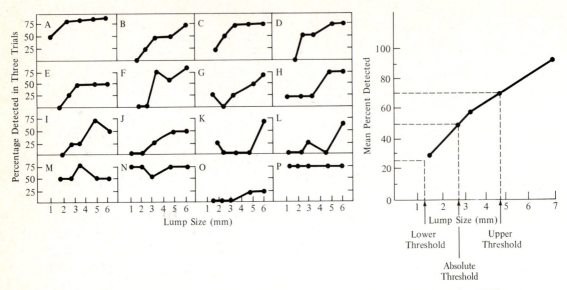

Figure 5–5 Psychophysical functions for detection of mammary lumps. (Data of Adams et al., 1976)

Comparison of Methods

There are a large number of psychophysical methods for measuring detection and discrimination, but most of them are variations on the two techniques just described. The continuous adjustment and random presentation methods have both withstood the test of time. Each method has its strengths and weaknesses based on differences in how the stimuli are presented to the subject, how the subject responds to them, and how the subject decides on a particular judgment.

For instance, consider the nature of the information available to the subject in each method. During the sequence of trials, the continuous adjustment method gives the subject a great deal of information about the relation between the standard and the comparison stimuli. The subject knows the previous value of the comparison stimulus, how he or she responded to it, and the direction of change in the stimulus value. Full attention can be concentrated on the relation between the standard and comparison stimuli. In the random presentation method there is more uncertainty. The subject cannot predict from one presentation to the next how the comparison will be related to the standard, nor by how much the two will differ. He or she does not know whether to concentrate on detecting a small difference or to relax, knowing that the difference will be readily perceivable. Because most people can maintain high levels of attention only briefly, it is not surprising to find that subjects appear more sensitive with the continuous adjustment method than with the random presentation method.

What is a strength from one perspective can become a weakness when viewed from another. In the continuous adjustment method, the subject's expectations can lead to problems. If the comparison stimulus is noticeably different from the standard at the beginning of a test series (e.g., series II in Figure 5–1), after a few trials the subject may suspect that the point of subjective equality *should* have been reached and may thus be inclined to make a premature judgment that the comparison stimulus is equal or shorter, even though the perceptual experience suggests that it is still a little longer. An opposing bias can occur when the series begins with a comparison stimulus that is close to the standard. These biases do not necessarily cause a systematic change in the point of subjective equality—the effects tend to average out—but they do increase the amount of variability and hence the difference threshold. Expectations play a smaller role in the random presentation method, although even here the subject may still be influenced by the sequence of events; if too many *longer* stimuli appear in succession, the subject may begin to think that it is about time for a *shorter* stimulus to make an appearance. Similarly, the radar operator expecting to spot aircraft in a particular airspace, trying to maintain vigilance when nothing is happening, is likely to sound the alarm at the slightest indication of a change in stimulus conditions—even if the "target" happens to be the moon rising over the horizon (Buckner and McGrath, 1963; Mackie, 1977).

Signal Detection Theory

As is apparent from the comments immediately preceding, the subject's judgments when performing a psychophysical task depend on the interplay of both *perceptual* and *decision* processes. The subject analyzes the perceptual experience, relates this analysis to the other contextual factors in the experience, and then decides how to combine all this information to select an actual response. Thus, seldom does the subject simply respond *veridically* (to the facts, and nothing but the facts); interpretation always takes into account the broader context. The previous sections focused on the perceptual aspects of the psychophysical task (detection and discrimination); now we examine the influence of decision processes on performance.

An example may help to make the concept clear. Suppose I ask two different people to monitor a radio channel tuned to pick up faint extraterrestrial messages. The first individual is paid fifty cents for each message reported, while the second person is paid five dollars per report. The second person is likely to report more messages, all other things being equal and assuming no penalties for false reports. While it might be that the amount paid makes the ear more acute, a more likely explanation is that the second person will adopt a very liberal criterion for deciding whether a message has been detected.

The relation between perception and decision have been described by **signal detection theory,** which provides an account of how the subject's performance is affected interactively by factors like the strength of the message (or **signal**), the rewards and penalties for being right or wrong, and the subject's knowledge and experience. Several versions of the theory exist; the model described here was developed by Atkinson and his colleagues (Atkinson, Bower, and Crothers, 1965; cf.

Coombs, Dawes, and Tversky, 1970, for other versions). This particular version is designed for the *yes–no detection task*:

> On each of a series of trials the subject hears a pulse of "white noise," which sounds like a burst of static. On some of the trials a "pure tone," something like a faint beep, is added to the white noise; on other trials only the white noise occurs. These are referred to as *signal-plus-noise* and *noise-only* events, respectively. The subject's task is to say "yes" if a signal is detected, and "no" if only noise is heard.

This task can be designed for a wide range of sense modalities, though for some reason most of the experimental work has concentrated on audition.

In the Atkinson model the stimulus experience, or *perceptual state*, is represented as an all-or-none event. It is assumed that after each stimulus presentation the person thinks either that he or she heard the signal in the noise (perceptual state $\mathcal{S}$), or that only noise was heard (perceptual state $\mathcal{N}$). These two perceptual states are probabilistically related to the stimulus events:

> Presentation of signal-plus-noise (a signal trial) is followed by state $\mathcal{S}$ with probability s, and is followed by state $\mathcal{N}$ with probability $1 - s$.

> Presentation of noise-only (a noise trial) is followed by state $\mathcal{S}$ with probability n, and is followed by state $\mathcal{N}$ with probability $1 - n$.

Probabilities express the likelihood of the occurrence of an event—the percentage of times the event happens. The detection probabilities s and n describe the perceptual process. Ordinarily we would expect s to be greater than n: the subject is more likely to think that he or she has heard a signal when one is present than when only noise is present. Notice that s is the likelihood of perceiving a signal when one is present, an appropriate perceptual reaction, whereas n is the probability of perceiving a signal when none is present, an inappropriate perceptual reaction. This way of defining the probability values may seem a bit odd, but it simplifies the estimation of the probabilities, as we shall see below.

Suppose $s = .80$ and $n = .10$. The probability value for s means that on 80 percent of the signal-plus-noise trials the subject will perceive the signal; on the other 20 percent of the signal-plus-noise trials nothing but noise will be perceived. Similarly, the probability value for n means that on 10 percent of the noise-only trials the subject will imagine a signal, whereas on the remaining 90 percent of the noise-only pulses only noise will be perceived.

Now let us turn to the decision process. How should it be represented in the model? The simplest assumption might be that the person always responds on the basis of the stimulus experience, giving a veridical report of the perceptual state: if in state $\mathcal{S}$, say "yes"; if in state $\mathcal{N}$, say "no." This assumption is unlikely to work for several reasons, none of which entail untruthfulness by the subject. Most important, the subject is generally aware that perception is not perfect: sometimes a person misses a signal, other times a signal is imagined when none is there. We all know that our sensitivity can be limited under certain conditions, and so we are right in sometimes doubting our experience. Thus, it makes sense to take into account other facets of the situation. In particular, rewards and penalties should be considered. If the payoff conditions punish false alarms (saying "yes" when nothing is there), then the subject may sensibly decide to say "no" on some trials when it seems a signal was present. This strategy reduces the number of penalties. Conversely, if the payoff conditions reward hits (saying "yes" when a signal is present), then the subject would probably say "yes" whenever a signal is experienced and throw in some extra "yes" responses even when nothing is experienced. The subject's decisions are also likely to be affected by the rate of signal-plus-noise and noise-only trials. If the experimental situation favors one or the other of these events, the subject will soon become aware of this and can adjust the decision strategy to favor one or the other of the events.

The line of reasoning laid out above is represented in the Atkinson model by two postulates that link the subject's responses to the perceptual states:

The liberal strategy (bias toward saying "yes")
The subject, if in state $\mathcal{S}$, always says "yes."
The subject, if in state $\mathcal{N}$, says "yes" with probability p, and says "no" with probability $1 - p$.

The conservative strategy (bias toward saying "no")
The subject, if in state $\mathcal{N}$, always says "no."
The subject, if in state $\mathcal{S}$, says "no" with probability q, and says "yes" with probability $1 - q$.

From these two sets of assumptions, one can construct the *detection graph* in Figure 5–6, which shows the predictions of the model for performance in this task. (Signal detection theory was originally introduced by engineers to model the characteristics of radio receivers, and you will sometimes find reference to a receiver-operating-characteristic, or ROC, graph.) The detection graph shows the relation between two fundamental measures mentioned earlier:

Hit rate: the proportion of times that the subject says "yes" on a signal-plus-noise trial.

False alarm rate: the proportion of times that the subject says "yes" on a noise-only trial.

The other two events, occasions when the subject says "no," do not need to be considered because the subject must say either "yes" or "no." If the model can account for the "yes" responses, then the "no" responses are also predicted.

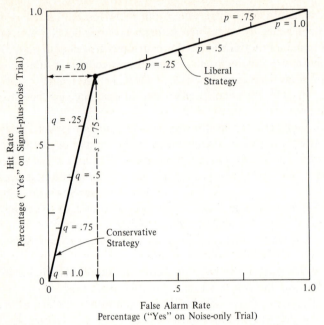

Figure 5–6 Detection graph showing the relations between hit rate and false alarm rate

The graph is constructed by drawing the hit rate and false alarm axes as shown, then locating a pair of specific values for the estimates of the probabilities for the perceptual states, s and n. We will see later how to estimate these values from actual data; for now, suppose that $s = .75$ and $n = .20$. If the subject gives a veridical report of perceptual experience, then s and n will be the hit and false alarm rates, respectively; this happens when p and q both equal zero. This situation, shown by the closed circle in the middle of the graph, occurs when the subject has no reason to bias judgments in either the liberal or conservative direction.

The straight lines drawn in either direction from the closed circle show how performance changes as the subject becomes more liberal or conservative. The limit of the liberal strategy is at the upper right corner. The subject will always say "yes," no matter what the perceptual state, so both the hit rate and the false alarm rate are at 100 percent (the proportion equals 1.0). A moderately liberal strategy (e.g., $p = .50$) falls half way along the "liberal" line. Similarly, a completely conservative strategy winds up in the lower left corner—the subject always says "no," no matter what the perceptual state—and moderately conservative biases will be at various points along the "conservative" line.

To illustrate how to use signal detection theory in designing a study and interpreting the results and how the probability measures are estimated from experimental data, let us look again at the research on the detection of breast lumps. The graphs in Figure 5–5 showing individual responses differ considerably from one another. We do not know whether these graphs reflect differences in perceptual sensitivity or in subjects' decision strategies. Suppose we train the individuals. How do we ensure that the training affects the perceptual process rather than leading the people to simply increase the number of times they say "I feel a lump?"

Figure 5–7 shows an experimental plan for tackling this question and demonstrates how to interpret the data. Three variations in the experimental conditions are laid out on the left side of the figure. The study might be carried out in the following manner. First, the observers are pretested as they come into the laboratory; then they are given an intensive training program on lump detection and on the importance of reporting a lump if they have any suspicion whatsoever (a liberal decision strategy is clearly appropriate in this situation). Second, the plan calls for variation in lump size. On some of the trials, a lump is not present; on other trials the artificial breast is embedded with either a relatively small lump or a relatively large one. This variation is designed to affect the perceptual probabilities, s and n. Third, we need to introduce a variation designed to influence the decision process; unless we can induce the subjects to switch between the liberal and conservative strategies in a systematic way, it is impossible to estimate the probabilities in the model. The variable selected for this purpose in the plan laid out in Figure 5–7 is the likelihood of a lump. In some blocks of trials, 80 percent of the stimuli include a lump. In other blocks of trials, 20 percent of the stimuli contain a lump. Subjects will quickly figure the odds if they are given feedback when they are right or wrong. Let us assume that feedback is given. If most of the stimuli in a series contain a lump, the subject should adopt a liberal strategy, and conversely.

For the subject the experiment proceeds as follows. There are four blocks of trials at the beginning of the test. Though the subject may not know it, these four blocks cover all four combinations of large and small lumps with high and low percentages of a lump. These four conditions provide the hit rate (HR) and false alarm rate (FAR) data for the top two graphs. The subject next goes through the training program and is then retested on the same four sets of conditions, generating the data for the two bottom graphs. (All of the data in this graph are fictitious, created for this illustration.)

Once the researcher has the data for hit and false alarm rates for both liberal and conservative strategies, the model comes into play. The hit rate and false alarm rate for each of the percentage conditions are plotted for every one of the combinations. Next, the lines for the liberal and conservative strategies are drawn through these data points. If the variations have actually led the subject to change strategies, then the point of intersection provides estimates of the perceptual probabilities. The placement of the data along the "liberal" and "conservative" lines can be used to estimate the decision probabilities. These estimates can be made visually, by more complex graphic procedures, or by algebra; we will rely on the visual approach in this illustration.

Now that the model has allowed us to go from the data to the probabilities of the underlying process, what do the results look like? First, the variations in the lump size and in the percentage of lumps have the desired effects in the pretests.

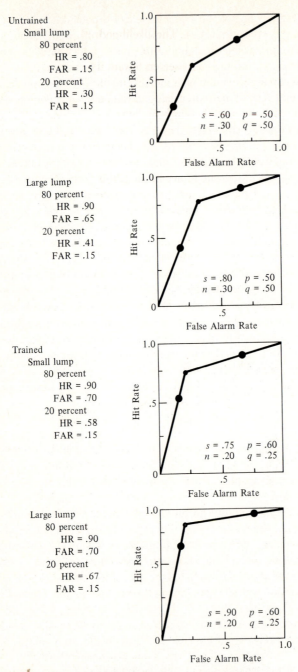

Figure 5–7 Hypothetical results of signal detection experiment with variation in signal, probability of signal, and training

The likelihood of feeling a lump when one is there is greater for larger lumps ($s = .80$) than for smaller lumps ($s = .60$). The likelihood of imagining a lump when none is present is equal in both conditions ($n = .30$). The percentage variation also has the desired effect, driving the observers toward the liberal and conservative strategies, and markedly so (p and q equal .50 under the two conditions).

Training has strong effects on both the perceptual and decision processes. The probabilities of detecting a lump increase for both large ($s = .90$) and small ($s = .75$) lumps, compared with the pretraining performance. The likelihood of imagining a lump goes down in both conditions to .20. There is also an overall shift toward a more liberal decision bias; performance in the high-occurrence condition has a larger p value ($p = .60$), and performance in the low-occurrence condition is less conservative ($q = .25$), compared with pretraining performance.

This illustration has been rather complex and extended, but it exemplifies the significant role that a theoretical model can play in the measurement of psychological processes. The "raw" data in Figure 5–7 are relatively meaningless as they stand; they may be numbers, but they are not interpretable. The model provides a mechanism for translating the original observations into values that can be meaningfully related to understandable concepts. Such ease of interpretation is the ultimate goal of any technique of measurement.

PSYCHOLOGICAL MAGNITUDES

The Human Use of Numbers

We have just seen how performance, either directly or by means of a theoretical model, can serve to provide measures of detection and discrimination. The examples were from the senses, but the same techniques can be used to measure memory strength, problem-solving difficulty, and a wide range of other domains (Egan, 1975). We now examine situations in which people use numbers directly as responses.

Most of us who were born into modern society encountered number concepts and learned to calculate with numbers at a fairly early age. By eight or nine, we had become reasonably competent at adding, subtracting, multiplying, and dividing. Moreover, we had a grasp of the practical applications of arithmetic. If one child says to another "You have twice as many jelly beans as I do!" the statement is more than a general complaint; it can be checked by counting the number of jelly beans in each youngster's possession and calculating the ratio.

Even very young children become accustomed to hearing adults use numbers in everyday situations. A mother says "If I've told you once, I've told you a million times—shut the screen door!" Johnny realizes that it makes no sense to search through past experience for the number of times his mother has actually uttered this command. He understands that "a million times" is serving figuratively to denote intensity of feeling—fairly strong in this instance!

A more scientific-sounding example appears in the following statement:

> The builders of the Y-99 jetliner claimed that it carried twice the payload of the Y-98, yet sounded only 75 percent as noisy during takeoff.

The payload capacity of the aircraft can be determined relatively easily, but what is meant by "only 75 percent as noisy?" The manufacturer can take readings with an intensity-level meter, but does a reading that shows 75 percent of previous intensity mean the same as "only 75 percent as noisy?" Suppose residents living near the airport complain that the new aircraft actually makes twice as much noise as the old model? Which is to be believed, the meter or the people? The people do most of the listening.

Here is another example. You are looking for an apartment. The features that matter most to you include roominess, attractiveness, proximity to your college, swimming pool, and cost. You can compare any two apartments quantitatively on each of these features, but it is unlikely that either will come out on top for all of them. How do you combine or "add up" the various pieces of information to reach an overall rating for each alternative? In wrestling with the issues entailed in these examples and others that could be given, we need to think a bit more about the nature of numbers.

Number Scales

In the examples above, people are asked to make judgments that call for them to act like a measuring instrument: a foot rule, a bathroom scale, an adding machine. They are like "subjective yardsticks." Before examining the psychology of such performance, let us consider some of the ways in which numbers are assigned to objects.

At the beginning of this section we looked at measurement operations in which numbers were generated by a counting operation—for instance, if we count the number of times a 1-meter stick can be laid end to end from one end of a carpet to the next, that count is the length in meters of the carpet. Measurement has been defined as the assignment of numbers to objects according to a rule (Stevens, 1951). Counting is one such rule, but there are others. We will consider five types of measurement scale in this section: nominal, ordinal, interval, ratio, and logarithmic.

Nominal Measurement. Social security numbers, automobile licenses, and the figures on the uniforms of football players are instances of **nominal scale**. The rule for this scale is that similar objects in a set be given the same or similar numbers. Regarding social security numbers, each individual has to be unique, and so everyone has a different number. Regarding football players, each position is generally assigned the same number in the tens-place (the center is 50-something, guards are 60-something, and so on), with the units-digit marking the specific player. Every player has a unique number in this system, but the values also provide information about the player's position. In nominal measurements like these, the numbers serve primarily to identify: they *name*, but they do not entail any of the other regularities associated with the number system. Accordingly, it is meaningless to perform arithmetic operations on nominally assigned numbers; two halfbacks do not equal a tackle, regardless of how the numbers come out.

Ordinal Measurement. On an **ordinal scale** the numbers reflect a regular ordering of the objects. Birth dates, serial numbers, and street address numbers are examples of an ordinal rule for assigning numbers. If you deliver messages to 101, 103, and 105 Maplewood Avenue, you may be assured that the houses are arranged in the order designated by the numbers. The first house may be close to the second while the third is another mile down the road; ordinal assignment guarantees nothing about intervals. Even the simplest arithmetic operations, addition and subtraction, cannot be performed on ordinally assigned numbers with any real assurance that the results will be meaningful.

Equal-Interval Measurement. If equal distances between objects on a particular scale correspond to equal numerical intervals, then the assignment meets the requirements of an **equal-interval scale.** Tract house numbers are often on an interval scale. The houses are so uniformly spaced that the distance between any two is exactly the same. The Centigrade and Fahrenheit temperature scales are also equal-interval scales. The same amount of energy is required to change the temperature of a volume of water from 10°F to 20°F as from 100°F to 110°F. Addition and subtraction are meaningful operations on an interval scale. If, for instance, the numbers of two pairs of tract houses differ by a fixed amount, then the two pairs will be a fixed distance apart. Multiplication and division are not legitimate operations on an interval scale, because the value corresponding to zero is not a true zero. Thus, it is not true that 100°F is twice as hot as 50°F because 0°F is not actually the bottom line for temperature (true zero on the Fahrenheit scale is about −460 degrees).

Ratio Measurement. When equal intervals are maintained *and* the scale begins at a true zero, the result is a **ratio scale** of measurement. All the standard numerical operations—addition, subtraction, multiplication, and division—can be meaningfully performed with such an assignment rule. The measurement of length meets the requirements for a ratio scale; if one board is four times as long as another, the first board can be cut into four equal segments and each will equal the length of the second board.

Logarithmic Measurement. The four scales described above are familiar to you by experience if not by name. You already know that adding the serial numbers for two refrigerators yields a number that is totally meaningless, while cutting a pound of salami in half produces two chunks that are exactly half a pound each.

The fifth type of scale is less familiar than the first four. Sometimes it is important to measure relative rather than absolute extents:

> Suppose a dog (10 pounds) and a horse (1000 pounds) each gain a pound during a specified period of time. In one sense, the two gains are equal; in another sense, however, the horse increased its weight only slightly, whereas the dog's increase was tremendous.
>
> If we assign numbers so that a change from 10 to 11 pounds is the same as a change from 1000 to 1001 pounds, we get one scale [a ratio scale, actually]. We get a second scale by assigning numbers so that the change from 10 to 11 is more nearly equal to a change from 1000 to 1100 [a 10 percent change in both instances, yielding the same relative increase in weight]. (Torgerson, 1960, pp. 24–25, slightly altered)

Relative changes are most conveniently measured by a **logarithmic scale.** A logarithm is defined as the power to which a base value must be raised to generate a particular number (we will use 10 as the base throughout this discussion). For instance, $100 = 10^2$, so $\log(100) = 2$; similarly, $1000 = 10^3$, and so $\log(1000) = 3$; finally, $10 = 10^1$, and so $\log(10) = 1$. On a logarithmic scale the distance from 10 to 100 is the same as the distance from 100 to 1000—both are one logarithmic unit apart. This is another way of saying that 100 is ten times larger than 10 and 1000 is ten times larger than 100; each set of numbers differs by the same *relative* amount. Likewise, the logarithms for the weight gains for the dog and the horse in the preceding example, who both increase by the same relative amount (10 percent), go from 1.0 to 1.04 for the dog and from 3.00 to 3.04 for the horse, equal logarithmic values.

To appreciate the utility of the logarithmic scale, it is helpful to think about the rather remarkable properties of the sensory systems: sensitivity to light and to sound and the ability to make judgments about length, weight, and time, among others. All these dimensions are *unbounded*; they have no upper limit, practically speaking. For example, the scale of length covers the distances between electrons as well as the distances between stars. Over this incredible range, the accuracy of the measure is typically relative to the magnitude. For the watchmaker a fraction of a millimeter is important; the astronomer is satisfied to achieve accuracy within a few light years when measuring the distance to neighboring galaxies. Implicit in this remark—and it is important to make the point explicit—is the fact that human sensitivity is also relative to magnitude in many situations.

Consider the scales of light and sound shown in Figure 5–8. The uppermost scale shows physical intensities, scaled logarithmically, and below it the logarithmic

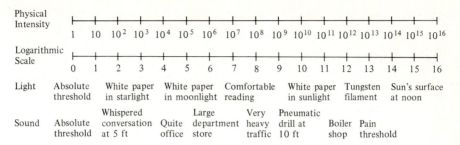

Figure 5–8 Physical and decibel scales for light and sound dimensions

scale. On both these scales, the "measured" distances on the paper are equal in relative values. The two bottom rows list commonplace experiences corresponding to various points on the scales.

It would be difficult to express the distances using the typical scales of measurement. For instance, the gap between the smallest and largest intensities that human beings are able to detect (at least for a brief time; one should not gaze at the surface of the sun for very long), a ratio of 10^1 to 10^{16} compares with the difference between a 1-inch-long thread and a chain stretching from the Earth to Jupiter. If the figure were on a regular ratio scale of intensity, the experiences on the lower end of the scale would be squeezed so tightly together that comparisons would be impossible—unless the figure was on a four-page foldout!

Human sensitivities are quite remarkable. Depending on the stimuli and the task, a person may respond to either the absolute or relative values of a stimulus. Either type of response can be meaningful to the researcher, as long as there is an awareness of the nature of the response and the implications of the "number" produced by the subjects. For instance, the Richter scale is used to describe the intensity of earthquakes. It is a logarithmic scale. People react relatively to earthquakes, and so the scale is appropriate to the response. When the Richter scale is interpreted in physical terms, each increase of 1 unit of intensity is an increase of 60 units in physical force; an earthquake of magnitude 4 (common in California) is 60 times more powerful than one of magnitude 3; the 1906 tremor in San Francisco (magnitude 8) was almost 13,000,000 times more powerful in physical energy than a magnitude 4 earthquake. The practical side of psychophysics. . . .

Psychological Scaling Tasks

Magnitude Estimation and Category Rating. Psychologists have devised a variety of methods for investigating the performance of human subjects on measurement tasks (Marks, 1974). In **magnitude estimation** the subject is asked to assign each stimulus a number according to its perceived intensity along some dimension.

The judgment may be more or less familiar to the subject from ordinary experience. For instance, many of us learned as Scouts to estimate the weight of objects in pounds; assigning numbers to stars of varying brilliance is commonplace to astronomers though not commonly done by most people.

The magnitude estimation task generally begins by giving subjects an *anchor point* that establishes the unit of measurement on the scale. For instance, subjects may be shown a 15-watt lamp (rather dim) and told to think of it as one unit of brightness. They are then shown lights of varying intensity (e.g., 40, 60, 75, 100, 250 watts and so on) and asked to assign a number to each. The task is generally easier for subjects if they do not have to work with fractional judgments (interesting, given that many students have trouble with fractions in school), and so the unit of measurement chosen as a base is typically smaller than any of the other stimuli being estimated. Another approach is to select a small stimulus value and tell the subject to assign it a value of 10; that way, a unit is established but fractions are avoided.

A second approach to subjective measurement is the **category rating task.** The subject is given a set of numbers and asked to rate each stimulus on a numerical scale. Generally the set of numbers ranges from 1 at the lower end to 10 or less at the upper end. The numbers may be given labels, and in some instances only the labels are used. For instance, the subject may be asked to rate a series of light intensities on a scale from 1 (very dim) to 10 (very bright).

In the category rating task, the responses available to the subject are bounded at both extremes, and so the scale is often *anchored* at both ends. For instance, the subject may be shown a 15-watt lamp and told to think of it as very dim and then shown a 250-watt lamp as an example of what to consider very bright. The other lamps in the series are then presented for judgment on the 10-point rating scale. When no anchors are provided in a category rating task, then subjects have to create their own frame of reference for judgment; later in the chapter we discuss what happens under these conditions.

Comparison of Methods. The magnitude estimation and category rating tasks both require the subject to assign numbers (or numberlike category values) to stimulus objects. The two methods are designed to tap the same underlying psychological processes. The methods differ, however, and these differences affect performance. In this section we examine three important differences between the methods and discuss several studies that demonstrate the effects of these differences.

The two methods obviously differ in the response scale available to the subject. Category rating tasks provide the subject with a scale that is bounded at both the lower and upper ends, whereas magnitude estimation uses a scale that is clearly unbounded at the upper end (there is no real limit to the number that the subject can assign to a very intense stimulus). The lower end of the magnitude estimation scale is unbounded in principle (fractions or negative numbers exist and could be employed by the subjects), but in practice the researcher typically tells the subject to avoid negative numbers, and subjects for their own reasons tend to avoid fractions. Thus, the lower end of the magnitude estimation is bounded for all practical purposes.

The two methods also differ in how the response scales are anchored to the stimulus dimension. By and large, the anchoring procedures reflect the boundedness of the response scales. In the category rating task, the subject is usually shown the largest and smallest stimuli to be rated and told to link these values to the upper and lower ends of the rating scale. Variations on this anchoring procedure are sometimes employed, depending on the purposes of the experiment. If the boundary stimuli are not presented at the beginning of a test series, most subjects are uncomfortable about making ratings until they get some sense of the values. Then they adjust their judgments as if they had been anchored by the experimenter in the usual fashion. In magnitude estimation the scale may be anchored by assigning the smallest stimulus value to a numerical value of 1 or 10. This assignment has the effect of anchoring the scale at the lower end only.

A third difference between the two methods is the relation between the response scale and the perceptual "measurements" of the objects. Category rating emphasizes equal intervals between objects, whereas magnitude estimation stresses constant ratios. This distinction sometimes shows up in the instructions given by the experimenter, which stress intervals in the rating task and ratios in the magnitude estimation task. It may also be that subjects are inherently disposed to use numbers in different ways in these two situations.

Numerous studies have compared subjects' performance on magnitude estimation and category tasks. Many of these experiments were conducted to determine the "true" relation between physical and psychological scales and to find out which of the two methods was closer to the "truth." A more productive approach to the studies is to reflect on how they demonstrate human beings' ability to perform as measuring instruments in a variety of situations and how the processes of psychological measurement vary with the task and the stimulus dimension.

One of the oldest studies of this problem is still one of the best. Stevens and Galanter (1957) employed the plan shown in Figure 5–9. One variable was the task: *magnitude estimation* versus *category rating*. Six stimulus dimensions were tested, three of which are relatively *familiar* and three of which are relatively *unfamiliar*

	Dimension					
	Familiar			Unfamiliar		
	Length	Duration	Weight	Area	Auditory intensity	Visual intensity
Magnitude Estimation						
Category Rating						

Figure 5–9 Design of experiments by Stevens and Galanter (1957) on magnitude estimation and category rating

(Stevens and Galanter did not emphasize this distinction, but it helps in understanding their findings). The subjects were all college students, and they were tested for many trials on each task for each dimension.

The basic findings are plotted in Figure 5–10. The response scale is on the vertical axis. The category and magnitude scales are lined up so that they match at

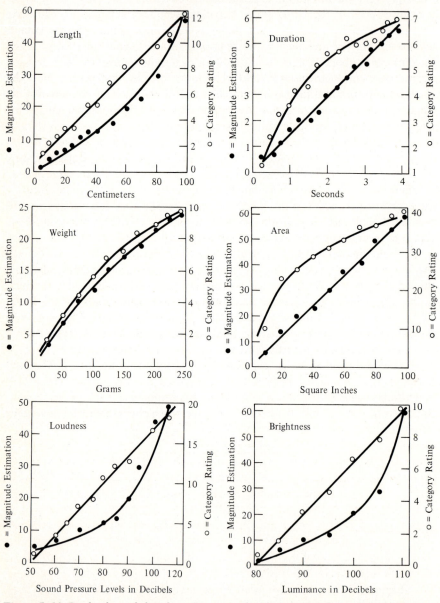

Figure 5–10 Psychophysical data from Stevens and Galanter (1957) plotted in standard coordinates

the upper and lower ends, with the magnitude scale on the left side of each graph and the category scale on the right. For instance, if the magnitude estimates for length range from 1 to 50 and for category scale from 1 to 10, the two scales are arranged so that the 1s match at the bottom and 50 on the magnitude scale lines up with 10 on the category scale at the top. The responses are on a ratio scale, starting at zero and with equal distances between equal numbers.

The physical stimulus scales are plotted on the horizontal axis. The four upper plots use a standard ratio scale for the stimulus dimensions. The two lower plots use decibel scales for sound and light intensity. The decibel scale is a type of logarithmic measure, such that as sound pressure goes from 40 to 50, for instance, the physical intensity actually goes up tenfold. Similarly, the change from 40 to 60 decibels amounts to a hundredfold increase, one tenfold increase followed by a second tenfold increase. The senses of sight and hearing, as mentioned earlier, respond in a relative manner to increases in light and sound, and so sensory researchers routinely rely on decibel scales.

Figure 5–10 contains a great deal of information. There are six graphs, one for each stimulus dimension. Each graph contains two plots, one for each of the tasks. The plots, which describe the relation between the physical stimulus dimension and the subjects' numerical judgments, trace a variety of shapes. Sometimes the relation is a straight line (e.g., magnitude estimation of area), sometimes it bends downward (e.g., category rating of duration), and sometimes it bends upward (e.g., magnitude estimation of length).

Which of these plots, if any, reveal the "true" psychophysical function? As already noted, this is probably the wrong question. On the other hand, it is difficult for the researcher to make sense of such complexity. An abiding tenet of scientists is that if a research study has been carried out in a competent manner, there must be some way of looking at the findings that will yield a simple interpretation. Sometimes a scientist creates a theoretical model that makes the complex simple; sometimes it is a matter of stumbling by chance onto a simple explanation. Both of these approaches play a role in the interpretation of the data in Figure 5–10.

First the "chance" approach. Some years ago, Stevens (1957) noted that if magnitude estimation data were plotted on log-log graph paper (both the horizontal and vertical axes scaled logarithmically), data like those in Figure 5–10 almost always appeared in *linear* form. Linear functions are important in scientific research because of their simplicity; the equation for a straight-line function, $X = a + bY$, is easy to understand (compared with most other algebraic functions), and it depends upon only two parameters, a and b (X and Y are supplied by the situation). Stevens had no theory in mind but was just toying around with different methods for plotting his data. His discovery was serendipitous (he found something he was not looking for), and he may not have fully appreciated the importance of the find. He was searching for the "true" psychophysical relation, and when he found that magnitude estimation data were simple straight-line functions when plotted on log-log paper, this simplicity (and some accompanying algebra) led him to conclude that the magnitude estimation task was the key to the "real thing" that he had been searching for.

Stevens distrusted the category rating method for a variety of reasons, and so it never occurred to him to plot these data on log-log paper. In fact, if you do this, as has been done in Figure 5–11, something very interesting appears: both the magnitude estimation and the category rating tasks are straight-line functions in log-log coordinates. The data in this figure are laid out as in the preceding one—they are

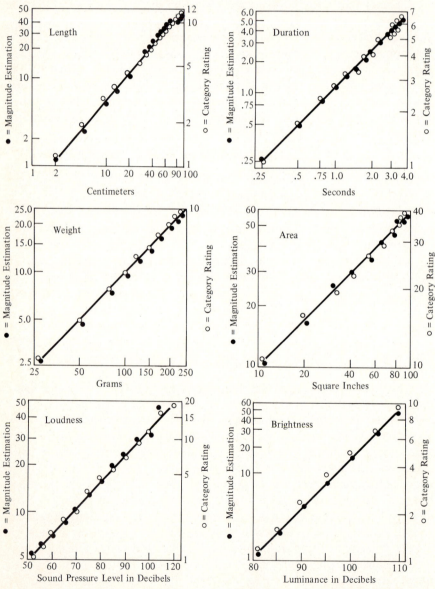

Figure 5–11 Psychophysical data from Stevens and Galanter (1957) plotted in log-log coordinates

the same data—but both the stimulus and response scales have been arranged logarithmically in every plot. Because the data are rather jumbled together, it is hard to separate the two tasks—and that is just the point. When both stimulus and response scales are laid out according to relative distances rather than equal intervals, the two tasks appear to be measuring the same thing.

When a researcher stumbles upon a regularity of the sort that appears in Figure 5–11, the best thing to do, after confirming that the results are reproducible, is to stop for a while and try to figure out what the regularity means. It is time to think and theorize. In fact, a theoretical model has been worked out that explains the relations in the figure (Calfee, 1975, Ch. 6; Birnbaum and Veit, 1974; Birnbaum, 1980). The model assumes that perceptual judgments are always based on relative magnitudes and that the numerical judgments that serve as responses require a perceptual judgment; in essence, both the category rating and the magnitude estimation tasks require the subject to try to match two stimulus scales, one of which the researcher calls a "stimulus" and the other the researcher calls a "response." The concept of a logarithm may not be especially well taught in school, but most of our judgments appear to be the result of comparing two dimensions in a logarithmic (that is, relativistic) manner, so that according to the model, the psychophysical relation between stimulus judgments and response judgments can be written as

$$a \log(\text{Stimulus}) = b \log(\text{Response})$$

which implies that

$$\log(\text{Stimulus}) = a/b \log(\text{Response})$$

The model predicts that the relation between stimulus and response should be a straight-line function in log-log coordinates. To be sure, it was the discovery of this relation that led to the development of the model. But the model does suggest some thoughts about other aspects of the findings in Figure 5–11. For instance, one would suspect that a depends primarily on the nature of the stimulus dimension, while b is related to the response dimension. For a familiar dimension like length or duration, college students are likely to have had considerable opportunity to learn something about the relation between a and b. They can accurately estimate the length of an object in feet or inches or yards and are able to convert these estimates from one scale to another. These experiences mean that the subject can adjust b so that the perception represented by a can be matched by adjustment in b; by setting b to equal a, the subjects behave like the "measuring stick" with which they are familiar. Under these conditions the slope of the straight-line function for familiar dimensions like inches or seconds should equal 1 for magnitude estimation tasks, and this prediction is borne out by the data in Figure 5–11 for these dimensions. For dimensions with which the subject is less familiar, b will seldom equal a—the subject does not have the experience to make the match—and so the slope will generally not equal 1.

Another interesting prediction of the model is that subjects go through the same judgment processes when comparing any two stimuli. For instance, suppose a number is presented, and the subject has to adjust the brightness of a light to match the number. Or the task requires the subject to match the loudness of a tone to the length of a line, the size of a square, or the brightness of a light. Many such experiments have been carried out over the past several years (e.g., Stevens and Guirao, 1963), not to test the model but as a matter of curiosity. The results are consistent with the model in every case that I have examined, and in several instances fairly detailed predictions have worked out (cf. Calfee, 1975, pp. 126ff, especially "the study of smells"). Once again, a full appreciation of the data comes when we have a theoretical model of the underlying processes.

INTEGRATION OF INFORMATION

You are told that someone is *friendly*, *appreciative*, and *reliable*. What is your overall impression of the person, based on this list of adjectives? What would your impression be of a person described as *considerate*, *restless*, and *critical*; someone who is *unfriendly*, *unappreciative*, and *reliable*?

Which of these descriptions would produce the best impression, and which the worst? To be sure, the answers might depend on the situation—whether you were hiring the person for a job or thinking about a date, for instance. In any event forming such judgments is an important part of the work of interviewers, personnel managers, social workers, clinical psychologists, and a wide range of other professionals who are regularly required to combine diverse sources of information to form an overall evaluation of a person. How do they do it? This question is the focus of this section.

Adding up the "Facts"

Over the past twenty years, Norman Anderson (1979) and his colleagues have developed a theory of impression formation based upon a simple notion: when human beings are given several pieces of information about someone or something, they assign a value to each piece, and if asked for an overall assessment, they simply average the different pieces. Nothing fancy—no complex, interactive judgments, but instead a task within the capability of a hand calculator. It turns out that the complex part of forming an impression is deciding on the values of the individual pieces of information.

Anderson and others have explored what is known as *information integration theory* over a wide array of situations, ranging from psychophysical scaling tasks to personality ratings. We will examine a few samples of this work to show how human beings perform relatively complex measurement tasks.

In one of the early experiments (Anderson, 1962), subjects rated the *likableness* of nine hypothetical persons, each of whom was described by a pair of adjectives. The experimental plan and the results of the study are shown in Figure 5–12. The first adjective in the pair is listed on the horizontal axis, with the most positive on the left and the least positive on the right. The second adjective in the pair is represented by the three plots in the figure, with the least positive at the bottom and the most positive at the top.

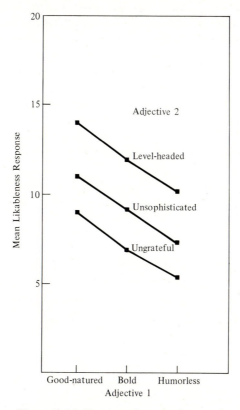

Figure 5–12 Design and results from study of impression formation by Anderson (1962). Subjects rated likability of nine persons described by all combinations of pairs from two sets of three adjectives. The plots are all parallel, which implies that impression is a simple average of the values for the two adjectives.

The results look rather simple: three parallel lines. As it turns out, the averaging model predicts exactly this result. Whatever the value of *level-headed* compared with *unsophisticated*, that value when combined with the three adjectives on the base line should produce the same change in the overall impression for each of the base-line adjectives (a little algebra should convince the doubter). For instance, *level-headed* increases the impression by three points whether the person being rated is *good-natured*, *bold*, or *humorless*.

This study is rather simple, but its implications are broad-ranging. For instance, in another set of experiments, Anderson (1973) used the same approach to investigate students' opinions of United States presidents. The research team identified eight relatively unknown presidents. Following the plan shown in Figure 5–13, a booklet of paragraphs was prepared describing each president. The paragraphs provided three basic descriptions that were connotatively either *unfavorable*, *neutral*, or *favorable*. These variations are shown on the horizontal axis. An extra set of paragraphs was then added to the basic description; the added information was either *favorable* or *unfavorable*. Each description was read by a sample of college students, whose task was to rate each president on overall statesmanship from 0 (poor) to 10 (excellent).

The findings in Figure 5–13 again support a simple averaging model: the effect of adding favorable rather than unfavorable information is the same, regardless of the level of the basic description.

The "presidents" experiment is somewhat artificial, to be sure. The reputations of Millard Fillmore and Warren Harding may be relatively easy to manipulate, but what about better-known and more recent presidents? What are the correlates of their reputations, and are these simply averaged to produce an overall impression?

To the best of my knowledge, a study along these lines has not been conducted, but the Anderson study suggests an approach that could be pursued: ask a sample of subjects to list the most important descriptors, both positive and negative, for a group of presidents who are better known. Then have a separate sample of

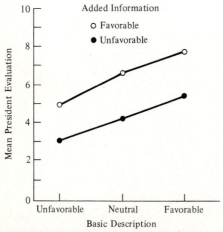

Figure 5–13 Judgments based on unfavorable, neutral, and favorable paragraphs about U.S. presidents. Absence of any interaction supports averaging model. (Data of Anderson, 1972)

subjects rate the value of each of the descriptors, without knowledge of how the ratings are to be used or where they came from. If the first sample does a good job of picking out the significant features for each president, and if the second sample rates the descriptors accurately, then it should be possible to predict the overall impressions of a third sample of subjects who are asked to evaluate the presidents.

The implications of this line of research are intriguing. A political candidate might give careful attention to the descriptors with the most positive values and cultivate those characteristics. On the other hand, the candidate with a large number of minor faults may find that these slowly but surely eat away at the public's impression. . . .

The averaging model does not always work, to be sure. For instance, Lampel and Anderson (1968) asked a sample of co-eds to rate the attractiveness of a potential dating partner based on a photograph and a pair of adjectives. The judgments did not converge on a simple average; rather, the photograph played a major role in the judgment, with the effect of the adjectives depending on the character of the photograph. If a date looked relatively unattractive, the adjectives had a negligible impact on the overall rating, which remained low even when the adjectives were positive. An attractive candidate, in contrast, had a lot to gain from the accompanying adjectives, up to an 8-point gain on a 20-point scale.

These complications muddy the water only slightly. The research findings suggest that, by and large, general impressions are the result of averaging information from various sources. Sometimes a particular piece of information is especially critical. More often, people make judgments based on the preponderance of the available information. Anyone's reputation may suffer from the accumulated weight of numerous derogatory statements; any product may "sell" if enough positive advertisements are placed before the public.

Context Effects on Judgment

Virtually every measuring instrument is influenced by the conditions under which it is used. Because metal rulers shrink or expand according to the temperature, measurements of length vary from a hot day to a cold day. These variations are very slight but can become noticeable in extreme conditions. Physical scientists know how these effects operate and can adjust for them.

The situational context strongly affects human judgment, and behavioral researchers are not always certain about how to predict these effects. Judgments are never made in isolation but always against the background of the subject's previous experiences and present expectations. For instance, how do you decide whether a particular object is heavy or light? To a watchmaker a brick seems tremendously heavy; to a bricklayer the same brick is about average; to a weightlifter its weight is negligible. Judgments of good and bad can also depend on the context. In *The Wall*, John Hersey (1950) describes a partisan's suffocating a newborn infant during the tragic seige of the Warsaw ghetto because the baby's crying threatens to alert a team of storm troopers to the partisans' basement hiding place. Ordinarily, we would view the murder of an infant with horror and dread. Against the larger backdrop of the atrocities being committed by the Nazis, the incident is terribly frightful but certainly does not strike the reader as evil.

Context can affect a person's judgments in either of two tasks. *Comparative judgments* entail the comparison of one object with another: *a* is better than *b*; *c* is smaller than *d*; *e* is more beautiful than *f*. In this task the two objects serve as standards for each other, and context effects tend to be modest. *Absolute judgments* are much more strongly influenced by the context. In these situations the subject has to respond in a nonrelative fashion ("good" or "bad," "large" or "small," "beautiful" or "ugly") to a single object.

Because there is no clear-cut standard of comparison in the absolute judgment task, the subject must construct a standard—a frame of reference—from the set of objects presented for judgment and from any other background stimuli or memories that may seem relevant to the judgment. The observer is told that a series of tones is to be presented, and each is to be rated as "loud" or "soft." The judgment of the first tone is a toss-up. The second tone will be judged relative to the first one and to the subject's response to the first one. Suppose the subject rates the first tone as "soft," and the second tone is even softer. The subject is likely to say "soft" again. But suppose all the subsequent tones are also lower in sound level than the first tone. Eventually the subject will adjust his or her standard for what is soft and what is loud, thereby constructing a judgmental frame of reference that allows all of the rating categories to be used; subjects dislike making one response to all stimuli ("soft, soft, soft . . .").

When confronted with an absolute judgment task, subjects often ask the tester to provide them with a standard for comparison, as if they appreciate the arbitrariness of adjectives and numbers. The subjects are right. A 6-foot human being is neither tall nor short; a 6-foot rabbit is very, very tall. If an observer has been rating the length of sticks ranging from 6 to 12 inches long and suddenly a 3-inch stick appears, it will seem quite short. The same 3-inch stick will seem quite long if the previous series of sticks ranged from ½ to 2 inches in length.

Parducci (1968) has investigated the influence of context on psychological measurement in a wide variety of situations, ranging from judgments regarding the size of numbers to whether sailboats are pleasurable. In a study that is typical of his research, subjects read one of the two lists in Figure 5–14 and assigned each of the statements in the list to one of the five ethical categories. Six critical statements common to both lists have been shaded for emphasis. The rest of the statements are designed to create a context. The contextual statements in the "mild" list are relatively innocuous, whereas those in the "severe" list are quite harsh. Some of the items may seem anachronistic because these materials were originally created in the 1930s.

The figure also shows the mean ratings for the statements common to the two lists. The last four common items are judged less evil in the severe list than in the mild list, by half a category width or more. Pocketing the waitress's tip may seem a vile act compared with wearing shorts illegally but shrinks into insignificance when

Mild Context

Registering in a hotel under a false name.
Bawling out servants publicly.
Contributing money to a cause in which you do not believe in order to escape criticism.
Keeping a dime you find in a telephone booth.
Publishing under your own name an investigation originated and carried out without remuneration by a graduate student working under you.
Failing to pay your bus fare when the conductor overlooks you.
Playing poker on Sunday.
Failing to put back in the water lobsters which are shorter than the legal limit.
Cheating at solitaire.
Fishing without a license.
Habitually borrowing small sums of money from friends and failing to return them.
Stealing towels from a hotel.
Stealing a loaf of bread from a store when you are starving.
Poisoning a neighbor's dog whose barking bothers you.
Lying about your whereabouts to protect a friend's reputation.
Wearing shorts on the street where it is illegal.
Pocketing the tip which the previous customer left for the waitress.
Getting your own way by playing on people's sympathies.

Severe Context

Using guns on striking workers.
Bawling out servants publicly.
Stealing ten dollars from an impecunious acquaintance.
Selling to a hospital milk from diseased cattle.
Publishing under your own name an investigation originated and carried out without remuneration by a graduate student working under you.
Spreading rumors that an acquaintance is a sexual pervert.
Having a sane person committed to a mental hospital in order to get rid of him.
Failing to put back in the water lobsters which are shorter than the legal limit.
Having sexual relations with a sibling (brother or sister).
Putting your deformed child in the circus.
Habitually borrowing small sums of money from friends and failing to return them.
Having incestuous relations with your parent.
Murdering your mother without justification or provocation.
Poisoning a neighbor's dog whose barking bothers you.
Testifying falsely against someone for pay.
Teaching adolescents to become dope addicts.
Pocketing the tip which the previous customer left for the waitress.
Sending another person to take a civil service exam for you.

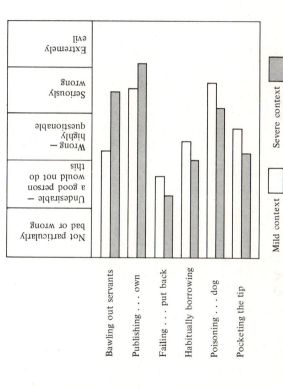

Figure 5–14 Effects of mild and severe context on moral judgment. Statements common to both lists, marked by darker background, were judged as more or less evil depending on context. (Data of Parducci, 1968)

compared with teaching adolescents to become drug addicts. The wickedness of any particular event depends in part on what else is on a person's mind at the time.

A second example of the effects of context on a person's attitude can be seen in a study by Dillehay and Jernigan (1970). College students responded to a survey of their opinions about the treatment of criminals. Figure 5–15 shows the three forms of the survey questionnaire: *lenient*, *harsh*, and *neutral*. Both the questions and the response choices were designed to produce different frames of reference for the student respondents. The approach is rather subtle; the context is not manipulated in an obvious way but by controlling the background against which the subject expresses his or her opinions. After the questionnaire had been completed, the respondents' attitudes toward the treatment of criminals was measured by a separate and relatively neutral rating scale; these data are shown on the right side of the

	Form	Mean Rating
Lenient	Is a policy of imprisonment for all crimes a good idea since it would involve locking up petty offenders who would never try another crime as well as persons who had one moment, or were victims of circumstance? a. Yes, any person who commits a crime, no matter how petty, should be put in prison. b. No, a policy of imprisonment for all crimes is impractical as well as unreasonable.	93
Neutral	Is a policy of imprisonment only for serious offenses or habitual criminality a good idea? a. Yes, a policy of imprisonment for serious offenders, or habitual criminals only, is a good idea. b. No, such a policy is not a good idea.	83
Harsh	Is a policy of imprisonment only for "serious" offenses or habitual criminality a good idea when it would probably encourage petty offenders and criminals who had never been caught to continue in their crimes? a. Yes, a policy of punishment for very serious offenders only is a good idea. b. No, it doesn't make good sense to adopt a policy which ways, in effect, "Small jobs are O.K. as long as you are not caught pulling them off more than a couple of times."	78

Figure 5–15 Sample items from prison reform questionnaires and mean ratings as a function of context. Higher scores are more lenient. (Data of Dillehay and Jernigan, 1970)

figure. The differences in the questionnaires had fairly substantial effects on the responses to the neutral-scale items. The lenient questionnaire led subjects to be more forgiving in their attitude than those who had completed the harsher questionnaire.

The findings in these studies reveal that people cannot make absolute judgments as such. Psychological measurements are made relative to an explicit standard when one is available, and otherwise to an implicit standard that the person establishes from whatever sources may be at his or her disposal. In forming a judgment about a particular stimulus, subjects not only average the pieces of information about the stimulus, they also add any contextual information that can be brought to bear (Anderson, 1982). This characteristic of human judgment complicates the interpretation of data, but it also means that psychological measurement is adaptive in a wide range of settings.

Attention and Judgment

An assumption has been made implicitly in the preceding section that subjects give equal attention to all information sources pertinent to the judgment of a stimulus. This assumption is an obvious oversimplification and breaks down totally in some situations. Shepard (1964) has noted that while human beings are skillful at evaluating the specific features of the most complex objects, we are less skilled at combining this information when its sources are internally inconsistent, or when the task of integration requires attention to too many different features. Tversky (1972) presents some interesting examples of this phenomenon, including a study on the problems involved in deciding on the admission of college applicants. This limitation to our ability to integrate distinctive sources of information reflects inherent limits on attentional capacity; at any one time, there are only so many things that we can simultaneously process, evaluate, and integrate. As a result, when several features of a stimulus are in conflict, some of the features are likely to be forgotten or disregarded.

An analysis somewhat along these lines may account for the unsettling findings of a study by Bjorkman (1963). He measured drivers' judgments of the point of impact for two cars moving toward a head-on collision. The situation is laid out in Figure 5–16. The subject, a passenger in car A, had the task of predicting which of the markers was closest to the probable point of impact with car B. The speed of the two cars varied according to the plan shown in the figure.

The findings were clear-cut. Regardless of the speed of the two cars, subjects consistently predicted the point of impact at half the distance between the two cars at the time of the judgment. When the two cars are moving at the same speed, this judgment is correct. When the oncoming car is moving more rapidly than car A (the one in which the subject is located), a collision will occur more quickly than the subject thinks. The actual point of impact depends on the ratio of the speed of

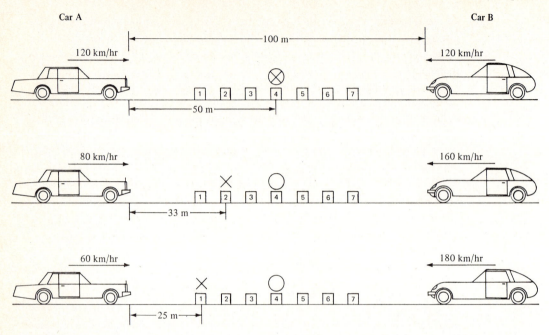

Figure 5–16 Experimental situation developed by Bjorkman (1963) to study psychological judgments of collision point of automobiles. Drivers predicted marker number where they thought collision would occur. X marks the actual point of collision; O marks the point judged by drivers.

the two cars. For instance, if car B is moving three times faster than car A, then the point of impact will be $1/(1 + 3)$ or one-quarter the distance between the two (see the bottom panel in the figure).

The implications of this finding can mean a tragic surprise for the driver. The critical factor in this situation is time rather than distance. If a driver is going 80 kilometers per hour (about 20 yards a second) and thinks that he or she will not hit an oncoming vehicle for another 100 yards, the person probably thinks that there are about 5 seconds to deal with the situation. If the point of impact is misjudged and there is only 50 yards to respond, then the driver has about 2 seconds to react—a significant discrepancy.

The mismeasurement was hard to correct. Bjorkman's subjects continued to make flawed and potentially hazardous judgments even after some practice at observing the mismatch between their estimates and the actual point of impact. Feedback was not enough, and systematic training was not attempted.

Let us try to analyze the subjects' thoughts in this situation. Three dimensions are relevant in solving this problem: (a) the distance between the two vehicles, (b) the velocity of the subject's car, and (c) the velocity of the oncoming car. The speedometer tells the subject the speed of his or her car, provided that this source of information is noticed. Distance judgments are fairly accurate, based on magnitude estimation findings (see the preceding section; also Gilinsky, 1951; Kunnapas, 1960). What about the velocity of the approaching vehicle? Semb (1969) found that psychological estimates of the velocity of an approaching vehicle were relatively unreliable at distances in excess of 300 yards, implying that this dimension is less salient than either the distance or the speed of the observer's car. This analysis suggests that the observer probably disregards the speed of an approaching car, even though this piece of information turns out to be critical in judging the point of collision.

This book is designed to teach you about research methods and only incidentally to present research findings. The last example, however, should leave you puzzling about what to do next: how can cars be designed or drivers trained to solve the problem? We must leave the problem, for to go further would take us too far afield. It should be clear from this brief account that while the ability of human beings to perform measurement tasks is remarkable for its flexibility and its integrative qualities, we are not infallible.

SUMMARY

This chapter describes methods for investigating the ability of human beings to *measure*—to make quantitative judgments about objects or events. The most basic type of psychological measurement entails the detection of a stimulus (was something there?) or the discrimination between two similar stimuli (was *a* the same or different from *b*?). In the psychophysical methods developed a century ago by Fechner, detection was equated with the zero point of the psychophysical scale for a stimulus dimension, and discriminability was equated with the unit of measurement.

While Fechner's theory is still debated, methods for measuring the absolute (detection) and difference (discrimination) thresholds have played an important role in psychological measurement, regardless of the validity of the theory. Two basic methods are presently employed to measure thresholds. In the continuous adjustment method small changes are made in the comparison stimulus until the subject notices a change. For instance, a pinpoint of light is gradually increased in intensity until the subject says "I can see it." Then the intensity is gradually decreased until the subject says, "I can't see it anymore." This process, which is used for measuring the absolute threshold, is continued until stable estimates can be made of the threshold (the average point of change). A similar process is used for obtaining estimates of the difference threshold. A comparison stimulus is moved up or down relative to a standard stimulus. The interval of uncertainty is the distance between the upper and lower average points of change, and the difference threshold is half the interval of uncertainty.

In the random presentation method a sample from the set of comparison stimuli is randomly selected on each of a series of trials. After each presentation the subject makes a judgment: "yes" or "no" for the absolute threshold and "greater" or "less" for the difference threshold. The 25th, 50th, and 75th percent points on the performance graph serve to define the lower threshold, the point of subjective equality, and the upper threshold respectively. The interval of uncertainty and the difference threshold are defined as in the comparison method.

Each of the methods has strengths and weaknesses. The comparison method measures the subject's optimal sensitivity to a stimulus but is likely to be biased by the subject's expectations. The random presentation method is less likely to be contaminated by expectations, but the subject has a more difficult attentional task.

Signal detection theory provides a mechanism for separating the sensory and decision effects in the psychophysical task. Several variants of the theory have been proposed. In the model presented in this chapter, it is assumed that after the presentation of a stimulus event, the subject enters a "detect" or "no detect" state, with probabilities that depend on whether a signal was present or not. The subject then makes a decision based on the sensory state, and on the degree to which the payoff and expectation conditions lead to a liberal ("say yes") or conservative ("say no") decision strategy. To validate the model and to obtain estimates of the theoretical probabilities, the experimenter must test the subject under a variety of conditions in which the sensory state and/or the decision strategy is altered by the treatment conditions.

The first section of the chapter, summarized above, describes indirect methods for investigating human ability to make quantitative judgments. In the second section of the chapter, we discuss what happens when the subject is asked to use numbers or quantitative categories as responses. In assigning numbers to an object or event, the measurement scale from this assignment can be classified into one of five types:

- Nominal scale: numbers serve for identification, as in assigning numbers to football players.

- Ordinal scale: numbers serve to put the items in order, but the distances between items may not match the distances between numbers, as in house addresses.

- Equal-interval scale: numbers line up objects in order, and the distances match for the items and the numbers, as in addresses in a housing tract; there is, however, no true zero on this scale.

- Ratio scale: all the properties of the preceding scale are pertinent to this scale, but the scale commences with a true zero; this is the scale you think of in most instances as measuring something, as in weight, length, volume, and so on.

- Logarithmic scale: relatively equal distances are assigned equal numbers, as in the Richter scale for measuring earthquakes or in the percentage method of describing pay raises ("All employees get a $100 raise" is measuring on a ratio scale; "All employees get a 10 percent raise" is measuring on a logarithmic scale).

What kind of measurement scale do subjects generate when asked to assign numbers to objects or events? Any kind the experimenter wants them to! The magnitude estimation and category rating methods, which have been extensively used in research on this question, suggest that subjects actually use a relative or logarithmic scale in most instances, but in a rather unusual manner. The stimulus value is judged internally in a relative fashion, and then the response values are subjected to a similar evaluation. If the stimulus and response dimensions are familiar to the subject, these two judgments are meshed; the subject can then make accurate judgments of length, weight, amount, and so on. With unfamiliar dimensions the judgments are less likely to be tied to a known physical scale. However, plotting the judgments on log-log graph paper reveals the consistency and simplicity of the underlying judgment process.

When subjects make quantitative judgments, these judgments may be relative to an explicit standard or may be absolute—no standard is provided. In all instances the subject is influenced by the context of judgment. People are not machines, and the subjects' previous experiences and their assessment of the current situation will influence the judgment. A 20-pound dog will be judged to be small; a 20-pound canary will be judged to be large.

The combining of stimulus judgments with other features of experience and context is a special case of the integration of information. One used car is spotless, in great running order, has lots of space, is a good buy, and gets 5 miles per gallon; a second car has some body damage, the motor sounds all right, it's a bit cramped, and it gets 35 miles per gallon. The theory of information integration states that a person would evaluate each of these features and then calculate an average over the various features in reaching a final assessment. This theory provides an accurate account of psychological measurement in many situations. In some instances, however, a person may disregard some of the dimensions. If gasoline prices suddenly climb, gas mileage may become the primary consideration; if fuel is cheap, or if you have plenty of money, prestige and comfort may dictate the judgment.

Though students in elementary and high school often express a dislike of mathematics, the research on psychological measurement suggests that, despite the expressions of confusion and frustration, people are pretty good at making quantitative judgments. They may not always be completely aware of how they are using numbers, but the responses reveal a considerable degree of sophistication in their use of measurement concepts.

6

Experimental Control

Asking a clear, precise, and answerable question is the first step in undertaking a research study. Framing an appropriate social context for the study and deciding on the appropriate measurements are also important concerns. These issues have been discussed in previous chapters. Now we turn to the process of designing the study. The present chapter focuses on methods for establishing *experimental control*, which involves various procedures for ensuring that the experiment is planned, conducted, analyzed, and interpreted so as to provide clear and trustworthy answers to the experimental question. In this chapter the concept of control is defined and illustrated. The next two chapters then describe the techniques of experimental design, the researcher's "tool kit" for establishing control in a study.

The Three Issues

Designing a research project entails choices about which factors to vary and which to leave constant, what levels of each factor to include in the design, what specific procedures to follow during the conduct of the research, and how to select subjects. In making these choices the investigator is wrestling with three issues: *variability, confounding,* and *interaction.* First we examine each of these issues in turn, focusing on how they affect decisions about the design of the study. Then we turn to procedures for conducting a study and methods of control in selecting a sample of subjects and assigning them to treatment conditions.

Two Examples

Consider the following two fictitious experiments. Sharon is interested in how the amount to be learned affects learning rate. She prepares two lists in which a consonant-vowel-consonant combination is paired with a two-digit number. Materials of this sort, in which the subject learns to associate a pair of nonsensically related items (hence the term *paired-associate learning*), are employed by psychologists to investigate "new" learning; presumably the subject can make little use of previous knowledge in acquiring these novel associations. One of Sharon's lists contains four pairs and the other has eight pairs:

Four-item list	Eight-item list	
PIZ—51	PIZ—51	HES—76
JOL—89	JOL—89	BYF—38
CAG—27	CAG—27	VUP—42
MEP—63	MEP—63	WOT—95

The training is done by a study–test procedure. Each stimulus–response pair is printed on a card; the cards are shuffled and then presented to the subject one at a time for a brief study interval. Next a set of cards containing only the stimulus are presented one at a time for the test; for instance, the subject sees PIZ—? and has to try to remember that the correct response is 51.

The shorter list is presented to Herbert (a fellow graduate student) for five trials, after which he is given a final recall test. Sharon then trains Phoebe (an undergrad acquaintance) for five trials using the longer list, followed by a recall test. Herbert recalls three of the four pairs (75 percent correct), while Phoebe remembers four of the eight pairs (50 percent correct). Sharon concludes that increasing the amount to be learned leads to poorer learning.

In the second example Jeffrey attempts to assess the effects of a new drug developed to enhance visual acuity. He first measures his own eyesight using a Snellen chart (similar to the eye chart found in many doctors' offices) and finds his vision is 20/40, slightly below normal. He then swallows a teaspoon of the drug and retests his vision an hour later. This time his eyesight is a normal 20/20. Jeffrey concludes that the drug improves visual acuity.

Both experimenters had fairly specific questions in mind when they undertook these two studies. Because of problems in the planning of the studies, however, neither set of results is very trustworthy and the conclusions are questionable. By examining the weaknesses of these two investigations, you will discover how to detect similar problems in other research.

VARIABILITY

Neither of the studies just cited, if repeated with different subjects and under different conditions, would be likely to yield exactly the same results as did the original investigation. The paired-associate experiment, if replicated with another sample of subjects, would probably show different patterns of learning for different individuals; levels of recall and pairs leading to errors would differ. Even if the same subjects were retested after a slight delay, there might be changes in performance. Likewise, repetition of the vision–drug study over several days might show some variation from one day to the next, both in the base-line acuity and in the effects of the drug.

Variability is an inherent characteristic of all living things. Behavioral variability can be traced to three sources: treatment variability, replicational variability, and unsystematic variability. **Treatment variability** is a systematic source of differences in performance that results from planned variations in the conditions of the experiment. The researcher varies the amount of time given to learn a passage or the complexity of a skilled task, expecting that these changes will produce systematic fluctuations from one condition to another. Ideally, the systematic sources of variation will be large and trustworthy, compared with the other sources of variation.

Replicational variability refers to the changes that occur when the "same" investigation is repeated several times under reasonably comparable conditions. When an investigation is replicated (i.e., repeated), there may be changes in either the subjects or situations that are sampled. If the findings fluctuate substantially from one sample or situation to another (i.e., if the results are not replicable), then the information may be of little value beyond the particular situations that have been explored.

Whenever a set of findings are limited to a specific set of contexts, the findings are said to lack **external validity** (Cook and Campbell, 1979). A weakness of much behavioral research, which undermines external validity, is the absence of well-established theoretical constructs. Several researchers carry out what appear to be similar investigations on reading comprehension and discover that the findings differ substantially. Careful examination of the various studies reveals significant differences in how *comprehension* has been defined, a problem arising because of the unavailability of a generally accepted theory of the reading process.

Unsystematic variability, also referred to as error or residual variability, falls into two subcategories: random variability, which arises because of fallibility in the instruments for measuring performance, and unexplainable variability, which results from sloppiness in research procedures. The more a particular study is plagued with variability springing from these sources, the less a researcher will be able to make sense of the results.

Because unsystematic variability is due to the conditions under which the particular study is conducted, the problems are of an internal character. The **internal validity** of an experiment is jeopardized when the measuring instruments are unreliable, when the procedures are not carefully followed, or when anything within the conditions of the study leads to confusion in the pattern of results (Cook and Campbell, 1979).

The contrast between replicational variability and unsystematic variability is an important one. Replicational variability can jeopardize the external validity of a study. If the findings change markedly when the study is repeated with a different sample of subjects or under a different set of conditions, then the conclusions are not valid beyond the conditions of the investigation. Unsystematic variability, on the other hand, compromises the internal validity of an experiment. If the study is poorly planned, then there will be so much "random noise" in the measurements that the researcher will be unable to make sense of the results, and no valid conclusions can be drawn. If a study lacks internal validity, then it will also lack external validity; findings that are not trustworthy under the conditions of the original study provide no guidance about other subjects and conditions.

Here is an analogy that may help you understand the concepts of internal and external validity. Suppose that, as an experiment, you have constructed a radio from parts salvaged in a junkyard. If you have done a good job, then you will pick up clear signals when you turn the radio on. If your reconstruction is poorly done, you will hear mostly noise. The difference between a good job and a poor one reflects the degree of internal validity. Suppose now you test the same rebuilt radio under a different set of conditions (weaker stations, or perhaps too many strong stations). Or suppose you go to a different junkyard and try to repeat the rebuilding process. If you can repeat your original success under a variety of different situations, then you will have demonstrated the external validity of the accomplishment. If you sometimes succeed and sometimes fail, external validity is compromised.

Controlling Unsystematic Variability

An Illustration. You probably have a commonsense appreciation of the fact that increasing the unsystematic variability in a data set makes it more difficult to tell what is going on. The brief example in this section demonstrates that uncontrolled fluctuations make it difficult to decide whether a treatment affects behavior.

Suppose we are interested in the effect of a newly developed first-grade reading program on achievement scores; the performance of children receiving standard instruction is to be compared with that of youngsters in the innovative program. An educational consultant suggests that the testing conditions may influence test performance, and so the research plan calls for administering the tests in two ways. One group of children is to be tested individually by an experienced tester who makes sure that each student understands the task and does his or her best. Children in the second group are to be tested as an entire class by the regular teacher under the usual classroom conditions (i.e., noisy and distracting).

Results for this fictitious study are displayed in Figure 6–1. The special program improves performance; in both the individual and group testing conditions, an average score of 110 is obtained when this program is used, compared with 100 when the standard program is used. The testing conditions, however, do affect the amount of variability in the scores. When the test is individually administered, scores vary no more than 10 points above and below the average. In contrast, when the test is administered to the class as a whole, scores range 20 points above and below the average.

When students are individually tested, the beneficial effects of the special program are fairly clear-cut (Figure 6–1, upper panel). Virtually every child in the special group outperforms the highest-scoring students in the regular group; the

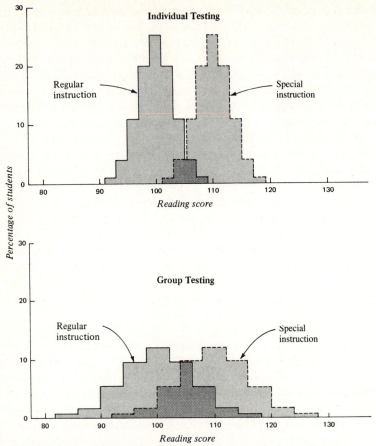

Figure 6–1 Distribution of reading achievement scores for students receiving regular or special instruction, when tested individually or in large groups. Greater variability between students when tested as a group obscures the benefits of special instruction.

overlap between the two distributions (the shaded area) is small. The results are less clear-cut with group testing; the increased variability leads to considerable overlap between the two treatments (Figure 6–1, lower panel). Some students in the special program score below the average of the regular group, and some students in the regular program are above the average of the special program.

The average difference between the two programs is the same in both testing conditions. The trustworthiness of the observed difference, however, depends on the amount of unsystematic variability. One index of trustworthiness is the amount of overlap between the two conditions. When the variability within conditions is reduced (in this example, by taking greater care in the testing procedures), there is less overlap, and the treatment effect is more clear-cut.

Methods of Control. The researcher can take several steps to minimize the deleterious effects of unsystematic variability. One of the simplest is to be especially careful in making observations, as the previous illustration shows. Sloppiness of any kind during data collection increases the amount of uncontrolled variability. Slipups can include the failure to explain the task fully to the subject, changes in motivation or attentional level, fluctuations in the calibration of the apparatus, and the misreading or misrecording of data. If the tester has not rehearsed the procedures sufficiently, mistakes and departures from the original plan are likely, and they may or may not be detected.

A second approach to the establishment of control is to increase the number of observations. With more data there is a decrease in the range of uncertainty around the average for each condition. (The appendix explains the statistical reasons for this decrease.) The influence of sample size on the stability of the average can be illustrated by a coin-tossing experiment. Suppose you toss a coin four times and three heads turn up. The results (75:25) differ from the expected odds (50:50), but the result is not too surprising. You know that there is a random element in coin tossing, and the outcome of each toss makes a big difference in such a small sample. As the number of observations is increased, however, you should expect the observed percentage of heads to be closer to the true value. Thus, if you toss a coin 100 times and 75 heads turn up, you should be surprised; this number of heads in 100 tosses is a very rare event and may mean that the coin is loaded.

The coin-tossing illustration also holds true in the research situation. If the researcher makes only a few observations, they may differ substantially from the "true value" because of unsystematic variation. As the number of observations is increased, the margin of error between the observed average and the true value becomes smaller. For research problems in the behavioral sciences, a sample of twenty to thirty observations per conditions seems to be the norm. With this many observations the average will be reasonably stable, unless the unsystematic variability is sizable.

A third method for minimizing unsystematic variability is to ensure that, except for the treatment conditions, everything else is kept constant. The extent of uncontrolled variability is smallest (in theory, at least) when the same subject is tested several times under identical conditions. Any departure from this ideal, which is admittedly difficult to attain, will almost always increase the unsystematic variability.

Constancy has its pros and cons. In general, it is a good idea to maintain a fixed experimental environment; sloppiness is always a bad practice. On the other hand, undue reliance on constancy can limit the generalizability of the findings, in which case external validity may be compromised. For instance, by programming a computer to present the instructions and the materials for a task, the researcher may ensure a high degree of constancy. But can the same results be obtained when a human researcher makes the presentation?

Mistakes (inconstancies) can lead to important discoveries. Penicillin was discovered in this fashion: a Petri dish for growing bacteria was accidentally exposed to bread mold, and before the "damaged" culture was thrown out, the researcher, Sir Alexander Fleming, noticed that the bread mold was killing the other bacteria. Inconstancies are a fact of life, but the researcher should seek to keep them to a tolerable level and should also stay alert to the occurrence of "accidents" and to their potential effects on the data.

We have examined a wide range of problems caused by unsystematic variability, along with some techniques for handling these problems. Given the nature of these threats to internal validity, our discussion is something of a grab bag. We now look at sources of variability that can threaten both internal and external validity. First we examine variability due to differences between individuals and then we discuss variability springing from factors that are not of primary interest to the investigator but that may nonetheless influence performance, so-called nuisance factors.

Control over Individual Differences

The presence of uncontrolled differences between people is a major source of variability in psychological research. Large differences between the individuals selected for a particular study can make it difficult to evaluate the effects of the treatment factor—a threat to internal validity—and big changes in these effects from one sample of subjects to the next can make it difficult to replicate a finding—a threat to external validity. Let us examine each of these issues in turn.

The influence of individual differences on a study depends in part on how the study is designed. Suppose the experimenter chooses to evaluate the effects of a factor by assigning different samples of subjects to each of the conditions. Then the effects of the factor must be measured against the amount of variability *between subjects* in each condition. This situation is illustrated by the reading experiment described earlier and in the paired-associate illustration presented at the beginning of the chapter. On the other hand, suppose the experimenter tests each subject several times, one or more times under each level of a particular factor. Then the effects of the factor can be measured against the differences *within a subject* over repeated exposures to variation in the factor. This situation was illustrated by the vision–drug experiment.

The decision to place different subjects at each level of a factor (a *between-subjects* plan) or to test each subject at all levels (a *within-subjects* plan) has a major bearing on the influence of individual differences in an experiment. The next two chapters provide information about how to design studies for each type of plan. The purpose here is to consider the importance of this decision in controlling individual differences.

An example may help you understand how individual variability influences the results of between-subjects and within-subjects designs. Suppose a miracle drug has been discovered that the inventor claims to increase short-term memory, the kind of memory you rely on when remembering a telephone number long enough

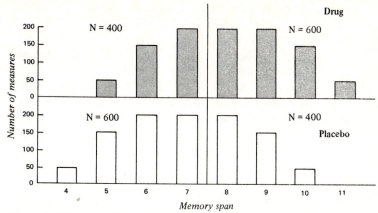

Figure 6–2 Results of between-subjects study of effects of memory drug on memory span. Scores of the drug condition are one digit greater compared with the placebo condition, but there is considerable overlap in performance.

to dial it. Short-term memory span is typically measured by asking the subject to recall number strings of varying lengths. The first string is generally quite short, three or four digits. Each succeeding string is one digit longer, and the test ends when the subject makes a mistake. The dependent measure is the longest string that the subject can repeat correctly.

Figure 6–2 shows the results of a fictitious experiment using a between-subjects plan to study the effects of the drug. The no-drug condition consists of a sample of 1,000 subjects who are tested under normal conditions. The scores range widely; some subjects can remember a string of only four numbers, whereas others can remember as many as ten digits. Let us assume that the drug is effective, such that every individual's short-term span is increased by exactly one digit. The drug condition shows the results based on this assumption. In a second random sample of 1,000 subjects, one expects a distribution of scores virtually identical to that of the no-drug condition but shifted up one digit, so that the range is between five and eleven digits.

Notice that although the drug has a clear effect, there is considerable overlap in the distributions for the no-drug and the drug conditions. If all 2,000 scores are divided at a midpoint (1,000 above and 1,000 below), 600 of the "high" scores are from the drug condition, but 400 are from the no-drug condition. The investigator might detect this pattern but remain uncertain about the trustworthiness of the results unless the sample was quite large, as in the example.

Now let us consider the situation for a within-subjects plan. We will begin by selecting a single subject from the large sample displayed in Figure 6–2. The fictitious data for this individual are shown in Figure 6–3; his typical score from 1,000 repeated no-drug tests is a memory span of six digits, although he occasionally gets

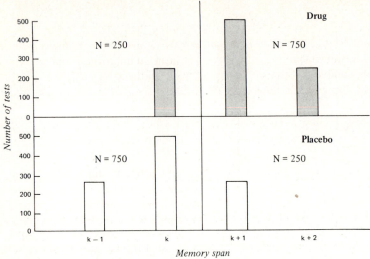

Figure 6–3 Results of within-subjects study of effects of memory drug on memory span. Performance in the drug condition is one digit greater compared with the placebo condition. However, because there is less variability within subjects, this difference is more impressive than in Figure 6–2.

scores of five or seven digits. This pattern of results, when compared with Figure 6–2, illustrates a noteworthy difference between the two approaches:

Differences among individual scores vary more widely than do differences among repeated tests on the same individual.

The top panel of Figure 6–3 shows what happens when the same individual is retested many times under the drug condition, assuming as before that the drug actually increases the memory span by one digit. There is much less overlap for the two treatment conditions in this design than there was in the between-subjects design. When all the scores are divided in half, there are three times more "high" scores from the drug condition than from the no-drug condition, and vice versa.

In this example we have assumed that the miracle drug treatment has a fixed effect for all subjects: the memory span is increased by one digit. This assumption is probably wrong; it is more likely that subjects will differ in how they are affected by the treatment. In a between-subjects design, because each subject is tested but once and under a single treatment condition, there is no way to determine whether there are individual differences in response to the treatment. A within-subjects design does permit measurement of this source of variability, as we shall see in Chapter 8. If subjects do differ markedly in their response to a treatment, even though a within-subjects design has been used, the treatment effects may not appear trustworthy.

Figure 6–4 illustrates this point. The three subjects in this example all perform identically under the no-drug condition; their average memory span is six digits and individual performance varies between five and seven digits. The data for subject A, shown earlier in Figure 6–3, indicate an improvement of one digit under the drug condition. Subject B shows no effect of the miracle drug, however, while subject C improves by three digits.

Does the miracle drug improve short-term memory? Let us assume that it *really* does for most people. What are the chances that the investigator will detect the effect? The answer to this question depends on the sources of variability and the degree to which they are controlled by the procedures and the design. If considerable variability exists among individuals when a between-subjects design is used (the situation in Figure 6–2), then small effects may be obscured by the individual differences. If in a within-subjects design individuals perform at a consistent level when tested repeatedly and respond consistently to the treatment, then even small treatment effects may be easily detected; but the investigator may find it difficult to make trustworthy judgments about the effects of the treatment factor if there are substantial individual differences in response to the treatment. As we shall see later, this problem can be solved by identifying the subject factors that are the source of the individual differences.

While the within-subjects plan generally has the advantage of reduced variability, it is sometimes impractical to measure the subject repeatedly. For instance, it may simply be impossible to test the subject under more than a single level of a factor, because the first treatment condition will contaminate the others that follow. The paired-associate example discussed earlier illustrates the problems that can arise. Learning one paired-associate list is almost certain to affect performance on subsequent lists. It may be easier to learn a second list because the subject has had practice at this unusual task; it may be more difficult because of interference from the associations formed when the first list was learned. If the experimenter is interested in relatively "pure" learning, then each subject can be tested only once. The situation is reversed, of course, if the research goal is to assess the positive or negative effects of one list on another; this problem *requires* a within-subjects plan.

Individual differences cannot be entirely eliminated as an influence in behavioral research. On the contrary, such differences may be the primary focus of a study. Nonetheless, the experimenter is usually well advised to give special attention to individual differences. Otherwise, the results may be overshadowed by this source of unexplainable variability.

Some methods for controlling individual differences have been mentioned already, but they merit reemphasis: clear and complete instructions, an opportunity to become familiar with the task, and assurance of adequate levels of attention and motivation. In addition, sometimes it may be necessary to select well-trained, highly motivated individuals and to pay them for their time. You will occasionally encounter studies in which the researcher and his or her colleagues serve as the subjects, and their investment in the research and experience with the procedures

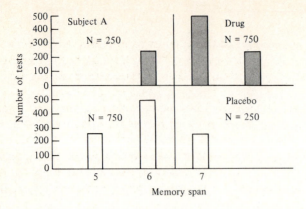

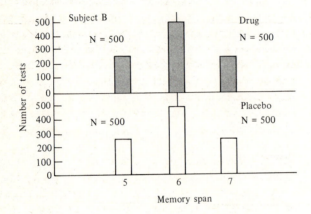

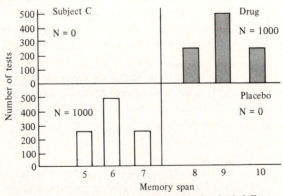

Figure 6–4 Example of the effects of individual differences on the sensitivity of a within-subjects design. The memory drug increases memory span by one item for subject A; has no effect on subject B; and produces a two-item increase in memory span for subject C. Does the drug have an effect? For some subjects, Yes; for other subjects, No.

generally ensure that individual differences will be minimal. On the negative side, this investment and experience may lead to bias. When the subject knows the research hypothesis, is strongly committed to the success of the experiment, and knows "how to behave" as a subject, safeguards must be established to minimize the influence of these background conditions.

Control over Nuisance Factors

Variability can be controlled by eliminating sloppiness in procedures and by minimizing the deleterious impact of individual differences, but it also is influenced by the experimenter's decisions about which factors to include in the design of an investigation. The researcher decides during the planning stage which factors to vary systematically as part of the research design, which factors to keep constant, and which factors to allow to vary at random. These decisions have a major bearing on the degree of control over the results. When powerful factors are allowed to fluctuate at random, the result will be an increase in the amount of unsystematic variability. It does not matter whether the experimenter happens to consider these factors a *nuisance*. If they are not controlled by the design of the study, then the findings will be more difficult to interpret because of the turbulence introduced by apparently random fluctuations.

The point being made is of critical importance in behavioral research and merits reemphasis as a basic principle:

> *Variability due to a particular factor does not disappear just because the researcher decides to disregard the factor; rather, such fluctuations become part of the unsystematic variability.*

Thus, it behooves the investigator to give serious consideration to all factors that may substantially influence performance and to include these factors in the design of the study, whether or not they are of special interest. This method for controlling unsystematic variability requires careful planning, but it is the most effective approach in the long run.

The reading study was used earlier in the chapter to illustrate the importance of reducing variability by procedural control; a similar example will be used to illustrate the importance of maintaining control over nuisance factors. Suppose an experimenter is interested in the effect of the testing environment on the verbal behavior of young children. Four- and five-year-old nursery school children are shown a series of pictures and asked to tell a story about each one. Half the children are tested in a relatively sterile environment: a small room with white walls, a table, and two chairs. The remaining children are tested in a more interesting room, with pictures on the walls, a table with toys and games, a shelf with picture books, and so on. The experimenter's hypothesis is that the children will talk more freely in the stimulating environment.

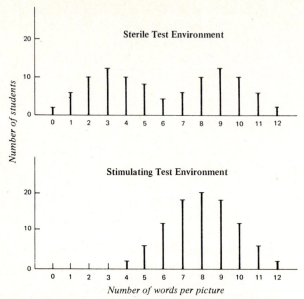

Figure 6–5 Effects of test environment on number of words children use to describe a picture. A stimulating environment leads to generally higher levels of perform-ance by many children, but variability forestalls any solid conclusions.

Figure 6–5 shows the results for this fictitious experiment. Performance is generally as predicted: more words per picture in the enriched environment. Indi-vidual differences are great in both groups, however, and hence the scores overlap considerably.

In planning the study the researcher chose to disregard the effects of age in the design. Suppose we redo the experiment, including age (4-year-olds versus 5-year-olds) as a factor; Figure 6–6 shows the results. Notice that the two age groups respond quite differently to the variation in test environments. Four-year-olds show a large gain in performance in the freer environment, with little overlap in scores between the two environments. Five-year-olds, in contrast, are only slightly affected by the environmental factor. Thus, a large portion of the variability among individ-uals in the sterile environment can be traced to the age factor.

A clear interpretation of the results in this experiment depends critically on the inclusion of age as a factor in the design, even though the researcher might consider it a nuisance to do so. When age is not controlled and both younger and older preschoolers are lumped together (Figure 6–5), the results are clouded. When age is included as a factor in the design, we can see more clearly the effects of the testing environment factor.

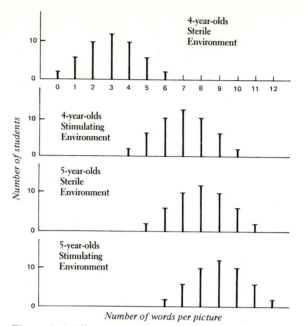

Figure 6–6 Effects of test environment on number of words children use to describe a picture; data of Figure 6–4 arranged according to age. Results now can be more easily interpreted. Four-year-olds are more productive in a stimulating environment, while five-year-olds are not so strongly affected.

CONFOUNDING

In designing an experiment the researcher's aim is to arrange matters so that each level of a factor represents only one particular condition. For the comparisons among levels of the factor to be valid, the levels must differ only along the dimension specified by the researcher. **Confounding** occurs when the levels differ in ways other than the one identified as critical by the researcher. When a factor is confounded with another variable, the results for that factor are totally compromised. The identified factor, the confounded variable, or both may lead to differences between levels—or may cancel one another.

Here is a commonsense example of confounding. Feeling that your colleagues in a new job are not friendly, you decide to run an experiment: you will flash a big smile whenever you see certain individuals while behaving normally with other people. Your dependent measure is the number of smiles you get in return.

What are some ways in which your "smile factor" might be confounded? Suppose you have bad teeth; whenever you flash a smile, you also expose your unattractive dentures. Or smiling may be unnatural to you so that you wrinkle up your features into a grimace. These two confoundings undercut the effects of the treatment variation in fairly obvious ways.

Other confoundings in your "smile" experiment may be less obvious. For instance, you may normally avoid eye contact with acquaintances except when you smile. If in your "smile" condition people appear more friendly, is it your smile or the eye contact? You may stay aloof most of the time but come closer and perhaps even give a hug to those people on your "smile list." Without careful examination of the entire set of variations that differentiate "smile" from "no-smile," you may easily misinterpret the results of the experiment.

Confounding is usually unintentional. Such is the case in the "smile" example; the paired-associate experiment discussed at the beginning of the chapter also illustrates the point. In this experiment list length is confounded with three other factors: gender, year in school, and (probably) age. The four-item list was learned by a male graduate student whereas the eight-item list was learned by a female undergraduate. Because graduate students are generally older than undergraduates, age is also likely to have been a confounding variable.

It is impossible to measure the influence of the confounded factors, and so the results are untrustworthy. Confounding in the paired-associate example could be eliminated by assigning to each list length several subjects representing a range of subject types. The problem is not always so easy to remedy.

The flaws in an experiment are not usually obvious, and published studies are seldom free of confoundings. The following examples illustrate the subtle ways in which confounding can occur; suggestions for eliminating the problem are provided.

> High school seniors who have taken a course in Latin are tested for achievement in English vocabulary and compared with seniors who have never had any Latin. The results show that the Latin group performs substantially better than the non-Latin group. The experimenter concludes that taking a Latin course improves performance in English.

The experimenter's conclusion is questionable because the two groups of students differ in ways other than whether they are enrolled in Latin courses. Because Latin is a difficult topic, students who sign up are usually above average in academic ability. To the extent that enrollment in Latin is confounded with overall ability, the results are uninterpretable.

This confounding might be eliminated by random assignment of students to language classes, though students might object to assignment by the flip of a coin. Another approach would be to encourage students at all levels of academic ability to sign up for Latin classes. The researcher can then measure the differential effects of Latin instruction for students of relatively high and low ability.

> Several studies have compared the effectiveness of *ita* (initial teaching alphabet) and *to* (traditional orthography) as alternate methods for teaching reading

to first-graders. The *ita* method uses a phonetic alphabet in which each letter corresponds to a single sound (Figure 6–7; page 154), whereas in regular English spelling the letters have many pronunciations. The usual finding is that in *ita* programs children learn to read more quickly and have a more positive attitude toward reading.

Several confoundings have plagued this line of research: (a) the *ita* teachers are given special training and supervision in reading instruction whereas the *to* teachers generally receive no such training; (b) the children receiving *ita* have special status as "experimental students" whereas the *to* children do not; (c) the *ita* materials—books, worksheets, and so on—are fresh and new; the *to* materials, in contrast, are old and dilapidated; and (d) *ita* usually emphasizes a "phonics" approach to reading instruction (the correspondences between spelling and pronunciation are stressed), whereas *to* relies more on a "look–say" whole-word approach. The superior performance of the *ita* groups could result from the special writing system, but the confounded factors are equally plausible explanations. A reading program in which teachers receive special training, students are told they are in a special project, the books are new, and a phonics approach is emphasized—but using regular English spelling—might be as effective as the *ita* approach.

Another confounding in the paired-associate example is somewhat less obvious than the problems mentioned earlier. The greater the number of pairs in a list, the greater the chance that two or more of the pairs will be similar to one another. In a two-item list, for example, it is easy to create pairs that have no letters in common. In the eight-item list, in contrast, some pairs must have common letters because there are only six vowel letters. The problem becomes worse the longer the list; in a twenty-item list, many letters would be shared because only twenty-six letters would be available to spell twenty three-letter words. It is certain, therefore, that similarity among the pairs will be confounded with list length. A number of studies have shown that inter-item similarity is an important factor in paired-associate learning, and so this confounding cannot be disregarded.

The vision–drug study includes several confoundings. First, the researcher–subject knew that the first test was without the drug whereas the second test was with the drug. His expectations and knowledge are likely to have influenced performance in subtle (and not so subtle) ways. Second, the drug test was administered on the second trial in the series and practice often leads to improved performance.

The researcher must be especially watchful for confoundings when the subject is tested under two or more conditions. Special attention is needed to control for changes over time, for variations due to materials, and for the effect of one level of a factor on another. Specific techniques for handling these confoundings will be discussed in Chapter 8.

Figure 6–7 James Pitman's forty-four-symbol initial teaching alphabet. Reproduced by permission of Initial Teaching Alphabet Foundation, Roslyn Heights, N.Y.

It is virtually impossible to eliminate all possible sources of confounding in a study. The researcher seldom knows for certain which factors have effects small enough to be safely ignored, and so must rely on informed judgment.

Confounding is sometimes unavoidable. School policy, for instance, may preclude random assignment of students to Latin classes. Confounding may also be intentional. In the "smile" experiment, after being confronted with the list of confoundings, you might reasonably decide that you were not interested in the effects of smiling but in an overall "friendliness" treatment that combined (i.e., confounded) several manifestations of friendliness and could be contrasted with your more usual way of dealing with people. Such a plan would be legitimate as long as your description of the research plan presented the components of the two conditions and your rationale for the design. Leave it to someone else to isolate the specific effects of smiling and the other components.

The potential influence of a confounded factor must be weighed against the cost of controlling it. If previous research findings or common sense suggest that a confounding factor may have a large effect, then the researcher should take all feasible steps to eliminate the possibility of a confounding. Other factors may not be worth the bother. Whatever the situation, the decision to disregard a potentially confounded factor should be made thoughtfully. It is one thing to ignore a confounding with forethought; it is another matter to ignore the problem until after the data have been collected.

The Control Group

Suppose a researcher is primarily interested in the impact of a single, innovative, "experimental" treatment. To measure the relative influence of this innovation, the typical scientific method calls for establishing a control condition, or **control group,** that serves as a base line for comparison with the treatment. This approach, in which a single experimental group is contrasted with a single control group, is fairly common practice in behavioral research. Such designs may be too simple in many instances to encompass the complexities of an experimental question, and the investigator is well advised to be especially alert for confoundings when this approach is used (Cronbach, 1963).

Confounding in experimental-control designs springs from several sources. The control group in these designs is frequently defined, by exclusion, as the absence of the innovative treatment. Stating what something is *not*, unfortunately, seldom tells exactly what it *is*. A more positive approach views the control condition as a treatment that is *different* from the experimental treatment, and different in some well-defined way. If the experimental treatment has many facets, then several control groups may be required (Campbell, 1957; Campbell and Stanley, 1963). If for practical reasons only a single control condition can be included in the design, then every effort should be made to ensure that the control group is handled in *exactly* the same manner as the experimental condition, with the exception of the single critical dimension under investigation.

For example, suppose a researcher is interested in the hypothesis that loud, fast music has an arousing effect on people, thereby increasing responsiveness and reaction time. (Reaction time is the amount of time needed to make a response after a stimulus is presented. For instance, a traffic light changes from green to yellow, and after some delay the driver's foot moves from the accelerator to the brake. That delay is the reaction time.) The hypothesis might be evaluated by having subjects in the experimental group listen to rock music as they perform a reaction-time task, while control subjects perform the same task in a noiseless environment. Comparison of the reaction times from the two groups should show whether the raucous music has the hypothesized effect.

The treatment factor is confounded in this example. If the two groups differ (e.g., if the music group responds more quickly than the silence group), it may be that music does have the presumed effect. If so, then other kinds of visual or auditory stimulation should also produce more rapid responses. On the other hand, the music also provides an incentive of sorts; it may be more pleasant to perform a dull task with a musical background. In this case other kinds of incentives should also improve performance.

The differential effects of the two confounded factors—arousal and incentive—could be separated by adding further treatments to the design. In addition to the rock music and nothing conditions, the researcher might include quiet music, flashing lights, quiet scenes, and so on. By modifying the design in this manner, the researcher is identifying the several dimensions that were combined in the original treatment. Confoundings usually occur because the researcher's attention is focused too sharply on a single factor; confoundings are reduced when the researcher is able to stand back from the problem and look at it from a broader perspective. The researcher who thinks that he or she has identified the "single most important factor" determining performance in a particular situation is almost certain to be disappointed.

Placebo and Novelty Effects

A frequent confounding in experimental-control designs, in which an innovative treatment is contrasted with a no-treatment control, is the **placebo effect.** A placebo (from the Latin, "I shall please") is a medicineless pill given to patients to soothe or placate them; the doctor might prescribe a placebo if the patient insists on some "medicine" even though the doctor believes that rest and relaxation are the best treatment. Patients often report that a placebo makes them feel better, even though the pill may contain only starch.

The placebo effect has several explanations, all of which entail confoundings. Suppose that subjects suffering from headaches are administered a "new improved remedy," after which they tend to report that they feel much better. Is the researcher justified in concluding that the drug is effective? No. It may be that (a) the drug actually works, or (b) the subject thinks that the drug should work, either of which reduces the perception of pain. It is also possible that (c) the subject thinks that the drug should work and reports feeling better even though the headache feels the same, (d) the experimenter's enthusiasm for the treatment convinces the subject that he or she feels better, or (e) this enthusiasm at least leads the subject to report an improvement.

Indirect influences like (b) through (e) can lead to the placebo effect. Influences (b) and (c) can be handled by a control condition in which subjects are administered a placebo treatment that includes everything but the critical ingredient. For instance, a placebo treatment for the *ita* reading program mentioned earlier might provide teachers with new textbooks and special training but have regular English spelling instead of the special *ita* format.

To rule out (d) and (e), which result from bias by the experimenter, **"blind" procedures** can be employed. In the **double-blind** procedure, for instance, neither the subject nor the person administering the treatment knows whether a particular subject is receiving the special treatment or the placebo. (In the **single-blind** procedure the subject is unaware of the treatment being administered.) In some instances it is virtually impossible to implement "blind" procedures, but these methods can be used effectively in studies of social and personality phenomena, where, for example, the tester's expectations may otherwise subtly influence subjects' behavior.

The novelty of an unusual treatment or the special status of being an "experimental" subject may also influence performance. A classic example of the **novelty effect** is the study of the effects of the duration and spacing of rest periods on the productivity of assembly-line workers at an electrical plant in Hawthorne, Illinois (Homans, 1965). A work team was transferred to a special room where rest conditions could be varied ·in a systematic manner. In one condition workers received five-minute rest periods in the morning and afternoon; the periods were lengthened to ten minutes in a second condition; a light snack was provided in a third condition. The findings were that regardless of the variation in the nature of the rest period, the team in the special room was more productive than groups on the regular assembly line, even when the special team was retested under the preexperimental no-treatment condition. It appeared that the novelty of being assigned to an experimental program was sufficient in itself to improve productivity. The Hawthorne effect was relatively slight, to be sure, and the original study has come under complex criticism in recent years (e.g., Parsons, 1974; Bramel and Friend, 1981; and "Comments" in the July 1982 issue of the *American Psychologist*).

The effects of novelty on performance may be either positive or negative. The strangeness of a new situation can be distracting, causing performance to be slower and more cautious. The subject may feel pressured to do especially well on a task, without being quite certain about the best strategy for handling the situation. Attention and motivation are often high at the beginning of a study but may decline as the novelty wears off—unless there is sudden change in the conditions (e.g., Wickens, 1970).

An experimental design should control for novelty and "special treatment" effects, especially for research where innovative programs are to be evaluated against "things as usual." The appropriate control group should incorporate all the elements found in the innovative program except for the critical ingredient. Having considered the nature of the appropriate control group, the researcher may decide that the research question requires some additional thought. Improvement over "things as usual" is seldom a simple matter.

INTERACTION

Two factors are said to interact when the effects of one factor change from level to level of a second factor. Whenever two factors interact, the researcher must be cautious in drawing conclusions about the effects of either factor. The complete picture comes only by considering the combined effects of *both* factors. **Interaction** means that the relations between two factors are complex.

This definition is a slight oversimplification. Because any number of factors may interact with one another, an accurate account of a particular factor may require the researcher to consider the interactive influence of two or more other factors. As a practical matter large interactions involving more than three factors are rare, and the most important instances of interactions generally entail only two factors. These relatively simple instances will be the focus in the discussion that follows.

To determine whether two factors interact, the investigator must plan the design to include combinations of both factors. An example of such a design is the study presented earlier in the chapter in which four- and five-year-old children described pictures in either a sterile or a stimulating test environment. Age and test environment are the two factors, each with two levels, for a total of four different conditions. The results of that study (Figure 6–6) illustrate the concept of an interaction. Does the test environment matter? This question can be answered only by taking into account the age factor: variation in the test environment has a large effect on the performance of four-year-olds but little influence on the performance of five-year-olds.

Examples of Some Typical Interactions

An interaction complicates matters, but interactions are not necessarily bad. Some interactional patterns make good sense, and a research study may be specifically designed to detect an interaction. The following examples illustrate the range of variation in patterns:

A number of studies have investigated the joint effects of task difficulty and motivation on problem-solving performance (Osgood, 1952, pp. 622ff). The

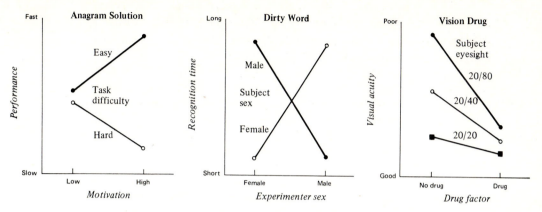

Figure 6–8 Examples of three different patterns of interactions

usual finding is that when subjects are given an easy problem, a high level of motivation improves performance, whereas with a difficult problem, performance declines when the pressure becomes too great. For instance, suppose the problem is to unscramble anagrams, a favorite task of laboratory researchers. Some anagrams (e.g., AKME) are easier than others (e.g., RMDA), the former taking less time to solve. Motivation can be varied by sounding a tone when the subject takes too long to solve the problem; a soft chime for low motivation and a loud buzzer for high motivation. The left panel in Figure 6–8 shows the interaction typically observed under these conditions. The dependent measure is on the vertical axis, the motivational factor is on the horizontal axis, and the difficulty factor is drawn as two lines in the plot. The points represent average performance. The graph shows that effects of the motivation factor depend upon the difficulty of the task; easy problems are solved more quickly under high motivation (the threat of an obnoxious buzzer) whereas difficult problems are easier to solve with a milder motivation (an inoffensive chime). Another way to describe the pattern is to note that task difficulty is not very important at low levels of motivation but makes a great deal of difference when motivation is high. The anagrams, by the way, are make and dram; anagrams for uncommon words are tougher to work out, in general.

In an experimental task that was popular several decades ago, a list of words was flashed on a screen, one word at a time for a brief interval. Some words in the list were completely innocuous, while others were a little risqué. The purpose of the investigation was to evaluate the subliminal awareness hypothesis, which holds that the subconscious protects the mind from undesirable stimuli and consequently that subjects should take longer to recognize a "dirty word." The findings from such studies tended to support the hypothesis; a word like *rape* required a longer exposure duration for recognition than a word like *rope*. More careful investigation of the problem, however, revealed an interaction between experimenter gender and subject gender, as shown in the middle panel of Figure 6–8. Male subjects took longer to recognize indelicate words when the experimenter was female, and female subjects were more cautious about reporting these words when the experimenter was male.

In the right panel of Figure 6–8 are fictitious results showing an interaction that might occur in the vision–drug experiment described early in the chapter. The researcher tests subjects who differ in how well they can see, first without the drug and then with it. The findings in the figure show an interaction between the drug treatment and the degree of visual deficit. The drug is most effective for subjects with very poor vision and has little effect on subjects with relatively normal eyesight. An understandable result. If it's not broken, don't fix it.

Interactions like those illustrated above are frequent in psychological research, and the investigator should always consider the possibility of interactions when planning an investigation and when interpreting the results. To state that two or more factors interact means that the findings cannot be described by reporting the effects of either factor in isolation. Rather, the pattern of the data has to be described much as in the examples presented above. Judgment is required in interpretation. One can almost always detect some degree of complexity in the pattern of relations between any two factors. In the examples in Figure 6–8 the interactions are strong compared with the main effects of the factors, and so the researcher needs to qualify the conclusions in light of these interactions. When the interactions are weak compared with the main effects, the interpretation should stress the main effects and comment briefly on the interaction.

Interaction and Experimental Control

Unless the design includes the appropriate combinations of factors, an interaction cannot be detected. When the design is inadequate in this sense (that is, an interaction is actually present but the plan does not allow it to be detected), the research findings may easily be misinterpreted. Here again, the basic problem is poor control.

To illustrate what can happen when design is inadequate, consider the likely conclusions if the three studies in Figure 6–8 were not designed to include both factors involved in the interaction:

College students solve relatively easy laboratory problems more quickly when threatened with a loud alarm than when simply encouraged to concentrate harder. It is therefore concluded (falsely) that the most effective way to motivate students is with the threat of punishments such as failing grades or expulsion from school. The flaw in the argument is the conclusion that the effect of strong motivation on *difficult problems* in schoolwork is the same as on the *easy problems* used in the laboratory. The design is inadequate to reveal the presence of a critical interaction that undermines this interpretation.

Male subjects are tested in the "dirty word" study by a male tester, and no difference in recognition time is found between regular and risqué words. The researcher concludes (falsely) that the social-emotional character of a word does not influence performance. With the inclusion of a female experimenter in the design, the evidence would have revealed a more complex pattern of results in which male subjects were not affected by the word type when tested by a male experimenter but were much slower to report risqué words when tested by a female experimenter.

The drug designed to improve vision is tested with a group of subjects whose eyesight is only slightly below normal, and it is concluded (falsely) that the drug is ineffectual. If subjects with poor vision were tested, then it might be concluded (again falsely) that the drug would aid everyone. Only if the design provides control over a range of base-line eyesight levels will the complete pattern be revealed.

In each example undetected interactions can lead to false generalizations. The truth of the findings is not being questioned; the problem arises when the researcher, in interpreting the results, extends the findings to situations other than those included in the particular experiment. The remedy is to ensure that the design includes an adequate representation of the situations and types of people to which the results are to be generalized.

The issue here is the external validity of a particular interpretation of an investigation. Any given set of results is of limited interest per se; the real benefit is realized to the extent that the findings can be applied to a larger set of circumstances. How does the researcher place reasonable limits on the domain of generalization so that an adequate design can be created? This is done by gaining familiarity with the existing literature, asking the advice of others who already "know the territory," and making good judgments when selecting the factors that can help in interpreting and applying the results.

But why guess? Why not incorporate in the design *all* factors that might be of importance? The answer is twofold: time and money. The researcher has to balance the costs of the experiment, the resources available to support the work, and the probable value of the findings. As we shall see in the following chapters, whenever additional factors are included in a design, the number of conditions increases along with the cost: equipment, materials, the selection and testing of subjects, and analysis of data all are more complex. Also, larger experiments can be more difficult to manage; efforts to enhance control may make it more difficult for the researcher to maintain a high level of quality.

Practically speaking, the researcher must make some tough decisions in planning a study. A relatively small number of factors must be selected for the design from those of potential interest; any other factors identified as possibly relevant can be either maintained at a constant level or allowed to vary at random. In making these decisions, the experimenter is betting (a) that there are no substantial interactions between the design factors and those that are being kept constant or (b) that if such interactions do exist, the constant factors are representative of the situations that will be important for interpretation.

The techniques of experimental design provide powerful and trustworthy tools for planning and conducting behavioral research. As in other human endeavors, however, experience is a valuable guide and good judgment a helpful companion.

EXPERIMENTAL PROCEDURES

The term **procedure** refers to the numerous nondesign details that must be arranged once the basic design has been planned. When deciding on procedural arrangements, as when planning the experimental design, the researcher must decide how to handle various factors that may influence performance. Whereas design decisions involve the selection and the level of factors, procedural decisions generally dictate the establishment of a single level for each of a number of factors—the constancies of the investigation.

For example, consider the paired-associate study described earlier in the chapter. The experimenter selects two levels of the primary factor—list length—and decides to assign different groups of subjects to each level of the factor. A single two-level factor with a between-subjects plan is the result. These decisions settle the design for this simple experiment, but several other decisions have to be made before the study begins. What specific items are to be used as stimuli? As responses? How long should the subject be allowed to study each of the pairs? For how many study trials? How will study and test trials be arranged? How much time will the subject be given to respond on test trials? What kind of test should be employed: multiple-choice recognition or recall of the answer?

Each of these questions, along with several others that might be raised, identifies a factor that may influence performance. Interactions between design factors and procedural factors are possible. For instance, list length may affect scores on a recall test but not on a recognition test. The researcher, in planning the procedures, should keep in mind how procedural decisions may affect the outcome. For each facet of the study, the researcher needs to consider the rationale for doing things one way rather than another, how else they might be done, and how the interpretability of the findings will be influenced by the decision.

Materials. A procedural matter of special importance is the selection of **materials.** Even when the design determines the general class of materials to be used in each condition, a final choice must usually be made from a wide array of possibilities. The criteria for selection, construction, and evaluation of materials depend on the exact nature of the problem under investigation, but the investigator needs to be aware of confoundings that may slip in unnoticed during the final selection. Special problems can arise in preparing language materials, which are inherently complex and multidimensional. As Clark (1973) has pointed out, it is all too easy for the researcher to (nonrandomly) pick out those materials that are biased toward a particular outcome, though not necessarily for the reasons specified in the formal design. Clark suggests that the researcher should always include in a study several random selections of materials appropriate to each condition and then observe whether the (unsystematic) variability within conditions is relatively small or large compared with the (systematic) variability between conditions. If the design variables provide adequate control, then the samples within each condition will yield roughly comparable data. The use of random selections ensures that the researcher will not fall prey to self-deception and mistakenly confound variables in the process of choosing specific samples.

The Task. Instructions and pretraining also need attention. Instructions should be prepared in advance, tried, and presented during the study in as natural a manner as possible. The tendency is to "overwrite" instructions, providing so much detail that the task actually becomes more difficult to understand. Be on the lookout for jargon and ambiguity.

Remember that the experiment is a social interaction between the experimenter and the subject and that the human factors need to be considered. It is easy to overestimate an individual's awareness of how to behave as an experimental subject. The experimental **task,** the testing conditions, and the strangeness of the situation all place unusual demands on the subject. On the other hand, it is a mistake to assume that the subject is altogether gullible. A postexperimental interview ("What do you think the study was all about?") can provide helpful insights into the subject's perceptions of the purposes and procedures of the study. When analyzed, individual differences in these perceptions can provide the means for improving control over the findings, especially if subjects differ markedly in their understanding of the experiments.

Data Collection. Finally, the researcher is well advised to evaluate the procedures from the perspective of the data collector. The occurrence of unexpected events during an experiment can reduce the efficiency of **data collection.** If one or two segments of each task take only a few seconds more than expected, the accumulated seconds can add several minutes to the session. Tester and subject begin to feel rushed, and control is jeopardized. Procedures for recording the data also need to be considered. Entries are written down in a poorly organized format, and so analysis takes longer and is more susceptible to error. The subjects are asked to write their own responses, and the experimenter discovers later that a considerable amount of the data is illegible.

Procedural problems seldom can be eliminated altogether. They can be kept to a minimum, however, by giving serious thought to the details of the experiment during the initial planning and by trying out the various procedures with a few "pilot" subjects as the arrangements are being worked out. Problems that surface during such rehearsals then can be remedied before the experiment proper begins.

CONTROL IN SUBJECT SELECTION AND ASSIGNMENT

The results of an experiment are seldom important in their own right but are of primary interest to the extent that they can be generalized to a broader set of people and situations than those represented in the particular study. The population to which the results can be generalized depends critically on the procedures for selecting subjects and for assigning them to conditions in the experiment. An experimenter is interested in the process by which young children learn to read. Field research in real schools is difficult to arrange, so the investigator plans a study in which undergraduates at a prestigious university are asked to learn to read Sanskrit. The findings may provide an insight into how relatively able young adults (presumably fluent readers) learn to read a new and unusual language; it is highly questionable whether the results tell us anything about the process by which young children from a wide range of backgrounds learn for the first time how to read.

Randomness in Subject Selection and Assignment

Randomness is an important concept for the establishment of control. Technically, to be **random** is to be established by chance or by drawing lots. In principle, the subjects for an experiment should be **randomly selected** from the population to which the results are to be generalized. Random selection means that every subject in the population is equally likely to be selected for the study. Likewise, subjects should be **randomly assigned** to treatment conditions when the study is carried out; every subject in the group selected for the study should have an equal chance of being assigned to any of the treatment conditions. Selection and assignment—let us therefore see how to ensure randomness in each of these procedures for dealing with subjects.

Random Selection. A good deal of psychological research has as its implicit goal the discovery of general behavioral principles that apply to "all people everywhere." As a practical matter it is difficult if not impossible to draw a random sample from this ill-defined population; a **random sample** from a group is a sample drawn entirely by chance. Instead, most researchers select a "handy random sample" from those individuals who happen to be in the neighborhood. The researcher then uses judgment, common sense, and statistics to draw inferences from the results. These inferences are most secure when the subjects in the sample closely resemble the population of special interest. As the population differs more and more from the sample, the inferences become increasingly open to challenge.

Psychologists tend to rely on convenient and readily available pools of subjects: college undergraduates in introductory psychology classes who are required to serve as subjects in a number of experiments; students who respond to advertisements offering compensation (usually small) for their services as experimental subjects; or acquaintances of the experimenter, who are cajoled, enticed, dragooned, or shanghaied into the job.

College student samples provide a reasonable basis for generalization to other adults educated in Western culture, which is probably the population of chief interest to many psychologists. While college training may not be essential for generalization to the adult population as a whole—high school graduates are similar in many respects to those with college degrees—the results for college students are probably less applicable to younger people or to those who have not attended high school.

Cross-cultural research, in which subjects from widely disparate societies are compared, shows that the findings from laboratory studies of Western-educated adults do not necessarily apply to the performance of other populations (Cole, Gay, Glick, and Sharp, 1971). The issue is not one of competence but of difference, of quality not quantity. Almost everyone finds the experience of the psychology laboratory to be strange and artificial, and most people develop methods for dealing with the situation. People who have adapted quite well to their own environments often approach the psychological experiment quite differently from American college students. What is important is that these approaches vary distinctively from one society to another and from culture to culture within a society.

While many texts on social science research encourage (indeed, even mandate) random selection of subjects from "the population," and while statistics courses emphasize the importance of randomness, the capability of most researchers to realize this ideal is severely limited. The handy random sample is probably the most common approach. Practically speaking, few problems are likely to arise from this state of affairs as long as the researcher appreciates the limits of generalization and as long as the subject sample and the methods of selection are clearly described for the reader. Unfortunately, adherence to these cautions is the exception rather than the rule.

When research is for the guidance of policy rather than the pursuit of pure knowledge, random selection of subjects from the appropriate population becomes an important consideration. Suppose the researcher's goal is to investigate the influence of television violence on aggressive behavior in children, with the results to be used for framing legislative limits on television programming. While college undergraduates are clearly inappropriate subjects for this investigation, the youngsters in a university laboratory school may also fail to fill the bill. In applied research a careful analysis of the target population is frequently a major undertaking. The researcher needs to conduct a descriptive survey of the groups of interest, a task that may entail a sample of hundreds or even thousands of people, after which the experimental sample can then be randomly and representatively selected (Williamson, Karp, Dalphin, and Gray, 1982, Ch. 6).

Random Assignment. Whereas random selection is often difficult to manage, random assignment to conditions is generally within the capability of the investigator. More important, if subjects in the sample are *not* randomly assigned to conditions, confounding of subject characteristics with the treatment factors is almost certain to result, in which case the interpretation of the findings will be severely compromised. Confounding is the problem; nonrandom assignment is the cause.

Random assignment to conditions can be accomplished in any of several ways. The simplest model is one of the oldest: write every subject's name on a slip of paper and draw names out of a hat. Technical versions of this method use a table of random numbers (see Edwards, 1968, pp. 94–95; also, most modern computers have a routine for generating random numbers).

This simple ideal can be difficult to implement in practice. Nonrandom assignment occurs by a variety of oversights, some of which are more obvious than others. For instance, nonrandom assignment can occur when the experimenter uses personal judgment in making subject assignments to "balance" the groups in each condition. Balanced arrangements of subjects in each condition is a good idea, but not at the cost of random assignment to conditions. Nonrandom assignment can also occur when all subjects in one treatment condition are tested before subjects in another treatment condition, a situation that should generally be avoided. Finally, nonrandom assignment is almost certain if subjects are allowed to enroll in the condition of their choice; this issue will be considered at greater length under the topic of quasi-experimental design.

With the exception of situations where subjects have some say about the condition to which they are to be assigned, there is little reason for nonrandom assignment. Randomness can be compromised for the best of reasons, however. Imagine an experiment on reaction times in naturalistic settings. In the driving condition, the subjects are tested on a simulated automobile and in the flying condition on a simulated airplane. Both conditions are computerized and require considerable preparation of equipment and materials. The easiest approach is to set up the procedures for one of the treatments, assign the first batch of subjects who show up at the laboratory to this condition, and then change the equipment to the second condition and test a second batch of subjects. Easy perhaps, but sure to lead to problems in interpretation. "Early bird" subjects are likely to differ from "late risers," so that subjects and treatment levels will be confounded. The nonrandom assignment of subjects may be convenient, but the researcher will regret it later.

A better approach, which balances efficiency with control, is to test the subjects in time blocks. Selected chunks of time are dedicated during each day to one treatment condition or another. Over days, the conditions are arranged so that each condition is sometimes early in the day and sometimes late. Subjects sign up for time blocks whenever they choose. Though the experimenter cannot assure that the sign-ups will be random, the assignment of treatment conditions is random, which serves the purpose of randomizing the placement of subjects in treatment conditions.

Nonrandom Assignment and Quasi-experimental Designs

Assignment Problems in Field Research. Sometimes practical considerations make it impossible to assign subjects to treatment conditions completely at random. For example, suppose the investigator receives a grant to determine the effectiveness of a Head Start preschool program. Participation in Head Start is limited to children from low-income families. The researcher plans to assign children at random to the treatment condition (Head Start) or the control condition (stay at home), only to discover that many of the parents in the community insist on the right to decide which program their preschoolers will be enrolled in.

Random assignment to conditions is impossible under these circumstances, which are typical of a good deal of applied research on social and educational issues. The consequence can be a critical confounding of subject and treatment factors. In the Head Start experiment, for instance, the factors that lead a family to want their child to attend a Head Start class are likely to be associated with other variables that influence the child's performance: the parents' interest in the child, their plans for his or her educational experiences, the home environment, and so on.

Another complication needs to be considered. What about parents who do not want their youngsters tested or who decide halfway through the experiment to remove them from the project? Subject attrition or drop-out is seldom a problem in laboratory experiments, but it is a serious problem in field research. There is no one solution to these problems, but there are a number of partial remedies.

First, the researcher can try to solve the problem directly. For instance, some parents may insist that their children be assigned to the special Head Start program; they see it as an important opportunity for their children, one that should not be forgone. The researcher, emphasizing the importance of the experiment in proving the value of the program, might arrange for these parents in the "stay-at-home" group to enroll their youngsters in a special summer program at the end of the experiment.

Second, what can be done about subjects who reject random selection or assignment at the outset of a study despite all the investigator's entreaties? The researcher can identify those individuals who "deselect" themselves from a sample as a whole or from assignment to particular treatment conditions. Who are they, what are their personal characteristics, and why have they made the decisions they have made? These questions are not directed toward the individuals as such but aim to determine how they are similar to or different from the rest of the group.

Third, what can be done about subjects who leave in the middle of a study? Here again, the best solution is to try to keep them in the study. Sometimes this requires special incentives. Sometimes it entails tracking down subjects to a new location. A special problem is the absence of certain data for some subjects: a student is absent on a test day; parents cannot show up for an interview. In some instances statistical procedures can be used to extrapolate the missing data from the information that is available. Whenever possible, the researcher should attempt to salvage the data.

Quasi-experimental Designs. In handling situations in which complete control over selection and assignment of subjects is not possible, the investigator is employing what is known as **quasi-experimental design** (Cook and Campbell, 1979; *quasi* means "almost" or "approximately"). "True" experiments and quasi-experiments both aim to evaluate the effects of treatment conditions on performance, and in both cases the researcher has the task of identifying critical factors to include in the design. The main difference between the two approaches is that random assignment of subjects, which is taken for granted in a true experiment, is likely to be difficult if not impossible in the quasi-experimental situation. Because of the greater likelihood of confounding subject-classification factors with treatment factors, special steps are taken in the quasi-experimental situation to isolate the effect of the treatments on behavior. Even so, the results of such investigations are typically less trustworthy than those of studies where assignment is random.

In planning a quasi-experimental design, one of the primary aims is to establish for each treatment condition a base-line level of performance against which the effect of the treatment condition can be measured. One option that is frequently employed is to establish a control group whose condition resembles the treatment condition except for one critical dimension. As noted earlier, this approach has the limitation that the treatment and control conditions may turn out to be confounded in ways not encompassed by the critical factor. Practically speaking, it may turn out to be impossible to establish a control group that eliminates all possible confoundings.

A more satisfactory approach may be to prepare a design with several control groups, each identified with one specific confounding factor. For instance, the Head Start design might include as controls (a) a group of students whose parents have chosen to send them to a day-care program providing custodial services only, (b) a group attending a nursery school that promotes social and emotional development, (c) a cohort that remains at home, and (d) children who are tended by friends or relatives. Each of these control groups comprises a slightly different treatment for the children. The challenge to the investigator is to determine by observation and interview the details of each condition to portray the distinctive contrasts between treatments. In essence, the investigator becomes a sort of naturalist who relies on the results of a more or less "natural experiment" to evaluate the most significant factors influencing performance.

Subject-classification Factors and Representative Sampling

A **representative sample** is one that has characteristics typical of the population. A representative sample of college students contains males and females in proportion to their numbers on the campus. A representative sample of American adults includes quite a few people over the age of forty, quite a few from ethnic minority backgrounds, a significant number of poor people, and some physically handicapped individuals.

One approach to obtaining a representative sample from a population is to take a *large* random sample from it. If a sample is drawn at random from a population and if the sample is sufficiently large, then the proportions in the sample will match those in the population.

In experimental studies a different approach is needed. The sample size tends to be relatively small, twenty to thirty subjects per condition, which is too few to guarantee representativeness. Accordingly, it is generally wise to plan a **stratified random sample.** For practical purposes, this second approach requires the creation of a subject-classification design, followed by the selection of subjects at random according to the classification combinations. To be sure, the technique is limited by the characteristics of the pool from which the sample is being drawn; a representative sample of American adults cannot be readily obtained on a college campus because the campus itself is unlikely to be representative of American adults. Taking this limitation into account, the design of a stratified random sample generally makes the best use of the subjects that are available.

The chief consideration in planning a representative sample of subjects for an experiment is the relation of the various subject-classification factors to the treatment factors being investigated. A wide variety of subject-classification factors *might* be included in a design: age, gender, ability, socioeconomic level, interests, aptitude, height, weight, physical appearance, and so on. The critical question is, Which of these is likely to influence performance *in the task under study* or to interact with other factors being investigated? The researcher's task is to plan a stratification design so that the most relevant subject-classification factors are represented.

For instance, men and women perform differently on a variety of tasks (McGuiness, 1979; but see Sherman, 1978). Suppose that a haphazard assignment of subjects to treatment conditions produces one group with eight men and two women and a second group with seven women and three men. The findings will be questionable because of the partial confounding of gender and treatment conditions. The difficulty is most easily alleviated by including gender as a subject-classification or stratification factor, so that proportionate numbers of males and females are assigned to each treatment condition. Another approach is to select only males or females for the experiment. The choice between these two strategies depends upon whether the results are to be generalized to both sexes.

Both the purpose of the experiment and the ease with which a particular subject-classification factor can be included in a design must be weighed in planning a study. If an experiment on short-term memory is to be conducted with kindergartners, gender is relatively easy to include as a factor. If intelligence test scores are readily available, this information may be worth including in the plan, especially if the study is related to school achievement. Ideally, each condition in the experiment is assigned an equal number of youngsters from each combination of the classification factors. This arrangement ensures a well-controlled, representative sample of students in each condition, thereby providing an optimal opportunity for assessing interactions between subject-classification and treatment factors. As always, the gain from the improvement in experimental control must be weighed against the costs of the increase in design complexity.

SUMMARY

Experimental control refers to all the methods used to ensure that a study is planned, conducted, analyzed, and interpreted so as to allow clear and trustworthy answers to the experimental questions. The present chapter discussed the concept of control and described three domains that are critical to the establishment of adequate control: variability, confounding, and interaction.

Variability in an experiment has three sources. First is systematic variability, which results from the manipulation of the treatment and subject-classification factors. Because the researcher has designed the investigation to capture this source of variability, it is presumably under the tightest control. Second is replicational variability, which arises when the experiment is redone in different situations or with different samples of subjects. If the study has been carried out in one situation and with one type of people and the researcher seeks to extend the findings to other situations and people, then the extent of replicational variability becomes an important indicator of the external validity of the study. Too much change in results from one context to another and the findings lack external validity. Third is the unsystematic variability in the study, which arises partly from fluctuations in the measuring instruments and partly from the effects of factors that are not included in the design and hence contribute randomly to performance. More generally, inadequacies in the design of a study and sloppiness in the procedures for carrying out the research increase the unsystematic variability within a study, thereby compromising the internal validity.

If an investigation contains a large amount of unsystematic variability (that is, if it lacks internal validity), then the external validity is also undercut. Thus, it is important to take steps to control unsystematic variability. Care should be taken in making observations of performance. Conditions not related to the treatment variations should be maintained at a constant level and variations in irrelevant factors should be recorded to aid in interpreting the findings. Finally, if the observations are inherently "noisy," stability can sometimes be improved by taking more measures.

Individual differences in people contribute to all three types of variability. If these differences are ignored, they contribute to unsystematic variability. They are also an important consideration in replicational variability. And subject-classification factors are an important source of systematic variability.

The experimenter can plan a research design so that treatment effects must be assessed relative to differences between individuals (a between-subjects plan). This approach has certain advantages (there is no possibility that one treatment condition will influence any other) but its disadvantage is that individual differences are often quite substantial and may obscure treatment effects. The design can also be arranged so that each subject is tested on all levels of the treatment factor (a within-subjects plan). With this plan individual performance tends to be relatively stable, compared with differences between individuals, and so this approach is usually more sensitive to treatment effects. There can be disadvantages, especially if one treatment interferes with or facilitates another.

Confounding is the second major threat to control. Two factors are confounded when variation in one factor is linked to variation in the second factor. The researcher's task is to ensure that conditions differ only along the dimension specified by the design and that the incidental contribution of other variables is minimized. Confounding can be a serious difficulty. If two factors are confounded, then the results (or lack thereof) can be attributed to the first factor, the second factor, or any combination of the two.

Investigations in which an experimental treatment is compared with a control condition are especially subject to confounding. In these and other more subtle instances, the solution to the problem is to identify the confounding factor and arrange the design so that the confounding is separated from the factor of primary interest. The researcher must rely on judgment and common sense. No experiment is free of confounding. Some confoundings matter more than others, but the researcher should make this assessment before rather than after the study.

Interaction also involves two factors. When the effects of one factor vary from level to level of a second factor, the resulting complexity is defined as an interaction. Interactions are problems only when they are ignored. Within an experiment, if two factors interact strongly, then the researcher's interpretation of the main effects of either factor must take into account the pattern of the relation between the two. In extending the results of a study to different situations or people than those encompassed by the original investigation, the researcher should consider the possibility that the treatment factor may interact with factors that vary across situations and people. By including in the design of an investigation representative samples of the factors, situations, and people to which the results are to be generalized, the investigator is more likely to detect interactions that are important for interpretation.

The procedures of a study, which are often not considered in the planning of the design, entail all the features of the study that are presumably constant over all treatment conditions and subjects. They include the choice of materials, specifications of the task, and methods for collecting and recording the data. Various suggestions were made for improving control in each of these areas.

Subject selection refers to the plans for obtaining a sample of individuals to participate in the study. The ideal is to define a population and then pick people completely at random from this population. In practice, this ideal is often difficult to achieve. More often, the researcher picks a "handy random" sample from the individuals who are available. Generalization to other populations then requires judgment as well as statistics. The more the sample resembles a particular population, the safer the generalization. The problem is thornier in field research, where the handiest populations may be inappropriate, in which case a stricter definition of the population may be called for.

Subject assignment takes place when, after the sample has been selected, individuals are assigned to treatment conditions. For laboratory experiments random assignment is generally quite easy to manage, though there are still pitfalls. In field research, problems arise when subjects have their own ideas about how they will participate, whether they will continue, or whether they will simply refuse altogether. Quasi-experimental procedures provide some solutions for improvement of control in these naturalistic situations, but the difficulties can be substantial. In such situations the researcher's judgments about control become especially critical.

7

Between-subjects Designs

This chapter describes the procedures used to plan research projects in which different individuals are assigned to each treatment condition. Since each condition contains a different sample of subjects, and since the effects of the factors must be gauged relative to individual differences between subjects, such designs are labeled *between-subjects designs*. They are also called *randomized-groups designs* because different groups are assigned at random to the various treatment conditions. Some of the pros and cons of testing each subject at a single level of a factor (between-subjects variation) versus testing subjects at all levels of a factor (within-subjects variation) were discussed in Chapter 6. Within-subjects designs, along with mixed designs in which some factors are between-subjects and others are within-subjects, will be presented in Chapter 8.

We begin this chapter by looking at the decisions the investigator must make when planning a **one-way**, or *single-factor*, design. Many research problems require control over several factors, but it is simpler to examine first the issues that arise when a single treatment factor is the focus of the investigation. The same issues must then be decided for each of the factors in a **factorial**, or *many-way*, **design.** The overall planning of a factorial design raises additional questions in its own right; they are discussed in the second half of the chapter.

ONE-WAY DESIGNS

The selection and assignment of subjects to treatment conditions and the preparation of appropriate control groups were discussed in Chapter 6 and will not be reexamined here. Instead we examine the basic decisions that must be made when planning a one-way between-subjects design, focusing on decisions about how to manipulate the treatment factor. Two experiments—a laboratory study of memory and a field study on "buckling up for safety"—are given to illustrate the planning and analysis of the one-way design.

Basic Issues in Planning a One-way Design

Suppose the experimenter is interested in determining the effects of a particular treatment factor on performance—for instance, the influence of the number of items in a paired-associate list on the percentage of items recalled after five study trials. (An experiment of this sort was described in Chapter 6.) For convenience, capital letters are often used to refer to a factor; accordingly let us label list length in this study as the L (for length) factor.

In choosing a one-way between-subjects experiment to investigate list length, the investigator has decided to focus on a single factor, to assign different subjects to each level of the factor, and to disregard the possible influence of other treatment factors on performance. Several decisions about the list length factor remain to be made, however. In particular, how many levels of the L factor—and *which* levels— are to be included in the design? And how many subjects should be assigned to each of the treatment conditions? These two decisions are especially important because they influence the costs of the experiment and its likely benefits. If the experiment is of critical importance and resources are plentiful, then the researcher might select several levels of L and assign a large number of subjects to each level. When the research problem is less crucial, or when resources (time and money) are limited, then the researcher must consider trade-offs. Practically speaking, there is usually a limit on the total number of subjects who can be tested, and so increasing the number of levels means decreasing the number of subjects per level, and vice versa. Each of these choices has its pros and cons. Limiting the number of levels of the treatment factors makes it difficult for the researcher to make sense of the pattern of results, but when only a handful of subjects is tested at each level, the averages are less stable and the validity of the interpretation is compromised. Let us look at each side of this issue more carefully.

Choice of Levels. In selecting the treatment levels of a factor, the researcher must decide how many levels to include and which ones. The significance of each decision is brought home by a couple of illustrations.

In the list length study, the subject studies a list of l word pairs for five trials and is then tested for recall; l is the number of word pairs in the treatment condition to which the subject has been assigned. How is the percentage of correctly recalled word pairs related to l, the number of pairs? That is the experimental question, and in planning the experiment the researcher must make some guesses about what answer is likely.

Suppose the "true" relationship is the one shown by the solid line in the left panel of Figure 7–1. These are the results that would be obtained if every college

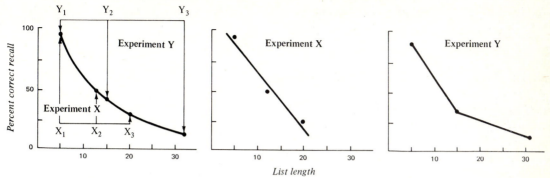

Figure 7–1 Example of how choice of levels can affect an experimental outcome. Experiment X suggests a linear relation between list length and recall, while experiment Y gives a more adequate picture of the relation.

undergraduate in the nation were to be tested. The experimenter's task is to select a few levels of the factor, run a small number of subjects at each level, and then use the handful of information that results to gain an approximation of the true underlying relation.

Figure 7–1 shows the results of investigations by two experimenters who differed in their choice of levels. Experimenter X decides to assess performance at list lengths of four, twelve, and twenty pairs; experimenter Y picks list lengths of four, sixteen, and thirty-two pairs. It would be interesting to know the reasoning behind these selections, but for now let us assume that the choices were based on reviews of the research literature, to which was added a dash of intuition.

As you can see from the findings in the middle and right panels, the investigations lead to different conclusions regarding the relationship between list length and recall percentage. In experiment X, recall decreases with increasing list length in almost a straight-line fashion. (Researchers find the simplicity of a straight-line relation quite appealing.) Extending the line, one might conclude that recall would be negligible for a list of twenty-five pairs. The results of experiment Y portray the actual relation more accurately. Recall declines with increasing list length, but the trend is clearly not a simple straight line and is still noticeably above zero even when there are thirty-two pairs in the list.

For our second example, consider a fictitious study on the effect of incentives on problem-solving skill. The subject's task is to solve anagrams (for instance, make a word out of NEWR). The investigator decides to vary the amount of money paid to the subject if he or she can solve the problem within a fixed time limit—if you come up with *wren* within 15 seconds, you get a reward of a penny, a nickel, or a dime.

Figure 7–2 shows the true relation between the amount of payoff and the success rate, where *true* is defined, as in the previous example, as the results of testing all college students in the country. Notice that the incentive factor is scaled logarithmically; each point on the scale is ten times the previous value. This layout

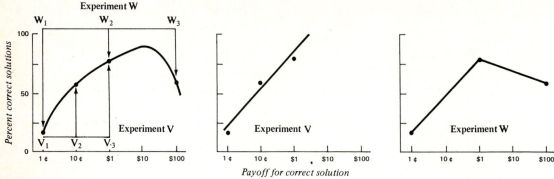

Figure 7–2 Example of how choice of levels can determine pattern of experimental outcome. Experiment V shows steady improvement in performance as payoff increases. In experiment W performance reaches a peak and then declines when the stakes get too high.

is consistent with the notion that relative increases in payoff, not absolute increases, are what matter (see Ch. 5). Notice also that the relation is curvilinear rather than straight-line; increasing incentive leads to improved performance up to a certain point, beyond which the strain of high stakes causes performance to deteriorate.

Once again, imagine that two experimenters plan studies that vary in the choice of levels, as shown in the figure. The results from experiment V lead to the conclusion that increasing incentive produces greater success, and in a more or less straight-line fashion. Experiment W, which shows that the pattern is more complex, is a more accurate portrayal of the underlying relationship.

How does the investigator decide which levels of a factor to include in a design? As the examples suggest, this decision may have a significant bearing on the outcome of the study. The most trustworthy decision would be based on a theory of the problem under investigation that would provide some clues about the nature of the relation between factors. Theoretical models of this degree of precision are still rare in psychology, although, as noted in Chapter 1, they are beginning to appear. In the absence of theory the investigator must rely upon previous studies, pilot investigations, and informed judgment.

Finding the **boundary conditions** of a relationship (the levels that correspond to its high and low points) is a significant consideration in deciding on the levels to be included in a study. In the list length experiment, for instance, it is useful to know the number of items at which performance begins to decline and the level at which recall has become negligible. (You might consider how the research question and the choice of levels would be changed if the dependent measure were the *number* of pairs, rather than the percentage, recalled.)

It is also important to determine whether the relation is a fairly simple one (are trends consistently up or down) or changes direction at certain points (as in the incentive example). Many relations in psychology are reasonably simple and can be adequately described by evaluating performance at three to six levels of a factor, provided that the levels chosen are informative ones.

Sample Size. How many subjects should be assigned to each treatment condition in an experiment? Since each subject tested represents an investment in time and effort, this question is an important one. If too little information is available, the measure of average performance for the condition will be unstable. If too much information is gathered, it can be a waste of resources (unless, of course, the information is very cheap).

One way to decide on sample size is to see what other experimenters are doing. In current practice experimenters generally assign between twenty and thirty subjects to each of the conditions in a one-way design.

Another consideration in deciding sample size has to do with the **power** of an experiment. To understand this concept, we have to digress briefly.

The researcher, in analyzing the results of a study, can commit either of two mistakes, as illustrated by Figure 7–3. First, the investigator may decide that a particular factor has an effect on performance when in fact it has no real effect and only random variation is being measured. Most statistical procedures keep such *false-positive* errors at a low rate, less than one in 20 to 100 events. Second, the investigator may decide that a factor has *no* effect on performance when in fact it does. This second type of error is related to the power of an experiment.

The power of a study is defined as the sensitivity of a research study to detect "real" effects (i.e., the likelihood that, when there are real effects, the experimenter

		True State of Nature	
		No Effect of Treatment Factor	Actual Effect of Treatment Factor
Researcher's Interpretation of Experimental Results	"No effect has been detected"	True-Negative Decision	False-Negative Decision (Type II Error)
	"An actual effect has been found"	False-Positive Decision (Type I Error)	True-Positive Decision (Power of the Experiment)

Figure 7–3 Outcomes of an experiment; the "decision space"

comes to the conclusion that they are there). Thus, the likelihood that the researcher avoids a false-negative error is a measure of the power of the experiment.

The power depends on (a) the actual magnitude of the effects, (b) the amount of unsystematic variability in the data, (c) the experimenter's conservatism in avoiding a false-positive error (announcing that something has been found when nothing is there), (d) the sensitivity of the statistical procedures used for data analysis, and (e) the sample size.

Items (a) and (b) are more or less self-evident: when the effects of a factor are weak, they will be difficult to detect and when strong, easier to detect; and the sloppier the results, the more difficult it will be to draw any conclusions with much assurance. Item (c), the experimenter's conservatism in making a false-positive error, is less obvious. Simply stated, the conservative strategy is to avoid arousing people's ire at false alarms by not crying wolf unless you are absolutely sure that the wolf is there. Unfortunately, this strategy increases the likelihood of making the false-negative mistake: the wolf may capture a sheep because everyone is afraid to sound the alarm.

Detailed discussion of item (d) would take us beyond the scope of this text. Briefly, the contents of any book on basic statistics reveal a variety of procedures for data analysis; some are more precise and sensitive than others. In general, the most sensitive procedures may require extensive computations, a consideration that has become irrelevant with modern computers.

Finally, there is item (e), the sample size—that is, the number of subjects assigned to each condition in the experiment. (In fact, as we shall see later in the chapter, the power of the experiment actually depends on the total number of observations in the study rather than the sample size per condition.) The basic principle is simple. If a sufficiently large number of subjects is tested, then very slight effects can be detected. Techniques exist for calculating the number of subjects required to achieve a particular degree of statistical power in an experiment, *if* you can estimate the effects that are to be detected and the amount of unsystematic variability and can specify the statistical procedure and the extent of conservatism in making the first type of error (Hays, 1981, pp. 247ff).

While precise techniques are available for determining the sample size needed to achieve a certain degree of power, these techniques are not useful in most instances. Researchers seldom have a well-defined estimate of the size of treatment effects to be expected, nor can they estimate the unsystematic variability with much precision. The sample size is, on the surface, an "easy" tactic for increasing power: run more subjects, collect more observations, and you are more likely to detect the effects of the treatment factor.

You may question an approach that relies on very large sample sizes in order to identify minuscule effects, and you are right. The practical judgment of most researchers at the present time seems to be that if an effect cannot be identified at a cost of twenty to thirty subjects per condition, then it is probably not large enough to warrant further attention. It would be interesting to consider whether this rule of thumb is defensible, but this text is not the appropriate place. The power of an experiment can be increased without increasing the number of subjects by reducing unsystematic variability through improved control over random sources of fluctuation or by making more efficient use of the subjects in an experiment. These methods, which rely on the factorial design technique, will be discussed later in the chapter.

Organizational Effects in Memory: A Laboratory Study

Our first example of a one-way between-subjects design is a laboratory study of the effects of categorical organization on a subject's ability to remember a long list of words. One might investigate this question through a simple demonstration, showing that a group studying an organized list of words had a higher recall rate than a group tested on an unorganized list. In the experiment described in this section, the researcher uses a one-way between-subjects plan in a more extended fashion to explore some of the facets of categorical recall. Because this is the first actual study to be presented in the text, it will be described in some detail.

Theoretical Background. Bower (1970) and his colleagues have carried out several experiments on the improvement of memory through mnemonic techniques—"tricks" for memorization. One of these studies provides an excellent example of the application of the one-way between-subjects design. Before going into the details of the study, providing some background on the problem may be helpful.

Theories of memory are based on one of three means of memorization: associations, episodes, and semantic networks. The associative approach can be thought of as a "magnet" theory. Certain experiences, because they are similar or occurred at the same time, become hooked together. Investigations of associative memory have a long history, beginning with Ebbinghaus (1885; also cf. Anderson and Bower, 1973). Research on paired-associate learning has been a laboratory favorite; Bower's early studies of this phenomenon (e.g., Atkinson, Bower, and Crothers, 1965) showed that memorization of paired associates could be accurately described by mathematical models of the learning process. Numerous other studies have uncovered several factors that strongly influence associative memory: the number of study opportunities, the preexisting strength of the association between stimulus and response, and interference from competing associations, among others (Hall, 1971).

In recent years researchers have turned their attention to the investigation of memory in more naturalistic situations, with increasing emphasis on the nature of the underlying mental processes. Out of these investigations has come the contrast between episodic and semantic memory (Tulving, 1972).

Episodic memory is the recall of a sequence of events experienced personally. You remember "how you spent your summer" and other flashes from the past, tall tales, special experiences, and even commonplace happenings. This type of memory is individualistic. The elements are seldom novel; more often, it is the remembrance of familiar people and objects newly arranged in time. When a friend asks, "How was your day?" or "What was the movie like?" you rely for your answer on episodic memory.

Semantic memory is illustrated by your mental experience when asked to describe the similarities and differences between a canary and an eagle. Both are birds, both have feathers and wings, both can fly, they differ in size, one is yellow and the other is not, one is appropriate as a pet and the other is not, and so on. Semantic memory is stored in the form of networks or linkages of information; animals, vegetables, and minerals provide the beginning of one such structure. The patterns of these networks tend to reflect cultural universals and are therefore much less idiosyncratic and individualistic than are episodic memories.

Design of the Study. Bower and his colleagues (Bower, Clark, Lesgold, and Winzenz, 1969) undertook an investigation of how well college students could employ preexisting information in semantic memory to recall a large amount of information after only a brief period of study. They employed the *free recall* technique, in which the subject briefly studies a list of words and afterward attempts to recall as many of the words as possible. College students can generally recall eight to twelve words from a list of unrelated words after the first study trial and then gain a few additional words after each subsequent trial.

Bower and his colleagues were interested in how subjects learned word lists that were not chosen at random but selected to fit into a clear-cut organizational structure. Figure 7-4 shows an example of one such list. As you can see, the "mineral" words take the shape of a hierarchical network with different levels of abstraction. Four such networks were prepared as stimulus materials, each containing 28 words, for a total of 112 words. A list with this many words would normally

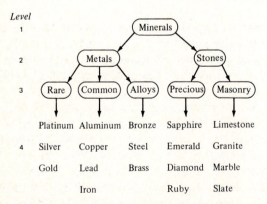

Figure 7–4 Example of hierarchical "tree" of words of the type used by Bower, Clark, Lesgold, and Winzenz (1969) to study effects of organization on free recall. Each subject studied four trees of this sort.

take quite a few trials for a college student to master if the words were chosen at random.

The treatment factor for this study is displayed in Figure 7–5, which shows samples of six different study arrangements of the words on display cards. In the two *whole-list* conditions, all 112 words were studied for each of four trials. In the whole-list structured condition, all the words for a given network were placed on a single card and organized to match the hierarchy as shown in Figure 7–4. This level of the factor was presumed to provide an optimal match to the students' preexisting memory of the concepts. In the whole-list random condition, the four sets of 112 words were scattered more or less at random over the positions on four cards, obscuring the hierarchical structure altogether.

The four remaining conditions used a *part-list* procedure in which only a portion of each list was presented on the first two study trials. The purpose of the part-list procedures was to determine whether gradual introduction of the hierarchical structure would be more efficient than presentation of the entire structure for all four categories from the very beginning. The part-list structured condition is the critical condition. As Figure 7–5 illustrates, the part-list structured condition is identical to the whole-list structured condition except that on trial 1 only the two upper categories, and on trial 2 only the three upper categories, are included.

The three remaining part-list conditions are control conditions. In the part-list random condition, words from the whole-list random condition were presented in the same physical locations as in the part-list structured condition. This condition shows the relative effectiveness of presenting a word list for study in a cumulative fashion, beginning with a small block of unrelated words and then adding batches on subsequent trials. In the part-list category-random condition, all of the words from a particular hierarchy (one "card") were presented on trial 1, and arranged physically to match the part-list format. A second "card" was added on trial 2, and the remaining words on trial 3. In the part-list unrelated condition, a set of 112 completely unrelated words (that is, a new set of 112 words that could *not* be arranged in networks) was selected and presented in the part-list fashion. (You might consider the value of adding a whole-list unrelated condition to the design.)

The Findings. The original report showed details of the learning rate for each of the conditions; our purposes can be served by examining performance on the fourth and final trial of the experiment. These results are shown in Figure 7–6. All groups were tested on 112 words on this trial, and so the six conditions can be directly compared. Compared with the previous arrangements, this graph has been tilted; the dependent measure is laid out on the abscissa (remember this axis by "flat on your abscissa," an example of a mnemonic); and the six levels of the treatment factor are arranged along the ordinate (the vertical axis).

While examining these data, you might keep two questions in mind: What is the effect on recall rate of studying words arranged in a hierarchy rather than in a random presentation? What is the relative efficiency of the whole-list compared with the part-list presentation technique?

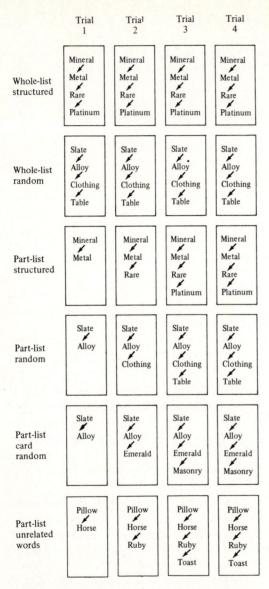

Figure 7–5 Arrangement of word trees in six conditions studied by Bower et al. (1969). A single word from each of four levels from one of four trees is presented here (there were actually 28 words on each card). In part-list conditions, two levels were presented on trial 1, three levels on trial 2, and all four levels on trials 3 and 4.

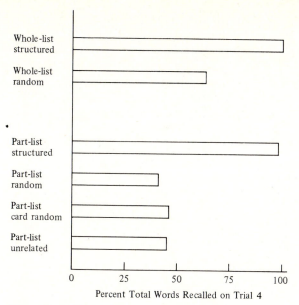

Figure 7–6 Performance in each of six experimental arrangements of hierarchical word lists. Data of Bower et al. (1969).

Three findings bear on these two questions. First, subjects presented with a hierarchically structured list, whether in whole-list or part-list fashion, recalled an incredible amount of information—virtually all words in the list of 112 were perfectly remembered by trial 4 in both these conditions. The subjects in the part-list structured condition had only one opportunity to study the entire list, yet this sufficed to produce a high degree of accuracy and completeness in recall. In fact, the original paper reported that the subjects in the whole-list structured condition had virtually mastered the list by trial 2 (94 percent correct recall). Examination of the recall by individual subjects showed that the subjects in the structured conditions clearly used the hierarchical network as a basis for organized recall; every subject consistently reproduced the word lists beginning with the top categories and then proceeding to lower-level entries.

Second, even though the words in several of the treatment conditions could have been reorganized into a hierarchical structure, the college undergraduates in this experiment were generally unable to discover the structure on their own; rapid learning depended on an arrangement that emphasized the structure. The critical data for this conclusion come from the part-list conditions. Performance in the part-list structured condition was superior to the other three control conditions, among which there was no noticeable difference. One would predict that, had subjects been sensitive to the underlying structure in the scrambled arrangements, the part-list category-random condition (in which all items from a hierarchy were presented on the same card, though in a scrambled arrangement) would yield the best performance, and the part-list unrelated condition (in which the words could not be related in any obvious way) would yield the poorest performance of the three conditions. But the data show that, if anything, the part-list unrelated words were recalled no better than the other two control lists. Moreover, the investigators found no evidence from the patterns of word recall in the random-arrangement conditions to suggest that subjects were using the higher-level categories (e.g., minerals, metals, stones) as cues for organizing their recollection.

Third, the data suggest that the part-list procedure is at least as efficient as the whole-list method. The experiment is not ideally designed for this comparison, and the conclusion requires a careful examination of the trial-by-trial results provided in the original paper. Practically speaking, however, it appears that presenting hierarchical lists in part-list fashion, starting with the upper categories and then adding successive lower-level entries, is a sensible strategy and may be a time-saver.

The results from this study, which are quite clear-cut, represent an excellent application of the one-way between-subjects design. Bower was convinced that the organizational factor would have a powerful effect and that the college undergraduates in the sample would perform fairly consistently (showing relatively small differences between individuals). He was correct on both counts. To be sure, the generalizability of the results is restricted to fairly able and well-educated young adults like those found on the Stanford campus, young people likely to be familiar with the hierarchies and to recognize the value of using such structures for recall. The subjects must not be too perceptive, of course; if the subjects in the unstructured conditions had perceived the underlying organization of the random-arrangement lists, they might have been able to improve their performance to match that of the structured groups.

A within-subjects design would clearly be inappropriate for this investigation. Once a subject has encountered a structured list, he or she is likely to examine all subsequent lists for the presence of structural features that might aid recall. Investigating transfer of organizational strategies might be an interesting question, but it was not the goal of the Bower study. A between-subjects design was essential.

Encouraging People to "Buckle Up": A Field Study

The laboratory study of memory just described exemplifies the theoretical side of experimental psychology. Research in psychology can also be pragmatic and atheoretical, directed toward solving practical problems that require fairly direct action. We now examine a study that illustrates the application of the one-way between-subjects design for investigation of one such problem.

Background. As you may be aware, fastening your seat belt dramatically improves your chances of survival in an automobile crash. Drivers unfortunately tend to disregard this fact; the inconvenience of wearing a belt apparently outweighs the benefits of increased safety. Buckling up requires thought and action in the here and now, whereas the consequences of not buckling up entail future events that many drivers consider unlikely: "I won't have an accident. I'm a good driver!" Efforts to force people to wear seat belts through mandatory-use laws, warning lights and buzzers, and starter-interlock devices have proven both unpopular and difficult to enforce. While the issue is in large measure a political matter, it makes sense to search for more effective methods to encourage people to use seat belts.

The Study. With this goal in mind, Elman and Killebrew (1978) sought to influence buckling up by direct application of reinforcement principles; an individual is more likely to do something when there is a chance of immediate reward. These investigators carried out three experiments, all using the same basic one-way between-subjects design but with slight variations in the specific conditions. The results will be reported as a single study; you should note that a special strength of this investigation was the effort to replicate the findings.

The research was carried out in the parking lot of a large shopping center. Drivers were handed a one-page leaflet as they got into their cars after shopping. Variations in the message on the leaflet, to be described below, comprised the levels of the treatment factor. Observers stationed at the parking lot exits noted whether the drivers had fastened their belts—the dependent measure.

The Design. Nine levels of the treatment factor were tested over the three replications of the study. The leaflet message for these conditions is shown in Figure 7–7 (page 186). The conditions on the left entailed various types of warnings that relied primarily on exhortation:

DRIVE CAREFULLY!
REMEMBER TO BUCKLE UP!
OBSERVERS ARE WATCHING YOU!

In the right column are several conditions in which drivers were told that they might be rewarded if their belts were fastened. The odds of receiving a gift certificate varied from 50 percent (every other driver) to 1 percent (1 out of every 100 drivers). The design also included a no-treatment control condition, which makes more sense in this experiment than it does in many others.

The Findings. The results are displayed in Figure 7–8 (page 187). The levels of the treatment factor have been arranged along the abscissa (the horizontal axis) in order of likely effectiveness, based on the researchers' judgments.

Certain patterns in the findings seem clear-cut: (a) people do not usually wear their seat belts—only one in seven in the no-treatment control condition did so; (b) reminders and threats had only a slight effect on performance, increasing the proportion of bucklers to about one in four; (c) the promise of a reward increased the proportion of people who buckled up by two and a half times the no-treatment control average; (d) the likelihood of reward affected the rate of compliance slightly— the big difference was between a warning condition and an incentive condition. You catch more flies with honey. . . .

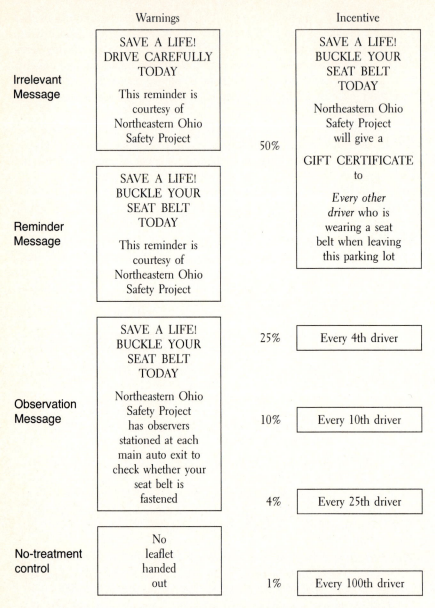

Figure 7–7 Leaflet messages for nine conditions in "buckle-up" study

This experiment demonstrates a practical application of the one-way between-subjects design. The treatments were simple and easy to operationalize. Different leaflets were handed out on different days, making this a between-subjects design (a few subjects may have been included in more than one condition, but most were first-timers).

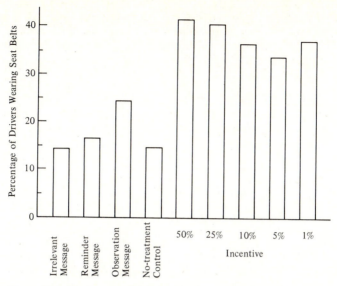

Figure 7–8 Percentage of drivers wearing seat belts for each treatment condition in the "buckle-up" study

The experiment is also an excellent example of the effective use of limited resources. The observers were relatively inexperienced and received only a small amount of training. The treatment factor was fairly powerful, and the results could be replicated even with a relatively insensitive design.

A more complex design might have been difficult to implement, considering the limited resources and the inexperience of the observers. Nonetheless, it is interesting to consider other factors that might have been included in the design, given its limitations. For instance, the observers noted the drivers' gender and the number of passengers in each car; none of this information was used in the analysis of the results. Another factor of potential importance could have been included at little or no additional cost: the type of car. Older cars are less likely to have seat belts installed and in working order; more recent models employ seat belt arrangements that facilitate buckling up, and so on. By capitalizing on opportunities to include such factors in the design, the researchers might have gained a more complete understanding of the effects of the primary treatment factor. Nonetheless, the experiment stands as an excellent example of the effective use of the one-way design.

FACTORIAL BETWEEN-SUBJECTS DESIGNS

In a factorial design, the researcher investigates the simultaneous effects of two or more factors. When one or more control factors are included in the design, experimental control is often greater than in a one-way plan even though the researcher's main interest may be centered on a single treatment dimension. The factorial approach is also an efficient strategy when the researcher is interested in more than one factor, and the technique is essential when interactions are of interest.

Basic Issues in Planning Factorial Designs

The researcher confronts a wide array of decisions in planning a factorial design. There are two or more factors to consider, and levels must be selected for each. Potential interactions between the factors must also be considered when making these decisions. A factorial design, because it includes combinations of factors, typically has more treatment conditions than a one-way design, and so management of the study is more demanding. Let us examine each of these issues in more detail.

Pros and Cons. A factorial design typically includes all combinations of two or more factors. There are three reasons for combining multiple factors in a design. First, the experimental question may entail more than a single factor. One reason behavioral phenomena are complex is that multiple causality is the rule rather than the exception. Second, even when the primary interest is in a single factor, further analysis often turns up secondary factors. As noted in Chapter 6, the decision about which secondary factors to include in an experiment is a difficult one. While the researcher seldom has the resources to investigate *all* the possibilities, by including several factors in a compact factorial design the investigator may obtain better control over a problem than with a one-way design of comparable size. Third, adequate experimental control often requires the inclusion of one or more nuisance factors in the design. More comprehensive designs provide improved control but may also entail greater cost and complexity. Factorial designs help the investigator in keeping costs down while realizing the benefits of improved control and increased information.

The simplest version of a factorial design consists of two factors with two levels each. This is called a *two-by-two (2 × 2) factorial design*. It includes four factorial combinations, each of which comprises a unique condition in the experiment. Examples of two-by-two designs described in Chapter 6 are displayed in Figure 7–9: high and low levels of motivation combined with easy and difficult anagram problems; four- and five-year-olds tested in a sterile or stimulating test environment. Larger and more complex designs may have either additional factors or more levels for some of the factors. Chapter 6 included one three-factor design: gender of the experimenter, gender of the subject, and word type (neutral or risqué). This two-by-two-by-two (2 × 2 × 2) design has eight treatment combinations, as shown in Figure 7–9.

In general, the number of combinations in a factorial design is obtained by multiplying the number of levels for each of the factors. While there is no theoretical limit to the size of a factorial design (an experimenter may combine any number of factors with any number of levels), there are practical constraints on the size. As

2 × 2 Designs

	Motivation	
	High	Low
Anagram Problem Difficulty — Easy		
Anagram Problem Difficulty — Difficult		

	Age	
	4-Years-Old	5-Years-Old
Test Environment — Stimulating		
Test Environment — Sterile		

2 × 2 × 2 Design

Gender of Subject		Gender of Experimenter			
		Male		Female	
		Male	Female	Male	Female
Test Word	Neutral				
Test Word	Risqué				

Figure 7–9 Examples of factorial design

just noted, the number of combinations increases with the number of factors and levels, and this increase is quite rapid. For example, a 3 × 4 × 5 design requires sixty combinations—a large management task. Even with the minimum of one subject per condition, sixty subjects must be tested. Adding another two-level factor doubles this number to 120, and so on.

A factorial design with a large number of factors and factorial combinations may overwhelm the experimenter with information. For instance, a design with five two-level factors has five main effects, ten two-way interactions, ten three-way interactions, five four-way interactions, and one five-way interaction. Practical experience suggests that interactions among more than four factors are rare in nature and are virtually impossible to interpret. In general, when reviewing a study you should give most attention to the main effects and to low-order (two- and three-way) interactions. If the researcher reports more complex interactions, these are likely to be of interest only to the extent that they make theoretical or practical sense.

Choice of Factors and Levels. As noted earlier, limited resources place restrictions on the number of conditions that can be included in any particular study, and so the experimenter, in planning a factorial design, must consider trade-

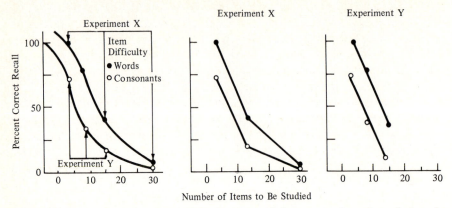

Figure 7–10 Example of how interaction in a factorial design may depend on choice of levels. Experiment X indicates an interaction between those two variables. Experiment Y suggests that amount of information does not interact with item difficulty (lines are aparallel).

offs between the number of factors and the number of levels per factor. For example, a study with *five factors*, each with *two levels*, yields a total of 2 × 2 × 2 × 2 × 2 or thirty-two combinations, about the same number of conditions (and thus a comparable investment in time and effort) as an investigation of *two factors*, each with *six levels*, totaling 6 × 6 or thirty-six combinations. Which is the more informative design? There is no general answer to this question. The researcher must consider the nature of the problem and decide whether it is best to study a small number of factors in considerable detail, examine several factors more superficially, or search for some combination of these two strategies (hence, in the instance just cited, a 4 × 2 × 2 × 2 design would represent a compromise of equal cost).

The choice of levels in a factorial design requires more planning than for a one-way design, partly because more factors are involved but also because the choices must take into account the potential for interactions. For instance, suppose the researcher is interested in how memory is affected by the number of items to be remembered and the difficulty of each item. The left panel in Figure 7–10 shows the hypothesized relation between recall and the number of items, where the items are either three-letter words (e.g., CAT, RUG) or three-consonant strings (e.g., CRG, MPJ). Words are likely to be easier to recall than the nonsense strings. Recall is also presumed to be poorer when there are more items in the list. At the shortest and longest levels of the list length factor, however, the effect of item difficulty becomes negligible.

The X and Y sets in Figure 7–10 show how two different experimenters chose levels of the list length factor, with the outcomes displayed in the middle and right panels of the figure. From the results of experiment X one would conclude that there was a substantial interaction between item difficulty and list length and that the nature of that interaction could be described. Experiment Y leads to the conclusion that there is little or no interaction between the two factors; the difference between words and consonant strings seems roughly equivalent at all list lengths. This latter conclusion is reasonable, *but only within the range of list lengths included in experiment* Y. The researcher is often tempted to generalize over a broader range of conditions than those actually included in the design of a study, in which case interactions become an important consideration in the design.

Both of these experiments yield useful information about the "real world," but the nature of the information differs. Regardless of the level of the difficulty factor (words or consonant strings), we can assume that the recall of short lists will be close to 100 percent. If an experimenter is exploring new territory and is primarily interested in determining the upper and lower bounds of performance, then the choice of levels in experiment X is probably the better choice. If previous research has already provided estimates of the upper and lower limits of performance, then experiment Y would yield useful details about the relation between the two factors within these limits.

Interactions and the Choice of Response Measures. The preceding example illustrates an important point: the researcher's selection of a dependent measure may determine whether or not two factors appear to interact. Two factors may interact within certain levels for one measure but not for another. Since an interaction complicates the description of a set of findings, one dependent measure may therefore lead to a simpler set of findings than another measure. Let us see how these patterns come about.

Suppose the goal of the experiment is to evaluate the effects on associative learning of list length and grade in school. Figure 7–11 presents the "true" effects of these two factors for two different measures: percentage of correct responses and time to make a response. The left panel of the figure, which shows the relation for percent correct, exhibits a clear interaction between the two factors. This complication is not very interesting; it results because college students do perfectly at all list lengths, whereas kindergartners can recall nothing at any list length. At the two intermediate grades, percent correct declines steadily with increasing list length.

The interaction described above is the result of **floor** and **ceiling limits** on the measure. It is impossible for the college students to exceed perfection (100 percent correct) or for the kindergartners to do worse than nothing (0 percent correct). Interactions that reflect floor and ceiling limits do not necessarily represent genuine complications in the combined effects of two factors. Rather, the interaction may simply reflect limitations on the performance measure.

When performance is at the upper or lower limits of one measure, sometimes another measure can be found that provides a more sensitive (and perhaps a simpler) picture of the factor effects. The right panel of Figure 7–11 shows the results that might be found in the same experiment using response time as the dependent measure. There is no effective upper limit to this measure, and the results can be adequately and simply described by the main effects of each factor: there is no interaction. The example suggests that the lower boundary on response time is not a

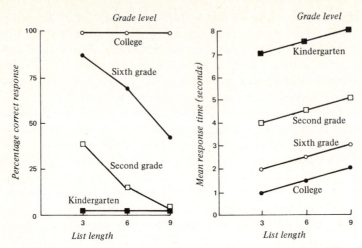

Figure 7–11 Example of results from a single experiment when different dependent variables are used. The interaction on the left reflects floor and ceiling effects. Time scores in the left panel show no interaction.

problem here; in other instances floor limits can be as serious a problem as ceiling limits.

Which is the better measure of performance in this example? Is there really an interaction between grade in school and list length or not? These questions cannot be answered in the abstract. Whether an interaction is observed depends upon the decisions made in planning the experiment, which include the choice of factor levels and of the dependent measure. The experimenter's conclusions about whether interactions occur beyond the immediate boundary conditions of the experiment are a matter of judgment and interpretation. In the study under discussion, the list lengths included in the design show little evidence of interaction in the range from second through sixth grade for the percent correct measure. This result might be of practical value for certain applications, but the researcher should be careful about generalizing this statement to longer list lengths: all grade levels must eventually level out at zero. The response time measure, on the other hand, shows little evidence of interaction anywhere within the range of the experiment, and hence the researcher is justified in extending the conclusion that there is no interaction to a broad range of conditions beyond those included in the study.

Whenever an interaction is observed in a study, the researcher has the task of interpretation, of making sense of the data. Generally speaking, it is easier to describe the results of a factorial experiment when no interactions are present; a parsimonious (i.e., simple) explanation expresses the main effects of each factor. The response time data in Figure 7–11 are therefore easier to interpret than the percentage data. The latter index might be more amenable to interpretation for theoretical or practical reasons, to be sure. Then the researcher must deal with the additional complications.

Sample Size in Factorial Designs. How many subjects should be assigned to each combination in a factorial design? The answer to this question differs in significant respects from the earlier presentation for one-way designs. Each condition in a one-way design must include sufficient data to provide a stable estimate of the treatment effect for that condition; each level of the factor must stand on its own. In a factorial design, observations for each of the factors are combined over the levels of the other factors and so the sample size in each combination can be relatively small. The critical question for sample size in a factorial design is, What comparisons are important for answering the research questions? Once this issue is decided, then the principles discussed earlier for one-way designs can be applied.

The situation will be illustrated with a concrete example. Suppose the basic design for a study includes four factors, each with two levels; this $2 \times 2 \times 2 \times 2$ factorial design with a total of sixteen combinations is displayed in Figure 7–12. Suppose two subjects are assigned to each combination. Is this sample size sufficient?

As noted earlier, the adequacy of any proposed sample size in a factorial design depends upon the comparisons that are to be made. Two subjects per condition seems quite small compared with the usual practice of using twenty to thirty observations per cell. That recommendation holds for one-way designs, however. If the experimenter in the present example is interested only in the main effects of each factor, then a sample size of two subjects per combination might be sufficient, especially if the study is exploratory in nature. As shown in Figure 7–12, when comparing the two levels for each factor the data are collapsed over all the other factors. The average for level 1 of the A factor, for instance, is based on eight combinations of the B, C, and D factors, each with two subjects, for a total of sixteen observations. All the main effects follow this same pattern; all have sixteen observations if the sample size is two subjects per factorial combination. Sixteen observations is a bit on the low side and might be too few for certain purposes, but three to four subjects per combination, which would yield twenty-four and thirty-two observations for each main effect, surely would be adequate.

Suppose the experimenter is interested in certain of the two-way interactions in this example, and two subjects are assigned to each condition. For evaluation of a two-way interaction, the data are divided into a set of four two-by-two tables, as shown in Figure 7–12 for the AB interaction. The division of the total of thirty-two observations into four combinations yields eight measures per cell, too few by conventional standards. To ensure stable averages in the two-way interaction tables, the experimenter should assign at least four subjects to each combination.

You can see the pattern. If the researcher wants to examine high-order interactions, then larger sample sizes per combination are required. Thus, investigating complex interactions quickly becomes an expensive proposition. If the researcher's goals are more modest, with primary emphasis on the main effects of a set of factors, then relatively small samples—sometimes only a single subject per combination—may suffice to yield stable estimates of the treatment effects.

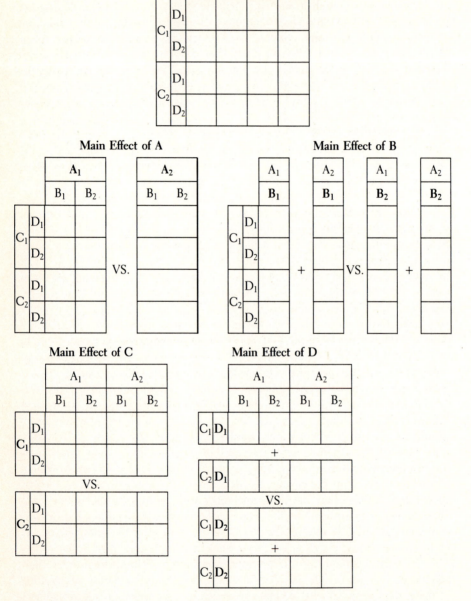

Figure 7–12 Plan of 2 x 2 x 2 x 2 design, showing how cells are divided for main effects

The factorial principle is an efficient research investment in any event. It provides the researcher the means to investigate multiple factors within an integrated design framework at relatively low cost. If the four factors in the example (A, B, C, and D) were each to be tested in a one-way design with 16 subjects per condition, a total of 128 subjects would be required, compared with a total of 32 subjects for the same information with the $2 \times 2 \times 2 \times 2$ factorial design. When interactions are an important part of the research question, then a factorial design is mandatory; interactions cannot be evaluated except by including in the design the various combinations of the interacting factors. The cost of the factorial approach, it should be remembered, is a more complex management task for the researcher because each condition in the experiment is a relatively complicated combination of factors. The opportunities for procedural mistakes become greater as the number of factors in the design is increased, and the researcher should keep this possibility in mind.

The Development of Communication Skills: A Laboratory Study

Background. "The Magic Years" is the title aptly chosen by Fraiberg (1959) to describe the experience of childhood. As she puts it: "Language originates in magic. The first 'words' of a baby are not words at all, but magic incantations, sounds uttered for pleasure and employed indiscriminately to bring about a desired event" (p. 112).

This state of affairs changes dramatically as the child develops the ability to communicate using the medium of language. By three or four years of age, virtually all children can carry on a conversation. Still, most youngsters are far from having mastered their language at this age. They are uncertain about the full implications of what others say to them. Their references are often ambiguous, phrases are left unfinished, and they tend to wander from one point to another. To be sure, all of us tend to talk in this fashion when the setting is informal. Our *private language* (Bernstein, 1961) is idiosyncratic, slangy, and depends on the context. We leave a great deal unsaid: "Ya know what I mean. . . ."

These remarks are not meant to criticize; private language works and is personal and effective in many situations. The developing child thrives on the apparent chaos found in informal language. From the diversity of personal languages (including "baby talk") surrounding preschoolers, each child chooses the elements and styles desired to construct his or her own language—a collage appropriate to the environment and a foundation for adapting to the other environments encountered later in life.

People also acquire one or more *public languages*, which conform to the vocabulary, grammar, and style designated as "proper" by members of a particular language community (Goody, 1977). The goal of formal schooling is to help students acquire the set of public languages that are needed for success in modern society. These languages are generally more precise and explicit than everyday conversation; they are more formal, less colloquial, more carefully phrased, more stilted, and less ambiguous. The student also learns about the suitability of various language styles to different occasions. Private language is appropriate to the home and close friends; public language is used in speaking with strangers (Rodriguez, 1981, provides a dramatic account of the tension that can grip the individual when the gap between personal and public language becomes too great).

Psychologists have studied the development of communication skills in young children, and this line of research provides some excellent examples of the application of factorial between-subject designs. We now look at two examples of such designs. While both studies were conducted in laboratory settings, the results have practical implications as well. Schoolchildren are participants in an ongoing communication "game" between themselves and the teacher, their classmates, and occasionally even the principal. Knowing how to communicate effectively and knowing when you are succeeding in that effort are important skills. The factorial experiments to be described below help clarify the dimensions of this situation, which turns out to be somewhat less complicated than one might imagine.

The Two-person Communication Task.

"How does a child learn to speak to strangers about strange things?" is a fitting title for the research undertaken by Glucksberg and Krauss (1967). Let us look first at the communication task that they devised and then examine some of their findings.

The communication task was disarmingly simple—a good thing, because most of the subjects were children. Two individuals sat on either side of a table, their view of one another obscured by an opaque screen, and played a game called "Stack the Blocks." The situation is shown in Figure 7–13. One person, the *speaker*, took a block from the dispenser, placed it on the peg, and tried to describe the design on the block clearly enough that the other person, the *listener*, could pick out the same block from the tray and place it on his or her peg. The degree to which speaker and listener had communicated was measured by how well their stacks matched at the end of the session.

Because the shapes used in this study were complex and unfamiliar, people could easily disagree about how to describe them. Preliminary studies by Glucksberg, Krauss, and Weisberg (1966) showed that children below the age of four had little success in playing the game, children between four and six years of age could learn to play the game when animal designs were used but had trouble with nonsense designs, and children over six could play the game reasonably well with nonsense designs.

Speaker and Listener Age: Design and Results.

These early findings also suggested that the ages of both the speaker and the listener influenced performance on the communication task. To pinpoint these effects and to investigate the possibility of an interaction between the two factors, Krauss and Glucksberg (1969a) planned a 3 × 3 factorial study. The layout of the design and the results of the study

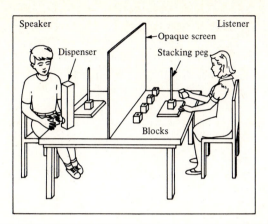

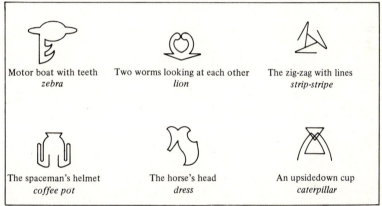

Figure 7–13 Experimental situation used by Glucksberg et al. (1966) to study the development of communication skills in young children. Bottom panel shows the designs that children had to describe and sample descriptions given by adult (roman) and kindergarten subjects (*italic*).

are shown in Figure 7–14 (page 198). Notice that by choosing three levels for each factor, Krauss and Glucksberg were able to evaluate the trends over age. There is a "floor" to the response measure because no one can do better than zero errors. Here is an instance in which measuring response time as well as errors might have made it easier to interpret the results. Within this limitation, however, the design shows whether the effects of variation in speaker changed at about the same rate as the listener age was varied.

As you can see, speaker age and listener age both affected communication rather substantially. Listener age had the greater effect, and there is little evidence of an interaction. A listener at any of the ages in the design made a more accurate match as the age of the message sender increased. Speakers and listeners of the same age have no special advantage.

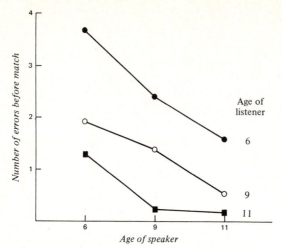

Figure 7–14 Number of errors made before a successful match in Glucksberg–Krauss task as a function of the age of speaker and listener. Data of Krauss and Glucksberg (1969a).

The Speaker Dimension: Background. Why is an older child better both at receiving a message and at sending a message? The findings in Figure 7–14 suggest that we can tackle these problems independently because there is no evidence of an interaction between the speaker and listener factors; an interaction would require all designs to include both factors. Of these two variables, we are well advised to examine the speaker factor first; we can objectively analyze what a person says, but measuring what someone "hears" is a more subtle problem.

Glucksberg and Krauss (1967) had given close attention to the descriptive features of the messages produced by their young speakers (a good example of supplementing quantitative analysis of a dependent measure by qualitative analysis) and discovered that older speakers were more likely to come up with a *key word* or *key phrase* that was particularly apt for the nonsense design. The adult responses beneath the patterns in Figure 7–13 illustrate the nature of these key words and phrases. Younger speakers were more likely to produce idiosyncratic clues that their listeners found difficult to interpret. Some examples of this style of message are also shown in the figure.

A Theoretical Model of the Speaker. How does a speaker create a descriptive message in the communication task? Krauss and Glucksberg (1969b) proposed a two-stage theoretical model to answer this question. In the first stage, after having examined the pattern, the speaker engages in a *sampling* process in which a "mental dictionary" is searched for possible labels. Next comes a *comparison* stage in which the speaker evaluates the appropriateness of each of the labels uncovered during the search and selects one or more of the labels to share with the listener.

Communicating About Words: The Task. Asher (1976) used a factorial between-subjects design to evaluate the two-stage theory. The primary goal of the study was to investigate the evaluation stage of the model by determining children's ability to assess the adequacy of various messages, including ones that they had produced as well as those produced by other subjects. Asher conducted two experiments, which I have combined for simplicity. Again, replication is a virtue.

In the variation of the communication game used in the Asher study, both the speaker and the listener were shown a pair of words (e.g., head–stomach or lift–carry). Both children were looking at the same pair of words, but one of the words on the speaker's card was underlined, and as in the previous game, a screen separated the two individuals. The speaker's task was to give clues to the listener about which of the two words was underlined. Some clues are more helpful than others for making this decision. For instance, if *head* is underlined and the speaker says "think," the listener should have no trouble in selecting *head* over *stomach* as the correct answer. In contrast, if *carry* is underlined and the speaker says "heavy," the listener is at a loss regarding the choice between *lift* and *carry*.

The researcher tape-recorded the game as it was being played, and after the game was finished, the speaker was asked to listen to a game tape. Some speakers heard their own game, some heard the dialogue from a game where the speaker was another youngster of the same age, and others heard a dialogue in which the speaker was an adult. The youngster was asked to evaluate each of the tape-recorded messages according to the following instructions:

> Now I will show you the word pairs while you listen to the clues that *you* [or *another child* or *a grownup*] gave. Tell me whether you think the other person would or would not be able to pick the underlined word from the clues in the message.

A group of adult judges independently assessed how informative was each message. The "assessment accuracy" score for each subject was the percentage of times that the subject's assessment matched that of the adult judge.

The Design and the Results. Figure 7–15 shows the design of the study, along with the results. The design had two factors: the message source described above and the subject's grade in school. The data showed that younger children had more difficulty than older children in judging the difference between a good clue and a poor clue. Not only did younger students appear to have more difficulty in generating adequate messages (the Krauss and Glucksberg finding), they were also less sensitive to the features of a good clue.

The second major trend in the data was that subjects at all ages were able to assess the messages generated by adults more accurately than their own messages or those of peers. The age of the person generating the message was thus the critical feature; a youngster was no better at judging the adequacy of his own messages than the messages of others of a similar age.

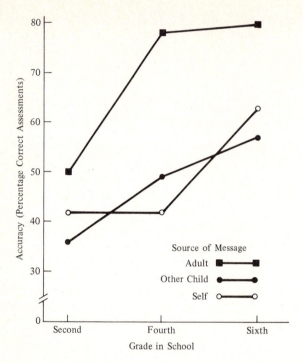

Figure 7–15 Effect of speaker age and source of message on ability to assess the adequacy of a message. Data of Asher (1976).

While the lines in the figure are not perfectly parallel, the slight interaction was not substantial enough to take seriously. The main trend in the data was the increasing ability to assess accurately the quality of a message as the student became older and had spent more time in school.

Both these experiments used a factorial between-subjects design to good advantage, but it is interesting to think about other ways in which they might have been planned. In the Krauss and Glucksberg experiment, speaker and listener age are necessarily between-subjects factors, given that the game is played by real participants (one or the other of the participants might have been "simulated" by an adult actor, but that would have been a different experiment). Grade in school is clearly a between-subjects factor. The message source factor, however, could have been planned as a within-subjects factor, with each youngster having an opportunity to assess the adequacy of messages delivered by each source. You might give some thought to the pros and cons of these two approaches to the design. Also, think about this question: Which of the factors should be categorized as treatment and which as subject-classification factors? Your answer should lead you to realize that these categories, while they are a good starting point for thinking about the dimensions of a research question, are by no means sacred.

Asking for Money: A Field Study

Background of the Problem. Next we look at a communication situation quite different from the one presented earlier: how does one solicit for charitable contributions, or to put it more bluntly, how does one succeed at the fine art of begging? Although government agencies have taken over some of the responsibilities that were in earlier times assumed by charities (the extent of this support varies with the administration in power, to be sure), many social programs are still underwritten by individual donors. Television, radio, and the mailbox have become the primary media for soliciting contributions, but door-to-door campaigns still play an important role.

The Design. What is the best way to make a pitch? This question was the focus of an experiment by Benson and Catt (1978). Their analysis of the problem led them to plan a factorial between-subjects design including five factors with two levels each:

Reason for Giving
Social Responsibility: "It's really your responsibility to help the less fortunate."

Feeling Good: "I know you will feel good to realize that you are helping those less fortunate than yourself."

Locus of Need
Internal: "True, most of these people have themselves to blame."

External: "You know, most of these people are innocent victims of circumstances."

Extent of Need
High: "These people really need your help."

Low: "These people could use your support."

Gender of Donor
Male

Female

Race of Donor
Black

White

The experimenters prepared a script requesting donations for a local charity according to each of the eight combinations of the first three treatment factors. Next, 240 households were identified in a residential neighborhood of the small city in which the researchers' university was located. One of the experimenters visited each household, made a request for funds according to one of the eight scenarios, and

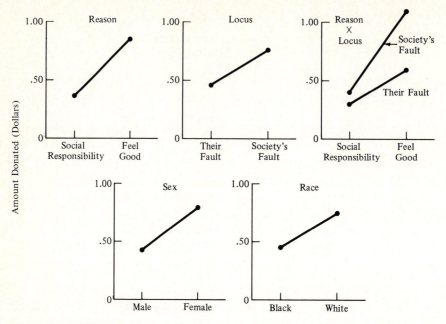

Figure 7–16 Effects of message and subject factors on amount donated to charity. Data of Benson and Catt (1978).

recorded the gender and race of the person who answered the door, along with the amount of the contribution. Approximately equal numbers of individuals from the four combinations of gender and race wound up in each of the treatment combinations; there were some fluctuations because of the ad hoc nature of the assignment (it depended on who came to the door). The amount of the contribution was the dependent measure.

The Findings. This experiment was relatively complex. There were thirty-two combinations of the 2 × 2 × 2 × 2 × 2 design, which opened the way for a substantial number of high-order interactions. Nevertheless, the results were relatively simple and could easily serve to guide the planning of a charitable campaign. Four of the five factors had effects that were identified by the statistical evaluation as large enough to take seriously, the exception being "extent of need." The two-way interaction between "reason for giving" and "locus of need" was the only interaction that was statistically trustworthy. The interaction pattern illustrates a theme that is typical in behavioral research: large interactions are most likely to appear when each of the main effects also has a large effect on performance.

The significant results are graphed in Figure 7–16. First, it does matter how you ask for money. The extremes ranged from "Please donate because it is your social responsibility to aid someone even though their problems are their own fault" (that pitch produces an average contribution of thirty cents per household) to

"Please donate because it will make you feel better to help someone who is the victim of social injustice" (that pitch yields an average of a dollar and ten cents per household—nearly four times greater than the preceding line!).

It also matters whom you ask. The largest contributions in this neighborhood were from white females (ninety-five cents on the average), the smallest from black males (twenty-seven cents on the average). Combining the effects of the treatment factors and the demographic variables, variations in the average contribution range from a zero contribution at one extreme (the weakest pitch to the most resistant audience) to a dollar and a half at the other extreme (the best pitch to the most generous audience)—quite a contrast!

An experiment of this sort may seem cold and calculating. Behavioral research often touches on sensitive issues. I must admit to an uneasiness about certain forms of encroachment, but it is pointless to ignore the fact that such research is ongoing. The investigation concerning charitable contributions was published, but one suspects that a great many studies of this sort are not released for public review. The best stance, it seems to me, is to seek to understand the process of psychological experimentation and to strive to direct it toward reasonable and defensible ends. The experiment just described makes it clear that an extremely complex problem is amenable to systematic application of factorial design principles.

SUMMARY

This chapter has described techniques for planning experiments in which different groups of subjects are assigned to each of the treatment conditions, producing between-subjects designs. Designs in which a single factor is investigated are called one-way designs. These designs, though too limited for the investigation of complex problems, provide a sound basis for describing several issues: decisions about the number of levels, the choice of those levels, and the number of subjects to be tested in each level.

Experimental design is a process of compromise. Assuming that resources permit only a fixed number of observations, increasing the number of levels of a factor in an experiment means decreasing the number of observations at each level (and hence the stability of the average for that level). Generally speaking, three to six levels of a treatment factor are sufficient to provide an adequate picture of the effects of the factor, assuming that the levels are properly chosen. When exploratory research is being done, it is important to establish the boundary limits of a factor, those levels at which performance is at the upper or lower limits of performance. The levels should also show the form of the relation between these limits, and when this question is meaningful, should indicate whether the relation is straight-line or curvilinear.

Current practice calls for a sample size of twenty to thirty observations per condition in a one-way design. More precise estimates of sample size depend on the experimental power sought by the researcher. Power is the likelihood that the researcher decides that a treatment factor has an effect, when in fact (that is, according to the "true state of affairs") it really does. Power depends on the size of the treatment effects, the amount of unsystematic variability, the experimenter's conservatism in avoiding false-positive errors (saying that a treatment factor has an effect when it does not), the sensitivity of the statistical procedures, and the sample size. If an acceptable level of power could be established and if all the other elements of this equation could be determined, then the researcher could compute the appropriate sample size. Unfortunately, in the typical research project, most of the elements of the equation are unknown, and so the researcher must rely on the conventional practice stated at the beginning of the paragraph.

In factorial designs two or more factors are simultaneously investigated. The design is constructed by combining all levels of all of the factors. With two factors, each with two levels, a 2×2 design of four combinations results; in general, a complete factorial design has combinations equaling the product of the number of levels of all the factors. It is usually good practice to limit the number of combinations to a reasonable size—less than fifty combinations is probably advisable. It is also advisable to concentrate attention on main effects and simple interactions.

In choosing the factors and levels for an experiment, the researcher faces the same issues in a factorial design as in a one-way design but must in addition keep interactions in mind. Factors may be related to one another in a simple fashion within certain boundary limits, even though they interact outside those limits. The researcher's choice of a dependent measure also determines whether or not an interaction will be observed. When the measure has upper or lower limits, interactions may reflect nothing more than boundary effects. Choice of a different response measure may yield a simpler picture of the relation between the factors.

Sample size in factorial designs follows some of the same principles as in one-way designs, but with one difference. In a factorial design the effective sample size depends upon the questions being asked. If attention focuses on the main effects, then the sample size for a given factor equals the number of observations for all the combinations of the other factors. A relatively small number of observations in each combination of a factorial design, when added together, may yield a sample size for the main effect of a factor that is quite substantial—a size more than adequate by conventional standards. If interactions are to be evaluated, the set of observations is divided more finely, and a larger number of observations per combination may be required.

The factorial method is an efficient technique. For a given investment in resources, a substantial amount of information is generated. Several factors can be investigated in a factorial design at a fraction of the cost of separate studies of the factors. Moreover, examination of interactions requires a factorial design. The major disadvantage of the factorial technique is the increased complexity of managing the multitude of combinations created by the plan. Once again, the researcher winds up weighing costs and benefits.

8

Within-subjects and Mixed Designs

Testing the individual subject under all levels of a treatment factor can have a number of advantages and may even be essential for obtaining a valid answer to the experimental question (Ch. 6). Experimental plans in which the subject undergoes multiple treatments are referred to as **within-subjects designs.**

In many investigations the researcher will decide that some variable should be planned as between-subjects factors while other variables are arranged as within-subjects factors. **Mixed designs,** as they are called, require no additional concepts beyond those covered in the discussion of the two basic design types—if you understand the concepts and techniques for between-subjects and within-subjects designs, you will be able to understand mixed designs. When you read in a research report that a mixed design was used for the investigation, this is a signal that you need to identify the status of each factor in the design: is it between-subjects or within-subjects? Psychological research that is "purely" one or the other type of design is becoming a rarity, so it is a good idea to assume that a design is mixed unless stated otherwise.

In this chapter we begin with a concrete example of a within-subjects design; the experiment is fictitious but will serve to introduce the concepts. Then the techniques for planning and analyzing one-way and factorial within-subjects designs are discussed. Next we examine mixed designs, after which two illustrations from the research literature are presented.

ONE-WAY AND FACTORIAL WITHIN-SUBJECTS DESIGNS

An Example: The Driving Study

Imagine an experiment in which the purpose is to determine the general effects of sleepiness and intoxication on driving performance, with special emphasis

205

Subject Number	Time (Session Number)		
	T_1	T_2	T_3
1	Normal	Martinis	No Sleep
2	No Sleep	Normal	Martinis
3	Normal	No Sleep	Martinis
4	Martinis	No Sleep	Normal
5	No Sleep	Martinis	Normal
6	Martinis	Normal	No Sleep

Figure 8–1 Design of one-way within-subjects study of effects of sleepiness and drinking on driving

on differences between individual subjects in response to these conditions. Because of the last requirement, a within-subjects design is essential.

Here are the procedures. Each subject participates in three sessions, during each of which they are tested for twenty minutes in an automobile simulator. The test sessions present the driver with a number of more or less serious emergency situations (a green light changes to amber at the last minute, a ball bounces out into the street, a stop sign is partly obscured by a tree, and so on). Observers rate the subject's performance on a scale from 0 (complete failure) to 100 (a perfect score), with an average of 50.

One of the three sessions is conducted with the subject in a relatively normal condition. In a second condition the subject is tested after being without sleep for forty-eight hours. In a third session subjects show up an hour early, at which time they are served three martinis at twenty-minute intervals. These three conditions correspond to the levels of the treatment factor, P (for physical condition) and will be identified as P_1, P_2, and P_3, respectively.

Six subjects are recruited for the study and tested in the order shown in Figure 8–1. Notice that the design has been planned so that each treatment condition is tested equally often during each session.

The results of the experiment are presented in Figures 8–2 and 8–3, along with the averages for each subject, for each treatment level, and for each session. Notice that the data have been rearranged according to the levels of the treatment factor rather than according to session number as in Figure 8–1.

What are the major trends in the data? Overall, the treatment factor has a noticeable effect on performance; driving is poorer when the subjects are either sleepy or drunk compared with the normal condition. Second, these effects appear in the data of every subject. Each subject shows a decline of 15 to 20 points or more under the abnormal conditions. Third, subjects vary considerably in how they normally perform on the average, with a high of 73 for subject 1 and a low of 32 for subject 2. Finally, martinis appear to influence subjects differentially, whereas the response to lack of sleep is fairly constant for all subjects. All subjects dropped about fifteen points from the normal to the sleepy condition. The drunk treatment led to an additional 5- to 10-point decline for some subjects, whereas other subjects performed about the same when drunk as when sleepy.

Subject	P_1 Normal	P_2 Sleepy	P_3 Drunk	Subject Averages
1	73	46	34	51
2	32	15	19	22
3	47	29	32	36
4	55	44	36	45
5	47	36	31	38
6	58	46	40	48

P Averages

52	36	32

Session Averages

T_1	T_2	T_3
42	37	41

Figure 8–2 Design and data matrix for driving study (fictitious data)

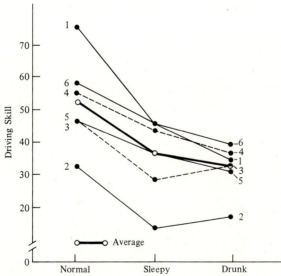

Figure 8–3 Graph of data for the driving study (fictitious data)

Planning a Within-subjects Design. What is the most appropriate description of the design for this study? It can be thought of as a one-way design because there is a single treatment factor. It can also be considered a two-factor design in which the subjects comprise the second factor; because all combinations of the treatment factor and the subject factor are included in the design, we can determine the extent of interactions between subjects and treatments. More about this point later. But there is also a third factor in the design: the session number. So we actually have a three-factor design.

Virtually every within-subjects design is a multifactor design. When a single treatment factor is the focus of the research, the initial planning of the study follows the scheme laid out in our discussion of one-way designs. The definition of the factor, the choice of levels, the selection of control groups all are virtually identical for between-subjects and within-subjects designs. When two or more treatment factors are to be included in a within-subject design, the guidelines for planning this part of the design would also follow the principles described in the preceding chapter. In addition to the selection of the factors and of levels of each factor, the investigator must give thought to the possibility of interactions. In both cases, after this portion of the planning is complete, additional steps must be implemented by the researcher using a within-subjects design.

Controlling for Order Effects

Because each subject is tested several times in a within-subjects design, it is essential to take into account the effects of changes over time. In some instances the materials may also change from one treatment to another; methods for controlling this factor are discussed later in the chapter.

Performance may change over repeated sessions for several reasons. The person may become better at the task through the opportunity to learn or through adaptation to the strangeness of the situation. Fatigue may set in over a long series of test trials. The novelty may disappear, with interest turning to boredom. Performance may improve and then decline, or any other pattern may appear, all for reasons unrelated to any treatment effects. The driving simulator may confuse the subject at first, then intrigue the subject when he or she gets the hang of it, and finally become a drag during the last session.

The effects of a treatment condition may depend upon the other conditions that have preceded it in the sequence. Suppose the driving sessions are on successive days. The subject whose normal condition comes after the martini session may perform less than optimally if that individual is prone to hangovers. And think about the person who has trouble handling liquor and is assigned to a sequence in which the martini session comes immediately before the no-sleep session!

The order factor may also influence the treatment effect, since the order factor and the treatment factor may interact. A treatment condition that produces no effect during the early sessions may have a substantial effect on performance once testing has gone on for a while, or vice versa. Subjects may experience so much difficulty learning how to handle the simulator during the first session that their physical condition has little effect on performance—or it may be especially important for the subject to be in tip-top shape during the initial experience with the task.

The main effects of the order factor can be handled relatively easily by **warm-up** and **counterbalancing** techniques. Interactions between the order factor and the treatment factor or complications due to the order of the treatment conditions are more difficult to control. They are hard to detect, and they hamper interpretation of the findings.

The researcher may choose to disregard order effects altogether, but this tactic is seldom wise. Suppose the order variable is neither controlled by the design nor taken into account during the analysis of the data. There is good chance that the treatment conditions will then be confounded with the order effects. In addition, changes over time will contribute to the unsystematic variability in the observations, making it more difficult to decide whether the treatment effects are trustworthy.

There are two basic techniques for controlling the effects of order. Both should be employed whenever possible.

Warm-up. The first step is to make sure that the subject is in a stable frame of mind before the experimental treatments begin. In general, within-subjects designs are not suitable for investigations of learning unless the goal is to examine how effectively one type of learning can be transferred to a different learning task. More often, the experimenter using such a design needs to minimize the amount of learning that takes place over the repeated sessions. It is therefore important to make sure that the subject understands the nature of the task before the experiment begins. The largest changes in performance often take place during the first few test sessions or trials; the subject is discovering what to do, anxiety is decreasing, novelty is wearing off. Most of these influences can be eliminated by a few practice trials under neutral conditions. In the driving study, for instance, it would probably be a good idea to give the subjects a practice drive prior to the beginning of the sequences shown in Figure 8–1, and then discard these data.

These warm-up precautions help to increase the control for any study. They are essential for within-subjects designs.

Counterbalancing. The second step in establishing control over order effects in within-subjects designs uses a technique known as **counterbalancing,** in which different subjects (or groups of subjects) are assigned to different sequential arrangements of the treatment conditions. In the driving study, the six different sequences provide a counterbalancing of the order factor. Whatever the main effects of order, they are equally distributed over the levels of the treatment factor and so cannot contaminate the measurement of the treatment effects. Interactions of order and treatment are not controlled by counterbalancing; neither are complications due to subject-by-order interactions or sequential effects. Counterbalancing does not eliminate the effects of the order factor; instead, it ensures that these effects are not confounded with the treatment conditions.

To understand better what counterbalanced designs can and cannot accomplish in the way of control, let us look at the simplest possible situation—one factor with two levels. As a concrete example, suppose the researcher is interested in the effect of type font on reading speed; the text is printed either in upper case (all CAPITAL LETTERS) or the more usual mixture of Upper and Lower case. The

Arrangement	Test I Passage A	Test II Passage B
m − U	Mixed Case	Upper Case
U − m	Upper Case	Mixed Case

Figure 8–4 Counterbalanced within-subject design for studying effects of typeface on reading speed. Treatment factor is balanced for effects of test order on passage.

experimenter prepares two passages of equal length and difficulty, one for the first reading and the other for the second.

Figure 8–4 shows a counterbalanced design that avoids confounding the treatment factor with the order of testing and the passage. In the m-U sequence, passage A in the mixed type font is read first, followed by passage B in upper case; sequence U-m reverses the order of the conditions. Note that order and passage have been purposely confounded in this study; the researcher is not interested in separating the effects of these two nuisance factors.

Two possible outcomes of this study are shown in Figure 8–5. Let us assume that several subjects are assigned to each of these sequences, so that the averages for each of the four conditions are stable. Outcome X, the left panel, shows that the treatment has a substantial and constant effect in both the sequences; the reading time is longer (reading is slower) for upper case at both the order–passage levels. The order–passage factor has an effect (there is improvement over time, or passage B is easier, or some combination of the two), but there is no evidence of an interaction between the treatment factor and the other two factors. These results are easily interpreted. The treatment is effective, and there is no reason to suspect either confoundings or interactions.

Outcome Y, the right panel, is problematical. There is an effect of type font (upper case is more difficult to read than mixed case, on the average), but the size of the effect changes considerably between the first test on passage A and the second test on passage B. One interpretation is that the uppercase text is difficult to handle when first encountered but that the effect diminishes as the subject gains experience with the type font. The passage might also be a determining influence, though this explanation seems less plausible. In any event generalizations about the effect of the type font cannot be made with any confidence from this pattern of results. Further research with a more comprehensive design is required, including the separation of the passage and the order factors, additional test sessions with additional passages, and more complete counterbalancing. Complicated patterns in the data require complicated research designs.

The Latin Square Method. In the driving and the type-font examples, counterbalancing was guaranteed by including in the design all possible sequences

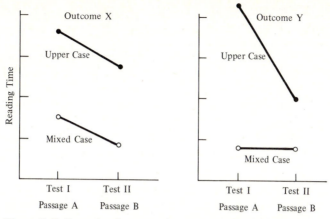

Figure 8–5 Example of two possible outcomes from study of effects of typeface on reading time. Interaction between control factors (order and passage) in panel Y raises problems in interpretation.

of the levels of the treatment factor. While this method ensures that the treatment and order factors are not confounded, it does create a problem: the number of different sequences goes up very rapidly as the number of levels increases. A two-level factor is simple, since there are only two sequences (the type-font study). With three levels the situation is still not too bad; as can be seen in the driving study, a three-level factor has six sequences, assuming that each level is tested just once.

When the treatment factor has four or more levels (or if a factorial treatment design has been planned), an experimental plan including all possible sequences rapidly becomes unmanageable and inefficient. A factor with k levels can be arranged in $k!$ (to be read as "k-factorial," which equals $k \times \{k - 1\} \times \{k - 2\} \ldots \times 2 \times 1$) sequences. For instance, a four-level factor has $4 \times 3 \times 2 \times 1$, or 24 sequences; a five-level factor requires $5 \times 4 \times 3 \times 2 \times 1$, or 120 sequences; and the list gets bigger very quickly. Testing more than twenty to forty subjects in a within-subjects design is generally inefficient, and so a four-level plan is the upper limit. Even in this instance, planning twenty-four different sequences is quite a chore.

The **Latin square method** provides an efficient alternative to the all-possible-sequences approach for counterbalancing the treatment factor and the order variable. As can be seen from the examples in Figure 8–6, a Latin square is literally in the shape of a square. A set of the possible sequences is selected, equal in number to the levels of the treatment factor and with the constraint that all levels of the treatment factor be included in each column and each row of the design. A three-level Latin square contains three of the six possible sequences, a four-level square has four of the twenty-four possible sequences, and so on.

To see how the method works, let us examine more carefully the 3×3 Latin square labeled plan X in the upper left corner of the figure, which is constructed

3 × 3

Latin Square X

Sequence	Time a	b	c
I	A₁	A₂	A₃
II	A₂	A₃	A₁
III	A₃	A₁	A₂

Latin Square Y

Sequence	Time a	b	c
I	B₁	B₃	B₂
II	B₃	B₂	B₁
III	B₂	B₁	B₃

Graeco-Latin Square

Sequence	Time a	b	c
I	A₁B₁	A₂B₂	A₃B₃
II	A₂B₃	A₃B₁	A₁B₂
III	A₃B₂	A₁B₃	A₂B₁

4 × 4

Latin Square X

Sequence	Time a	b	c	d
I	A₁	A₂	A₃	A₄
II	A₂	A₃	A₄	A₁
III	A₃	A₄	A₁	A₂
IV	A₄	A₁	A₂	A₃

Latin Square Y

Sequence	Time a	b	c	d
I	B₁	B₂	B₃	B₄
II	B₄	B₃	B₂	B₁
III	B₂	B₁	B₄	B₃
IV	B₃	B₄	B₁	B₂

Graeco-Latin Square

Sequence	Time a	b	c	d
I	A₁B₁	A₂B₂	A₃B₃	A₄B₄
II	A₂B₄	A₁B₃	A₄B₂	A₃B₁
III	A₃B₂	A₄B₁	A₁B₄	A₂B₃
IV	A₄B₃	A₃B₄	A₂B₁	A₁B₂

5 × 5

Latin Square X

Sequence	Time a	b	c	d	e
I	A₁	A₂	A₃	A₄	A₅
II	A₂	A₃	A₄	A₅	A₁
III	A₃	A₄	A₅	A₁	A₂
IV	A₄	A₅	A₁	A₂	A₃
V	A₅	A₁	A₂	A₃	A₄

Latin Square Y

Sequence	Time a	b	c	d	e
I	B₁	B₂	B₃	B₄	B₅
II	B₂	B₅	B₄	B₁	B₃
III	B₃	B₄	B₅	B₂	B₁
IV	B₄	B₃	B₁	B₅	B₂
V	B₅	B₁	B₂	B₃	B₄

Graeco-Latin Square

Sequence	Time a	b	c	d	e
I	A₁B₁	A₂B₂	A₃B₃	A₄B₄	A₅B₅
II	A₂B₃	A₃B₄	A₄B₅	A₅B₁	A₁B₂
III	A₃B₅	A₄B₁	A₅B₂	A₁B₃	A₂B₄
IV	A₄B₂	A₅B₃	A₁B₄	A₂B₅	A₃B₁
V	A₅B₄	A₁B₅	A₂B₁	A₃B₂	A₄B₃

6 × 6

Latin Square X

Sequence	Time a	b	c	d	e	f
I	A₁	A₂	A₃	A₄	A₅	A₆
II	A₂	A₃	A₆	A₁	A₄	A₅
III	A₃	A₆	A₂	A₅	A₁	A₄
IV	A₄	A₁	A₅	A₂	A₆	A₃
V	A₅	A₄	A₁	A₆	A₃	A₂
VI	A₆	A₅	A₄	A₃	A₂	A₁

Latin Square Y

Sequence	Time a	b	c	d	e	f
I	B₁	B₂	B₃	B₄	B₅	B₆
II	B₂	B₁	B₅	B₃	B₆	B₄
III	B₃	B₅	B₁	B₆	B₄	B₂
IV	B₄	B₃	B₆	B₁	B₂	B₅
V	B₅	B₆	B₄	B₂	B₁	B₃
VI	B₆	B₄	B₂	B₅	B₃	B₁

Figure 8–6 Latin and Graeco-Latin Squares for designs with three-, four-, and five-level factors and Latin Squares for six-level factor.

from three of the possible sequences of the treatment factor. Each sequence of this plan contains all three treatment levels, and each level occurs just once at each trial position. The three remaining sequences are used to construct plan Y, where once again each level of the treatment factor appears exactly once in each row (sequence) and column (trial). The reason for labeling the treatment factor as A in plan X and as B in plan Y will be made clear below in the discussion of the Graeco-Latin square.

Looking next at the 4 × 4 squares, you can see again that both plan X and plan Y are constructed so that each treatment level appears exactly once in each row and column, and similarly for the 5 × 5 and 6 × 6 squares. The 4 × 4 squares in the figure are only two of the possible plans that can be constructed; there are twenty-four different sequences, and so six different squares can be built. Complete sets of squares are described in a number of references (Fisher and Yates, 1970), but the selections in Figure 8–6 suffice for most purposes.

Here is how a Latin square plan is used to design an experiment. The size of the design (three-level, four-level, and so forth) is determined by the number of levels of the treatment factor. If there are five treatments, then the experimenter can select either plan X or plan Y at random (toss a coin; heads is X and tails is Y). Next, randomly shuffle the levels of the trial factor (*b* might wind up as trial 1, *d* as trial 2, *c* as trial 3, and *a* as trial 4). Experimenters tend to be systematic in numbering the levels of the treatment factor (level 1 is the easiest condition, level 2 next most difficult, and so on). The randomization of the levels of the time factor breaks up any such tendencies and also serves to eliminate any patterning due to the way the squares in the figure have been constructed. After the design has been selected and prepared, one or more subjects are assigned at random to sequences, an equal number to each sequence.

If a factorial treatment design is being used, a "dummy" factor can be constructed from the combinations and substituted into the plans in Figure 8–6. For instance, suppose a pair of two-level treatment factors are to be investigated—a two-by-two design. The four combinations in this plan are relabeled in random fashion as four levels of the dummy factor, and the procedures described above for constructing a 4 × 4 Latin square design are then followed. If the design is a two-by-three factorial (six combinations), then a 6 × 6 square is needed, and so on. For more extensive factorial designs, the experimenter should refer to the other sources mentioned above.

To summarize, the Latin square design is recommended when four or more treatment conditions are to be evaluated, when the experiment calls for a within-subjects design, and when efficient use of a relatively small number of subjects makes sense. The Latin square method requires blocks of subjects equal in number to the levels of the treatment factors; a four-condition study requires at least four subjects, a five-condition study at least five subjects, and so on. The basic design can then be replicated in blocks of the same size; a 4 × 4 design can be planned with four, eight, or twelve subjects or any other multiple of four subjects. These designs are compact, and replication is highly recommended.

The Graeco-Latin Square Method. The Latin square method provides an efficient technique for ensuring that the treatment and time factors are not confounded. As noted previously, within-subjects designs also may entail a change in materials from one test trial to another. The experimenter may choose to confound materials and time so that every subject receives the same sequence of materials; since time is counterbalanced with treatment, materials will also be counterbalanced. This approach was used in the study on the effect of upper- and lowercase type on reading time.

The experimenter may decide, on the other hand, that it is vital to separate the effects of all three factors: treatment, time, and materials. The Graeco-Latin method, an extension of the Latin square, can handle this job. Examples of Graeco-Latin squares for three-, four-, and five-level designs are displayed to the right in Figure 8–6. The experimenter might assign the treatment conditions to the levels of the A factor, and the four sets of materials to the levels of the B factor. The Graeco-Latin plan is constructed so that the A and B factors are balanced with each other as well as with both the rows and the columns. In fact, the Graeco-Latin squares in the figure are generally combinations of the X and Y plans (a caution—one cannot do this with every pair of Latin squares).

Graeco-Latin squares are used to design an experiment, utilizing the same procedures as with Latin squares—randomization of the time and materials and random assignment of one or more subjects to each of the sequences. These plans are highly compact, and although they do not permit the evaluation of interactions between any of the factors (and should not be employed if one suspects substantial interactions), they allow the investigator with limited time and resources to study multiple factors in an efficient and well-controlled situation.

An Example of a Graeco-Latin Experiment. The application of the Graeco-Latin method will be illustrated by a fictitious investigation of the effect of the layout of a telephone dial on the error rate in making a call. Figure 8–7 shows the four layouts. Types 1 and 2 are push-button styles whereas types 3 and 4 are rotary-dial styles; in types 1 and 3 the numbers are placed above the push buttons or outside the finger holes whereas in types 2 and 4 the numbers are on the buttons or inside the finger holes and hence are obscured when the number is dialed. We are representing dial type as a four-level treatment factor, but we could also view the plan as a 2×2 factorial, with push-button–rotary-dial and "view"–"nonview" as the levels of the two factors.

The experimenter decides on a within-subjects design, based on the judgment that there will be no carry-over effects from one level to another and the desire to obtain a sensitive assessment of the treatment factor. Subjects are presumed to have had considerable previous experience in dialing telephone numbers so that little change over test trials is expected. Nonetheless, the experimenter considers it prudent to use the Latin square method to control the time factor.

The materials for this study are the telephone numbers to be dialed. Are different numbers likely to affect the error rate? Perhaps so. Some telephone num-

Dial Type			
D$_1$	D$_2$	D$_3$	D$_4$

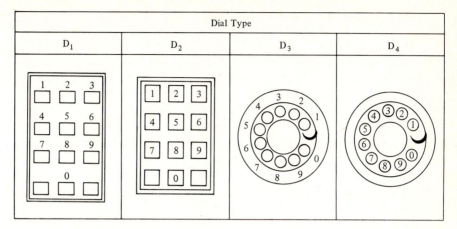

Figure 8–7 Stimulus materials for dialing study

bers are clearly easier to remember than others; 978-4391 is more likely to cause problems than 555-1001. The investigator selects four lists of fifty telephone numbers each in a midrange of difficulty, and even though the lists appear to be comparable in memorability, decides to use the Graeco-Latin method to control the number-list factor so that the effects of this factor can be separately evaluated. Accordingly, the four lists of numbers are assigned to the B factor in the Graeco-Latin plan. The four dial layouts are assigned to the levels of the A factor.

Figure 8–8 shows the layout of the 4 × 4 Graeco-Latin plan prepared for this study. The design from Figure 8–6 is the basis for the plan. The column factor (test trial) has been randomly rearranged, as recommended earlier (*b* is trial 1, *d* is trial 2, *a* is trial 3, and *c* is trial 4). Dial type (the A factor) and number list (the B factor) are displayed as combinations within the square. One subject is assigned at random to each of the four sequences that comprise the column factor.

Having decided on the design, the following procedures are employed: on each of the four trials, the subject is asked to dial each of fifty ten-digit numbers under the appropriate dial-type condition, with instructions that emphasize speed. The dependent measure is the number of dialings with one or more errors.

Also shown in the figure are the values of the dependent measure for this (admittedly fictitious) experiment. Only sixteen numbers; what can the researcher learn from them? The averages for each factor are shown in the figure, and inspection of these averages reveals some interesting patterns (and nonpatterns). Statistical tests provide quantitative backup to these generalizations (see the appendix), but the human eye is also a useful device for detecting trends.

The treatment factor, dial type, is of primary interest. Remember that the dependent measure is the number of errors—push-button layouts lead to fewer errors than rotary-dial types in this set of findings (D$_1$ and D$_2$ versus D$_3$ and D$_4$), and more errors are made if the dialer covers the number while dialing (D$_1$ and D$_3$

Sequence/ Subject	Trial Number				Sequence/ Subject
	1	2	3	4	
I	A_2B_2 22	A_4B_4 27	A_1B_1 18	A_3B_3 21	22.0
II	A_1B_3 17	A_3B_4 22	A_2B_4 17	A_4B_2 24	20.0
III	A_4B_1 31	A_2B_3 20	A_3B_2 19	A_1B_4 14	21.0
IV	A_3B_4 22	A_1B_2 15	A_4B_3 18	A_2B_1 13	17.0

Trial Number	1	2	3	4	Overall Mean
	23.0	21.0	18.8	18.0	20.0

A Factor (Dial Type)	1	2	3	4
	16.0	18.0	21.0	25.0

B Factor (Number List)	1	2	3	4
	21.0	20.0	19.0	20.0

Figure 8–8 Data and averages for dialing study

versus D_2 and D_4). The variation in this factor ranges from a low of sixteen errors to a high of twenty-five errors (about a 50 percent increase).

The trial factor has the next largest range of variation in errors (from eighteen to twenty-three). The general trend is for the error rate to decrease consistently over sessions; subjects become more accurate with practice, leveling out by the third and fourth sessions. The subject factor shows about the same variation as the trial factor, but since subjects are selected at random, it is difficult to say anything about this factor. The materials factor (the lists of phone numbers) makes little differ-ence in error rate; variation in the lists might have affected performance, but it did not.

This fictitious experiment contains only sixteen observations, but it demon-strates that from a handful of data, properly controlled, quite a bit of systematic information can be gleaned. In the present example, the use of the Latin square method permits the evaluation of four dimensions to the problem. While this method is efficient, it is important to be aware of both its strengths and weaknesses.

Pros and Cons of the Latin Square Method. As an efficient plan for evaluating the main effects of one or more factors while ensuring adequate control over other variables in a within-subjects design, the Latin square method has no equal. When time is short and resources are limited, this set of techniques provides maximum information at minimum expense. The inexperienced researcher tends to conduct preliminary investigations rather carelessly, with little attention to de-sign; the costs of a complete factorial design seem too much to pay when you are just a beginner or when you are planning a preliminary study in a new area of investigation. The Latin square method is preferable to the usual "no design at all." Nor is the method difficult to implement; the plans can be found in most statistical handbooks and the analysis is straightforward.

The Latin square method has its limitations, however. Whether this method is appropriate depends on the degree of independence between the interlocked factors; if there are interactions between subjects, sequence, treatments, trials, or materials, then the interpretation of the findings can be severely compromised. Since these designs do not permit evaluation of the interactions, there is no way for the researcher to determine from the data whether the assumption of negligible interactions is justified or not. Thus, if interactions are contributing to complica-tions in the data, the researcher may remain unaware of the problem.

For these reasons it is especially important to establish the highest degree of procedural control when using a Latin square plan. Instructions should be clear and subjects should be practiced before any data are collected. The researcher also needs to exercise special care in the management of the study. The designs are complex, rather like a house of cards, and a mistake in implementing any of the design combinations can jeopardize the counterbalancing of the plan.

MIXED DESIGNS

The decision to assign different subjects to each level of a factor or to test each subject on all levels of a factor must be made for each factor in a design. In the discussion thus far, we have considered designs in which all factors were either between-subjects or within-subjects. When, as is usually true in behavioral re-search, the experimental question calls for inclusion of two or more factors in the design, the investigator may decide to vary some factors in a between-subjects plan and other factors in a within-subjects arrangement. Such plans are called **mixed designs,** and a large proportion of current psychological research falls into this category.

When a research design is labeled "mixed," further description of the plan is required. The label means only that some factors are between-subjects and others are within-subjects; it is up to you as the reader to find out the status of each factor in the plan. In addition, you should keep in mind the need to counterbalance the within-subjects portion of the arrangement for the effects of time and/or materials, the latter two often being nuisance factors that may be overlooked in planning.

Mixed designs combine the efficiency and sensitivity of the within-subjects approach for those factors where this method is appropriate, with the resistance to carry-over effects of the between-subjects approach where this method is more suitable. In addition, subject-classification factors are inherently between-subjects, and so one often encounters studies in which one or more treatment factors are varied within-subjects, with individual differences being controlled by means of one or more subject-classification factors that are necessarily between-subjects.

We now use an elaboration of the dialing study to illustrate the concept of a mixed design and to demonstrate the descriptive methods for analyzing data from a mixed design. We then review the pros and cons of the between-subjects and within-subjects methods.

An Extension of the Dialing Study

The investigation of the relative efficiency of different configurations of the telephone dial presented earlier in the chapter had several shortcomings. First, the results would have been more easily interpretable if the four configurations had been treated as a 2×2 design rather than as a single four-level factor. This point was mentioned in passing; we now explore the advantages of the factorial approach. Second, with only a single subject assigned to each of the four sequences, the study lacked power; replication is called for. Third, the differences between subjects in overall error rate indicate that it might be useful to introduce a subject-classification factor into the design.

Figure 8–9 shows an improved plan for the dialing study, along with the data from the new design. This plan is one of the most complex that you will encounter in the text, so we will review the factors and the arrangement with some care.

In mixed designs it is a good idea to begin by describing the between-subjects portion of the plan and then lay out the within-subjects portion. There are three between-subjects factors in the present example. First there is the home-phone factor: whether a subject's home phone had a push-button or rotary dial. This factor serves as a control over the subjects' previous experience with the two styles. The choice of this factor to gain control over variability between subjects illustrates an important point: in deciding which subject-classification factors to include in a

		Sequence/ Subject	Trial Number				Sequence/ Subject
			1	2	3	4	
Home Phone	Push-button	I	$A_{BN}L_2$ 13	$A_{RN}L_4$ 29	$A_{BV}L_1$ 15	$A_{RV}L_3$ 23	20.0
		II	$A_{BV}L_3$ 9	$A_{RV}L_1$ 19	$A_{BN}L_4$ 17	$A_{RN}L_2$ 27	18.0
		III	$A_{RN}L_1$ 23	$A_{BN}L_3$ 11	$A_{RV}L_2$ 15	$A_{BV}L_4$ 11	15.0
		IV	$A_{RV}L_4$ 23	$A_{BV}L_2$ 13	$A_{RN}L_3$ 25	$A_{BN}L_1$ 15	19.0
	Rotary-dial	I	$A_{BN}L_2$ 19	$A_{RN}L_4$ 27	$A_{BV}L_1$ 21	$A_{RV}L_3$ 21	22.0
		II	$A_{BV}L_3$ 17	$A_{RV}L_1$ 19	$A_{BN}L_4$ 25	$A_{RN}L_2$ 27	22.0
		III	$A_{RN}L_1$ 29	$A_{BN}L_3$ 25	$A_{RV}L_2$ 21	$A_{BV}L_4$ 25	25.0
		IV	$A_{RV}L_4$ 19	$A_{BV}L_2$ 17	$A_{RN}L_3$ 21	$A_{BV}L_1$ 19	19.0

Trial Number				Overall Mean
1	2	3	4	
19.0	20.0	20.0	21.0	20.0

Figure 8–9 Plan for mixed design, effects of dial layout and home phone on error rate in dialing. Dependent measure is errors in a list of fifty numbers.

design, give priority to those factors that are *most directly related* to the problem under investigation. Gender, verbal ability, and a dozen other subject-classification factors might have routinely been chosen for use in this study simply because they are usually included as background factors in research; the type of phone the person uses most of the time, though an unusual factor, is especially appropriate for this study.

The investigator finds four subjects whose home phone is a push-button style and four whose phone is a rotary-dial type, and assigns the subjects in each of the two groups at random to the four sequences of the Graeco-Latin square from the previous study. The same square will be used for both subject groups; one might choose a different square for each of the groups, but it is not necessary. The four sequences comprise a between-subjects factor, as do the subjects assigned to each sequence. These factors will not be considered in the analysis, but they comprise the second and third between-subject factors in the design.

Now let us turn to the within-subjects factors. There are two treatment factors with two levels each: dial type (push-button versus rotary-dial) and placement of the numbers (in view or not in view). The four combinations of the dial and placement factors are assigned to the levels of A variable of the original Graeco-Latin square in Figure 8–8 as follows:

	A_1	A_2	A_3	A_4
Dial Type	Button	Button	Rotary	Rotary
Placement	View	Nonview	View	Nonview
Level	A_{BV}	A_{BN}	A_{RV}	A_{RN}

Notice that the A factor in Figure 8–9 has been subscripted for convenience with both the dial type and placement levels. The B variable from the original plan is used as in the previous study to control placement of the materials (the lists of telephone numbers) and has been relabeled for convenience as the L (for list) factor in Figure 8–9.

Putting all the pieces together, the within-subjects portion of the design has four factors: dial type, placement of numbers, lists, and trials. The first two factors are treatment variables of primary interest; the last two factors are nuisance variables. The treatment factors are crossed with one another, and each subject is tested on all four combinations. Confounding of the nuisance factors is controlled by the Graeco-Latin square design, which is replicated for the two levels of the home-phone factor.

Analysis of the Extended Dialing Study

In addition to displaying the design layout, Figure 8–9 shows fictitious data for this study. There is a pattern to the findings (I know, because I created the findings). Thirty-two observations are woven into a complex web by the intricate design. How can we untangle the web to find meaning in the data?

The answer to this question turns out to be rather simple. To analyze the data, the researcher begins by examining the main-effect averages for each factor, after which any interactions of particular interest are calculated. Anything left over represents the unsystematic variability from the study. Statistical procedures for carrying out this analysis in a formal manner are presented in the appendix; for now, a descriptive approach using averages will work well. The averages of most immediate interest are laid out in Figure 8–10. (The findings for trials, lists, and subjects—all

Dial Type		Push-button		Rotary-dial	
		Numbers in View	Numbers not in View	Numbers in View	Numbers not in View
Home Phone	Push-button	12.0	14.0	20.0	22.0
	Rotary-dial	20.0	26.0	20.0	26.0

		Dial Type	
		Button	Rotary
Home Phone	Push-button	13.0	23.0
	Rotary-dial	21.1	23.0

		Dial Placement	
		In View	Not in View
Home Phone	Push-button	16.0	20.0
	Rotary-dial	20.0	24.0

		Dial Type	
		Button	Rotary
Dial Placement	Not in View	16.0	20.0
	in View	18.0	26.0

Dial Type	
Button	Rotary
17.0	23.0

Dial Placement	
In View	Not in View
18.0	22.0

Home Phone	
Button	Rotary
18.0	22.0

Figure 8–10 Average performance for home phone study; interactions and main effects

nuisance factors—will be ignored in this analysis. In fact, they all turn out to be negligible sources of variation.) The table at the top of the figure shows the averages for the combinations of the treatment factor and the background information. Each of these eight averages is based on four observations—not too stable.

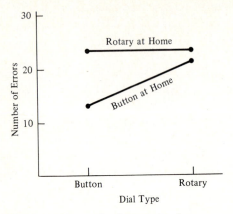

Figure 8–11 Graph of interaction between home-phone and dial-type factors

Spotting a pattern in "noisy" data is easy for the practiced eye, but it is safer to average over larger chunks of data—hence the two-way interaction tables below the top graph. But even before looking at these, let us first examine the main effects of the factors shown in the lower right corner. (Data analysis often proceeds in this fashion, averaging small chunks of data, then averaging those chunks, and so on until the main effect averages are calculated and then reversing the process, looking first at the biggest chunks, then at the simplest interactions, and so on to the most complex interactions of interest.)

Examination of the main trends from the tables in the lower right portion of the figure shows that the push-button layout produces fewer errors than the rotary-dial layout (17.0 versus 23.0 errors); fewer errors occur when the numbers are in view while dialing than when the finger hides the number (18.0 versus 22.0 errors); and subjects who are accustomed to the push-button style at home make fewer errors than those with rotary-dial phones at home (18.0 versus 22.0 errors). If there were no interactions, the difference between the best and the worst combinations would be quite substantial. A few errors here and there may not seem much, but they add up.

In fact, there is one interaction of consequence, which can be seen in the dial-type versus home-phone table. There is a 10-point difference in errors between the two dial types for subjects in the "push-button at home" category (13.0 versus 23.0 errors) and only a 2-point difference for the "rotary-dial at home" category. Interactions are often easier to comprehend when displayed visually, and so this interaction has been graphed in Figure 8–11. If you study the figure for a moment, you will see that in this laboratory experiment subjects who are accustomed to a rotary-dial make numerous errors with both dial types whereas individuals who have experience with the push-button style are much more accurate on this layout in the laboratory, while performing about the same on the rotary-dial as the other group of subjects. Once you have become accustomed to the push-button style, you are less likely to make errors in dialing on that style.

When both the main effects and the interaction are taken into account, it turns out that the systematic factors in this experiment make quite a difference in performance. If you examine the table of averages at the top of Figure 8–10, you will see that there is better than a two-to-one advantage of the optimum combination over the least effective combination; the error rate of the "dial button–numbers in view–home button" combination is less than half that of the "dial rotary–not in view–home rotary" combination (12.0 versus 26.0 errors).

The bottom line(s)? People are more accurate on the push-button configuration when dialing rapidly, but only when they have had considerable experience with this layout. The rotary-dial layout leads to more errors, especially when the numbers are placed inside the holes or on the buttons. A potentially complex "human engineering" problem, an efficient and tightly controlled design, and a simple set of findings (fictitious, to be sure).

CHOICE OF BETWEEN- OR WITHIN-SUBJECTS VARIATION IN A FACTOR

Now that you have seen examples of between- and within-subjects designs, as well as mixtures of the two, a comparison of the advantages and disadvantages of the two approaches is in order. Both methods are important in psychological research, and it is important for the researcher to recognize when the situation calls for one or the other method. Some of the pros and cons were established in Chapter 6 and are only reviewed here. Other points are new and are discussed in detail.

Advantages of the Within-subjects Method

Reduction in Unsystematic Variance. A major advantage of the within-subjects method for a factor is that its systematic effects can be weighed against the relatively small unsystematic variability from repeated measurements on the same subject rather than the relatively larger unsystematic variability due to individual differences between subjects. Making several observations on a single subject yields less variable data than the same number of observations on different subjects. This point was illustrated in Chapter 6 by the experiment on the effects of a "miracle drug" on short-term memory, an example that typified the benefits of reduced variability in a within-subjects design. Other things being equal, a within-subjects design gives a clearer picture of the treatment effects because the unsystematic variability within treatment conditions will be less than for a comparable between-subjects design. It is not unusual for within-subjects variability to be one-half to one-fifth the magnitude of between-subjects variability.

Convenience. A second reason for preferring a within-subjects design is the convenience of obtaining multiple measures from each individual. If considerable time is required for instructions and preliminary training on a task, then it makes sense to collect as much data as possible once the subject is prepared for the experiment. One must also take into account the amount of time required for each observation. If the measurement takes only a moment or so, as in the short-term memory task, then one can easily repeat the tests two or three dozen times and still use less than an hour to complete the entire experiment for a particular individual. On the other hand, suppose that the students in a psychology class have agreed to participate in an experiment, but the instructor has allowed only five minutes at the beginning of the class. Time is now at a premium, permitting only a few observations to be made. The limitation on time and the availability of a large number of subjects make it more convenient to plan a design in which most of the factors are between-subjects.

Essentiality. The nature of the experimental question may require that one or more factors be arranged according to a within-subjects plan. For instance, certain factors influence performance only when the subject has been assigned to different levels. The "incentive contrast" phenomenon illustrates this type of question. An experimenter is interested in the effects of payoff on problem-solving performance: do subjects improve when given a greater incentive? One group of subjects is simply asked to solve as many anagram problems as possible within a fixed time period. Three other groups are given the same task but are told that they will receive a penny, a nickel, or a dime, respectively, for each correct answer. Different subjects are assigned to each of the treatment conditions, which means that the incentive factor is a between-subjects variation. The research literature (Grice, 1966) suggests that the three groups will differ slightly or not at all. Given the relatively small amount of money involved, one should not be too surprised to discover that the incentive factor has no effect on performance.

Quite different results are likely to be obtained if the investigator employs a within-subjects design. Suppose each subject is tested in counterbalanced order under all four incentive conditions. The data are likely to reveal that the incentive factor has a marked effect. Moreover, the effects will vary depending on the ordering of the payoff conditions. Hence, this experimental question is *not* well suited to the Latin square method. If the subject receives a small payoff followed by a larger one, performance will improve (positive contrast). If the reverse sequence is used—a large payoff followed by a smaller one—then performance will decline (negative contrast). A penny may not seem like much in the abstract. If you have just been working for a nickel, however, it seems even smaller, whereas if you have been working for nothing, then a penny may seem like a lot. Subjects can make these comparisons only when they have experienced all levels of the incentive factor in a within-subjects design.

The within-subjects method may also be essential to evaluating a theoretical model. Consider a task in which the subject is given a fixed amount of time to study a list of words, after which recall is tested. Suppose the investigator has theorized that the number of facts recalled will increase in a straight-line fashion with the amount of study time permitted. The results in Figure 8–12 are consistent with the

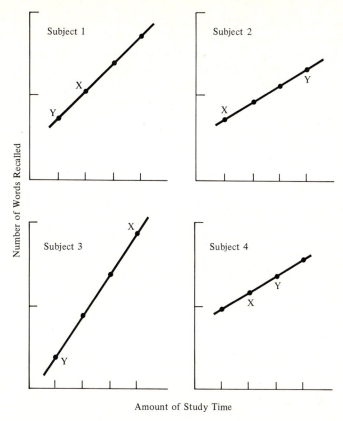

Figure 8–12 Data from four subjects in experiment on relation of study time to amount recalled. Some subjects learn at a faster rate than others, but the relationship is a straight line for every subject.

theory. These data are from a within-subjects design; measures are available for each subject at all levels of the study-time factor, and so individual patterns can be plotted and evaluated. Every subject exhibits the predicted straight-line relation between recall and study time. The rate of increase is greater for some subjects than for others, but the theory is nonetheless supported by the findings.

What if this study were carried out using a between-subjects plan? We will again resort to the "two experimenters" approach. Suppose two experimenters collected the data shown by the X and Y markers in the figure, with each subject tested at the level indicated by the markers. The results of the two between-subjects experiments are plotted in Figure 8–13. Experimenter X might be inclined to find support for the theoretical model because the data trace out a fairly straight path. Experimenter Y would be more likely to reject the theory or perhaps would conclude that there was an upper limit to the relation. In fact, neither experimenter would be justified in drawing either conclusion; the model can be tested only by within-

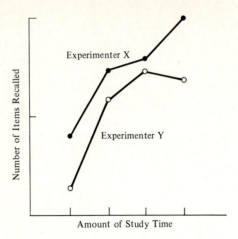

Figure 8–13 A between-subjects design may or may not reveal the character of the individual subject's performance (data are from Figure 8–12). Experimenter X's relation between study time and performance is a straight line. Experimenter Y suggests an upper limit on performance.

subjects variation in the study-time factor *unless* one can assume that individuals do not vary in response to the study-time factor—a most unlikely assumption.

Disadvantages of the Within-subjects Method

The major flaw of the within-subjects approach is the possibility that one treatment condition will contaminate another and will do so in such a fashion that the investigator will be unable to assess these contaminations. As seen in the incentive-contrast experiment, sometimes the researcher may be interested in such contaminations. If carry-over effects are *not* of interest, however, or if the researcher mistakenly assumes that such effects are negligible, then the results of a within-subjects variation may be seriously compromised. Under these conditions the between-subjects methods is preferable.

Within-subjects plans are also jeopardized when the researcher fails to control for the effects of time and materials. Techniques for counterbalancing these factors were described above, but sometimes they may seem to be too much trouble. A "penny saved" perhaps, but poor economy in many instances: "penny wise and pound foolish."

Finally, the potential increase in sensitivity from a within-subjects design will be realized only to the extent that most subjects respond in roughly comparable fashion to the treatment factor. It is possible, however, that subjects will react to treatments in diverse ways. Such diversity may be a genuine characteristic of the factor, and the discovery of individual differences in response to variation in a factor can be of considerable importance. In other instances the differences may simply reflect a lack of control over the subjects' understanding, motivation, and background. The experimenter can take several steps to reduce unwanted interactions between subjects and treatments: selection of subjects who are more or less comparable (or introduction of subject-classification factors to control for differences in selection), practice in performing the experimental task so that everyone is equally familiar with the situation, clear instructions, and the establishment of a constant level of motivation and attention for all subjects. If these precautions are observed and subject–treatment interactions still appear in the data, the researcher may reasonably conclude that the interactions are genuine and merit more intensive investigation.

Pros and Cons of the Between-subjects Method

The chief advantage of the between-subjects approach is that there is little chance for performance under one level of the factor to be influenced by other levels—the subject experiences only one level of the factor. Neither is there need for much concern about practice or fatigue, or any of the other changes that may occur over repeated tests. But the experimenter still needs to worry about individual differences in readiness, motivation, and attention, even though the subject is tested only once.

The nature of the experimental problem may dictate that the subject be tested under only a single level of the treatment factor. For instance, people learn, and they also learn how to learn. Once a subject has acquired a paired-associate list under one set of conditions, the learning of subsequent lists is likely to be influenced by the initial experience. The experimenter may be interested in the patterns of transfer, in which case a within-subjects plan is called for. Otherwise, learning studies typically require a between-subjects plan.

Even a between-subjects plan is not a guarantee of no contamination between treatment conditions. People talk to one another. If subjects all pass through the same waiting room, then the chances for "crosstalk" can be substantial, and subjects may perform differently depending on the particular levels they are expecting and the levels they actually experience. Even though the investigator takes appropriate precautions to keep crosstalk to a minimum, the between-subjects arrangement still does not ensure the independence of treatments. Some years ago, a researcher on a college campus began to study the effects of various mnemonic strategies on the rate of learning strings of unrelated words. For instance, suppose you are asked to recall the following list: *monkey, umbrella, bicycle, cigar, cape, tiger, saddle*. The task becomes much easier if you form a visual image of the items in the list—imagine a monkey, put an umbrella in its hand, place it on a bicycle, stick a cigar in its mouth, add a cape flowing in the breeze, bring a tiger into the picture in full pursuit, and finally saddle the tiger. A bizarre image, but a vivid one that helps you to recall the list.

Once a college student has learned a strategy like the one just described, it is virtually impossible to forget it—not just the word list but the strategy. Whenever a list of unrelated words is presented, the subject will be inclined to visualize the words in relation to one another. Thus, comparison of mnemonic and non-mnemonic conditions clearly requires a between-subjects plan. In addition, the experimenter must hope that subjects do not talk to one another; otherwise subjects assigned to the nonmnemonic conditions may actually be using the mnemonic approach. Even more problematically, what about other experimenters on the same campus who want to study the free recall of lists of unrelated words? In one instance with which I am familiar, in which mnemonic techniques were investigated, other psychologists on the same campus began to encounter subjects who recalled their experimental lists perfectly after only one or two trials. The mnemonic experiment made it impossible to investigate "nonsense learning" on the entire campus! Even a between-subjects design was not sufficient in this instance; a between-campus variation was needed.

VISUAL AND MEMORY SEARCH: A LABORATORY EXPERIMENT

Several examples of within-subjects designs have been used thus far in the chapter to illustrate the principles of the within-subjects approach, both in "pure" form and in mixed designs. All the examples have been fictitious for purposes of simplicity and also because researchers often provide only a brief sketch of the actual design in writing up research using within-subjects variation in factors. In the remainder of the chapter, two "real" studies are reported. A laboratory study in which all factors were within-subjects is discussed in this section and will be followed by a field study using a mixed design.

Background. You glance quickly through a phone directory for a friend's name. What mental activities are ongoing as you search through the list? You have bought four tickets in a door-prize contest. Along with others at the party, you listen as the prize number is announced—242–42–78–70. It takes a moment for you to confirm that you are not the winner. Again, what happens in your mind as you compare the announcement with your memory for the numbers on your ticket stub?

The two situations described above typify tasks that have been studied under the rubrics of visual and memory search. Investigation of performance on these laboratory tasks has led to the development of some remarkably simple theories about how human beings process information. The full story has implications that go far beyond the simple experiments to be presented here. For present purposes,

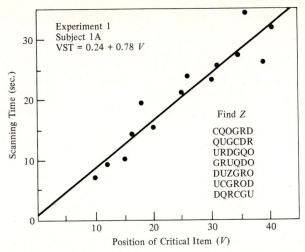

Figure 8–14 Visual search scanning time as a function of the position of the target items in a list. Visual search time per item is the slope of the straight line. (Data of Neisser, 1963)

however, we focus only on the role of within-subjects methods in this area of research.

Visual Search. In 1963 Ulric Neisser reported the first of several studies that he and his colleagues were to conduct over the next several years. The task and a sample finding are shown in Figure 8–14. The subject was told to look for a target letter (for instance, "Find Z") and then a list of letter strings was displayed. The subject scanned the list from top to bottom; as soon as the target letter was spotted, he or she pushed a button. Several lists were scanned in this fashion, with the position of the target letter varying from one list to the next; sometimes it was near the top, sometimes in the middle, sometimes near the bottom.

The results in Figure 8–14, which are typical, begin with a graph of the search time as a function of the position of the critical letter in the list. For instance, if the Z is in the fifteenth line from the top, subject 1A takes about ten seconds to locate it, a Z in the thirtieth string down is spotted in a little less than twenty-five seconds, and so on.

The most interesting feature of these data is that the *visual search time* increases in a straight-line fashion with the position of the target letter in the list. The simplest explanation of the findings is that the subject examines each string for a brief but constant amount of time, during which the letters in each string are compared with the target letter stored in memory. If the target letter is in position V, then the visual search time will be

Visual Search Time = $b + cV$

In this equation b is the "base" time for getting started and making the response, V is the number of strings that have to be scanned, and c is the time to compare the letters in each string with the target letter in memory.

The graph of the Neisser data is reported in seconds. In fact, because the mental processes operate in split-second fashion in this task, the times are more often reported in milliseconds (thousandths of a second). The results in Figure 8–14 show that the subject's base level was 240 milliseconds (roughly a quarter-second) and that the subject took 780 milliseconds (about three-quarters of a second) to search each line to determine whether it contained the target letter. Since there were six letters per line, this subject (who was slower than average) took 130 milliseconds per letter to compare each letter in the string with Z, the target letter.

Neisser and his colleagues carried out several other investigations to determine the generality of the model. In most situations and for most subjects, visual search appeared to be a serial, "one line at a time" mental process, as predicted by the theoretical equation. With practice, subjects did become faster at scanning each string. The base time remained fairly constant, but the value of c, the search time, dropped to 100 milliseconds per string after a few weeks of training.

Memory Search. About the same time that Neisser was reporting his work on visual search, Sternberg (1963) reported the results of several studies on memory search. In Sternberg's task, the subject was given a list of either letters or numbers to memorize; each list usually contained no more than six items. After memorizing the list, the subject was given a series of test trials, each of which displayed a test item. The subject was to respond as quickly as possible, "yes" if the test item was on the memorized list and "no" if it was not.

Figure 8–15 shows the results of Sternberg's first investigation of memory search. *Memory search time*, the reaction time for responding after the display of the test item, is plotted as a function of the number of items in memory. These and other results showed that reaction time in this task increased in a straight-line fashion with the number of test items stored in memory. Sternberg proposed a simple model of performance, remarkably similar to Neisser's model for visual search, in which memory search time is a combination of a base time and a series of memory comparisons:

Memory Search Time = $b + cM$

In this equation, b is the base time (to get started and to make the response), M is the number of items in the memorized list, and c is the time to check each item in memory.

The results in Figure 8–15 were confirmed in a large number of studies. Estimates of c, the comparison time, ranged on the average from 35 to 50 milliseconds. Visual search studies by Neisser and others found that the comparison time per letter by relatively inexperienced subjects ranged on the average from 20 to 60

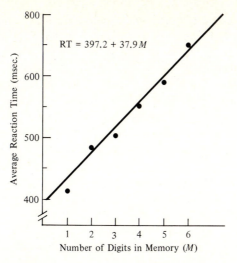

Figure 8–15 Memory search time as a function of the number of target items in memory. Memory search time per item is the slope of the straight line. (Data of Sternberg, 1963)

milliseconds. The similarity of the comparison times in the Neisser and Sternberg studies led several investigators to conclude that the critical stage in both visual and memory search tasks is the comparison stage, the amount of time that it takes the subject to determine if a pattern stored in memory matches a stimulus in the visual field.

Combining Visual and Memory Search. What happens when visual and memory search tasks are combined in a single investigation? The subject memorizes a list items and then sees a visual array with several items. Do any of the items in the visual display match any of the items in memory? A straightforward extension of the two preceding models leads to a simple prediction: search time for the combined task should be the sum of the base time and the total number of comparisons to be made:

Combined Visual–Memory Search Time = $b + c$VM

As in the previous models for visual and for memory search, b is the base time, V is the number of items in the visual set, M is the number of items in the memory set, and c is the time to make each comparison. This model describes reaction time for the "negative" trials, on which none of the memory items matches any item in the visual display. Why must V × M comparisons be made? Let us consider the situation in which the subject has stored two items in memory and sees four items in the visual display. The subject selects the first item in the display and compares it in turn with each item in memory; two comparisons are made (it is a negative trial, and so we can be sure that there will be no matches along the way). This operation is repeated for each of the three remaining items in the visual display, making a total of 4 × 2 or 8 comparisons. In general, the subject must make M comparisons for each of the V items in the array, hence V × M comparisons, each requiring c milliseconds.

The equation above describes a *plane* (a flat, two-dimensional "sheet") in three-dimensional space—Figure 8–16 shows what the equation looks like for a situation with visual and memory set sizes of 1, 2, and 4 items. The "subfloor" of the graph lays out the two treatment factors, visual set size and memory set size. On top of this subfloor is the base time, which is the foundation for comparisons. Finally, the plane of the comparison times rests on top of the foundation, showing how performance varies with the different combinations of the two factors, assuming that the rather simplistic model is a reasonable approximation to what actually happens in the mind.

The Schneider–Shiffrin Experiment

Design. Several experiments have been carried out to test this model. A study by Schneider and Shiffrin (1977) provides an especially good example of the application of the within-subjects method for investigating this task.

Two factors are combined in a factorial within-subjects plan: visual set size (1, 2, or 4 letters) and memory set size (1, 2, or 4 letters). Figure 8–17 shows the procedure for two cells from this design. A series of displays was presented to the subject in a carefully programmed sequence. The subject controlled the display of each card in the series. First the memory set was presented for study. Then the subject was shown a fixation point—a dot to steady the gaze. Next a test card was presented, which either contained an item from the memory set (a positive trial) or had no items from the memory set (a negative trial). The negative trials are especially critical for evaluating the model, because on these trials the subject must examine every item in the visual display. The dependent measure was the reaction time between display of the test card and the subject's response. Twenty trials were carried out in this fashion for a given memory set, ten positive and ten negative trials. A new memory set was then presented for study. All nine combinations were tested several times, with a large number of random selections of materials; the investigator depended on the numerous replications to control for the effects of order and materials.

Findings. The results of the Schneider–Shiffrin study are displayed in Figure 8–18 (page 235). The dots at the top of the "posts" in the three-dimensional plot show the reaction time for negative trials on each of the nine combinations of the 3 × 3 factorial design. The reaction times are superimposed on the theoretical

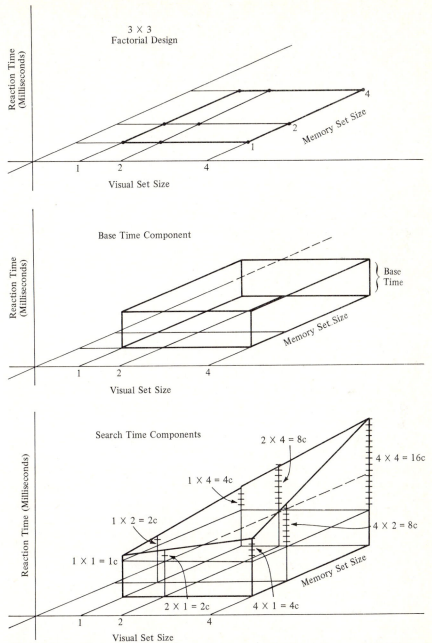

Figure 8–16 Design (top panel) and theoretical model (middle and lower panels) for within-subjects experiment on visual and memory search. Middle panel shows addition of base time to design; lower panel shows addition of memory and visual search time components to base time.

MEMORY SET SIZE 2   VISUAL SET SIZE 4

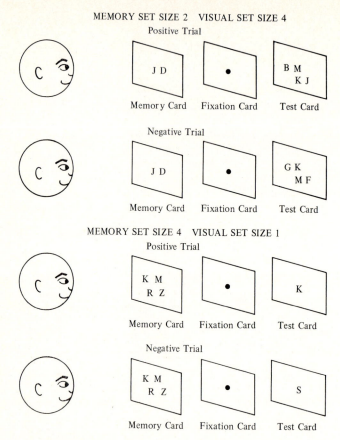

Figure 8–17 Experimental procedure used by Schneider and Shiffrin (1977) to study visual and memory search

predictions shown earlier, which were calculated to provide the best fit of the model to this particular set of data. The base time is 420 milliseconds and the comparison time 55 milliseconds. Simple though the theory may be, it provides a good account of the results of this study. The margin of error, compared with the range of variation due to the effects of the treatment factors, is negligible. One can imagine far more complex theories of the mental activities underlying visual–memory search time, but this simple, almost mechanistic model provides a satisfactory explanation of the performance in this experiment.

Several other experiments are described in the Schneider–Shiffrin paper. The procedures, materials, and subjects vary, but the results are all similar to those reported above. The authors present a theoretical analysis akin to the one presented in this chapter, with some refinements. Their conclusion is similar: one can describe performance on the visual–memory search task by a relatively simple model based on sequential comparisons. The predictions of the Schneider–Shiffrin model

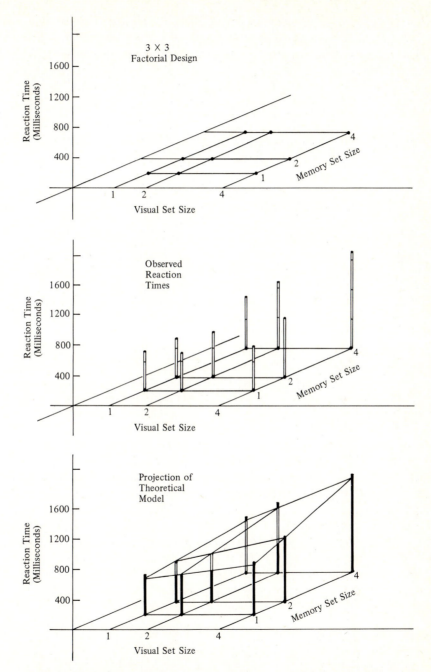

Figure 8–18 Design (top panel), results (middle panel), and theoretical predictions (bottom panel) for within-subjects experiment on visual and memory search. (Data of Schneider and Shiffren, 1977)

are accurate, both on the average *and* for individuals. The within-subjects method is critical both in the planning and the interpretation of the experiment. Assigning different subjects to the various combinations would not have guaranteed the sensitivity needed to detect effects in the millisecond range, nor would the results have provided assessment of individual differences in performance. Using the within-subjects method, both goals were achieved with remarkable success.

ENHANCING RECALL THROUGH NOVELTY: A FIELD STUDY OF MEMORY FOR TELEVISION NEWS

The von Restorff Effect

Any event that grabs our attention is likely to be well remembered. Von Restorff was the first to document this effect (1933; Wallace, 1965). His subjects studied a list of paired-associates that they knew they would be asked to recall later on. Midway through the study list, a pair was displayed that differed in some distinctive way from the preceding pairs—the words in the novel pair might be printed in red ink or in capital letters, for instance. The results showed that subjects made virtually no errors in recall of the novel pair.

Researchers have employed the von Restorff technique in numerous investigations of the effects of attention on memory (for an unusual application, see Loftus and Marburger, 1983). The operation of this effect is now reasonably well understood. For instance, emphasizing a stimulus will lead the subject to give it higher priority in memory, but at the cost of assigning lower priority to other stimuli; the subject may rob Peter to pay Paul, but without any real increase in the total amount recalled. The effect is therefore greatest when a single stimulus is distinguished in some manner—von Restorff's original technique. If two stimuli are selected for emphasis, both tend to be better recalled than the other items in the list, but neither is as well recalled as when a single item is emphasized. Waugh (1969) found that the von Restorff effect was still observable, but only barely so, when as many as ten items were emphasized in a free recall task. The research also suggests that the effect is automatic. The subject does not have to be put on the alert for unusual stimuli, nor is the effect noticeably enhanced if the subject is informed about the procedure.

Release from Proactive Interference

The von Restorff effect has also been investigated under the rubric of "release from proactive interference." This mouthful of jargon calls for translation. *Interference* in memory occurs when the subject's effort to remember one piece of information gets in the way of storing or retrieving another piece of information. *Proactive* means "forward reaching." Thus, proactive interference refers to situations in which the subject studies one piece of information and then has difficulty in successfully studying another chunk of information presented later in the session because the first piece of information "reaches forward" in time to influence the second. It is, of course, the person's memory of the first piece of information that does the "reaching."

For instance, you memorize the telephone number of a friend (998-6843) at 9:00 in the morning; you must call the person at 3:00 P.M. regarding a dinner engagement. After lunch, you find your car has been sideswiped, and so your lunch partner gives you the telephone number of a body work specialist. It is 989-6438. Later in the afternoon, when you try to make the two calls, you discover that you are unsure about the repair shop number.

Proactive interference is a common phenomenon in within-subjects studies of memory. When a series of word lists is studied one after the other, recall is best for the first list in the series and declines steadily over subsequent lists. Keppel and Underwood (1962), who were among the first to describe this phenomenon, theorized that each list leaves a residue in the memory that hampers the storage and retrieval of new information. The interference effect stabilizes fairly quickly; after half a dozen lists, performance levels out and there are no further declines.

Release from proactive interference (Wickens, 1970) occurs when the experimenter changes the situation so as to eliminate the deleterious influence of previous lists. You can think of the phenomenon as a von Restorff effect for word lists. In a typical laboratory experiment on *release*, Wittlinger (1967) tested short-term memory using a within-subjects design. Several experiments were carried out. In one, the subject briefly studied a string of three consonants (e.g., J V M), spent twenty seconds on a difficult discrimination task, and then tried to write down the list of consonants in the correct order. Eight lists were studied and recalled in this fashion.

Release events were introduced on the fourth and seventh lists in the series. On the fourth list, numbers (e.g., 3 7 2) appeared rather than consonants; on the seventh list, consonants then replaced the numbers. Wittlinger's findings in Figure 8–19 show the development of proactive interference (the drop in percent recalled from the first to the second list), and the release caused by changing the materials on the fourth and seventh lists.

Wittlinger's results are fairly typical. Bjork (1970) made an intriguing contribution to this question when he showed that release would occur if the tester simply told the subject at some point in a list to "forget everything you have studied up to this point in the experiment." Subjects were able to comply with the request, showing clear improvement in recall of the list following the instructions to forget.

Bjork concluded that the experiment demonstrated the "power of positive forgetting":

> The positive function of any such forgetting mechanism is to prevent information no longer needed from interfering with the handling of current information. Consider the information-processing task faced by the typical short-order cook. He [or she, et seq.] must process one by one a sequence of orders that have high interorder similarity [i.e., many of the orders have elements in

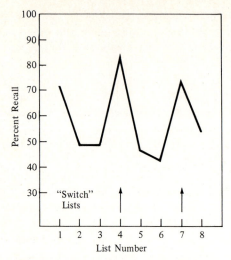

Figure 8–19 Release from proactive interference. Subject is switched from consonant trigrams to three-digit numbers (or vice versa) at lists 4 and 7. (Data of Wittlinger, 1967)

common]. Once he is through with "scramble two, crisp bacon, and an English," his later processing of similar but not identical orders can only suffer to the degree that he has not, in effect, disregarded that order. (Bjork, 1970, p. 265)

The Television News Study

Design. The experiment to be described here uses the release-from-proactive-interference procedure to investigate the factors that affect memory for television news. Practical interest in the findings is obvious. News programs can be boring, and it is of commercial importance to discover how variations in style and content can keep viewers alert, interested, and "tuned in."

Gunter, Clifford, and Berry (1980) used a mixed design to investigate the problem. The between-subjects factors were *release* (change or no-change), *type of change* (topic or format), and *initial conditions* (politics or sports for topic, studio-only or studio-plus-still-photographs for format). The within-subjects factors were *item/trial number* (1 through 4), and *time of recall* (immediate or delayed).

The complete layout of the design (Figure 8–20) appears formidable at first glance. Let us therefore go through the first few rows, after which the rest of the plan should be apparent. The top rows lay out the plan for the within-subjects factors, immediate or delayed recall and the trial number. The next row describes the sequence of events for the first of the between-subjects combinations: change in

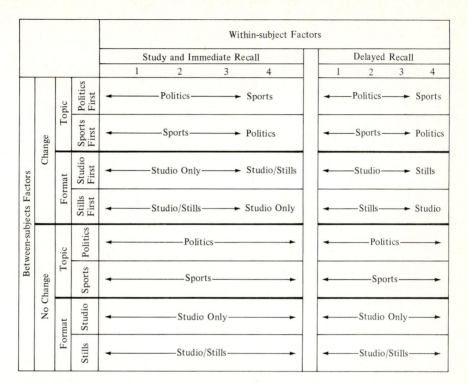

Figure 8–20 Design of release from proactive interference in television news viewing (Gunter et al., 1980). Within-subject factors are listed as column headings, between-subject factors as row headings.

topic with politics first. Subjects in this condition began by studying a series of three news items on the topic of politics. Each news item was a fifteen- to thirty-second television broadcast consisting of three separate segments. After each broadcast the subject had two minutes to write as much as he or she could remember from the broadcast. By the end of the third broadcast in the series, the subjects had viewed a total of nine snippets dealing with political events. The fourth broadcast was then presented without comment; it also contained three segments, but the topic changed to sports. After completing the report of the fourth broadcast, the subject was distracted momentarily and was then asked to recall the entire series of four broadcasts. The delayed recall was unexpected; subjects had been led to believe that they had finished the study after they recalled the fourth broadcast.

The same basic procedures were followed for all the other between-subjects combinations. Some of the combinations provide counterbalancing (that is, the combination below the one just described is identical except that sports is the first topic with a change to politics).

The change-in-format conditions relied on a different technique to generate release from proactive interference. Subjects either saw a newscaster reading the news in a bare studio (studio-only) or saw the newscaster with still photographs interspersed to provide a visual backup to the news (studio-plus-stills). One or the other of these conditions was in effect for the first three broadcasts, and then there was a switch to the other condition on the fourth broadcast. The no-change conditions were similar to the change conditions described above except that neither topic nor format changed.

Findings. The major findings of the study are presented in Figure 8–21, which shows performance averaged over the counterbalancing variations. The results are consistent, clear-cut, and rather intriguing. Recall of the broadcasts declined steadily over the series, reflecting the impact of proactive interference. Immediate recall dropped from 85 percent on the first broadcast to 50 percent on the fourth broadcast in the no-change condition. Changing conditions on the fourth broadcast markedly reversed this decline. A change in topic greatly increased recall; changing the format produced a smaller but still noticeable improvement in performance. The detailed report in the original article indicated that the relatively small enhancement with a change in format results when studio-plus-still was changed to studio-only. In this condition the character of the broadcast was not so much changed as diminished; the still photographs were eliminated and only the newscaster remained. This "change" did not stop the decline in performance, probably because the treatment was not perceived as a change.

The trends described above for immediate recall are even more noticeable on the delayed test. Recall of the fourth broadcast is virtually doubled when a change is introduced, compared with the no-change condition. Moreover, this enhancement occurs at little or no cost to the recall of the three preceding broadcasts—remember that the von Restorff effect usually entails a decline in memory for the non-novel items in a list.

Rapidly paced and constantly changing scenes are generally thought to increase the attractiveness and interest value of a television program; you will see this principle in action if you watch "Sesame Street." The Gunter et al. (1980) study shows that these variations also improve the recall of the substance of the broadcasts. The effectiveness of this strategy may have its limitations. Even novelty can become old hat. Nor do the results of this experiment establish the long-term benefits of the technique. Recall after a few moments is one thing, but what about recall after an hour, a day, or a week? Moreover, the critic can properly complain that the design does not rule out a variety of alternative interpretations. Is the improved performance due to a reduction in memory interference (as claimed), a lessening of boredom ("See one sportscast and you've seen them all"), an increase in motivation ("Wow, that was new and exciting!"), or any number of other possibilities? By now, you can probably imagine ways to improve the design to assess these other interpretations.

This study demonstrates the importance of both the between-subjects and the within-subjects methods and the application of the counterbalancing principle. The release phenomenon can be observed only when the subjects are repeatedly tested.

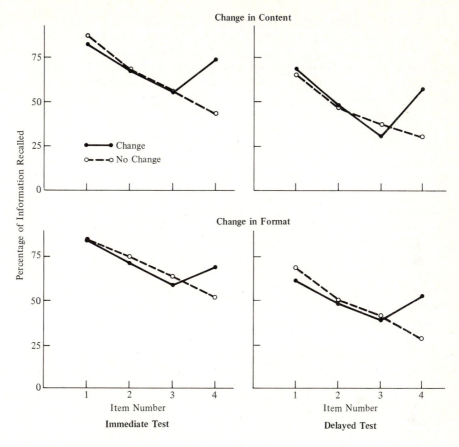

Figure 8–21 Release from proactive interference in television newscasts. Subjects in change conditions saw different content or format on fourth item, with positive effects on immediate and delayed recall compared with no-change conditions.

Though the experimenters in this study decided to assign different subjects to the content and format shifts, variation in the type of change might have been planned either as a between- or a within-subjects variation. Counterbalancing required between-subjects variations. The study illustrates nicely how to handle a complex set of decisions in the selection of factors and the arrangement of the conditions. The payoff is a simple but trustworthy set of findings, easily interpreted, and with the potential of practical benefit.

SUMMARY

This chapter discussed designs in which, for one or more of the factors in an experimental plan, individual subjects were tested on all levels of a factor. Within-subjects designs (in which all factors are arranged in this fashion) and mixed designs (in which some factors are arranged in this fashion, and other factors are arranged with different subjects assigned to each treatment condition) play an important role in psychological research. Variation over repeated measures on the same individual are generally smaller than differences between individuals, and so within-subjects variation provides a more sensitive index of treatment effects than does between-subjects variation, a point made in Chapter 6.

Within-subjects variation in a factor may be more convenient. If it takes a substantial amount of time to prepare a subject to perform in a study, and only a moment or two to make an observation in a particular treatment condition, then it makes sense to test the subject under several treatment combinations. Certain experimental questions can be answered only when comparisons are made within the individual. For instance, the effect of a treatment factor may appear only when the subject can make comparisons between treatment conditions, as in the incentive-contrast experiment. As another example, evaluation of theoretical predictions about patterns of individual performance may require within-subjects variation in a factor.

Within-subjects variation is to be avoided if contamination of one treatment condition by another will alter the treatment effects. Learning studies are generally not good candidates for within-subjects designs unless the intention is to investigate the transfer of learning under one set of conditions to learning in a new situation.

When a within-subjects plan is employed for a factor, the researcher needs to be concerned about confoundings with time and materials factors. These two factors often fall into the nuisance category, but they need to be controlled nonetheless. Two procedures exist for handling this problem. First, the influence of time can be minimized by providing warm-up—preliminary practice on the task to ensure that the subject understands what is to be done and to minimize the effects of novelty. Second, the researcher can distribute the effects of time and materials over the levels of the treatment factors by counterbalanced designs. One approach to counterbalancing is to assign different groups of subjects to all possible sequential arrangements. This approach works well when the number of treatment conditions is small but becomes unworkable when four or more conditions are to be evaluated because of the rapid increase in the number of different sequences.

Latin square and Graeco-Latin square designs provide an efficient method of counterbalancing when the number of conditions is five or more, especially when resources are limited. The Latin square approach employs designs in which subjects are assigned to carefully arranged plans, in which each treatment appears exactly once for each subject and for each trial. These designs do not permit the assessment of interactions between the treatment and the trial factors, nor can the experimenter tell if there are sequential interactions such that the effect of one treatment condition depends on the other treatment conditions that have been previously experienced. When the researcher is reasonably certain that the various factors operate independently of one another, the Latin square is an efficient technique for obtaining a great deal of well-controlled information at relatively low cost. It is not appropriate when the relations between factors may be complex.

Mixed designs are those in which some factors are within-subjects and other factors are between-subjects. Such designs, which are increasingly common in psychological research, require the reader to determine the status of each factor. A frequent pattern is for each subject to be tested on all combinations of one or more treatment factors (the within-subjects portion of the design), with groups of subjects selected according to one or more subject-classification factors comprising the between-subjects portion of the design. In analyzing more complex designs of this type, the best practice is to begin by examining the main effects for each of the factors in the design, then look at the various two-way interactions for evidence of additional complexities and proceed on to the higher-order interactions only if necessary.

9

How to Study a Research Report

In Chapter 2 a distinction was made between skimming a research report and studying it. When the goal is to decide quickly whether you need to study it, you should search rapidly for key words and ideas while simultaneously evaluating the overall relevance and quality of the article. For this task you will rely primarily on summary information, topic sentences from selected paragraphs, and tables and figures.

Once you have decided to study a report, the task is to untangle a tightly written composition, one that has a predictable structure but that requires you to examine each element with a searching and critical eye. Studying a research paper is an active process of organizing the elements in a way that makes sense to you. The task of reading the first paper may take hours, a discouraging prospect. When you tackle the next article, however, the territory will seem more familiar, and with experience and practice you will become more adept. Technical literature is demanding by nature, though, and reading a research paper never becomes easy.

In this chapter you will learn how a research report is put together, what pieces of information to look for in the various sections of a report, and how to extract what you need to know. You will also learn a strategy for studying a report. A critical feature of this strategy is that you begin by reflecting on your specific purposes for studying the article. Different purposes call for different actions, and it is important to be as clear as possible at the outset about what you consider to be your needs.

THE CONTENTS OF THE RESEARCH REPORT

What to Look for in a Report

There are six basic pieces of information that you should look for when studying a research paper:

1. What is the experimental problem?

2. What is the design?

3. What is the subject's task?

4. How have the data been analyzed?

5. What are the results?

6. What do the results mean?

Each of these questions will be examined in turn, and you will then learn where in a research paper to look for the answers. You may sense some redundancy in the next two portions of the chapter. This is intentional. There *is* some overlap between the way you as the reader search for information in a research paper and the way such reports are organized by the writer. The two matters are not, however, identical. The ideal situation is described in the APA publication manual: ". . . the sections [of a research report] are distinct, [but] their content is interrelated, so smooth transitions and integration of the parts of a paper are essential to a clear presentation of ideas" (APA, 1974, p. 13). When, as sometimes happens, this ideal is not attained, you as the reader must be prepared to fill the gaps.

The Problem. The first task in comprehending any piece of scholarly writing is to discover the main point. In many areas of scholarship, this main point goes under the label of the *thesis statement,* and its formulation is the focus of considerable attention (Inglish and Jackson, 1977). The guidelines for a well-phrased problem statement are fairly straightforward. The statement (or statements) should be placed early in a paper and should be reasonably short, clear, and to the point. The underlying assumptions and supporting evidence should then be presented clearly. The reader should have no difficulty in following the logic leading from the problem as stated to the investigation as actually carried out.

The supporting evidence and other elaborations may take a considerable amount of writing, since the author may need some time to build the appropriate background to the problem and to link the work to previous investigations. Sometimes the question will first be illuminated by laying out one or more theoretical positions or by exploring the potential relevance of the question to practical applications. No matter how long the introductory presentation, it is important for you to determine early in the examination of a report the answer to one critical question: "What is the problem?" Can you put it into a single, easily comprehended sentence? Can you state it in words that make sense to you? Do you see how the problem statement is likely to lead to the design and the analysis of the research project?

Surprisingly, this step may prove to be one of the toughest tasks in studying a research article. More than a few writers tend to assume that the experimental question will be obvious to the reader—a state of mind that is understandable when you consider that the researcher may have spent a year or more wrestling with the question, but an explanation that does little to help the reader who is not also a mind reader. You may have to search for the problem statement and, once you have found it, additional work may be necessary to translate it into a form that is meaningful to you.

Design, Procedure, Analysis, and Results. After you have become clear about the problem, the next thing to look for is the description of how the study was carried out. What factors were varied? What were the levels of each, and how were they arranged? Which variations were between-subjects and which within-subjects? Which factors were maintained at a constant value? Eventually you should be able to gain sufficient understanding of the design and the procedures to feel confident that you could reproduce the conditions of the experiment, that you could retrace what happened to the subjects at each stage of the investigation.

Because statistics is one of the best-developed areas of social science methodology, experimenters usually provide considerable detail about the techniques used to measure and summarize performance. Examine the descriptive statistics carefully, until they make sense to you. Researchers sometimes tend to stress statistical significance without adequately describing what actually happened.

Summary measures of performance are usually presented in tables or graphs, but just as it takes effort to comprehend prose, so it takes considerable work and translation to "get the picture." Look for averages, the most important summary measure. Sometimes they will be tabled, sometimes they will be in graphs. Tables are preferred when the goal is to provide the essential information in a compact format. Figures take more space, but a plot is much more effective than a table in displaying the pattern of results. Previous chapters in this book have discussed how to read a figure. The first task is to examine the horizontal and vertical axes: what is plotted on each scale? If the interior of the plot has several components, you will need to determine what they show. Tables require even more work, and you frequently will find it helpful to prepare your own graphs of tabled data.

The presentation of the research methodology and the results comprise the bulk of most research reports; you will find that this information takes up a lot of space and generally requires the greatest amount of study. For the novice, wading through the details can be time-consuming and frustrating. The bits and pieces seem unfamiliar and hence tedious, the print is smaller than average in certain especially relevant sections, and you may discover that some of the information you are searching for is hard to find or even missing. The procedures may be unclear, the instructions to the subjects uncertain, or the data analysis incomplete. Sometimes you can refer to previous reports to fill the gaps; if the study is fairly recent, you may contact the author for further information. Researchers are generally pleased to learn that someone is interested in their work and are usually willing to respond to queries.

Interpreting the Findings. Every report must eventually tackle the ultimate question: what do the results mean? It is generally a good idea to try to formulate your own answer to this question as you wend your way through the paper. The author will present a viewpoint, of course, and may present an interpretation that you find thought-provoking. Many reports contain a discussion of the broader implications of the research and directions for future investigations. Such discussions go far beyond the actual data, and these extensions are legitimate as long as the author clearly distinguishes between evidence and opinion, between logical conclusions and generalizations based on informed judgment.

Most behavioral research is limited in scope. The economics of research funding in the social sciences often means that the investigator must work with a "handy random sample" of subjects and with treatments, materials, and so on that are dictated by convenience as much or more than any other consideration. The experienced researcher, based on a personal knowledge of other studies, can make sensible guesses about the broader implications of the work and can say something about the practical value of the endeavor. You will discover that some writers are able to share some of these opinions and reflections with the reader. Such reflections can be informative and provocative, but unfortunately editorial policies tend to rule them out because of the limitations on space available for scientific publication.

Sections of the Research Report

Most research reports are arranged according to the conventions laid out in the *Publication Manual of the American Psychological Association* (APA, 1983). The report must consist of the sections presented below, and in the order listed, with very few deviations. We now describe each of these sections in turn, with an emphasis on where in each one to find answers to the list of questions presented at the beginning of the chapter.

Title and Author(s). The usual practice in psychological reports is for the title to mention the most important factors and the dependent measures:

Visual Search and Reading of Rapid Serial Presentations of Letter Strings, Words, and Text

Adult Age Differences in Reasoning from New Information

> The Effects of Television Commercial Form and Commercial Placement on Children's Social Behavior and Attention
>
> Distance Estimates of Children as a Function of Type of Activity in the Environment

This convention allows readers to determine quickly whether a particular study is relevant to their interests. Sometimes the title will take a different turn, referring to the task, to a theoretical question, or to some other study that served as a critical starting point. Occasionally you will even run across a title that is clever, refreshing, *and* even informative:

> Comparing Memory for Natural and Laboratory Reading
>
> Nonsocial Play in Preschoolers: Necessarily Evil?
>
> The Moon Illusion: How High Is the Sky?

Glancing at the authors' names and affiliations can be worthwhile. If a study strikes you as particularly valuable, or if the same names and institutions appear again and again, this is probably a sign that the source is worth tracking down (a job for a citation index, Ch. 2). Incidentally, current practice is for one of the authors to place his or her address as a footnote to the title—a handy piece of information.

Abstract. Since the early 1960s APA journals have required authors to prepare an abstract that is placed at the beginning of the paper. The ideal Abstract is a compact but readable summary of the major facets of the article. When well crafted, it quickly tells you what you can expect to learn from the paper. Does the article contain information relevant to your interests and therefore warrant a detailed examination? Most Abstracts are carefully written, and although the condensed telegraphic style makes for slow reading, you will discover that with some practice the overview provided by the Abstract makes it easier to comprehend the details in the body of the paper.

As noted above, the Abstract comes at the beginning of the paper, and so it would seem quite natural to read it first. Because it is difficult reading, and because journals persist in using a small type font for this section, you may be inclined to pass it by. In the long run this is a bad practice, but how does the novice get started? One way is to first skim the Abstract, next get into the meat of the article until you think you understand it, and then go back and reread the Abstract. With practice you will become accustomed to this very specialized style of writing.

Introduction. Following the Abstract and generally without any heading comes the Introduction to the paper. In a well-written paper the first paragraph sets the stage for exposition of the problem and gives the motivation for conducting the research: an extension of previous work, an examination of a theoretical question, or perhaps an investigation of a practical matter.

The remainder of the Introduction can vary somewhat. There is likely to be at least a brief review of pertinent literature. Sometimes there is a theoretical analysis of the issues, with a presentation of one or more theoretical models. At the conclusion of this section, the author often provides an overview of the plan of the study, including a brief sketch of the major factors, a statement of the hypotheses and rationale for the design, and a presentation of the expected results.

Method. This section contains details of the methodology of the study: how was the experiment actually carried out? The Method section should include discussion of the subjects, the apparatus (if any), the procedures, the design, and the measurement techniques (if unusually complex). The amount of detail given on each of these topics, the order in which they are discussed, and sometimes even the labels for the subsections can vary from one paper to another, depending on the character of the study and the author's purposes.

Experimental papers should always provide a clear presentation of the design, even if there is no section headed by that label. You should find enough information to reproduce the design structure and to evaluate the adequacy of the controls. The plan for the selection of subjects is often rather limited; unless the subject factors are of some importance, you are likely to find only a brief mention to the effect that "volunteers were sampled from introductory psychology classes"— archetypal of the "handy random sample."

Especially important are the descriptions of the procedures, including the instructions and pretraining given to the subjects. What did the subjects actually do at each stage in the experiment, and how were they informed about the nature of the task? What methods were used to measure performance, and how appropriate were the measurement techniques for each of the experimental conditions? These details are important for assessing the validity of an experiment. Again, you can expect in many instances to encounter extremely small print, but do not take this as a sign that the material should be ignored.

Results. The purpose of this section is to inform the reader of the findings of the study. Some authors begin with descriptive information—averages, presented either as tables or graphs—after which they present the inferential analyses that confirm the statistical significance of the descriptive patterns (t tests, F-ratios, and the like; see the appendix for a review of statistical concepts). Other authors prefer to begin by establishing statistical significance and then proceed to report the descriptive results. Sometimes you will find Results sections that have been organized in several segments, the most important measures presented first, followed by one or more supplementary analyses.

In any event you should be prepared to spend a considerable amount of time unpacking the information in this section of the research report. In particular, you will need to examine the tables and figures with special care; the heart of the study is often located in these sources. Work them over, organize them in different ways, check the various numbers for consistency, and then back away from time to time so you can see what things look like from a distance.

Discussion. This section generally begins with an overview of the findings, put in more or less plain English and placed within the context of the original problem statement and the expected findings. Next is likely to come a consideration of the fine points: puzzling features in the data, inconsistent or unexpected findings, and occasionally mullings about what might have happened if the study had been slightly different.

The Discussion section usually ends with an interpretation of the results in light of the existing literature and with some notion of the broader implications of the findings. Most researchers tend to be relatively cautious, but a few are rather venturesome in considering broader issues. What are the limitations of the study? What appear to be the most promising leads for pursuing the problem? When you find an article in which the author is willing to share his or her reservations, insights, and hunches, give this material special attention.

References. Scattered throughout a research report you will find citations to other studies. Footnotes are not used in reporting psychological research; instead, the author's name (or names) and the date of publication are inserted in the text and then a complete list of references is presented at the end of the report—the style used in this textbook. At first you may find this approach rather confusing because you don't know who or what is being referred to. After a while, as you become accustomed to an area, you will find yourself making excursions to the reference list only when something especially noteworthy strikes your eye.

The reference list for research reports is generally quite abbreviated. Because journal space is at a premium, editors require the author to be as economical as possible, listing only those references that are directly pertinent. This limitation means that you are likely to uncover only a few references in any given report, but you can be assured that the ones that you do find will usually be the best and most relevant. The search for other papers on the topic then becomes something like a chain letter; article A provides you with references to article B, where you will find references to article C, and so on. The citation index provides an alternate route for this process, but you may find it easier to backtrack through the original research papers, as discussed in Chapter 2.

A Strategy for Studying a Report

At the beginning of this chapter was a list of questions designed for guidance in studying a report—the problem, the design, the procedure, the analysis, the findings, and the interpretation. After that, you learned about the sections of the report—the Title, the Abstract, the Introduction, the Method, the Results, the

Discussion, and the References. Buried somewhere in each report are answers to the list of questions, but as you can see the correspondence between the list of questions and the organization of the research report is not a one-to-one match. Your job in understanding a paper is to reorganize the information to fit your purposes, and this almost always entails locating the answers wherever they may be found and bringing them together into a unified schema. For instance, the problem may be encountered first in the Introduction and then reappear in altered form during the Discussion, but it may be only when you reach the end of the report that you will have achieved a full understanding of the problem! Likewise, various facets of the design may be examined in the Introduction, the Method, the Results, and again in the Discussion sections, with slightly different features of the design emphasized in each.

For these reasons, finding what you need in a research report is seldom achieved by reading it in linear fashion from beginning to end. Before you begin the abstract, you need to have in mind the structure that you are about to explore. Think about what you need to know and where you are most likely to find that information. Then give the report a preliminary reading in which you determine where the most relevant pieces of information are actually located in the article. You may decide at this point to revise your study strategy slightly—you may want to reread portions of the study in more detail, you may have to wrestle with some pieces until they fit, or you may realize that the framework you are trying to construct requires additional work. Comprehending a report takes almost as much effort as writing one—the two activities are similar in some fundamental respects.

If you have ever taken a course in study skills, you will recognize similarities between the strategy sketched above and the SQ3R method (Robinson, 1970):

SURVEY . . .   Read the Title and skim the Abstract, look over the Introduction (especially the beginning and the end), and glance at the figures and tables. This should give you a rough idea of what the study is about.

QUESTION . . . Reflect for a moment about the information that you need to locate. A mental framework will help here, perhaps something close to an outline but with the addition of some substantive questions.

READ . . .   Go back through the paper from beginning to end, familiarize yourself with the relevant details, and note particular features and puzzlements.

RECITE . . .   Restate the material in your own words and check whether the information from the report is adequately organized for your own specific purposes.

REVIEW . . .   Literally, "look again." Once you have achieved a full understanding of the report, you are in a position to evaluate it critically, to assess the strengths and weakness of the study. Remember that a critical review is of little value when its force is spent on trivial details; criticism is most valuable when it "goes for the jugular" and when it includes constructive suggestions.

If the preceding summary leads you to believe that understanding a research paper takes a considerable amount of effort, then it has served its purpose. Speed-reading is a great strategy for the quick comprehension of relatively low-level writing—and adopting this strategy for the initial *skimming* of a research report is quite appropriate. In most instances, however, your purpose in *studying* a research paper is likely to go beyond the need to pass a multiple-choice test, and that sort of deeper understanding is not easily achieved. The secret, once you know the basic format, is simple but time-consuming—practice, practice, practice. . . .

TWO EXAMPLES

Thus far, this chapter has remained at a relatively abstract level in its discussion of techniques for reviewing the literature. Now we analyze two articles in some detail to illustrate the application of the principles presented above. The two research reports are substantially different in character, and the contrasts between them should help clarify various points. The first study is a laboratory experiment representing what is now known as the *information-processing* approach to thinking; the second is a field study of classroom learning conducted in a fairly naturalistic setting and directed toward the solution of a practical problem. Portions of the reports have been deleted in order to reduce the amount of prose, including some of the references and a few technical details that would be useful for replication of the studies but that are not essential for the purposes of illustration.

Journal of Experimental Psychology
1973, Vol. 97, No. 1, 22–27

SEARCHING FOR OBJECTS IN REAL-WORLD SCENES

IRVING BIEDERMAN, ARNOLD L. GLASS, and E. WEBB STACY, JR.
State University of New York at Buffalo

The speed at which a single object can be detected in a real-world scene was reduced when the scene was jumbled compared to when it was coherent. Jumbling was most disruptive when the target object was not in the scene but had a high probability of occurring in that kind of scene. These results are discussed in terms of the possible role played by schemas in the processing of information from real-world scenes.

The **Abstract** has been slightly altered from the original; it is quite succinct in present form but provides clues about the question, the design, and the findings.

This experiment was designed to show how people search for objects in real-world scenes. The literature on visual search has focused on the speed and accuracy of processing displays of unrelated items. Models for this research typically conceptualize an independent processing of the various parts of the display (e.g., Egeth, Jonides, & Wall, 1972; Rumelhart, 1970).

Biederman (1972) has recently demonstrated that the relation of an object to its setting affects recognition accuracy. In that experiment, subjects briefly viewed pictures of many varied scenes. Their task was to identify which object occupied a particular position in the scene. Immediately after the presentation of the scene, an arrow pointed to a position where an object had been. The subject's task was to tell which of four pictures had been in that position. Coherency was manipulated through a scene-jumbling procedure (described below), which destroyed the natural spatial relations of the scene. Jumbling reduced recognition accuracy, even when the subject knew what to look for, and to a lesser extent, where to look. Thus, jumbling probably affects perceptual recognition and not just memory of response selection.

The present experiment explored the effect of jumbling on a speeded search task. The subject also had an opportunity to use his overall characterization of the scene.

METHOD

Subjects. The subjects were 36 students from the State University of New York at Buffalo. Participation was part of their psychology course requirement.

Scenes. The scenes were projected from 35-mm. black and white slides. A wide variety of scenes was sampled, e.g., streets, kitchens, desk tops, store counters, etc. Coherent and jumbled versions of each scene were made by photographing a 20×35 cm. print, which had been cut into six sections (generally with one horizontal and two vertical cuts) in such a manner as to leave at least four well-defined objects intact (Figures 1 and 2). . . . The jumbled version was rearranged so as to destroy the natural spatial relations of the components, but one section was always left in its original position, containing a well-defined object. The position of the section remaining constant was balanced across different scenes.

Design and Procedure. Each subject viewed 112 scenes, half jumbled and half coherent, in random order. The first 16 scenes were practice trials and were not included in the data analyses.

Before viewing each scene, subjects perused (for approximately 5 sec.) a card with the picture of an object on it. This object was cut out of the original photographs used in making the slides. Upon presentation of the scene, subject pressed either a "yes" or "no" finger key as soon as he judged whether the object was or was not in that scene.

This is the **Introduction.** It briefly presents . . .

the *problem,* which is to learn more about how the arrangement of a photograph affects the speed with which a person can locate a specific object in a photograph, and . . .

the *procedure,* which was used in a previous study. The subject studies a "target object," then is shown a regular or jumbled photo and decides whether or not the object is in the scene. There is also a brief reference to relevant theory.

The overview is sparser than usual and not altogether adequate for the novice.

The **Method** section describes: The number of *subjects* and the method of selecting them.

The *materials* used in the experiment.

A description of one of the *primary factors,* scene coherence (either regular or jumbled photographs).

The **Design and Procedure** subsection begins with an almost offhand remark about the primary factor, scene coherence, which is a within-subjects factor.

Next the task is described in detail.

FIG. 1. Sample of coherent scene. (Note that the target object, a relatively easy one in this example, is the fire hydrant.)

FIG. 2. Sample of jumbled scene. (Note that the lower right section, which contains the target object, is the same as in Figure 1.)

Another primary factor is then mentioned, scene plausibility. Each test photograph either (a) contained the target object, (b) could have plausibly contained the object, or (c) could not have contained the object.

The remainder of the section deals with details of the design, arrangements to ensure that there was adequate counterbalancing. You can see that a fair amount of work is required to bring together the various parts of the design.

The **Results** section first describes the summary of the scores and presents *descriptive statistics*.

Next are the findings of the *analysis of variance*, a technique described in the appendix for determining statistical significance.

On one third of the trials, the object was, in fact, in the scene ("yes" responses). On these trials, the target object was from its original position. On another third of the trials, the object was not in the scene but could have been in it ("possible-no" responses). For example, the target object might have been an automobile and a street scene might have been projected, but the automobile was not one of the automobiles in the scene. On the remaining third of the trials ("impossible-no" responses), the object was one that was highly unlikely to have appeared in the scene. Examples of impossible-no trials would be a cup as a target in a street scene, or an automobile as a target in a kitchen scene.

Each subject viewed only one of the two versions of a given scene (jumbled or coherent) and responded to that version under only one of the three response categories. . . . The trials were self-paced; the scenes remained projected until a response was made or 8 sec. elapsed.

RESULTS

For each subject, median correct reaction times (RT's) were calculated for each of the six kinds of trials. The means of these medians, as well as the mean percent errors, are shown in Figure 3. Approximately 1.5 sec. are required to find an object that is in a scene. The main effects on RT's of coherency, $F(1, 35) = 12.22$, $p < .01$, and response category,

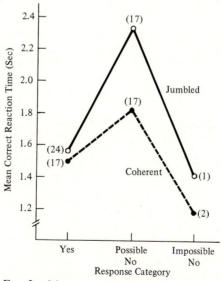

FIG. 3. Mean correct reaction times as a function of scene version and response category. (Numbers in parentheses are percent errors.)

$F(2, 70) = 34.46$, $p < .001$, were both significant, as was their interaction, $F(2, 70) = 3.68$, $p < .05$. Quite striking was the effect of probability in the "no" response categories: The "impossible-no" responses were, on the average, about .75 sec. faster than the "possible-no" responses.

Errors were almost nonexistent in the "impossible-no" response category, but very high in the "yes" and "possible-no" categories. A significant Coherency × Response Category interaction $F(2, 70) = 8.05$, $p < .001$, in the error rates is attributable to the higher error rates in the jumbled yes responses compared with the coherent yes responses. If a speed for accuracy trade-off were operating for the yes responses, then the effect of coherency on this response category was underestimated.

Next are the findings of the analysis of variance.

The analysis and the data in Figure 3 show that (a) jumbled pictures take longer to search than coherent pictures and (b) plausible alternatives take longer to discard, (c) especially when the photo is jumbled—the interaction is significant. All these results must be read from the figure. Finally, (d) errors are more likely when the photo is plausible. Notice that error times are not included in the earlier analysis. How might this decision affect the interpretation?

DISCUSSION

A number of recent theories of stimulus recognition (e.g., Eden, 1962; Halle & Stevens, 1964; Neisser, 1967) postulate a multistage theory in which an initial characterization of the stimulus as a whole biases the subsequent testing, weighting, and combination of detailed features and the subsequent memory representation. One set of speculations to account for the results of both the present and Biederman (1972) experiments that is consistent with such a multistage theory would emphasize the importance of the finding that the "possible-no" responses were more affected by jumbling than "impossible-no" responses (504 vs. 227 msec). In the "impossible-no" condition, as soon as the subject could achieve an overall characterization (or schema) of the scene—as soon as he could recognize the scene as a street, desk top, or kitchen—he had sufficient information to respond. That the subject did tend to exit at this point is evidenced by the short "impossible-no" RT's (relative to the "possible-no" RT's).

That jumbling might also have slowed the recognition of specific objects is consistent with the additional effect of jumbling on the "possible-no" RT's. Here achieving a schema was insufficient and the subject would have to engage in detailed feature processing and object identification to determine if the target was in the scene. . . .

In this brief paper, the **Discussion** section does not include a summary of the findings. The gist of the interpretation is that subjects first create an image of the scene as a whole and then use this image to decide what to look for in the scene. Various (technical) implications of this interpretation are considered; the prose here is tough to decipher. However, you might think about how to test the interpretation by further experiments. For instance, what might be the effects of the size of the photograph, the complexity, the amount of time for study, or the familiarity of the scene? The segment beginning "as soon as he (sic) could recognize . . ." is a critical comment in this regard.

[In summary there are two effects of a schema on perceptual recognition.]

1. There are a greater number of object fragments in a jumbled scene compared with its coherent version. While the fragments did not overlap with the target object they could have "drained" some of the processing capacity. This interpretation can be tested through a procedure whereby scenes are drawn or cropped in such a manner that jumbling leaves the number of entities intact.

The effects of jumbling serve as a basis for conjectures—again, how might these be tested?

2. Jumbling might have disrupted an informative external scanning of the scene. For example, if the target was a cup in a kitchen scene, one would tend to look at the counter tops rather than on the floor.

These two explanations are consistent with a theory positing an independent perceptual processing of the various positions of a scene within each fixation. Further research will be necessary to resolve the issue as to the role of higher order units in the perceptual recognition of scenes.

REFERENCES

Biederman, I. Perceiving real-world scenes. *Science*, 1972, *177*, 77–80.

Bruner, J. S., & Potter, M. D. Interference in visual recognition. *Science*, 1964, *144*, 424–425.

Bugelski, B. R., & Alampay, D. A. The role of frequency in developing perceptual sets. *Canadian Journal of Psychology*, 1961, *15*, 205–211.

Eden, M. Handwriting and pattern recognition. *I. R. E. Transactions on Information Theory*, 1962, IT-8, 160–166.

Egeth, H., Jonides, J., & Wall, S. Parallel processing of multielement displays. *Cognitive Psychology*, 1972, *3*, 674–698.

Halle, M., & Stevens, K. N. Speech recognition: A model and a program for research. In J. A. Fodor & J. J. Katz (Eds.), *The structure of language: Readings in the philosophy of language*. Englewood Cliffs, NJ: Prentice-Hall, 1964.

Neisser, U. *Cognitive psychology*. New York: Appleton-Century-Crofts, 1967.

Rumelhart, D. E. A multicomponent theory of the perception of briefly exposed visual displays. *Journal of Mathematical Psychology*, 1970, *7*, 191–218.

The **References** include some earlier work by Biederman, as well as related experiments and background. Which of these might be useful for locating additional research findings?

Journal of Educational Psychology
1978, Vol. 70, No. 2, 175–179

EFFECTS OF THREE TYPES OF UNIVERSITY LECTURE NOTES ON STUDENT ACHIEVEMENT

Vaughan Collingwood and David C. Hughes

University of Canterbury, Christchurch, New Zealand

This **Abstract** describes a longer and more complex set of problems, but you should nonetheless keep your eye open for the experimental question, the design, and the findings.

During a series of three electronics lectures, university students made use of three different kinds of lecture notes. These were (a) duplicates of the lecturer's detailed notes; (b) copies of the headings, key points, diagram outlines, tables, and references from the lecturer's notes with spaces for the students to add additional notes as appropriate; and (c) the students' own notes taken during the lectures. An analysis of variance indicated that there were significant differences between the notes as measured by a delayed achievement test, the order being from high to low, a, b, and c. The students' preferences for the three types of notes were obtained before and after the experimental lectures. A significant interaction between initial student preference and treatment was found. However, student preference changed in favor of (a) following exposure to the three types of notes during the experimental lectures.

The lecture method is widely used in university teaching and will undoubtedly continue to be used in the future. Therefore, any procedures that enhance the effectiveness of lectures are likely to have significant effects on student learning. One important lecture variable is the type of student notes that is used. At one extreme students are required to make their own lecture notes and are provided with nothing by way of handouts, whereas at the other extreme they are provided with duplicates of the instructor's lecture notes. In between are various kinds of summary handouts.

It is generally accepted that lecture notes can serve either or both of two functions. The first is an *encoding function* in which the lecture material is transformed into a more meaningful form for the learner and hence is easier to remember. The second is an *external storage function* in which the student is provided with material for later review. . . .

The encoding function should be maximized when students are asked to make their own notes. However, since student-made notes contain omissions, errors, and over-simplifications (Hartley & Marshall, 1974; Maddox & Hoole, 1975), the external storage function should be maximized when duplicates of the lecturer's notes are given out, although in this situation the encoding function is lessened. . . .

In the 2 decades since Cronbach (1957) introduced the term *Aptitude × Treatment interaction*, there have been many studies designed to identify interaction between instructional treatments and individual differences between students (Berliner & Cahen, 1973; Bracht, 1970; Tobias, 1976). At the beginning of the present study, the subjects were asked which of three types of lecture notes they would prefer to have and which they thought would be most efficient in terms of passing examinations. . . . Approximately 25% of the students indicated that they thought making their own notes was most effective, the same proportion said that having a copy of the lecturer's notes was most effective, and the rest (50%) believed that an outline of the lecturer's notes with spaces for additional student notes was most effective.

The difference of opinion suggests that different students may use the encoding and external storage functions of lecture notes to different degrees. That is, students who believe that making their own notes is most effective may be those for whom the encoding function is of prime importance, whereas those who prefer a copy of the lecturer's notes may rely heavily on the external storage function. If this is the case, then an

----

The **Introduction** to this study begins with a general discussion of types of lecture notes, . . .

and a theoretical discussion of the differential effects of notetaking.

The implications of the mini-theory are spelled out.

As the introduction continues, it becomes clear that one of the experimental questions is "how do student predispositions affect the effectiveness of different kinds of lecture notes" —the hypothesis being that there is an interaction between student preference and type of notes used by the student.

In this article the authors bring the experimental question into view in a fairly roundabout manner.

interaction would be expected between the students' preference for a particular kind of lecture notes and the kind of notes they actually receive. . . .

METHOD

The **Method** section covers the number and selection of *subjects* . . .

Subjects. The subjects were 57 University of Canterbury, Christchurch, New Zealand, undergraduate engineering students taking the second professional year course, Electrical Engineering 2. The subjects received the experimental treatments during three digital electronics lectures that were part of the normal digital electronics course.

and the preparation of *materials.*

Materials. A sequence of three lectures covering the topic *bistables, registers,* and *counters* was used for this investigation. The three lectures formed a complete unit and were judged by the lecturer to be similar in difficulty level and material covered. The lecturer's detailed notes for the topic were obtained, and two handouts were prepared for each of the three lectures.

It also describes one of the *primary factors,* the type of lecture notes (complete or full notes by the lecturer, partial outline notes, or no notes at all).

The first handout was a complete typewritten copy of the lecturer's notes including neat diagrams (hereafter called *full notes*). No special spaces were left for the students to add their own notes to the full notes. The second handout was an edited typewritten copy with all detailed text removed, leaving only the headings, key points, unlabeled diagram outlines, tables, and references (hereafter called *partial notes*). Space equal to the amount used in the full notes was left beneath the headings and key points in the partial notes for the students to add their own notes as appropriate. This note form requires the students to encode the material, but it also provides a structure that should improve the quality of the notes as an external store.

Measurement Instruments

The tests for the second primary factor, *student preferences,* are described, along with additional information on procedural precautions.

Prequestionnaire and postquestionnaire.
Both the prequestionnaire and postquestionnaire asked the students which of three types of notes they considered would be most efficient in terms of passing exams. It was thought that students might select the type of lecture notes that demanded the least effort of them, as their answer to the first question, while actually believing that another lecture note form would be better in terms of passing the exams, hence the inclusion of the second question. . . .

The tests for the *dependent measure* are described.

The achievement test.
A . . . multiple-choice achievement test sampling the content of the experimental lectures was devised jointly with the lecturer. The test was incorporated as part of the midterm examination, which also contained two essay questions. . . .

Design

. . . . Subjects were randomly assigned to three treatment groups. Each group received the same combination of lecture note types but for different lectures as shown in Table 1. The three types were full notes, partial notes, and no handouts at all so that students were required to make their "own notes."

TABLE 1
Experimental Design

Grp	Lecture 1	Lecture 2	Lecture 3
1	Own notes	Partial notes	Full notes
2	Partial notes	Full notes	Own notes
3	Full notes	Own notes	Partial notes

Procedure

The prequestionnaire was administered during the last electronics lecture of the first term of 1976. . . .

[Then,] during the afternoon laboratory session of the day prior to the first lecture in the sequence, the subjects were handed their appropriate notes for the experimental lecture sequence. . . . The subjects were told to bring the notes to the lecture the next day.

At the start of the first lecture, the subjects were told of the different types of lecture notes that they had received and that this was related to the questionnaire they had completed during the first term. No particular instructions on how to use the handouts were given. . . . The whole procedure was made as close to the normal teaching situation as possible. . . .

Three days after the last lecture in the experimental sequence, the postquestionnaire was administered during a normal lecture period. Four weeks after the completion of the last lecture, the subjects sat the midterm examination, which included the multiple-choice test.

Analysis

Achievement. The experimental subjects were the 57 students who had (a) completed the prequestionnaire, (b) attended all the lectures, (c) completed the postquestionnaire, and (d) completed the multiple-choice test.

The test papers were marked to provide three scores for each subject. These scores measured the subject's performance on the content

---

A preliminary statement of the **Design**—the primary factors and their arrangement.

Additional design features for counterbalancing time and treatment are shown. The design also includes student preference, which is necessarily a between-subjects factor.

The *tasks* for the subjects are described, along with additional detail on procedures.

An unusual section—included not so much to talk about the subjects (the first paragraph would have been better earlier in the **Subjects** subsection), but to clarify a few points about the treatment of the achievement and preference scores. This portion of the **Analysis** subsection could have been placed also in **Results**.

A rather uncommon method was used to standardize the scores for the different lectures, and the analysis of variance was a bit unusual. Both are discussed here.

contained in each lecture. These three scores were each converted to standard scores with a mean of 500 and a standard deviation of 100. A two-way analysis of variance with unweighted means suitable for a design with repeated measures on one factor was carried out. The two factors were treatment and preference.

Preference. It was assumed that the three types of lecture notes used in the study represent three points on a continuum that ranges from own notes to full notes. Therefore, the changes in preference from the prequestionnaire to the postquestionnaire were treated as having direction, and the sign test was used to test the changes for significance.

The sign test is a special statistical procedure.

Results

Achievement

The **Results** section presents *descriptive statistics* both tabularly and graphically.

Table 2 shows the mean achievement scores obtained in the experiment. . . . [In Table 3] the differences between the treatment means were significant at the .05 level. . . . The interaction between preferences and treatments was also significant at the .05 level. The interaction is shown in Figure 1.

TABLE 2

Mean Achievement Scores and
Standard Deviations Following Three Types of Lecture Notes

	Treatment			
Preference	Own notes	Partial notes	Full notes	Total
Own notes (12)				
M	497.0	533.7	505.6	512.1
SD	76.2	66.8	119.1	91.6
Partial notes (31)				
M	475.3	512.9	498.3	495.5
SD	103.3	111.8	94.0	104.4
Full notes (41)				
M	458.4	475.8	560.2	498.1
SD	94.0	106.6	36.5	95.7
Total				
M	475.7	508.2	515.0	499.6
SD	96.8	104.6	93.8	100.0

Note. Numbers in parentheses are *ns.*

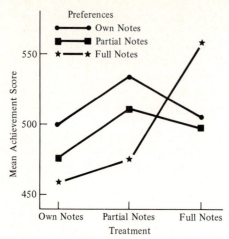

Figure 1. The Preferences × Treatment interaction

TABLE 3

Analysis of Variance for Differences in Achievement Following Three Types of Lecture Notes

Source of variation	df	MS	F
Between subjects	56		
Preference (A)	2	3,826	<1
Subjects within groups	54	15,554	
Within subjects	114		
Treatment (B)	2	24,881	3.60*
A ×B	4	17,178	2.48*
B × Subjects Within Groups	108	6,919	

*$p < .05$.

Preferences

Table 4 shows the responses to the first two questions in the questionnaires. Question 1 asked the students which of the three types of lecture notes they would prefer, and Question 2 asked them which type of notes they considered would be best for passing exams.

The supplementary analysis of the questionnaire is presented here. The pre–post pattern could have been presented more informatively without any substantial increase in space requirements—do you see how to change Table 4?

TABLE 4

Responses to Questions 1 and 2 on the Prequestionnaire and Postquestionnaire

	Notes preference		
Item	Own	Partial	Full
Prequestionnaire			
Question 1	12	31	14
Question 2	15	28	14
Postquestionnaire			
Question 1	8	19	30
Question 2	7	22	28

A synopsis of the pattern of findings would be helpful at this point: (a) full notes yield the best performances and students' own notes the poorest; (b) these effects are largest for subjects who originally preferred their own notes (the interaction is significant); and (c) at the end of the study most subjects indicated preference for full notes.

Fifty of the 57 students responded in the same way to Questions 1 and 2 in the prequestionnaire, whereas 49 did so in the postquestionnaire. The changes in the distributions of responses from the prequestionnaire to the postquestionnaire were significant at the .001 for both questions.

Discussion

The **Discussion** recapitulates the presentation of the findings, emphasizing the importance of the external storage function of notes.

You might consider the importance of the choice of within-subjects variation in type of notes. Also, the achievement test stressed information covered in the lectures. What might be the pattern of findings for a test that stressed application to new problems, or a test after a delay of some sort?

The results indicate that the kinds of notes used in this study are significantly different in their effects on achievement. Further, the results suggest that the external storage function of notes in the normal university situation is an important one, with the order of the treatment means being full notes, partial notes, and own notes. However, there was also a significant disordinal interaction between preference and treatment. Those students whose preference was for full notes had the lowest mean on the own notes and partial notes treatments, but they had the highest mean when given the full notes treatment. Both the partial notes preference students and the own notes preference students had higher scores when given the partial notes treatment, which obviates the conclusion that students routinely do best when given their lecture note preference. Clearly all groups had higher achievement when given some form of lecture notes handouts.

The responses to the questionnaire show that almost all students preferred the lecture notes that they thought would be most efficient for passing examinations and that following exposure to the three kinds of notes, their opinions about which type of notes is most effective shifted in favor of the full notes, although a substantial proportion of the students still preferred the partial notes. These changes in preference are in accord with the achievement data.

In conclusion the results of this investigation suggest that the efficiency of lectures can be improved by the distribution of some form of notes. The results suggest that, given the note forms used in the present study, students should be offered a choice between partial or full notes whenever this is practical. However, it would be easy to adapt the partial notes and full notes used in the present study by, for example, adding content to the partial notes or leaving spaces in the full notes so that students can add their own notes. It might be that an adaptation of this kind could cater to all students without the need for different preferences. However, whether this is the case or not can only be decided on the basis of future research.

Some interesting ideas for future work—it would seem appropriate to tie these ideas back into the theoretical analysis.

References

Berliner, D. C., & Cahen, L. S. Trait-treatment interaction and learning. In F. N. Kerlinger (Ed.), *Review of research in education* (Vol. 1). Itasca, Ill.: Peacock, 1973.

Bracht, G. H. Experimental factors related to aptitude–treatment interactions. *Review of Educational Research*, 1970, 40, 627–645.

Cronbach, L. J. The two disciplines of scientific psychology. *American Psychologist*, 1957, 12, 271–684.

Hartley, J., & Marshall, S. On notes and notetaking. *Universities Quarterly*, 1974, 28, 225–235.

Maddox, H., & Hoole, E. Performance decrement in the lecture. *Educational Review*, 1975, 28, 17–30.

Tobias, S. Achievement treatment interactions. *Review of Educational Research*, 1976, 46, 61–74.

A POSTSCRIPT

The two examples presented above typify the variety in style and substance found in journal articles describing experimental research in psychology. The papers should give you a fuller appreciation of the points covered earlier in the chapter.

Understanding a research paper cannot be a passive task; you must make your way through the article with some definite ideas about what you are looking for. A critical eye and questioning mind are essential. In both of the papers presented, important information was sometimes located in unexpected places, some essential details were hard to find anywhere, and certain statements required critical examination. You should expect most articles that you read to make similar demands on you as a reader. Though scientific papers are written by skilled individuals, reviewed by skeptical peers, and monitored by critical editors, they are still a human endeavor and hence subject to human shortcomings.

The reading of research papers becomes easier with practice. At first the task will be time-consuming and mind-wrenching, but the situation is by no means hopeless. You will save time and energy by being careful in the articles that you select for close examination when you first begin studying a particular research area. As you become familiar with the area, and as you come to know a particular investigator's style, understanding will come more quickly and more easily. After dissecting a few papers, the structure will begin to become apparent—just like carving a Thanksgiving turkey.

SUMMARY

Studying a research report, in contrast to skimming it, requires a careful dissection of the article. The reader's goal is to locate information on six critical topics—the experimental question, the design, the task procedures, the methods of data analysis, the results, and the interpretation of the results. Research papers published according to the guidelines of the American Psychological Association are organized in seven sections: the Title and the Authors, the Abstract, the Introduction, the Method, the Results, the Discussion, and the References. While there is a general correspondence between the list of questions and the sections of the research report, the match is not perfect. The reader's task is to use his or her knowledge of the overall structure of the research paper as a framework for locating information on the six critical questions.

Reading a research report is a technical job requiring a systematic strategy. The SQ3R method of study works well in this situation: SURVEY (skim the entire paper), QUESTION (decide what questions you need to answer), READ (. . . the entire paper, with special attention to the most relevant parts), RECITE (restate the important information in your own words), and REVIEW (look over your work and check its adequacy). This method will take time at the beginning, but with practice you will become more adept at the task.

10

Writing a Research Report

Writing a paper to describe a psychological experiment is something like studying the paper in reverse. First you must have in mind an image of the project—the experimental question, the design, the procedures, the basic findings, and the first steps toward a reasonable interpretation. All these must have become familiar to you through repeated critical thinking about the study. At some point you will be ready to prepare an outline and to write a preliminary draft of the report. The last step—and here the process differs somewhat from studying an article—is to revise, refine, and edit the paper until it is clear, accurate, and concise.

In this chapter you will go through the various phases of writing a report. Certain preparatory steps that are important are described first. To aid you in preparing the preliminary draft, I suggest a process that works well for both experienced research authors and beginning students. An essential feature of the process is the idea of forcing yourself through the completion of an initial draft—get some words on paper. You will not be striving for perfection in this first version, but it helps to have certain basic guidelines in mind as you prepare the draft. For the final version, you will need to attend to the specifications for technical writing in psychology that are spelled out in the *Publication Manual of the American Psychological Association* (APA, 1983), the most important of which are described below. The chapter ends with an example of how to edit and revise a research paper.

Before going into the "official" details about how to prepare yourself to write a paper, one "unofficial" matter. Every piece of writing is directed toward an audience, and you should give some thought to the person (or persons) who are most likely to read your work. It may be your professor or a graduate teaching assistant, or you may plan to submit the paper to a professional journal. In any event, your primary aim is to communicate to this audience (a) what you have done, (b) why you did it, (c) what you found, and (d) what you think it means—almost a specialized version of newspaper reporting. You can generally assume that the audience has some degree of technical expertise, and you should prepare the paper accordingly. There is little advantage in writing at length on a matter that your audience already knows. For example, you can generally assume that the reader already knows something about the logic of behavioral research and accepts the assumptions of the scientific study of psychology. On the other hand, unless the experiment is a class assignment, you should *not* assume that the reader knows about your rationale for carrying out the study. The importance of the topic may be obvious to you, but even the most talented psychologists are seldom skilled at mind reading. Sometimes it is helpful to make a dry run with a classmate or companion, someone who knows a little about your project but not too much—such a person can provide an excellent audience. Be alert to the distinction between the immediate and the larger audience. Your professor may know exactly what your project is all about, but your task is to write a paper that is sufficiently explicit to allow other professionals who are unfamiliar with the situation to understand the study.

PREPARING TO WRITE A REPORT

The Basic Structure

The first step in writing almost anything of substance is to construct an outline of the work. Part of this task has already been done for you; the publication manual specifies that the basic structure of the paper must include the following elements in the order listed:

The Introduction. Begin with the statement of the problem. Present earlier research and theory if they have a direct bearing on *your* problem. Be sure that this review of the literature is coherent—simply listing the articles you found in a search of the literature is no help. What do you think about the value and the limitations of the papers? How do they fit together, in what ways do the studies complement and contradict one another, and where are the "holes" in the literature? State your hypotheses (or expectations) along with competing hypotheses and explanations. The last paragraph of this section should describe succinctly the nature of your investigation: what factors have been varied, who are the subjects, what is being measured? Do a good job here, and it will help you later in writing the Abstract. The summary paragraph should be no more than 200 to 300 words long.

The Method. This section describes how the study was conducted. In an experimental study it is often a good idea to begin by laying out the design; the order of the other parts of this section should then be determined by their relative importance to the research question. Describe the pertinent features of the stimulus materials and the apparatus. Discuss the procedures—if I were to serve as a subject, what would I experience during each stage of the experiment? Be sure to mention the instructions; if these are complicated, you may want to present them verbatim, word for word. When you have finished this section, other psychologists should be able to repeat the study in its fundamental details.

The Results. Unless the study is simple, it often helps to begin this section with a brief, one-paragraph overview. What can the reader expect to encounter throughout the section? As noted in the preceding chapter, you have several options about how to organize the results. My personal preference in most instances is first to present the descriptive statistics for the measures of most central importance to the research question: what was the effect of the design factors on performance? After that, I follow with the inferential tests (ANOVA and *t*-tests; see the appendix for a review) that establish the trustworthiness of the descriptive statistics.

Tables and figures are often the most efficient way to present the descriptive statistics. You will usually have to construct quite a number of charts and tables before you find the most informative layout. Figures are most helpful when you need a visual aid to explain a complex pattern in the data; tables are more appropriate for presenting lots of information in a compact form. The primary purpose of the Results section is to present the facts, but try to avoid redundancy. Don't use words simply to repeat what you have already shown in graphic form. Rather, point out highlights of the findings and help the reader to focus on the patterns that are of greatest value (in your opinion) for interpretation. You are treading a fine line here between discussing the data (making interpretations that go more properly into the next section) and aiding the reader (helping him or her see what is important for understanding the meaning of the data).

The Discussion. What do you think the results mean? Do they support or contradict your original hypotheses? How do your findings compare with previous findings? What did you discover during the experiment that was unexpected? What do you see as the most promising directions for future work? Are there shortcomings that might make it necessary to qualify the findings, and if so how might these be remedied in future experiments? These are the questions to be considered in the Discussion. Your first efforts, in all likelihood, will be confused and incoherent. But stick with it. Science is a process of accumulation. Facts build upon one another, but the efforts of experimenters to make sense of these facts are what represent the real progress. Research follows a pattern—the "incubation" stage, in which ideas germinate and take shape; the "activity" stage, in which the design is prepared, data collected, and results analyzed; and the "what does it mean" stage in which the researcher attempts to make sense of the findings. If the first draft is less than perfect, stick with it—this is the hardest part. The questions posed above are a goal, not an automatic procedure for generating the Discussion.

The Outline

Before undertaking the construction of an outline, you should first assemble all the relevant pieces of information and arrange them according to the basic framework listed above. You will probably have made numerous notes about the rationale for the research question and about the literature. The details of the method—design, subject selection, apparatus, procedure, measuring instruments, and so on—will be partly on paper and partly in your head. You will have completed the statistical analysis, and your files should brim with descriptive statistics. From the note cards, the sketches of figures and tables, and the smattering of computer printouts, you will have begun to formulate some hunches about what it all means.

Lay out these materials somewhere: a dining-room table, the living-room floor, your bed—a place with lots of space. You need to get the total picture.

Outlining is more than preparing an ordered list of topics. It is a time for rumination, for digesting the work that you have done. As the outline takes shape, you may decide to reread a few selected articles or perhaps to search through one or two new sources. You will want to examine your method once again for flaws and limitations. You should move toward the preparation of tables and figures in close-to-finished form; you will still be displaying more graphics than are likely to appear in the final paper.

In constructing the outline, you are filling in many of the blanks from the guidelines of the publication manual. For instance, the Introduction can take any of several forms: a logical argument built upon an orderly progression of assumptions and conclusions, an historical accounting of previous studies leading up to the present work, a description of a practical (or not so practical) problem that caught your attention, a simple curiosity that would not go away. How can you set the stage so that the reader understands the rationale behind the experiment? Even though the paper may be an assignment and even though the basic framework may have already been spelled out for you, choices about approach and style are still up to you.

Similarly, you are likely to be faced with decisions about how to present and interpret the results. What is the most notable finding? What arrangement of the data provides the clearest and most coherent picture? Should theory guide the presentation of the results or should you let the facts first speak for themselves?

A well-crafted outline provides the skeleton for the paper. The "bones"—the basic elements of the report—should be sufficiently detailed to allow you to write a paragraph around each element in the outline.

Once the outline has been completed, it is a good idea to set it aside for a day or two and find something else to do, if you can afford the time. The passage of even a little time can give you a fresh perspective. You may be distressed to discover that some ideas don't seem as clear and compelling as they appeared a few days prior, but it is better to tackle this matter *before* you have written paragraphs rather than afterward. You may decide to let certain points fall by the wayside. A reorganization may suggest itself. A question or doubt may arise in your mind—tantalizing, but with no clear resolution. Make a note of it, and press on.

You are ready to write.

THE FIRST DRAFT

Writing is hard work. For most people it is slow and frustrating, and as with other painful activities, we tend to avoid the matter by delaying whenever possible.

The best advice is *write*, even if it hurts and even if you can find lots of reasons to put it off. Set aside a time and a place for writing. Use the outline to get started and to keep going. Build sentences. A handful of these and you will have made a paragraph. Get the core ideas onto paper in some form—later you can go back and make them better. Set yourself a goal (five pages a day?) and decide how you will reward yourself when you have reached it.

While the chief aim is to get words onto paper, a few stylistic guidelines are worth keeping in mind even at this stage. The paragraph is the basic unit in most technical writing. Each paragraph should begin with a strong thematic statement. This is called the *lead*, or *topic*, sentence. This first sentence should be followed by three to six other sentences that elaborate the theme. If a paragraph begins to exceed these limits, you are probably trying to cram too much into it. Except for certain sections (Summaries and Abstracts, for instance), a well-written paragraph should contain a single idea. Trying to force two or more ideas into the same paragraph makes it hard for the reader to comprehend your meaning.

The paragraph may be the "idea unit" of a paper, but it is no better than the words and sentences of which it is constructed. Keep your sentences short and active. Rarely should a sentence contain more than two dozen words, and even then it should probably be broken into clauses. Build around nouns and verbs— these are the strong parts of speech. Avoid fancy words and jargon—spice is nice, but not when overdone. Challenge each word for precision of meaning, and dump any word that is not carrying its weight. Avoid colloquialisms and informal expressions; these are stylistically inappropriate in technical writing—if you know what I mean. . . .

Whenever possible, build on the work of others. If someone else has compiled a comprehensive review of a particular area, you should take advantage of this effort. Extract the most salient points for your purposes, link them to your study, and move on. Remember to give credit where credit is due—keep track of references.

In general, try to stay on the track laid out in your outline. Avoid general and tangential issues—they will only mislead the audience. You may become suddenly excited by a new thought, or anxious to explain an interesting gimmick in the procedure, or disturbed by a funny quirk in the data. Make a note and go on. You will have opportunities to explore sidepaths later. On occasion, you may decide that your original ideas call for some reorganization—the outline needs modification. If the changes are major, then you may have to stop the entire writing process and go back to step 1. More often, you will realize while writing that your thoughts have steered you into a more natural channel for expressing a set of ideas. Go with the flow. You can come back later and alter the outline as necessary.

Don't let any of these cautions slow down the writing process. Keep moving ahead. A note in the margin will remind you of the problem later during revision. Margins can be helpful in many ways, so be sure that they are adequate. Leave plenty of space along each side of the paper. You should double- or even triple-space the first draft so that there is plenty of room between the lines for editing later. Incidentally, APA style requires that *everything* in a manuscript be double-spaced in the final version—the body of the text, but also the abstract, quotations, the references, everything!

You may be tempted to assign table and figure numbers early during the initial draft; this may lead you to the comfortable feeling that the manuscript is almost finished. It isn't. A more practical approach is to give each table and figure a brief name ("ANOVA results," "plot of correct responses"), jot this label in the margin or write it in parentheses, and worry about the numbering scheme later when you are close to completion. Follow the same approach for references. Going to the library to look up the details of a reference is a great way to avoid writing. Jot the author's name, the date, and the source in the margin and attend to the details later. You may have deleted the reference by the final version and so will not need the details.

Above all, *keep writing*.

REVISING THE FINAL REPORT

It is the rare writer who produces readable prose on the first try, and seldom is even a single revision sufficient. Most people turn out a finished paper only after considerable editing and revision. Until you have gained some experience at technical writing, you should plan on several trips through the manuscript. I find it most efficient to focus on a different task during each pass. In the first revision I concentrate on overall organization by preparing a new outline based on what I have actually written; in the second I challenge each paragraph for style and coherence; in the third I work at the word level, cleaning up imprecise usage and checking spelling; and finally I make a last broad reading. A few details on each of these steps may be helpful.

A Scan for Structure

As noted earlier, before revising a paper it helps to gain the perspective of time. Organizational difficulties are especially hard to spot when the words are still hot on the paper. Everything seems so clear to you. With the passing of a day—

better yet two—you begin to see where the argument is sloppy, where the prose is muddy, where the interpretation is overly enthusiastic. If you need help in spotting the flaws and don't have a lot of time, try to persuade a friend to read the draft with a critical eye.

In any event, your first pass through the initial draft should be quick and should aim toward an analysis of the overall structure. It may help to jot down the points covered by the topic sentences on a separate piece of paper—almost a matter of outlining in reverse. You will often discover that you have departed from your original plan—either for better or for worse. A reorganization may suggest itself; you may see a need to add a new section or may spot an opportunity to rid yourself of a redundant or irrelevant passage. It is hard to throw away anything gained at such cost, but do it.

Grammar and Style

Now make another pass through the paper, concentrating on the appropriateness of each paragraph, sentence, and word; this may take more than one pass. As mentioned above, every paragraph should begin with a clear, strong, topic sentence, and the rest of the paragraph should follow that lead. If a paragraph is too long and complex (more than six to eight sentences), it probably contains more than one idea. Or perhaps you are overexplaining (when you are not yet sure about what you want to say, it is amazing how many words it takes to say it). In either event, the paragraph will be hard for most readers to comprehend.

Check each sentence. Long sentences (more than twenty to thirty words) should be chopped into two or more parts. A thought may flit through your mind— "I don't like that sentence" or "I don't need that sentence." Stop and examine the thought. It is difficult, after you have spent time creating a piece of priceless prose, to think about tossing it. Maybe it is neither as priceless nor as essential as you first thought. When in doubt, toss excess verbiage overboard. With time, ridding yourself of unneeded baggage will become less painful.

Take this opportunity to change passive sentences into active ones wherever possible. Check each sentence to ensure that closely associated words are placed near one another. For example, avoid constructions like "The paragraphs were shown on 3 × 5 cards to the subjects, which were printed in uppercase letters." Subjects are not printed in uppercase; words are. The writer intends to say, "The subjects saw paragraphs printed in uppercase letters on 3 × 5 cards."

Watch for *indefinite referents*—*this, that, it,* and *they* standing alone and without any clear topic or reference. In general, whenever any of these four words appears by itself, this (this what?—this event!) is a sign that you should automatically change the sentence so that the reader can tell what is being discussed.

That and *which* can also be a source of problems when they introduce a clause. *That* is generally used to begin a *restrictive clause*, one that restricts the expression and cannot be eliminated without substantially altering the meaning:

"The information that was given at the beginning of the experiment was brief, but more detailed instructions were provided after a practice run." Try taking out the restrictive clause "that was given at the beginning of the experiment," and you will discover that the sentence is harder to understand. *Which* introduces a *nonrestrictive clause*, one that is not essential and that can be eliminated without substantial change in meaning: "The instructions, which were given at the beginning of the experiment, were brief, but the subjects appeared to have no trouble with the task." The sentence reads clearly even though the "which" clause is dropped. Notice that nonrestrictive clauses are usually set off by commas, an indication of their optional status; commas are not used with restrictive "that" clauses.

As the previous examples show, you need to examine each word, especially nouns, verbs, and adjectives. Throw away wasteful terms; if a sentence reads as well without a word or phrase, get rid of it. The reader will be grateful. Check each word to ensure that it is the right word for the thought. Precise word choice is one of the keys to clear writing. To assist you in writing concisely, make sure you have a good thesaurus. Often a single word can replace a phrase: *for the purpose of* can be replaced with *for*; *in the case of* with *if*; *on the grounds that* with *since*; *on the basis of* with *by*; *prior to* with *before*; *subsequent to* with *after*; and *with regard to* deleted altogether—these are only a few examples.

Technical Revisions

On the next pass through the draft, check that the report satisfies the technical guidelines presented in the APA publication manual (APA, 1983). This manual is the ultimate arbiter of style for references, abbreviations, headings, preparation of figures and tables, and the final composition of the paper. The papers in Chapter 9 provide models for some of the standard conventions in the manual. Remember that *everything* in the manuscript should be double-spaced.

Nonsexist Language

The American Psychological Association has established guidelines for the nonsexist use of language. The publication manual encourages writers to "be aware of the current move to avoid generic use of male nouns and pronouns when content refers to both sexes" (p. 28). The APA Publications and Communications Board has some specific suggestions on this issue (APA, 1983).

Problems of designation. When you refer to a person or persons, choose words that are accurate, clear, and free from bias. Long-established cultural practice can exert a powerful, insidious influence over even the most conscientious author. . . . Choose nouns, pronouns, and adjectives to eliminate, or at least to minimize, the possibility of ambiguity in sex identity or sex role. . . . Problems of designation are divided into two subcategories: *ambiguity of referent*, when it is unclear whether the author means one sex or both sexes; and *stereotyping*, when the writing conveys unsupported or biased connotations about sex roles and identity.

Problems of evaluation. Scientific writing . . . should be free of implied or irrelevant evaluation of the sexes. Difficulties may derive from the habitual use of clichés or familiar expressions, such as "man and wife." The use of *man* and *wife* together implies differences in the freedom and activities of each and may inappropriately prompt the reader to evaluate the roles. Thus, *husband* and *wife* are parallel, and *man* and *woman* are parallel, but *man* and *wife* are not. . . . Problems of evaluation . . . are divided into *ambiguity of referent* and *stereotyping*.

. . . Ambiguity of Referent

Man's search for knowledge has led *him* into ways of learning that bear examination.	*The search* for knowledge has led *us* into ways of learning that bear examination.
Subjects were 16 girls and 16 boys. Each *child* was to place a car on *his* board so that two cars and boards looked alike.	Each child was to place a car on *his* or *her* board so that two cars and boards looked alike.

. . . Stereotyping

Research scientists often neglect their *wives* and *children*.	Research scientists often neglect their *spouses* and *children*.
the psychologist . . . *he*	psychologists . . . *they*; the psychologist . . . *she*
the therapist . . . *he*	therapists . . . *they*; the therapist . . . *she*
the nurse . . . *she*	nurses . . . *they*; nurse . . . *he*
the teacher . . . *she*	teachers . . . *they*; teacher . . . *he*

(APA, 1983, 44–47)

A Final Word

Attempting to introduce nonsexist language at the cost of awkwardness, obscurity, or euphemistic phrasing does not improve scientific communication. . . . Under no circumstances should an author hide sex identity in an attempt to be unbiased if knowledge of sex may be important to the reader.

(APA, 1977b, 8)

Alpha and Omega

The first and last elements of a research paper require special polishing at this time:

The Title. In fifteen words or fewer, summarize the topic of the study in clear, precise words. You should mention the primary factors (subject and/or treatment) and the task. Avoid any word that does not contribute directly to understanding the paper. For instance, avoid expressions like "a study of," "an experiment on," "the investigation of," and so on. Abbreviations are not to be used in the title.

The Abstract. This is generally the last section to be written—and it can be the toughest. The aim is to summarize the entire paper in 100 to 200 words. You should mention the purpose, the main hypotheses, design, subjects, procedures, major findings (no numbers, just results), and the main ideas from the interpretation. The writing style must be that of a telegram—every word is costly and so the *little words* are generally left out. The final product should be succinct but able to stand on its own. A difficult undertaking, and one not to be attempted until the report is virtually completed.

The References. Citations of other articles are placed at the appropriate location within the body of the text, with the authors' names and the date of publication listed in parentheses. If there are more than two authors, all are listed when the article is initially mentioned (e.g., Smith, Jones, Brown, & Peters, 1979), but only the first author and "et al." on subsequent occasions (Smith et al., 1979). When a paper is by two authors, both names are always listed in the citation.

The complete list of references goes at the end of the paper. Three types of citations account for most references, and you can follow the models given below for these:

Journal article:

Biederman, I., Glass, A. L., & Stacy, E. W., Jr. (1973). Searching for objects in real-world scenes. Journal of Experimental Psychology, 97, 22-77.

Book:

Calfee, R. C. (1975). Human experimental psychology. New York: Holt, Rinehart and Winston.

Chapter in an edited book:

Engen, T. (1971). Psychophysics: Discrimination and detection. In L. A. Riggs & J. W. Kling (Eds.), Experimental psychology. New York: Holt, Rinehart and Winston.

Except for the line spacing, every detail in these models is important—the capitalization, the abbreviations (and nonabbreviations), the underlining, the order of the elements, and so on.

AN EXAMPLE OF EDITING AND REVISION

Next you will see an example of editing and revising a draft manuscript. Editing is the task of detecting problems in a manuscript; revising is the job of correcting the problems.

First you will see a draft that I coauthored several years ago. Some obvious mistakes have been put into the draft for purposes of illustration, but the process of revision is never complete. Looking back at the paper, I found numerous ways to improve on our "final" draft.

The Rough Draft

The original draft of the manuscript is shown on the next five pages. You may assume that this version was the result of several preliminary sketches and is in near-final form. Now the job is to polish it. Read through the draft to get an overall impression. In the margin you will notice a list of code letters and words. Disregard these for the moment. When you have finished, you will find out what the codes mean and how they are used in the final revision.

SHORT-TERM MEMORY IN CHILDREN AS A FUNCTION OF DISPLAY SIZE

Dr. Robert C. Calfee

Professor E. Mavis Hetherington

Phyllis Waltzer

Department of Psychology

University of Wisconsin

T

Abstract

Display size was vareid in a card-guessing game with
young children by presenting either 3, 4 or 5 animal cards
in serial order, and testing for recall on one of the cards.
Marked recencry effects were observed at all stages of training,
and during the early trials, some primacy was noted. Retrieval appeared to be an all-or-none phenomenon, in contrast to previous studies with 8-item displays, which found
generalization and above-chance guessing on the second choice.

G - SP

G - Sr

S - BIG WORD

Introduction

Recent studies by Atkinson et al. (1964) and Hansen
(1965) have used a card-guessing game to investigate short-
term memory (STM) processes in young children. In this technique, a series of cards with colored drawings of animals were
presented one at a time in a serial order. Each card, after
being presented to the child, is turned face down so that a
horizontal array is formed. The child is then shown a separate cue card, and is asked to turn over the matching card in
the face-down array. 8-card lists were used in both of the
studies referred to above.

S - JARGON

G - TENSE

G - ACTIVE

T

Short-Term Memory -2-

    The method used in these studies has been used by other
researchers, but these two studies are the most important
ones for our purpose. A pronounced recency effect was evi-
dent in the Atkinson et al. study (the last card laid down
had the highest probability of being chosen correctly as a
match), but no primacy was observed. Generalization behaviors were also found; when an error was made, the incorrect
choice tends to be close to the correct position. In the
Hansen study, presentation rate was varied (1 sec. and 3 sec.)
with the result that the slower rate imporved recall of the
last cards presented, and the faster rate improved recall of
the first cards. Marked recency effects were observed with
both rates. There was also a slight primacy effect, especially at the slower rate.

    The present study was designed to investigate within-
subject list length short-term memory effects for preschool
children using a similar experimental task. It is well known
that primacy and recency effects vary over trials, and so this
was a question of interest.

Method

    The Ss were 38 preschool children between 3.5 and 5
years of age ($\overline{X}$=4.1, SD=.51) from the Unitarian Society Nursery School, Madison, Wisconsin. Each child was asked if he
would like to play a game; if the child was willing, he was
brought to the experimental room. There he was shown a collection of small toys, and told that he might choose one toy
as a prize for playing the game well. This was given to S at
the end of the session.

Handwritten margin annotations:
- O - LEAD
- G- ACTIVE
- S- JARGON
- G- TENSE
- S-TOSS
- G-SP
- S-TRAIN
- S- OBVIOUS
- S-JARGON (ss)
- G-THIS

Short-Term Memory -3-

The stimulus materials consisted of a set of 11 brightly
colored animal cards. Each card was shown to S, who was asked
to name the animal until S was familiar with each card in the
deck. The experiment consisted of 24 trials, each trail   *G-SP*
requiring about 1 min., for a total session time of about
1/2 hr.

On each trial a subset of 3, 4 or 5 cards was randomly
selected for presentation. The sequence for a child was
randomly arranged so that each display size was used for 8   *S-VAR*
trials, and each serial position was tested at least once for   *G-AWK*
every display size. The selected cards were shown one at a
time to S for a 1-sec. interval, S called out the name of the
animal, and then the card was placed face-down in a horizontal
array in front of S. After the last card was presented, a cue
card which was identical to one member of the presentation set
was held up, and S was asked to turn up the matching card in
the array. If this was incorrect, S continued to turn up   *G-THIS*
additional cards until a match was obtained. The intertrial
interval was about 40 sec., during which time E arranged cards
for the next trial and chatted with S.

Results and Discussion

Figure 1 presents the mean proportion of correct responses
at each position for the three display sizes. Position 1 corresponds to the last card displayed prior to the retention
test. The proportion of correct responses is a decreasing
function of the number of cards intervening between the test
position and recall. The probability that the last card in the

- - - - - - - - - - - -

Insert Figure 1 about here

- - - - - - - - - - - -

display is correctly identified when it is in the test position varies between .85 and .90, and appears to be unrelated
to display size. It may be taht this performance represents   G-SP
the best obtainable with preschool children in this task.
Hansen's 5 yr. olds gave about .65 correct responses at Posi-   T
tion 1 with an 8-item list, and the corresponding value in
the Atkinson et al. study was about .90. The proportion of
correct responses in Position 2, the next-to-last card presented, varies from .34 to .67, and is monotonically related   S-BIG WORD
to display size. As the display size is decreased (i.e.,
fewer cards are presented), S is more likely to recall the
card presented in Position 2, and the amount of this improvement is greater than can be accounted for by changes in the
guessing rate.

In order to evaluate changes in the serial position curve
over trials, the probability of an initial correct choice was
found for the first (F) and last (L) positions, and for all
middle (M) positions taken together, averaged over display

Short-Term Memory -5-

sizes in 6-trial blocks. The results of this analysis are in
agreement with Murdock's (1964) results; primacy as well as
recency is observed during the first two blocks, following
which there is only recency in the last two blocks.

    Comparison of the present study with the results of
Atkinson et al. and Hansen indicates that the data from these
studies are not trustworthy. An 8-card list is too long to
show how STM operates in children. It is clear that at list
lengths of 5 items or less the children behaved in the expected
fashion.

O = PICTURE

O - DATA

S - OBVIOUS

T

References

Atkinson, R. C., Hansen, D. N., & Bernbach, H. A. Short-
    term memory with young children. Psychon. Sci.,
    1964, 2, 255-256.

Hansen, D. N. Short-term memory and presentation rates with
    young children. Psychon. Sci., 1965, 3, 253-254.

Murdock, B. B., Jr. Proactive inhibition in short-term
    memory. J. Exp. Psychol., 1964, 68, 184-189.

From this draft you should have grasped the major points of the article. The manuscript is in reasonably decent shape—the title is appropriate, the overall organization is good, and so on. There are lots of little problems, however, and it is hard to understand some of the details because the paper is not as readable as it should be.

The first task in fixing the problems is to identify them. When you have been given the job of editing a paper, you should probably start by reading through it, jotting notes in the margin whenever something is wrong or you have trouble understanding a point.

Editing is time-consuming and requires a great deal of concentration under the best of circumstances. Some of the work is fairly routine, and to mechanize this part of the job, it helps to categorize and code certain recurring problems rather than always writing extensive notes in the margin. The most common problems can be classified under four headings:

> *Content* refers to the substance and overall structure of the paper and to the clarity of the paragraphs.

> *Grammar* includes proper sentence construction and other rules of syntax and word usage.

> *Style* covers problems of inappropriate or imprecise usage; the writing may be understandable, but it breaks some of the rules or can be changed so that it flows more smoothly.

> *Technical errors* are instances in which the manuscript does not conform to the specific guidelines of the publication manual.

The four categories are presented below with several types of specific problems that commonly occur in each category. The problem types are described, and an abbreviation is suggested for use in the margin. As you can see, these codes were used in the manuscript that you just read. You can use this checklist for reviewing your own papers; your instructor may already use some variation of this system for critiquing your assignments.

If you look back over the rough draft, you will find most of the codes illustrated by one or more examples. Those that are not exemplified are relatively self-explanatory and could not be further clarified without extensive discussion.

Content

ORDER
: The sections of a research paper generally follow a conventional order. All deviations—to depart from the established sequence, to leave out sections, or to intermix topics—make a paper hard to understand.

POINT
: Each section of a paper should have a theme. Rambling discussions should be avoided; stick to the point.

UNSMOOTH
: The first step in constructing a section is to decide on one or more themes. Then you assemble the information relevant to the themes, often on 3 × 5 cards. Next you "stitch" all these cards together. The last stop is to smooth out the transitions so the stitches don't show. You haven't completed this last step.

LEAD — Each paragraph should begin with a strong, topical sentence. The rest of the paragraph should support this lead sentence.

PICTURE — A picture, a graph, or a table can be worth a thousand words. It can also be worth less than a plugged nickel.

STRAW — Avoid the "straw man" approach to defending your own position or criticizing someone else's. If you want to argue with a person, make his or her argument as strong as possible.

EVIDENCE — Be careful to tell the difference between criticizing evidence and questioning the interpretation of the evidence.

Grammar

LONG — The sentence is too long.

COMPLICATED — In writing, among the many ways to boggle the reader's mind by making him or her maintain too many chunks in working memory waiting for the subject of the sentence is the embedded or left-recursive sentence. Avoid complicated sentences.

BAD GRAMMAR — Incorrect or questionable sentence structure.

ACTIVE — Use the active voice whenever possible.

THIS? — Avoid indefinite referents. Especially with *this* and *that*, be sure that a noun usually follows so that the referent does not stand alone.

TENSE — Check the usage and agreement of verb tense. Use past tense when referring to things happening in the past. Use future tense in stating hypotheses or conclusions that apply in the future. In any event, tense usage should be consistent.

SP — Check the spelling.

Style

AWK — An awkward sentence. Rephrase.

BIG WORD — You have utilized an unnecessarily extended verbalization. Don't use a big word when a short one will do.

TOSS — Toss out unneeded and redundant words.

VARIETY — Variety is the spice of life. Try not to use the same words or expressions over and over and over in close proximity.

PRECISE — Is this word really the one you mean? Consult a dictionary or thesaurus for a more precise term.

JARGON ". . . the medium through which the maximization of proper utilization of communications techniques to facilitate comprehension within a designated peer group and/or specific environment can be achieved. In other words, shop talk" (Grosswirth, 1978, Small Systems World). Avoid jargon, uncommon abbreviations, acronyms, nonsense syllables, and other incomprehensible terms.

TRAIN A string of nouns, called a "freight train," should be avoided.

OBVIOUS Almost nothing is really obvious. Do not use phrases like "it is well known that" or "as everyone realizes." Document the point by appropriate references.

Technical Errors

T Because there are numerous technical details in preparing a paper, a list of codes would be ungainly. Hence, the letter T is used to cover all such errors, with annotation where the problem is not readily apparent. The most important technical details are summarized below.
Headings. Up to three levels of headings are used in research papers. The primary headings correspond to the major elements. The secondary and tertiary headings aid the reader in seeing other organizational elements.
Abbreviations. Current practice is to be sparing of abbreviations. Use them only if they are familiar, are in conventional use, or will save a great deal of space because they occur frequently.
Metrication. Present policy is to use the metric system for measurement whenever possible.
Statistics. The notation used throughout this text follows the APA style. Underline symbols like F, t, and s. Analysis of variance results should be placed in a table rather than in text, except for the simplest designs.
Numbers. Zero through nine are usually written out, as is any number that begins a sentence. Use figures otherwise for two-digit numbers, for lists of numbers, and for units of measurement and percentages (a 6-year-old, 25 percent).
Tables and figures. Use graphic representation whenever economy and clarity can be achieved. The results should be supplemented but not duplicated in text. Headings and captions should be succinct, but sufficient so that the graphic can stand alone.
Quotations. Fewer than three lines go into the text; four lines or more should be set off as an indented block.
Footnotes. Avoid whenever possible. Use for acknowledgement, occasionally for expansion of a substantive point, and rarely for references.
Punctuation. Use sparingly in scientific writing. Where one has a choice about whether or not to use a comma, a semicolon, a hyphen, italics, or even capital letters, the rule is to dispense with punctuation.

Preparation. Double space *everything*, and leave *wide* margins (1.5 inches or 3.8 centimeters).

Authorship. Avoid titles like Dr. or Prof. The primary author is listed first, followed by any others who have made a substantial contribution. Minor contributions are recognized by a note.

Nonsexist use of language. The policy is to avoid generic use of male nouns and pronouns where both sexes are intended. There are several techniques for achieving this goal. Neologisms and constructions like he/she are generally frowned upon.

Marking the Manuscript for Revision

Once the editing is complete, you must again put on your hat as writer and attempt to deal with each problem. As you reexamine the text, you will undoubtedly find additional ways to improve the writing; the process of revision is never complete. If the manuscript has been edited professionally, it is likely to be covered with special symbols known as proofreaders' marks. The most useful of these symbols are presented in Figure 10–1 for your convenience; a complete list of proofreaders' marks is found in the backmatter of many dictionaries.

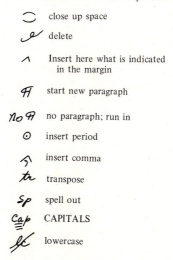

⌒	close up space
ℓ	delete
⋀	Insert here what is indicated in the margin
¶	start new paragraph
𝑛𝑜 ¶	no paragraph; run in
⊙	insert period
⋀	insert comma
𝑡𝑟	transpose
𝑠𝑝	spell out
𝐶𝑎𝑝	CAPITALS
ℓ𝑐	lowercase

Figure 10–1 Commonly occurring proofreaders' marks

On pages 286 and 287 are the first and last page of the revised manuscript, which illustrate the process. I have edited this sample more intensively than is common to demonstrate the variety of signs. The edited version follows APA standards for revision and illustrates how you might proceed in your own editing of a manuscript, or what you might expect to receive from a conscientious professor who has read your first draft.

SHORT-TERM MEMORY IN CHILDREN AS A FUNCTION OF DISPLAY SIZE

~~Dr.~~ Robert C. Calfee

~~Professor~~ E. Mavis Hetherington

and Phyllis Waltzer

Department of Psychology

University of Wisconsin

Abstract

Display size was varied ~~in a card-guessing game with~~ young children by presenting ~~either~~ 3, 4 or 5 animal cards *a list of* ~~in serial order~~, and testing ~~for~~ recall on ~~one of~~ the cards. ~~Marked~~ recency effects were observed at all ~~stages of training~~ *on/trials* ~~and~~ during the early trials some primacy was noted. Retrieval appeared to be ~~an~~ all-or-none ~~phenomenon~~, in contrast to previous studies with 8-item displays, which ~~found~~ *showed* generalization and above-chance guessing on the second choice.

Introduction

Recent studies by Atkinson ~~et al.~~ (1964) and Hansen *,and Bernbach* (1965) ~~have~~ used a card-guessing game to investigate short-term memory (STM) ~~processes~~ in young children. In this *game/list* ~~technique~~, a ~~series~~ of cards with colored drawings of animals ~~were~~ *is* presented one at a time ~~in a serial order~~. Each card, ~~after being presented to the child~~, is turned face down ~~so that~~ a *then/to form* horizontal array ~~is formed~~. The child is then shown a ~~separate~~ cue card, and is asked to turn over the matching card in the face-down array. ~~8-card lists were used in both of the~~ *these* studies ~~referred to above.~~ *used an 8-card list.*

Short-Term Memory   -5-

~~sizes in 6-trial blocks.~~ The results of this analysis are ~~in~~ shown in Figure 2 the same as ~~agreement with~~ Murdock's (1964) ~~results~~; primacy ~~as well as~~ findings and/both occur recency ~~is observed~~ during the first two blocks, ~~following~~ but afterward ~~which there is~~ only recency ~~in the last two blocks.~~ fig 2 appears about here

Comparison of the present study with the results of Atkinson et al. and Hansen indicates that ~~the data from these studies are not trustworthy. An 8-card list is too long to show how STM operates in children. It is clear that at list lengths of 5 items or less the children behaved in the expected fashion.~~ children may remember long and short lists differently. Short lists may be stored in a "tape recorder" format. Longer lists may have to be organized for successful retention. Further study over a wide range of display sizes is needed to resolve this question.

#! <u>References</u> ———————→

Atkinson, R. C., Hansen, D. N., & Bernbach, H. A. (1964). Short-term memory with young children. Psychon. Sci, ~~1964,~~ 2, 255-256. omic/ence ital

Hansen, D. N. (1965). Short-term memory and presentation rates with young children. Psychon. Sci, ~~1965,~~ 3, 253-254. omic/ence ital

Murdock, B. B., Jr. (1964). Proactive inhibition in short-term memory. J. Exp. Psychol, ~~1964,~~ 68, 184-189. Journal of Experimental Psychology ital

Note: location of dates after author name changed in APA Pub Manual, 1983

THE FINAL DRAFT

The revisions in the original draft were fairly extensive in this example. Starting below is a retyped copy of the final version, in the form in which it would be submitted for publication in a journal—the finished job.

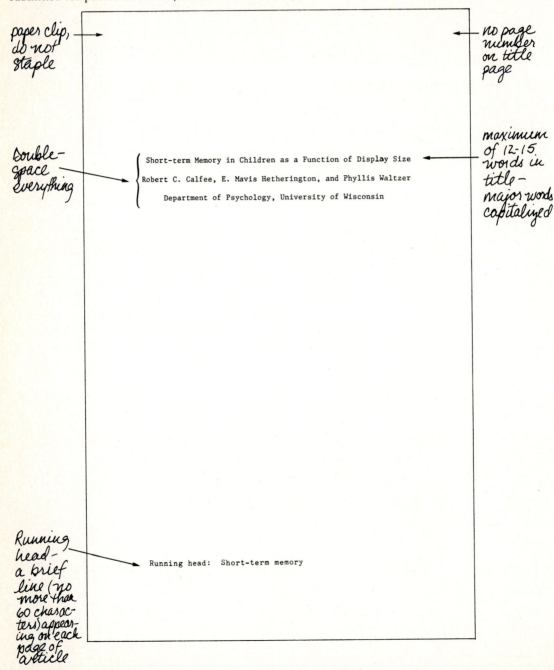

paper clip, do not staple

no page number on title page

Double-space everything

Short-term Memory in Children as a Function of Display Size

Robert C. Calfee, E. Mavis Hetherington, and Phyllis Waltzer

Department of Psychology, University of Wisconsin

maximum of 12-15 words in title—major words capitalized

Running head— a brief line (no more than 60 characters) appearing on each page of article

Running head: Short-term memory

Short-term Memory

1

Abstract

Display size was varied by presenting young children a list of 3, 4, or 5 animal cards, and testing recall of one card. Recency effects were observed on all trials. Some primacy was noted during the early trials. Retrieval appeared to be all-or-none, in contrast to previous studies with 8-item displays, which showed generalization and above-chance guessing on the second choice.

Running head and page number in upper right corner — paging begins with abstract

Single paragraph, no indentation — journals sometimes specify length

Authors' names do not appear past title page

Title is repeated (no author)

After the first time in full, et al. may be used

Abbreviations or acronyms may be used alone after having been spelled out

"S"(subject) "E"(experimenter) are no longer used

Common statistical terms may be abbreviated (m is mean s is standard)

Margins on all four sides of text are 1"-1½"

List all authors (3 or more) first time cited

Use abbreviations or acronyms sparingly, only when used several times later in the paper

Abbreviations are used for standard measures. Use the metric system where appropriate

The introduction often ends with an overview and a statement of the research goals

Center main headings. Check publication manual for second- and third- level headings

Short-term Memory

2

Short-term Memory in Children as a Function of Display Size

Recent studies by Atkinson, Hansen, and Bernbach (1964) and Hansen (1965) used a card-guessing game to investigate short-term memory (STM) in young children. In this game, a list of cards with colored drawings of animals is presented one at a time. Each card is then turned face down to form a horizontal array. The child is then shown a cue card, and is asked to turn over the matching card in the face-down array. Both of these studies used an 8-card list.

Atkinson et al. (1964) found a pronounced recency effect (the last card laid down had the highest probability of being chosen correctly as a match), but observed no primacy. They also noted generalization behaviors; when an error was made, the incorrect choice tended to be close to the correct position. Hansen (1965) varied presentation rate (1 sec. and 3 sec.) and found that the slower rate improved recall of the last cards, whereas the faster rate improved recall of the first cards. He found marked recency effects at both rates.

In our study we investigated the effects of variation in list length on the STM of preschool children using a card-guessing task. We were also interested in how primacy and recency effects vary over trials, because Murdock (1964) had found significant changes in the shape of the serial position curve over trials. Both primacy and recency appeared during early trials, but only recency during the later testing.

Method

The subjects were 38 preschool children between 3.5 and 5 years of age (m = 4.1, s = .51) from the Unitarian Society Nursery School, Madison, Wisconsin. Each child was asked to play a game, and if willing, was taken to the experimental room where there was a collection of small toys. The child was told to choose one toy as a prize for playing the game well. The prize was given to the subject at the end of the session.

The stimulus materials were 11 brightly colored animal cards. Each card was shown to the subject who was asked to name the animal until famil- ial with all the cards in the deck. The experiment consisted of 24 trials. Each trial required about one minute, so the total session lasted about half an hour.

On each trial a subset of 3, 4, or 5 cards was randomly selected for presentation. Each display size was used on eight trials, and each serial position was tested at least once for every display size. On a given trial, cards were shown one at a time for one second, the child named the animal, and then the card was placed face-down in a horizontal array. After the last card, a cue card was held up and the child tried to turn up the match- ing card in the array. If the choice was incorrect, the subject continued to turn up additional cards until he made a match. The intertrial inter- val was about 40 secs. During this time, the tester arranged cards for the next trial and chatted with the subject.

Results and Discussion

Figure 1 presents the mean proportion of correct responses at each serial position for the three display sizes. Position 1 is the last card displayed prior to the test. The proportion of correct responses decreases with the number of cards between the test position and recall. The prob- ability of identifying the last card in the display varies between .85 and .90, and is unrelated to display size. This performance may represent the best that preschool children can do in this task. Hansen's (1965) 5-year olds were right about 65 percent of the time at Position 1 with an 8-item

Use numerals for numbers larger than 10 — or for lists of numbers write out otherwise

Because this is a brief article the results and discussion sections have been combined

Short-term Memory

4

list, and the corresponding value in the Atkinson et al. (1964) study was about 90 percent. The proportion of the correct responses in Position 2, the next-to-last card presented, varies from .35 to .67 with increasing display size. When fewer cards are presented, the subject is more likely to recall the next-to-last card presented, and the amount of improvement in STM is greater than can be accounted for by changes in the guessing rate.

- - - - - - - - - - - - -

Insert Figure 1 about here

- - - - - - - - - - - - -

To evaluate changes over trials in the shape of the serial position curve, we calculated averages over 6-trial blocks of the probability of correct choice for the first, last, and middle positions. The results of this analysis shown in Table 1 are the same as Murdock's (1964) findings; primacy and recency both occur during the first two blocks, after which recency appears.

- - - - - - - - - - - - -

Insert Table 1 about here

- - - - - - - - - - - - -

Comparison of the present study with the results of Atkinson et al. (1964) and Hansen (1965) indicates that children may remember long and short lists differently. Short lists may be stored in a "tape recorder" format. Longer lists may have to be organized for successful retention. Further study with a wider range of display sizes is needed to resolve this issue.

Don't hesitate to use first person when appropriate — but keep it under control

Putting the year after each reference becomes tedious but it is the style

Notice the style for showing where figures and tables are to appear in the text. This practice aids the typesetter, though it makes it difficult to read the paper! Arabic numerals are used for both figures and tables.

The ampersand is used in the reference section and when a reference is in parentheses within the text

For the style of other references, check the publications manual or see examples at the end of this text

Underlining is used for book titles, journals, and for the journal volume number—to the typesetter it means to use italics

Short-term Memory

5

References

Atkinson, R. C., Hansen, D. N., & Bernbach, H. A. (1964). Short-term memory with young children. Psychonomic Science, 2, 255–256.

Hansen, D. N. (1965). Short-term memory and presentation rates with young children. Psychonomic Science, 3, 253–254.

Murdock, B. B., Jr. (1964). Proactive inhibition in short-term memory. Journal of Experimental Psychology, 68, 184–189.

Table 1

Percentage of Correct Responses

as a Function of Trial Block and

Position of Test Item in Study List

Trial	Position of Test Item		
Block	First	Middle	Last
1 – 6	96	38	49
7 –12	93	39	40
13 –18	77	45	20
19 –24	91	50	20

Tables are typed double-spaced and table number and title are included with the table

Short-term Memory

Figure Captions

Figure 1.   Proportion of items correctly recalled on first attempt at
each serial position for three display sizes.

Figure captions are submitted on a separate page placed before the figures. This is for the convenience of the typesetter.

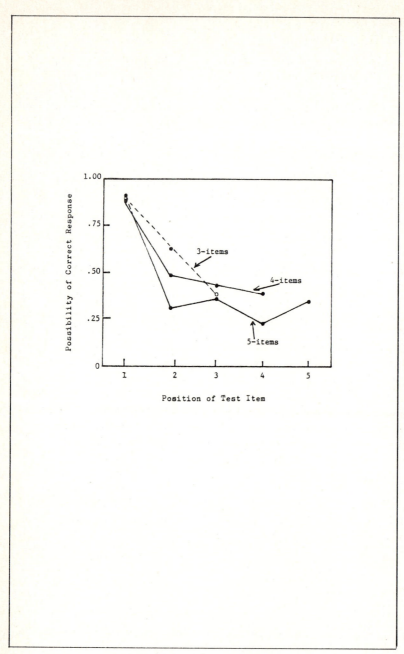

Figures are either photographs or black-and-white drawings. The figure number and running head are written lightly in pencil on the back of the figure. Also on the back is indicated the TOP of the figure.

TOP
FIG 1
Short-term
Memory

SUMMARY

Writing a research report is something like studying the paper in reverse. The starting point is an image of the study in the writer's mind—the question, the design, the procedures, the findings, and (poorly formed when the writing begins) the interpretation of the findings. The writer also needs to think about the audience for the report, and the formal structure that is spelled out in the APA publication manual.

In preparing oneself to write a research report, it is best to begin with an outline based on the major elements of the formal structure—the introduction, the method, the results, and the discussion. The outline should be fairly detailed so that the writer can use it as a starting point for creating paragraphs.

The initial draft, based on the outline, is a matter of constructing paragraphs from the leads provided by the outline. Paragraphs, the "idea units" of a paper, should begin with a topic sentence that is followed by several sentences of supporting detail. In preparing the first draft, the writer's main goal is to get words onto paper, but some concepts of style are worth keeping in mind. Sentences should be kept relatively short and simple. Tables, figures, and references should be noted in the text, though not necessarily in complete detail. Double- or triple-space everything, and leave wide margins. Most important, it is essential to keep writing.

Revision is a multistage process. The first stage is a reading from a broad perspective to evaluate the overall structure of the paper; it may help to outline "in reverse," using the topic sentences as cues. The next stages in revision are at the paragraph level (does each paragraph deal with a single coherent idea?), and at the sentence and word levels. The writer should then review the paper for technical adequacy based on the requirements of the APA publication manual. The final pass through the finished product should again be from a broad perspective to make certain that the final draft is complete and readable. At this point the title, the list of authors, the abstract, and the references are added to the paper.

The publication manual is the bible for research reports in psychology (and for many other areas of social science), and the writer should consult this manual when preparing a report, for guidance, and also for examples. Some of the most important guidelines are illustrated by the example at the end of the chapter, which shows the steps in taking a research report from the first draft through to the final product.

APPENDIX
STATISTICAL ANALYSIS

Experimental design is often identified with statistical analysis. Advanced courses in experimental design may present relatively little information about design, the focus being almost entirely on statistical methods. This linkage has its roots in history, a fact that is of little help to the student. This book has concentrated on research methods, both descriptive and experimental. The appendix covers some statistical procedures that go along with these methods. It is intended as a review, and so if you have never had a course in statistics, you will find this material difficult and may need to consult an introductory textbook on statistics. Many of the concepts and techniques reviewed here are discussed in my earlier text on experimental psychology (Calfee, 1975).

This appendix takes a conceptual rather than computational orientation. For present purposes it is more important that you understand how statistics support the findings from an experimental design than that you demonstrate skill in calculating a t-test or an F-ratio. Not too many years ago, prior to the advent of the digital computer, calculational expertise was more critical—knowing the formulas was important for the behavioral scientist. In this day of the computer—mini, micro, and macro—conceptual understanding is essential for the student to make intelligent use of the resources available.

The appendix begins with a nonexperimental situation. Suppose you need to analyze a set of numbers (analysis of nonnumerical data is possible but will not be covered here). The techniques for analyzing one set of numbers are broadly applicable to the analysis of experimental data, that is, data in which one or more factors have been controlled by the experimenter, so that several sets of numbers have to be analyzed. After the discussion of the single-sample situation, the analysis of one-way and two-way designs is presented. It is assumed that all of the plans are between-subjects, the simplest case; the analysis of within-subjects and mixed designs is somewhat more complex, though the same basic principles apply.

Statistical Description of a Data Set

Central Tendency and Variability. Suppose you have been presented the set of numbers in the list below:

3 2 4 1 5 3 9 8 7 6 6 6

What should you do with them? How can you summarize them? The statistician's answer to this question would be this: calculate a measure of central tendency for the set; and calculate a measure of the variability in the set. *Central tendency* refers to the middlemost value of the set, and *variability* is the scatter around the index of central tendency.

We might, for instance, arrange the numbers from smallest to largest.

1 2 3 3 4 5   6 6 6 7 8 9

This rearrangement makes it easy to see (a) that half the numbers are 5 or smaller and half are 6 or greater, and (b) that the numbers range between 1 and 9. The "breakpoint" or *median* is one measure of central tendency, and the difference between the largest and smallest numbers or *range* is one measure of variability.

The Sample Mean and the Sample Variance. While the median and the range are handy for some purposes, they are not the best indices for statistical purposes, primarily because they tend to be rather erratic, especially when the number of observations is small. (Notice that the data set is now being referred to as a sample; the reason for this switch in terminology will become clear in the next section.) The best indices that can be found—the most consistent and precise—are the sample mean and the sample variance.

You probably know the *sample mean* by another name—the average. You probably also know how to calculate it: add together all the observations in a sample and divide by the number of observations. This operation is described by the formula

$$m = \frac{\sum_{i=1}^{n} X_i}{n}$$

The sample mean is abbreviated as m. Each observation in the set is given an index number, X_i. The Greek letter *sigma* or Σ is a command to add whatever follows; the values at the top and bottom of the command indicate the beginning and ending indices. Assuming that there are n observations, the formula says, "To calculate the mean, m, line up the observations from the first (number 1) to the last (number n), add them together, and divide by n"—a compact though unfamiliar code for describing how to compute an average. In the example, the sum of the observations is 60, there are 12 observations, and so the sample mean is 5.0—close to the median.

The *sample variance*, or s^2, is probably new to you. If you have had an introductory course in statistics, you may have encountered the *standard deviation*, or *s*. These two indices of variability are really one and the same: the standard deviation is the square root of the variance, and the variance is the square of the standard deviation. The choice of one index or the other depends on the nature of the statistical analysis being performed, as we shall see below.

The variance has no intuitive basis, and laying out the theory behind this index would take us far afield, but here is the computational formula:

$$s^2 = \frac{\sum_{i=1}^{n} (X_i - m)^2}{n - 1}$$

The instructions direct you to perform the following operations. First, calculate the sample mean, *m*. Second, subtract each observation from the mean and square the difference. This is the interpretation of $(X_i - m)^2$. Third, add together all of the squared deviations that you have just computed, the direction given by the Greek sigma. Finally, divide the sum by $(n - 1)$, 1 less than the number of observations in the sample.

The variance is a rather strange beast, but some of its characteristics are worth noticing. First, it is always a positive number. Whenever you square a number, the result is positive; since you are adding a bunch of positive numbers and dividing by a positive number, the final result is positive. Second, it takes at least two numbers to compute a variance; otherwise, you wind up dividing by zero, which leads to problems. Third, the greater the scatter in a set of numbers, the greater the variance—and even a few observations that depart greatly from the mean can markedly increase the variance because it is the square of these numbers that is being added up.

In the data set we have been using for an example, the sum of squared deviations is 66.0, the denominator is 11 (one less than the 12 observations), and so the variance is $66.0 \div 11$ or 6. The standard deviation is the square root of 6, which equals 2.45. You can now compute the mean, the variance, and the standard deviation. But what do you do with these results? That is the topic of the next section.

The Sample and the Population

A sample is seldom of interest in its own right but only as we can learn something about the larger collection from which it is a random selection. The larger collection is referred to in statistics as the *population*. Notice the distinction between the definition of population as a group of people, and its use in statistics to describe a collection of numerical observations.

Imagine that someone tosses a coin; heads are scored 0 and tails 1. The population is the collection of all 1s and 0s from tossing this coin an infinite number of times. The scores from ten tosses are a sample from the population. Another population is the set of all scores by college freshmen in the United States on a ten-item vocabulary test taken during September 1984. A sample would be the test scores of 100 freshmen selected at random from the population. Another sample might be the test scores of 100 students selected at random from the freshman class at San Francisco State University; this is not a true random sample from the original population, but it might be informative and it would certainly be handier to obtain than a true random sample. Notice that a population is described by a data collection procedure: toss a coin an infinite number of times; administer a ten-item vocabulary test to all college freshmen in September 1984; and so on. In most instances it is either impossible or impractical to collect the data for an entire population. Instead, a sample of observations is obtained, and the researcher uses the sample data to make inferences about certain characteristics of the population.

The population characteristics of primary interest are, as you might have guessed, indices of central tendency and variability. The *population mean* is calculated in exactly the same manner as the mean of a population. To be sure, this calculation would take a long time to perform, especially when the number of observations is infinite. The population mean is generally a theoretical value, however, and the researcher is playing a guessing game—"What is the most likely value of the population mean, given the information in the sample?"

The *population variance* is also calculated by the same formula as the sample variance, with one slight change: the sum of squared deviations is divided by n rather than by $n - 1$. Remember that we are talking about populations, in which the number of observations is very large, and so the difference between n and $n - 1$ is negligible.

The population mean is generally labeled by the Greek letter μ, and the population variance by the Greek letter σ^2, corresponding to the roman letters for the sample mean and variance. The population *parameters*, μ and σ^2, are the most important characteristics of the population, and in the case of some theoretical populations, all that one needs to know.

As it turns out, the mean and variance from a sample can be used as estimates of the population mean and variance. To understand how the estimation works, we need to introduce the concept of a *sampling distribution*. Suppose a population has been defined, a sample of a particular size has been obtained, and the sample mean and variance have been calculated. Imagine that the sampling procedure is carried out a second time—a second sample of the same size is drawn, and sample mean and variance are calculated. Imagine a third and fourth sample being collected. In fact, let's repeat the sampling procedure an infinite number of times. The set of sample means comprises the *sampling distribution of the mean*, and the set of sample variances is the *sampling distribution of the variance*.

A concrete example may help. We will use the population of coin tosses. Suppose that a coin is tossed 50 times, the sample mean and variance are calculated, and this procedure is repeated one million times—not quite infinite, but very large. The outcome of each sample will range between a total score of 0 (no heads in the sample) and 50 (all heads); the sample means will therefore range between

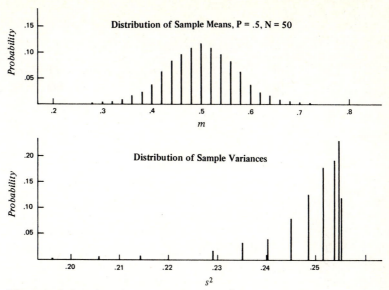

Figure A–1 Sampling distribution of m and s^2 for a coin-tossing experiment with 50 tosses per sample

0/50 = 0.0 and 50/50 = 1.0, with intermediate values like 1/50 = .02, 2/50 = .04, and so on. If the coin is unbiased, the average number of heads will be 25/50, which is equivalent to a mean of .50. If a computer were to actually generate the million samples, the distribution of sample means would be as shown in Figure A–1.

The sample means have the shape of the bell-shaped *normal distribution*, with which you may be already familiar from introductory statistics. The average of the sampling distribution is .5, which is also the mean of the entire population of coin tosses. Two features apparent in the figure are also characteristic of the sampling distribution of the mean, along with a third characteristic that is quite valuable for drawing inferences:

The sample means are normally distributed.

The mean of the sampling distribution of m equals the population mean μ.

The variance of the sampling distribution of m, σ_m^2, equals σ^2/n; σ^2 is the population variance, and n is the number of observations in the sample.

These relations are known collectively as the *central limit theorem* of statistics, and they are the foundation for drawing inferences about a population from a sample. We know that the sample mean is an unbiased estimate of the population mean, we know the shape of the distribution of sample means, and we know the variance of that sampling distribution, which can be calculated from the variance estimate.

The *t*-statistic

Another sampling distribution of importance is the t-*distribution*, which is closely related to the sampling distribution of *m*. Suppose that a sample is drawn from a population, that the sample mean and variance are calculated, and that these estimates are used to compute the *t*-statistic:

$$t = \frac{m}{\sqrt{\dfrac{s^2}{n}}} = \frac{m}{s_m}$$

The sample mean and variance you are familiar with. What about the relations in the formula above? The sample variance when divided by the sample size is actually an estimate of the variance of the sampling distribution of the mean, as mentioned above in the discussion of the central limit theorem. The square root of this variance, s_m, is referred to as the *standard error of the mean*; it is the "standard deviation" of the sampling distribution of the mean. Thus, we now have a short-hand description of the *t*-statistic: *t* equals the sample mean divided by the standard error of the mean.

The distribution of the *t*-statistic resembles the sampling distribution of the mean, with two exceptions. First, because the mean has been divided by the standard error, the variance of the *t*-distribution equals 1.0. Thus, no matter what the variance of the original population, all *t*-distributions have the same variance. Second, the *t*-distribution is bell-shaped to the eye, but it varies slightly from a true normal distribution, depending on the stability of the variance estimate. More precisely, the *t*-distribution depends on the denominator of the variance estimate, $n - 1$ in the present case. This quantity, known as the *degrees of freedom* (or *df*) for the variance estimate, determines the stability of this estimate. When the degrees of freedom are large (30 or more), the *t*-distribution is virtually indistinguishable from the normal curve. As the degrees of freedom become smaller, the top of the curve is pushed down and the outlying "edges" tend to rise. Typical values become less common, and deviations become more likely, a pattern that arises from the instability of the variance estimate.

Statistical Inferences

The game of statistical inference is just that—a game. The researcher formulates a hypothesis, collects a sample of data, and uses the information from the data together with the rules of the inference game to decide whether the hypothesis is tenable. The issue is not truth, but plausibility. To see how the game is played, let us use the sample of data analyzed earlier in the appendix. Suppose these scores describe the improvement in test performance after administration of a magic memory drug—each subject was given a twenty-item vocabulary test, took two pills, and then was given a second twenty-item test. A score of 3 indicates that the subject was correct on three additional items on the second test, and so on.

How shall we formulate the hypothesis? An approach commonly used by social science researchers is to propose the *null hypothesis*: start with the assumption that the pills have no effect, in which case the difference in performance from the first to the second test should be zero. According to this hypothesis, the twelve observations are a sample from a population in which the mean μ equals zero.

Let us now think about the *t*-distribution under the null hypothesis. The hypothetical mean is 0.0, and the standard error for the sample can be estimated from the variance estimate:

$$s_m = \sqrt{\frac{s^2}{n}} = \sqrt{\frac{6.0}{12}} = .707$$

The sample mean, *m*, is 5.0, and so is 5.0/.707 or 7.07 standard error units away from the hypothesized population mean of 0.0.

Now we need to refer to the values of the *t*-statistic displayed in Table A–1 at the end of the appendix. This table does not actually show the *t*-distribution; instead, it presents *critical values* of the *t*-statistic for making decisions. You should keep Figure A–1 in mind as we examine Table A–1. The degrees of freedom for the variance estimate are $12 - 1$ or 11; look at the line in the table corresponding to 11 *df* in the left column. The next number to the right is 2.201, which is in a column labeled .05.

The value of 2.201 is the critical value of the *t*-statistic for a *significance level* of .05. If a *t*-statistic is greater than 2.201, then the index has moved out of the range of typical values in the sampling distribution and into the range where rare or *statistically significant* events are occurring. If you refer to Figure A–1, you will notice that sample means greater than .6 occur rarely in the coin-tossing situation; if more than thirty heads turn up in a sample of fifty coin tosses, something unusual has happened. The table of critical *t*-statistics establishes boundaries for rare events. A significance level of .05 corresponds to 1 event in 20. If a *t*-statistic exceeds 2.201 under these assumptions, then something has happened that should occur only once in twenty samples (or experiments). The rightmost value on the line for 11 *df* equals 4.437, which corresponds to a significance level of .001. If a *t*-statistic exceeds 4.437, then we have observed an event that should occur less than 1 in 1,000 times, given that the assumptions are sound.

The *t*-statistic of 7.07 calculated under the null hypothesis (the drug has no effect) is indeed an unusual event; it goes entirely off the scale of the table of critical *t*-values. (Incidentally, this table is for *two-tailed tests*; either a positive *or* negative deviation as large as the critical *t*-statistic is suspect.) What should the researcher do? One decision might be to conclude that something truly rare has been observed. A second decision would be to conclude that the null hypothesis is untenable, thereby leading the researcher to reject the null hypothesis and to conclude that the drug actually affects performance. The argument takes a rather backward approach, because the researcher probably ran the experiment not to confirm the null hypothesis, but in the hope that this hypothesis could be rejected. The researcher is therefore delighted when he or she is proven wrong!

Suppose the observations in our sample actually had a mean of 1.0, with the same variance. The t-statistic for the sample would now be $1.0/.707 = 1.41$; this value falls well within the band of critical values, and so the null hypothesis cannot be rejected. You can now see the basis for the discussion in the text about the power of an experiment. The null hypothesis is more likely to be rejected (a) if the treatment has a big effect, (b) if the variance is small, and (c) if the sample size is large (big samples produce small standard errors). In addition, the researcher's choice of a critical significance level also influences the likelihood of rejecting the null hypothesis. If a relatively liberal significance level is chosen (e.g., .05, or 1 in 20 chances), then the critical band is not so selective—the researcher may decide that something is happening when nothing is there, but is also more likely to detect true effects when they exist. If the significance level is relatively conservative (.001, or 1 in 1,000 chances), then the researcher is unlikely to ever cry wolf but may fail to spot some promising treatments.

Statistical Analysis of the Experimental-Control Design

In this section we apply the descriptive and inferential methods described above to the analysis of one-way between-subjects designs. We begin with the simplest situation—the experimental-control comparison. As noted in the text, this design is especially vulnerable to confounding, but it is easy to analyze. Then we apply the methods to one-way designs with three or more treatment conditions.

Suppose that the first six numbers from the data set at the beginning of the appendix are scores for a control group (no memory drug) and that the last six numbers are from an experimental group (memory drug before second test). Here are the scores for each group, along with the descriptive statistics (sample mean and variance).

Group	Scores						m	s^2
Control	3	2	4	1	5	3	3.0	2.0
Experimental	9	8	7	6	6	6	7.0	1.6

The means for the two groups are quite different, in the direction of better performance by the experimental group; the researcher breathes a sigh of relief. The variance for the two groups is about the same. Many statisticians would be happy about this feature of the data.

Does the memory drug "really" make a difference? This question asks about the population from which this study is a sample. Stated more precisely, if the study were to be repeated a large number of times, would there be a difference between the two conditions? Expressed as a formula, what is the value of $\mu_E - \mu_C$? Might it be possible that, despite the observed difference between the two conditions in this sample, the null hypothesis is nonetheless tenable? Or can the researcher reject the null hypothesis and conclude that the drug has some effect?

The *t*-statistic can be used in this situation. The formula for evaluating the difference between two means is:

$$t = \frac{m_E - m_C}{\sqrt{\dfrac{s_E^2 + s_C^2}{n}}}$$

The control mean is subtracted from the experimental mean; the standard error of the difference is computed from the sum of the variances for the two groups (it may help if you remember the "difference over the sum" or "subtract means and add variances"). Calculations from the descriptive statistics computed earlier yield a *t*-statistic of 5.16 with 10 degrees of freedom (each of the variance estimates has 5 *df*, so the total *df* for the overall estimate is 10). If you look in Table A–1, you will find that on the line for 10 *df*, the critical value of the *t*-statistic for a significance level of .001 is 4.59. The observed difference between the experimental and control groups yields a *t*-statistic greater than this critical value, and so the chances are less than 1 in 1,000 that this difference would occur if there were actually no effect of the memory drug. The experimenter is probably well advised to decide that the drug has a positive effect on performance. Sound decisions can be based on a small amount of data if the pattern is clear—if you are tossing pennies with a friend, and the first twenty tosses are heads, you should examine the coin. . . .

The Additive Model. The extension of the *t*-statistic to the two-group situation works well for some situations, but a more general approach exists for describing data and drawing inferences about experimental effects. This method, referred to as the *additive model*, is the foundation for both the *t*-statistic and the *analysis of variance*, the latter technique for handling factorial designs as well as one-way designs.

The additive model assumes that each observation in a study is the sum of several components, each component reflecting a source of variability in the data. The base line is an overall mean, μ, which is the grand average of the entire population of observations. Each factor in the design contributes a main effect, which may be negligible, of course. Some of the factors are systematic (treatment, subject-classification, or nuisance), and others are unsystematic. The model for any particular study depends on the factors in the design of the study. In the present example, there are two factors: the treatment factor (two levels, experimental and control), and the subject factor (unsystematic, six levels within each of the two treatment groups). Accordingly, the additive model for this experiment is

$$X_{ij} = \mu + \tau_i + \epsilon_{ij}$$

The Greek letters in the model indicate the theoretical status of the model. To describe the elements in the model, and to draw inferences about each component, it is necessary to estimate each of the components. The estimation of the overall mean μ is simple enough—use the overall mean of the sample, m, which we have previously determined to equal 5.0. The equation below shows the estimation, with the "hat" over μ indicating that it is an estimate:

$$\hat{\mu} = m = 5.0$$

What about the effects of the treatment factor, which we have labeled with the Greek τ for treatment? The model assumes that effects add together, and so the estimates are based on subtraction:

$$\hat{\tau}_E = m_E - \hat{\mu} = 7.0 - 5.0 = 2.0$$
$$\hat{\tau}_C = m_E - \hat{\mu} = 3.0 - 5.0 = -2.0$$

You should notice two features of these estimates. First, the positive and negative effects offset each other; more generally, if the number of observations in each condition is the same, then the sum of effects for each factor will be zero so that there is a perfect balance around the overall mean. Second, the distance between the two effects is the same as the difference between the two means. The effects with two levels of a factor are simply another way of expressing the difference between the means.

The final component of the model is the unsystematic subject factor. This effect is estimated separately for each subject in order to complete the fit of the model to the data; the approach may seem circular, but it is not, as you will see. The subject effect is estimated by subtracting from each observation the estimates for the other components:

$$\hat{\epsilon}_{E1} = X_{E1} - \hat{\mu} - \hat{\tau}_E = 9 - 5.0 - 2.0 = 2.0$$
$$\hat{\epsilon}_{E2} = X_{E2} - \hat{\mu} - \hat{\tau}_E = 8 - 5.0 - 2.0 = 1.0$$

$$\cdots$$

$$\hat{\epsilon}_{C6} = X_{C6} - \hat{\mu} - \hat{\tau}_C = 6 - 5.0 - (-2.0) = -1.0$$

Notice that each observation and each of the subject effects has two indices, i for the treatment condition and j for the subject within the treatment.

Decomposing the Set of Observations. The bookkeeping has become burdensome by this point; Figure A–2 shows the whole picture. The process entails decomposition by stages: first the overall mean is pulled out, then the treatment effects, and finally the residual (whatever is left over). The numbers in the right panels are the estimates for each component in the model; each observation can then be reconstructed by adding together the components for a particular subject.

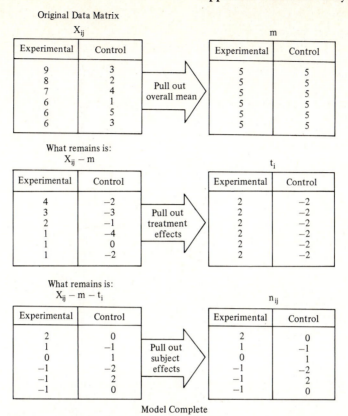

Figure A–2 Steps in decomposing data matrix into components of the additive model, one-way, two-level design

A minor point, but one with important implications: notice that the subject effects in each group are actually deviations from the group mean, $X_{ij} - m_i$. Thus, if you square these components, add them together, and divide by the degrees of freedom for each group, you will have actually computed the variance for that group.

The Analysis of Variance for a Two-group Design. Suppose you square each observation in the experimental–control data set and add these squares together. This quantity, which equals 366, is referred to as the *total sum of squares*. Next, square the estimates for each component of the model in Figure A–2 and add together the squared values over all subjects. A summary of these calculations is presented in Figure A–3 in the column labeled SS for "sum of squares." There are twelve 5s in the component for the mean; squaring 5 yields 25, times 12 is 300, which is the value under SS for the source labeled "mean." The other SSs are calculated in similar fashion. Notice that if you add together the SS for the three components of the model, the result equals the total SS. An interesting feature of

Source	df	SS	MS	F
Mean	1	300.0	300.0	
Treatment	1	48.0	48.0	26.7
Subjects in Treatment	10	18.0	1.8	
(Total)	(12)	(366)		

Figure A–3 Summary table for analysis of variance of data in Figure A–2

the additive model is that it provides for a perfect division or "partitioning" of the sum of squares in a data set.

Now look at the column labeled *df* (for degrees of freedom). This term has been mentioned before; now it will be given a new interpretation. The degrees of freedom for a source in the additive model is the number of estimates that are unique and free to vary. Let's play a guessing game. I have twelve numbers in mind—what are they? More particularly, what is the mean of the set? You cannot tell, so I will calculate the mean and inform you that it is 5.0. This estimate has 1 *df* because it is a single estimate without any constraints until it is computed. What about the treatment effects? Again, you have no way of telling until I calculate the mean of one or the other group. Suppose I tell you that the mean of the experimental group is 7.0. Now you can estimate the effect of the experimental treatment and also the effect of the control treatment (the two must offset each other); since the experimental effect is $+2.0$, the control effect must be -2.0). There are two estimates, but only one is free to vary, and so there is 1 *df*. Finally there are the df for the subject source. Within each group there are 5 *df*—I can tell you the scores for each subject up through the fifth one, and then you can figure out what the sixth score must be because it must balance the other five to equal the mean for the group. Notice that the total degrees of freedom for the model equals the total number of observations. Each observation in a study provides you with one degree of freedom for the statistical analysis.

Now let us put all these pieces together, so that you can see where the exercise has led us. The definition of a variance estimate presented earlier can be described as a sum of squares divided by the appropriate degrees of freedom. For each component of the model, we now have both of the elements needed to compute a variance source for that component. The entries in the *MS* column are actually variance estimates. The label for a variance estimate was originally "mean square," hence the designation *MS*. Recall that the variances for the experimental and control groups equaled 1.6 and 2.0, respectively; notice that the *MS* (subjects in treatment) is the average of these two variances.

The F-ratio. The ratio of any two sample variances has a sampling distribution, much like the sample mean, the sample variance, or the difference between two sample means. The variance ratio, referred to as the *F-ratio* after the statistician, Sir Ronald Fisher, also has a sampling distribution. Since variances are always positive, the F-ratio is also positive. If two sample variances are from the same population, then the F-ratio should be in the neighborhood of 1.0, because the two estimates will be approximately equal. Table A–2 at the end of the appendix shows critical values of the sampling distribution of F. The table has certain features in common with the table of critical values for the t-statistic. The F distribution depends on the stability of both variance estimates, and so must be entered by noting the df for both the numerator and the denominator.

Suppose, for instance, that we compare the variance estimate for the treatment source with the variance estimate for subjects in treatment. This ratio, shown in the F column of the summary table, equals 26.7. The treatment variance has 1 df and the subjects variance 10 df. If you look up the entry for this combination in the table of critical F-values, you will discover that the entries are 4.96 for a decision probability of .05, 10.04 for a decision probability of .01, and 21.04 for a decision probability of .001. The observed F-ratio of 26.7 is extremely large and would occur less than 1 in 1,000 events if the two variance estimates were actually from the same population.

What sources of variability contribute to the two estimates in the ratio that we have computed? In the denominator is an estimate of unsystematic variability between subjects, including all the "noise" due to error of measurement and other unpredictable sources. This source serves as a measure of the internal validity of the experiment. In the numerator is an estimate of the systematic variability introduced by the treatment conditions. If the null hypothesis is true, then the difference between treatment conditions should reflect only random variation, and the F-ratio should be close to 1.0. If there is a genuine treatment effect, however, then the variability due to this source might indeed be expected to be rather large, leading to an increase in the F-ratio.

In fact, the F-ratio comparing the treatment source to the subject source parallels the previous test using the t-statistic. Both compare the magnitude of the treatment effect to a measure of residual or unsystematic variability and then turn to a table of critical values of a summary statistic as a basis for making a decision. The two approaches are in fact equal when there are only two levels of a treatment factor; if you compute the square root of the F-ratio in the summary table, you will discover that it equals 5.17, which is the value of the t-statistic computed earlier. While the t-statistic and the observed F-ratio are identical when there are two levels of a factor, the F-ratio provides additional flexibility in that it can handle designs with three or more levels of a factor.

Statistical Analysis of a One-way Four-level Study

To illustrate the last point above, we will analyze the previous data set using a different design; the numbers may be the same, but the information they generate depends greatly on the design.

DATA MATRIX

	TREATMENT FACTOR			
	T_1 Grammatical	T_2 Adjectives	T_3 Nouns	T_4 Verbs
SUBJECTS IN TREATMENTS	$X_{11} = 3$ $X_{12} = 2$ $X_{13} = 4$	$X_{21} = 1$ $X_{22} = 5$ $X_{23} = 3$	$X_{31} = 9$ $X_{32} = 8$ $X_{33} = 7$	$X_{41} = 6$ $X_{42} = 6$ $X_{43} = 6$

DESCRIPTIVE STATISTICS FOR EACH TREATMENT FACTOR

Mean m_i	3.0	3.0	8.0	6.0
Variance s_i^2	1.0	4.0	1.0	0.0
Standard Deviation s_i	1.0	2.0	1.0	0.0

Figure A–4 Data matrix and summary statistics for misspelling study

To add some realism to the illustration, let us assume that the following study has been conducted. College undergrads have been assigned the task of looking through a list of twenty words for misspellings. The list, which was displayed for ten seconds, contained ten words that were correctly spelled and ten words with a single misspelling. The treatment factor, T, is the type of words in the list: List T_1 contained grammatical words like *therefore, morover,* and *whereupon*; list T_2 had adjectives like *wonderous, pennyless,* and *coqently*; list T_3 included nouns such as *technique, excelence,* and *foundasion*; and, finally, list T_4 contained verbs like *manipulate, terroreize,* and *nulify*. The purpose of the study was to investigate how completely the readers decoded the letter patterns when skimming words. The dependent measure was the number of misspelled words detected by the subjects.

The *data matrix* from the study is displayed in the top panel of Figure A–4. The columns and rows of the matrix correspond to the levels of the treatment factor and to the set of subjects within each treatment, respectively. Each observation, X_{ij}, has two indices; i is the treatment level index and j the index for the subject within a given treatment level. The observations, as noted above, are the same numbers used previously for illustration.

Descriptive statistics for each treatment level are shown in the panel below the data matrix. Each of the descriptive statistics is indexed with the treatment level; m_1 refers to the average number of misspellings for grammatical words, and so on. The pattern in the means shows that subjects appear to detect fewer misspellings in the

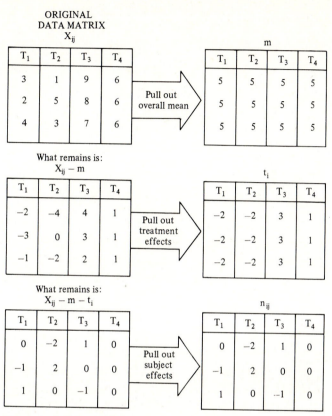

Figure A–5 Steps in decomposing data matrix into components of the additive model, one-way, four-level design

grammatical words and adjectives than in nouns and verbs. Notice that these last two types of words generally provide more substantive information about meaning. Whether this contrastive pattern is trustworthy remains to be established, of course. The variances differ somewhat from one level to another, but the number of observations per level is small, leading one to expect some instability.

The additive model for this design is the same as for the experimental–control design discussed earlier, except that now there are four treatment effects to be estimated. The model is shown in Figure A–5, which also displays the process of decomposing the observations to obtain estimates for each component of the model. As in the experimental–control example, the estimates are computed by successive subtraction.

Figure A–6 shows the results from the analysis of variance based on the estimates for the additive model. As in the preceding example, the sum of squares for each component is calculated by squaring each estimate and adding together the

Source	df	SS	MS	F
M	1	300	—	—
T	3	54	18.0	12.0
N(T)	8	12	1.5	—
Total	(12)	(366)	—	—

Note: F (3, 8, .05) = 4.1
      F (3, 8, .01) = 7.6
      F (3, 8, .001) = 15.8

Figure A–6 Summary table for analysis of variance of misspelling study

squared estimates. The degrees of freedom are calculated following the principle of the number of independent estimates. For the mean there is a single estimate, hence 1 *df*. For the treatment source there are four estimates; once the first three have been estimated, the fourth is determined because the set of four must add to zero: three independent estimates means that there are 3 *df*. Within each treatment level there are three subject estimates; once two of these have been estimated, the third is determined—two independent estimates for each of four treatment conditions adds up to 8 *df*. As in the previous example, the *df* add up to the total number of observations and the SS add up to the total of the squared observations.

The variance estimate, or *MS*, is calculated by dividing the *df* into the SS for each source. The *F*-ratio comparing the treatment variance to the subject variance equals 12.0. Critical values of the *F*-ratio for the appropriate degrees of freedom in the numerator and denominator are shown in the note to Figure A–6. The observed *F*-ratio is greater than the critical value for a decision probability of .01 but less than a value of .001—an *F*-ratio as large as 12.0 might occur by chance 1 in 1,000 times even though the null hypothesis is true (no effects of the treatment factor), but it would occur less than 1 in 100 times. The researcher has reason to reject the null hypothesis and to conclude that the treatments do affect performance—odds of 1 in 100 are not worth accepting.

The results from the analysis of variance give the researcher confidence in concluding that something is happening as a result of variation among the four levels of the treatment factor. The results do *not* tell the researcher which conditions differ significantly from one another, but there are several techniques for determining which of the levels differ from one another. A complete discussion of this topic would take us too far afield for present purposes, but the *t*-statistic for comparing means is one way of handling this situation.

To calculate a *t*-test, the researcher must decide which means to contrast, and then must calculate the standard error of the difference. A variation on the previous formula for comparing two treatment conditions takes advantage of the fact that $MS\{N(A)\}$ is the most stable estimate of residual variance:

$$t = \frac{m_k - m_l}{\sqrt{\dfrac{MS\{N(A)\}}{n_k} + \dfrac{MS\{N(A)\}}{n_l}}}$$

The k and l indices refer to two nonoverlapping means calculated from the data. Using this formula the researcher can compare any two means or sets of means. For instance, suppose the researcher wishes to compare the first two levels with the last two levels. The value of m_{1+2} is 3.0, and m_{3+4} equals 7.0. Each of the means is based on six observations. When these values are put into the formula, we have

$$t = \frac{3.0 - 7.0}{\sqrt{\dfrac{1.5}{6} + \dfrac{1.5}{6}}} = \frac{-4.0}{.707} = -5.66$$

The critical value of the t-statistic with 8 df for a decision probability of .001 is 5.04, and so the observed difference between these two means would occur by chance less than once in 1,000 times if the null hypothesis is true. The researcher should probably reject the hypothesis and conclude that there is a difference between the two sets of conditions. (Remember that the critical values of t are for either a positive or negative difference.)

There is clearly no difference between the first two conditions, grammatical versus adjectives; both have a mean of 3.0. What about the difference between nouns and verbs? Each mean is based on 3 observations, yielding a t-statistic of

$$t = \frac{8.0 - 6.0}{\sqrt{\dfrac{1.5}{3} + \dfrac{1.5}{3}}} = \frac{2.0}{1.0} = 2.0$$

The critical value of t with 8 df and a decision probability of .05 is 2.31, and so a t-statistic as large as 2.0 could occur by chance at least 1 in 20 times, even though the null hypothesis is true. To be sure, the comparison is between means based on very few observations and so lacks statistical power. The researcher cannot reject the null hypothesis, but neither is there much confidence in accepting it.

Statistical Analysis of a Two-by-two Design

We will now take one final look at our data set, this time as a two-by-two between-subjects factorial design with three subjects per condition. The treatment factors will be simply labeled A and B—you can devise your own cover story for the experiment. The data matrix is shown in the upper left panel of Figure A–7, along with the decomposition into the estimates for the additive model. The model, shown along the right side of the figure, includes components for the mean, for the main effects of the A and B factors, for the interaction between A and B, and for the residual effects of subjects.

The estimation process has more steps in a complex design than in the simpler one-way examples. Extracting the mean is straightforward. Next, compute the average for the entries in A_1 and then for A_2; these are the main effects of the A factor. Notice that the two estimates offset one another. Pull out the A effects, and then compute the average for B_1 and for B_2; these are the estimates for the main effects of the B factor. Again, subtract the B estimates, and record the remainder. The AB interaction effects are then estimated by calculating the average for each of the four conditions. The overall mean, along with the A and B effects, are subtracted from these averages. The remainder is an interaction estimate. The remainder from each observation is left as an estimate of the subject effects. Notice that these latter are the residuals from the one-way design discussed previously; in each instance the subject estimate is based on the deviation from the cell mean.

After the decomposition process is completed, the next step is to calculate the analysis of variance. As before, the sum of squares for each source is computed by squaring the estimates for that source in the decomposition table. The results are shown in Figure A–8. Each source has 1 df except subjects. There are two estimates for each main effect; as soon as one of the estimates is calculated, the other is determined. The interaction source also has a single degree of freedom; the estimates must offset one another along both rows and columns so that after one of the estimates is calculated, the other three are determined.

F-ratios are calculated for each of the treatment sources by comparison with the subject source. The observed F-ratios in the summary table are then evaluated against the critical values of F shown in the note to the table. As you can see, the A factor yields an F-ratio that would occur less than 1 time in 1,000 if the null hypothesis is actually true. The researcher can safely reject the null hypothesis for this source. The two remaining sources, B and AB, produce little systematic variance, and the researcher cannot reject the null hypothesis for these sources.

Analysis of More Complex Designs

Designs can be more complicated than those discussed above in one of three ways. First, factorial designs may include combinations of three or more factors. The additive model can be extended to these situations by including components for each main effect and for interactions for the various combinations of the factors. As noted in the text, the number of sources increases rapidly with the number of factors, and the estimation process can quickly become tedious and even overwhelming. No new concepts or techniques are required to cover this situation, however.

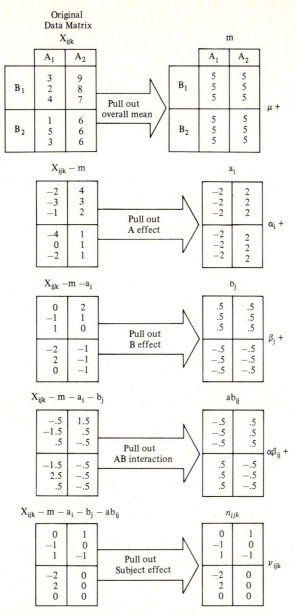

Figure A–7 Steps in decomposing data matrix into components of the additive model, two-way, 2×2 design

Second, within-subjects and mixed designs must be handled in a slightly different fashion than the between-subjects designs just discussed. In between-subjects designs the observations in one condition are not related to the observations in any other condition; in within-subjects and mixed designs a subject who does

Source	df	SS	MS	F
Mean	1	300.0	—	
A	1	48.0	48.0	32.0
B	1	3.0	3.0	2.0
AB	1	3.0	3.0	2.0
N(AB)	8	12.0	1.5	—
Total	(12)	(366)		

Note: F (1, 8, .05) = 5.32
F (1, 8, .01) = 11.26
F (1, 8, .001) = 25.42

Figure A–8 Summary table for analysis of variance of data in Figure A–7

especially well or poorly in one condition is also more likely to do well or poorly in other conditions. The researcher needs to be aware of the influence of these patterns on the validity of the analysis and to take steps to ensure that the patterns are described for the reader and that the analysis is adjusted according to these patterns. Several statistical texts discuss this matter (Kirk, 1982, Chs. 10, 11; Myers, 1979, Chs. 7, 8), and should be consulted for details.

The third area of complexity, also related to within-subjects variation in a factor, is the analysis of Latin and Graeco-Latin square designs. While actually simpler to analyze than complete factorial designs, these designs do make strong assumptions about the absence of interactions, and the researcher needs to be alert during the analysis for failures in these assumptions. The references listed in the preceding paragraph give advice on this matter.

Correlation, Prediction, and Reliability

This final section of the statistical appendix describes techniques for measuring the association between two variables. These techniques play a relatively minor role in the analysis of experimental data, but you will see that they do tie in at some crucial points.

Before describing the concept of correlation, we need to introduce the notion of a *standardized*, or *z, score*. To standardize a set of scores, one subtracts the mean of the set from each observation and then divides by the standard deviation; if the data are from a sample, then the sample mean and standard deviation are used:

$$z = \frac{X_i - m}{s}$$

Standardized scores have a number of features that appeal to statisticians; for instance, the mean of a set of standardized scores is always 0.0 and the variance and standard deviation are always 1.0. This property is an algebraic consequence of the formula used to compute the z-score. Another feature of standardized scores is the ease with which one can calculate the degree of relationship between two sets of measures. Let us see how this works.

Correlation. We will begin with a simple data set:

$$1 \quad 2 \quad 3 \quad 4 \quad 5 \quad 6 \quad 7 \quad 8 \quad 9$$

The mean of this data set is 5.0, the variance is 7.5 and the standard deviation is 2.74. Standardizing the original scores yields the following values:

$$-1.5 \quad -1.1 \quad -.73 \quad -.37 \quad 0.0 \quad .37 \quad .73 \quad 1.1 \quad 1.5$$

If you calculate the mean and standard deviation of this transformed data set, you will discover that they do indeed equal 0.0 and 1.0, respectively. You can see that these numbers balance around a centerpoint of 0, although the pattern is less apparent when the distribution is not symmetric.

Now let us consider a second data set with *two* variables—two dependent measures, if you will:

First variable	1	2	3	4	5	6	7	8	9
Second variable	1	2	3	4	5	6	7	8	9

A rather strange data set, but designed to make a point. These two variables have clearcut relation to one another—the second variable is perfectly predictable from the first one, and vice versa. In the leftmost panel of Figure A–9, the two variables are plotted against each other; the X and Y coordinates show both the original and the standardized values. Because the two variables are perfectly related to each other, they trace out a straight line from one corner of the graph to the other corner at a 45-degree angle.

The Pearson product-moment correlation coefficient, r, is the measure of association most commonly employed to assess the relation between two variables. There are quite a few ways to compute this index; with standardized scores the formula is relatively simple:

$$r = \frac{\sum_{i=1}^{n} x_i y_i}{n - 1}$$

In words, multiply the two standardized variables for each observation, add together the products, and divide by the number of observations less 1. Notice that this formula works only for standardized scores. If the scores are not standardized, the formula is more complicated.

In the present example, the computation yields

$$r = \frac{(-1.5)(-1.5) + (-1.1)(-1.1) + \ldots + (1.5)(1.5)}{8} = 8.0/8 = 1.0$$

A correlation of 1.0 means that a straight line with a slope of 1.0 (a 45-degree angle) best describes the relation between two variables. Moreover, a correlation of 1.0 means that the straight-line relation is a perfect one; knowing x, you can predict y exactly.

Figure A–9 shows two other patterns. The center panel shows what happens when the order of the second variable is reversed relative to the first variable so that the highest scores for the second variable are paired with the lowest values of the first variable, and vice versa. The relation is again perfect, but opposite or inverse. The r for this situation reflects the pattern—a correlation of -1.0 indicates a perfect inverse relation between two variables.

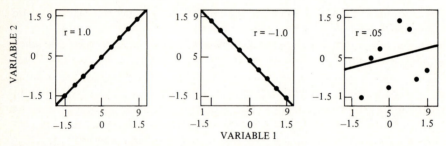

Figure A–9 Scatterplots showing different correlational patterns

The right panel shows what happens when there is little or no relation between variables. This pattern was created by randomly pairing the two sets of scores. The points are scattered throughout the two-dimensional space, so that predicting one variable from the other is virtually impossible. By calculating r we find that there is a very slight positive relation, but the coefficient of .05 is very close to 0.0, which represents a "perfect" nonrelation between two variables.

Prediction Based on Correlation. The correlation coefficient can be used for several purposes. For instance, if two variables are closely related, then the coefficient can be used to predict one variable from the other. Even if the relation is not very close, the prediction from the correlation is the best that can be done—the predicted value is likely to be off the mark when the correlation is as small as .05, to be sure.

A special form of prediction is the assessment of the predictive validity of a measure. Suppose a researcher claims to have developed a new measure of aggressiveness based on the number of teeth that an adult has lost (perhaps the researcher has friends who play hockey or football). Let us also assume that a trustworthy index of aggressiveness exists (finding this index might be a problem, to be sure). To validate the lost-teeth measure, the researcher calculates the correlation between this measure and the index of aggressiveness. If the correlation coefficient is close to 1.0, then the researcher has evidence supporting the validity of counting lost teeth to measure aggressiveness. As noted in the text, predictive validity is only one index of the validity of a measure, and not necessarily the best indicator.

Reliability: the Split-half Index. Just as there are several definitions of the concept of validity, so reliability can be defined in several ways. One of the most basic definitions is the technique of *split-half correlation*. This method is fairly simple. Let us assume that the researcher has constructed an eight-item test and has administered the test to a sample of ten subjects. The split-half reliability is computed by (a) dividing the test items into two sets of equal size (the odd and even items will do quite nicely), (b) calculating the total scores for each of the split-half sets, and (c) computing the correlation between the two split-half scores. If the correlation is close to 1.0, then the first half of the test rates the subjects about the same as the other half of the test, which means that the test items are internally consistent.

Figure A–10 illustrates the difference between consistent patterns in which the test items contribute uniformly to the total test score, along with an inconsistent pattern in which there is "disagreement" between items. The figure also demonstrates the use of the split-half reliability to evaluate a set of test items. Two data matrices are shown in the figure; the one on the left is reliable while the one on the right is not. The ten subjects and eight items have been arranged from highest to lowest scores. Notice that the scores (1 = an error on the item; 0 = a success on the item) appear as a visually simple diagonal pattern, a characteristic of internally consistent patterns of response. The scores for odd and even items are also presented; the correlation between the two halves is .75, a fairly high correlation given the small amount of data for the test. The researcher is justified in taking seriously the differences in the total scores for the sample of subjects.

The data matrix on the right has no apparent pattern of 0s and 1s. The items are all about equally difficult (not necessarily an indicator that a test is unreliable, but often suggestive of inconsistency). The distribution of total scores for subjects is identical to that in the left panel. The score for odd and even items has been calculated for this test; it is $-.50$, a slightly negative correlation indicative of internal inconsistencies among items. Whether a particular subject is performing well or poorly depends on the items selected for assessment, and if a new set of test items were to be added to the test, the subjects' performance might shift rather markedly—the differences between the subjects' total scores are not trustworthy.

The data matrices in Figure A–10 may remind you of an analysis of variance and, in fact, the analysis of variance can be used to determine the reliability of a test. The details would take us too far afield, but briefly, a test is reliable if the

	HIGH RELIABILITY TEST				
Subject Number	Item Number 1 2 3 4 5 6 7 8	Total	Odd Items	Even Items	
1	1 1 1 1 1 1 0 0	6	3	3	
2	1 1 1 1 1 1 0 0	6	3	3	
3	1 1 1 1 1 0 0 0	5	3	2	
4	1 1 1 1 1 0 0 0	5	3	2	
5	1 1 1 1 0 0 0 0	4	2	2	
6	1 1 1 1 0 0 0 0	4	2	2	
7	1 1 1 0 0 0 0 0	3	2	1	
8	1 1 1 0 0 0 0 0	3	2	1	
9	1 1 0 0 0 0 0 0	2	1	1	
10	1 1 0 0 0 0 0 0	2	1	1	
	10 10 8 6 4 2 0 0		r = .75		

	LOW RELIABILITY TEST				
Subject Number	Item Number 1 2 3 4 5 6 7 8	Total	Odd Items	Even Items	
1	1 1 1 0 1 1 1 0	6	4	2	
2	1 1 1 1 0 1 0 1	6	2	4	
3	0 1 0 1 0 1 1 1	5	1	4	
4	1 1 1 0 1 0 1 0	5	4	1	
5	0 1 0 1 0 1 0 1	4	0	4	
6	1 0 1 0 1 0 1 0	4	4	0	
7	1 0 0 1 1 0 0 0	3	2	1	
8	0 0 1 1 0 0 0 1	3	1	2	
9	1 1 0 0 0 0 0 0	2	1	1	
10	0 0 0 1 0 0 0 1	2	0	2	
	6 6 5 6 4 4 4 5		r = −.50		

Figure A–10 Examples of subject-item matrices for tests of high and low reliability

variance due to the subject factor is large compared to the interaction between subjects and items. The main effects of subjects and of items adequately describe the data in the left matrix, and so the interaction is relatively small—a reliable pattern of relationships between subjects and items, and hence the main effects (in this case, differences between subjects) are trustworthy. In the right panel the main effect of the item factor is small (the items do not differ greatly from one another), which leaves a considerable amount of variability in the interaction component. The differences between subjects must therefore be taken with a grain of salt.

The topic of reliability is discussed at greater length in several statistics texts. Besides the references listed earlier, you might also want to consult Hays (1981). As you learn more about statistical analysis, you will begin to appreciate the interrelatedness of the various methods. Virtually all the techniques discussed above are based on some form of the additive model and on the principle of dividing the total variability in a set of observations into components associated with either systematic or unsystematic factors. Many statistics texts still place emphasis on computational formulas. As noted at the beginning of this appendix, in the day of the digital computer, it makes more sense to let the machine do the actual computing and to emphasize the conceptual foundations of the technique, and this is the approach taken here.

Table A-1
Critical Significance Values of the *t* Distribution

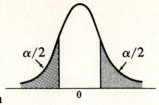

df	α=0.1	0.05	0.02	0.01	0.002
1	6.314	12.706	31.821	63.657	318.31
2	2.920	4.303	6.965	9.925	22.326
3	2.353	3.182	4.541	5.841	10.213
4	2.132	2.776	3.747	4.604	7.173
5	2.015	2.571	3.365	4.032	5.893
6	1.943	2.447	3.143	3.707	5.208
7	1.895	2.365	2.998	3.499	4.785
8	1.860	2.306	2.896	3.355	4.501
9	1.833	2.262	2.821	3.250	4.297
10	1.812	2.228	2.764	3.169	4.144
11	1.796	2.201	2.718	3.106	4.025
12	1.782	2.179	2.681	3.055	3.930
13	1.771	2.160	2.650	3.012	3.852
14	1.761	2.145	2.624	2.977	3.787
15	1.753	2.131	2.602	2.947	3.733
16	1.746	2.120	2.583	2.921	3.686
17	1.740	2.110	2.567	2.898	3.646
18	1.734	2.101	2.552	2.878	3.610
19	1.729	2.093	2.539	2.861	3.579
20	1.725	2.086	2.528	2.845	3.552
21	1.721	2.080	2.518	2.831	3.527
22	1.717	2.074	2.508	2.819	3.505
23	1.714	2.069	2.500	2.807	3.485
24	1.711	2.064	2.492	2.797	3.467
25	1.708	2.060	2.485	2.787	3.450
26	1.706	2.056	2.479	2.779	3.435
27	1.703	2.052	2.473	2.771	3.421
28	1.701	2.048	2.467	2.763	3.408
29	1.699	2.045	2.462	2.756	3.396
30	1.697	2.042	2.457	2.750	3.385
40	1.684	2.021	2.423	2.704	3.307
60	1.671	2.000	2.390	2.660	3.232
120	1.658	1.980	2.358	2.617	3.160
∞	1.645	1.960	2.326	2.576	3.090

Table A-2 The 5 (Roman Type) and 1 (Boldface Type) Percent Points for the Distribution of F

n_1 degrees of freedom for numerator mean square

n_2	1	2	3	4	5	6	7	8	9	10	11	12	14	16	20	24	30	40	50	75	100	200	500	∞
1	161 / **4,052**	200 / **4,999**	216 / **5,403**	225 / **5,625**	230 / **5,764**	234 / **5,859**	237 / **5,928**	239 / **5,981**	241 / **6,022**	242 / **6,056**	243 / **6,082**	244 / **6,106**	245 / **6,142**	246 / **6,169**	248 / **6,208**	249 / **6,234**	250 / **6,258**	251 / **6,286**	252 / **6,302**	253 / **6,323**	253 / **6,334**	254 / **6,352**	254 / **6,361**	254 / **6,366**
2	18.51 / **98.49**	19.00 / **99.00**	19.16 / **99.17**	19.25 / **99.25**	19.30 / **99.30**	19.33 / **99.33**	19.36 / **99.34**	19.37 / **99.36**	19.38 / **99.38**	19.39 / **99.40**	19.40 / **99.41**	19.41 / **99.42**	19.42 / **99.43**	19.43 / **99.44**	19.44 / **99.45**	19.45 / **99.46**	19.46 / **99.47**	19.47 / **99.48**	19.47 / **99.48**	19.48 / **99.49**	19.49 / **99.49**	19.49 / **99.49**	19.50 / **99.50**	19.50 / **99.50**
3	10.13 / **34.12**	9.55 / **30.82**	9.28 / **29.46**	9.12 / **28.71**	9.01 / **28.24**	8.94 / **27.91**	8.88 / **27.67**	8.84 / **27.49**	8.81 / **27.34**	8.78 / **27.23**	8.76 / **27.13**	8.74 / **27.05**	8.71 / **26.92**	8.69 / **26.83**	8.66 / **26.69**	8.64 / **26.60**	8.62 / **26.50**	8.60 / **26.41**	8.58 / **26.35**	8.57 / **26.27**	8.56 / **26.23**	8.54 / **26.18**	8.54 / **26.14**	8.53 / **26.12**
4	7.71 / **21.20**	6.94 / **18.00**	6.59 / **16.69**	6.39 / **15.98**	6.26 / **15.52**	6.16 / **15.21**	6.09 / **14.98**	6.04 / **14.80**	6.00 / **14.66**	5.96 / **14.54**	5.93 / **14.45**	5.91 / **14.37**	5.87 / **14.24**	5.84 / **14.15**	5.80 / **14.02**	5.77 / **13.93**	5.74 / **13.83**	5.71 / **13.74**	5.70 / **13.69**	5.68 / **13.61**	5.66 / **13.57**	5.65 / **13.52**	5.64 / **13.48**	5.63 / **13.46**
5	6.61 / **16.26**	5.79 / **13.27**	5.41 / **12.06**	5.19 / **11.39**	5.05 / **10.97**	4.95 / **10.67**	4.88 / **10.45**	4.82 / **10.27**	4.78 / **10.15**	4.74 / **10.05**	4.70 / **9.96**	4.68 / **9.89**	4.64 / **9.77**	4.60 / **9.68**	4.56 / **9.55**	4.53 / **9.47**	4.50 / **9.38**	4.46 / **9.29**	4.44 / **9.24**	4.42 / **9.17**	4.40 / **9.13**	4.38 / **9.07**	4.37 / **9.04**	4.36 / **9.02**
6	5.99 / **13.74**	5.14 / **10.92**	4.76 / **9.78**	4.53 / **9.15**	4.39 / **8.75**	4.28 / **8.47**	4.21 / **8.26**	4.15 / **8.10**	4.10 / **7.98**	4.06 / **7.87**	4.03 / **7.79**	4.00 / **7.72**	3.96 / **7.60**	3.92 / **7.52**	3.87 / **7.39**	3.84 / **7.31**	3.81 / **7.23**	3.77 / **7.14**	3.75 / **7.09**	3.72 / **7.02**	3.71 / **6.99**	3.69 / **6.94**	3.68 / **6.90**	3.67 / **6.88**
7	5.59 / **12.25**	4.74 / **9.55**	4.35 / **8.45**	4.12 / **7.85**	3.97 / **7.46**	3.87 / **7.19**	3.79 / **7.00**	3.73 / **6.84**	3.68 / **6.71**	3.63 / **6.62**	3.60 / **6.54**	3.57 / **6.47**	3.52 / **6.35**	3.49 / **6.27**	3.44 / **6.15**	3.41 / **6.07**	3.38 / **5.98**	3.34 / **5.90**	3.32 / **5.85**	3.29 / **5.78**	3.28 / **5.75**	3.25 / **5.70**	3.24 / **5.67**	3.23 / **5.65**
8	5.32 / **11.26**	4.46 / **8.65**	4.07 / **7.59**	3.84 / **7.01**	3.69 / **6.63**	3.58 / **6.37**	3.50 / **6.19**	3.44 / **6.03**	3.39 / **5.91**	3.34 / **5.82**	3.31 / **5.74**	3.28 / **5.67**	3.23 / **5.56**	3.20 / **5.48**	3.15 / **5.36**	3.12 / **5.28**	3.08 / **5.20**	3.05 / **5.11**	3.03 / **5.06**	3.00 / **5.00**	2.98 / **4.96**	2.96 / **4.91**	2.94 / **4.88**	2.93 / **4.86**
9	5.12 / **10.56**	4.26 / **8.02**	3.86 / **6.99**	3.63 / **6.42**	3.48 / **6.06**	3.37 / **5.80**	3.29 / **5.62**	3.23 / **5.47**	3.18 / **5.35**	3.13 / **5.26**	3.10 / **5.18**	3.07 / **5.11**	3.02 / **5.00**	2.98 / **4.92**	2.93 / **4.80**	2.90 / **4.73**	2.86 / **4.64**	2.82 / **4.56**	2.80 / **4.51**	2.77 / **4.45**	2.76 / **4.41**	2.73 / **4.36**	2.72 / **4.33**	2.71 / **4.31**
10	4.96 / **10.04**	4.10 / **7.56**	3.71 / **6.55**	3.48 / **5.99**	3.33 / **5.64**	3.22 / **5.39**	3.14 / **5.21**	3.07 / **5.06**	3.02 / **4.95**	2.97 / **4.85**	2.94 / **4.78**	2.91 / **4.71**	2.86 / **4.60**	2.82 / **4.52**	2.77 / **4.41**	2.74 / **4.33**	2.70 / **4.25**	2.67 / **4.17**	2.64 / **4.12**	2.61 / **4.05**	2.59 / **4.01**	2.56 / **3.96**	2.55 / **3.93**	2.54 / **3.91**
11	4.84 / **9.65**	3.98 / **7.20**	3.59 / **6.22**	3.36 / **5.67**	3.20 / **5.32**	3.09 / **5.07**	3.01 / **4.88**	2.95 / **4.74**	2.90 / **4.63**	2.86 / **4.54**	2.82 / **4.46**	2.79 / **4.40**	2.74 / **4.29**	2.70 / **4.21**	2.65 / **4.10**	2.61 / **4.02**	2.57 / **3.94**	2.53 / **3.86**	2.50 / **3.80**	2.47 / **3.74**	2.45 / **3.70**	2.42 / **3.66**	2.41 / **3.62**	2.40 / **3.60**
12	4.75 / **9.33**	3.88 / **6.93**	3.49 / **5.95**	3.26 / **5.41**	3.11 / **5.06**	3.00 / **4.82**	2.92 / **4.65**	2.85 / **4.50**	2.80 / **4.39**	2.76 / **4.30**	2.72 / **4.22**	2.69 / **4.16**	2.64 / **4.05**	2.60 / **3.98**	2.54 / **3.86**	2.50 / **3.78**	2.46 / **3.70**	2.42 / **3.61**	2.40 / **3.56**	2.36 / **3.49**	2.35 / **3.46**	2.32 / **3.41**	2.31 / **3.38**	2.30 / **3.36**
13	4.67 / **9.07**	3.80 / **6.70**	3.41 / **5.74**	3.18 / **5.20**	3.02 / **4.86**	2.92 / **4.62**	2.84 / **4.44**	2.77 / **4.30**	2.72 / **4.19**	2.67 / **4.10**	2.63 / **4.02**	2.60 / **3.96**	2.55 / **3.85**	2.51 / **3.78**	2.46 / **3.67**	2.42 / **3.59**	2.38 / **3.51**	2.34 / **3.42**	2.32 / **3.37**	2.28 / **3.30**	2.26 / **3.27**	2.24 / **3.21**	2.22 / **3.18**	2.21 / **3.16**

Reprinted by permission from *Statistical Methods* by G. W. Snedecor and W. G. Cochran, sixth edition © 1967 by Iowa State University Press, Ames, Iowa.

The 5 (Roman Type) and 1 (**Boldface Type**) Percent Points for the Distribution of F—continued

n_1 degrees of freedom for numerator mean square

n_2	1	2	3	4	5	6	7	8	9	10	11	12	14	16	20	24	30	40	50	75	100	200	500	∞
14	4.60 **8.86**	3.74 **6.51**	3.34 **5.56**	3.11 **5.03**	2.96 **4.69**	2.85 **4.46**	2.77 **4.28**	2.70 **4.14**	2.65 **4.03**	2.60 **3.94**	2.56 **3.86**	2.53 **3.80**	2.48 **3.70**	2.44 **3.62**	2.39 **3.51**	2.35 **3.43**	2.31 **3.34**	2.27 **3.26**	2.24 **3.21**	2.21 **3.14**	2.19 **3.11**	2.16 **3.06**	2.14 **3.02**	2.13 **3.00**
15	4.54 **8.68**	3.68 **6.36**	3.29 **5.42**	3.06 **4.89**	2.90 **4.56**	2.79 **4.32**	2.70 **4.14**	2.64 **4.00**	2.59 **3.89**	2.55 **3.80**	2.51 **3.73**	2.48 **3.67**	2.43 **3.56**	2.39 **3.48**	2.33 **3.36**	2.29 **3.29**	2.25 **3.20**	2.21 **3.12**	2.18 **3.07**	2.15 **3.00**	2.12 **2.97**	2.10 **2.92**	2.08 **2.89**	2.07 **2.87**
16	4.49 **8.53**	3.63 **6.23**	3.24 **5.29**	3.01 **4.77**	2.85 **4.44**	2.74 **4.20**	2.66 **4.03**	2.59 **3.89**	2.54 **3.78**	2.49 **3.69**	2.45 **3.61**	2.42 **3.55**	2.37 **3.45**	2.33 **3.37**	2.28 **3.25**	2.24 **3.18**	2.20 **3.10**	2.16 **3.01**	2.13 **2.96**	2.09 **2.89**	2.07 **2.86**	2.04 **2.80**	2.02 **2.77**	2.01 **2.75**
17	4.45 **8.40**	3.59 **6.11**	3.20 **5.18**	2.96 **4.67**	2.81 **4.34**	2.70 **4.10**	2.62 **3.93**	2.55 **3.79**	2.50 **3.68**	2.45 **3.59**	2.41 **3.52**	2.38 **3.45**	2.33 **3.35**	2.29 **3.27**	2.23 **3.16**	2.19 **3.08**	2.15 **3.00**	2.11 **2.92**	2.08 **2.86**	2.04 **2.79**	2.02 **2.76**	1.99 **2.70**	1.97 **2.67**	1.96 **2.65**
18	4.41 **8.28**	3.55 **6.01**	3.16 **5.09**	2.93 **4.58**	2.77 **4.25**	2.66 **4.01**	2.58 **3.85**	2.51 **3.71**	2.46 **3.60**	2.41 **3.51**	2.37 **3.44**	2.34 **3.37**	2.29 **3.27**	2.25 **3.19**	2.19 **3.07**	2.15 **3.00**	2.11 **2.91**	2.07 **2.83**	2.04 **2.78**	2.00 **2.71**	1.98 **2.68**	1.95 **2.62**	1.93 **2.59**	1.92 **2.57**
19	4.38 **8.18**	3.52 **5.93**	3.13 **5.01**	2.90 **4.50**	2.74 **4.17**	2.63 **3.94**	2.55 **3.77**	2.48 **3.63**	2.43 **3.52**	2.38 **3.43**	2.34 **3.36**	2.31 **3.30**	2.26 **3.19**	2.21 **3.12**	2.15 **3.00**	2.11 **2.92**	2.07 **2.84**	2.02 **2.76**	2.00 **2.70**	1.96 **2.63**	1.94 **2.60**	1.91 **2.54**	1.90 **2.51**	1.88 **2.49**
20	4.35 **8.10**	3.49 **5.85**	3.10 **4.94**	2.87 **4.43**	2.71 **4.10**	2.60 **3.87**	2.52 **3.71**	2.45 **3.56**	2.40 **3.45**	2.35 **3.37**	2.31 **3.30**	2.28 **3.23**	2.23 **3.13**	2.18 **3.05**	2.12 **2.94**	2.08 **2.86**	2.04 **2.77**	1.99 **2.69**	1.96 **2.63**	1.92 **2.56**	1.90 **2.53**	1.87 **2.47**	1.85 **2.44**	1.84 **2.42**
21	4.32 **8.02**	3.47 **5.78**	3.07 **4.87**	2.84 **4.37**	2.68 **4.04**	2.57 **3.81**	2.49 **3.65**	2.42 **3.51**	2.37 **3.40**	2.32 **3.31**	2.28 **3.24**	2.25 **3.17**	2.20 **3.07**	2.15 **2.99**	2.09 **2.88**	2.05 **2.80**	2.00 **2.72**	1.96 **2.63**	1.93 **2.58**	1.89 **2.51**	1.87 **2.47**	1.84 **2.42**	1.82 **2.38**	1.81 **2.36**
22	4.30 **7.94**	3.44 **5.72**	3.05 **4.82**	2.82 **4.31**	2.66 **3.99**	2.55 **3.76**	2.47 **3.59**	2.40 **3.45**	2.35 **3.35**	2.30 **3.26**	2.26 **3.18**	2.23 **3.12**	2.18 **3.02**	2.13 **2.94**	2.07 **2.83**	2.03 **2.75**	1.98 **2.67**	1.93 **2.58**	1.91 **2.53**	1.87 **2.46**	1.84 **2.42**	1.81 **2.37**	1.80 **2.33**	1.78 **2.31**
23	4.28 **7.88**	3.42 **5.66**	3.03 **4.76**	2.80 **4.26**	2.64 **3.94**	2.53 **3.71**	2.45 **3.54**	2.38 **3.41**	2.32 **3.30**	2.28 **3.21**	2.24 **3.14**	2.20 **3.07**	2.14 **2.97**	2.10 **2.89**	2.04 **2.78**	2.00 **2.70**	1.96 **2.62**	1.91 **2.53**	1.88 **2.48**	1.84 **2.41**	1.82 **2.37**	1.79 **2.32**	1.77 **2.28**	1.76 **2.26**
24	4.26 **7.82**	3.40 **5.61**	3.01 **4.72**	2.78 **4.22**	2.62 **3.90**	2.51 **3.67**	2.43 **3.50**	2.36 **3.36**	2.30 **3.25**	2.26 **3.17**	2.22 **3.09**	2.18 **3.03**	2.13 **2.93**	2.09 **2.85**	2.02 **2.74**	1.98 **2.66**	1.94 **2.58**	1.89 **2.49**	1.86 **2.44**	1.82 **2.36**	1.80 **2.33**	1.76 **2.27**	1.74 **2.23**	1.73 **2.21**
25	4.24 **7.77**	3.38 **5.57**	2.99 **4.68**	2.76 **4.18**	2.60 **3.86**	2.49 **3.63**	2.41 **3.46**	2.34 **3.32**	2.28 **3.21**	2.24 **3.13**	2.20 **3.05**	2.16 **2.99**	2.11 **2.89**	2.06 **2.81**	2.00 **2.70**	1.96 **2.62**	1.92 **2.54**	1.87 **2.45**	1.84 **2.40**	1.80 **2.32**	1.77 **2.29**	1.74 **2.23**	1.72 **2.19**	1.71 **2.17**
26	4.22 **7.72**	3.37 **5.53**	2.98 **4.64**	2.74 **4.14**	2.59 **3.82**	2.47 **3.59**	2.39 **3.42**	2.32 **3.29**	2.27 **3.17**	2.22 **3.09**	2.18 **3.02**	2.15 **2.96**	2.10 **2.86**	2.05 **2.77**	1.99 **2.66**	1.95 **2.58**	1.90 **2.50**	1.85 **2.41**	1.82 **2.36**	1.78 **2.28**	1.76 **2.25**	1.72 **2.19**	1.70 **2.15**	1.69 **2.13**

n_2 degrees of freedom for denominator mean square

Reprinted by permission from *Statistical Methods* by G. W. Snedecor and W. G. Cochran, sixth edition
© 1967 by Iowa State University Press, Ames, Iowa.

The 5 (Roman Type) and 1 (**Boldface Type**) Percent Points for the Distribution of F—continued

n_1 degrees of freedom for numerator mean square

n_2	1	2	3	4	5	6	7	8	9	10	11	12	14	16	20	24	30	40	50	75	100	200	500	∞
27	4.21/**7.68**	3.35/**5.49**	2.96/**4.60**	2.73/**4.11**	2.57/**3.79**	2.46/**3.56**	2.37/**3.39**	2.30/**3.26**	2.25/**3.14**	2.20/**3.06**	2.16/**2.98**	2.13/**2.93**	2.08/**2.83**	2.03/**2.74**	1.97/**2.63**	1.93/**2.55**	1.88/**2.47**	1.84/**2.38**	1.80/**2.33**	1.76/**2.25**	1.74/**2.21**	1.71/**2.16**	1.68/**2.12**	1.67/**2.10**
28	4.20/**7.64**	3.34/**5.45**	2.95/**4.57**	2.71/**4.07**	2.56/**3.76**	2.44/**3.53**	2.36/**3.36**	2.29/**3.23**	2.24/**3.11**	2.19/**3.03**	2.15/**2.95**	2.12/**2.90**	2.06/**2.80**	2.02/**2.71**	1.96/**2.60**	1.91/**2.52**	1.87/**2.44**	1.81/**2.35**	1.78/**2.30**	1.75/**2.22**	1.72/**2.18**	1.69/**2.13**	1.67/**2.09**	1.65/**2.06**
29	4.18/**7.60**	3.33/**5.42**	2.93/**4.54**	2.70/**4.04**	2.54/**3.73**	2.43/**3.50**	2.35/**3.33**	2.28/**3.20**	2.22/**3.08**	2.18/**3.00**	2.14/**2.92**	2.10/**2.87**	2.05/**2.77**	2.00/**2.68**	1.94/**2.57**	1.90/**2.49**	1.85/**2.41**	1.80/**2.32**	1.77/**2.27**	1.73/**2.19**	1.71/**2.15**	1.68/**2.10**	1.65/**2.06**	1.64/**2.03**
30	4.17/**7.56**	3.32/**5.39**	2.92/**4.51**	2.69/**4.02**	2.53/**3.70**	2.42/**3.47**	2.34/**3.30**	2.27/**3.17**	2.21/**3.06**	2.16/**2.98**	2.12/**2.90**	2.09/**2.84**	2.04/**2.74**	1.99/**2.66**	1.93/**2.55**	1.89/**2.47**	1.84/**2.38**	1.79/**2.29**	1.76/**2.24**	1.72/**2.16**	1.69/**2.13**	1.66/**2.07**	1.64/**2.03**	1.62/**2.01**
32	4.15/**7.50**	3.30/**5.34**	2.90/**4.46**	2.67/**3.97**	2.51/**3.66**	2.40/**3.42**	2.32/**3.25**	2.25/**3.12**	2.19/**3.01**	2.14/**2.94**	2.10/**2.86**	2.07/**2.80**	2.02/**2.70**	1.97/**2.62**	1.91/**2.51**	1.86/**2.42**	1.82/**2.34**	1.76/**2.25**	1.74/**2.20**	1.69/**2.12**	1.67/**2.08**	1.64/**2.02**	1.61/**1.98**	1.59/**1.96**
34	4.13/**7.44**	3.28/**5.29**	2.88/**4.42**	2.65/**3.93**	2.49/**3.61**	2.38/**3.38**	2.30/**3.21**	2.23/**3.08**	2.17/**2.97**	2.12/**2.89**	2.08/**2.82**	2.05/**2.76**	2.00/**2.66**	1.95/**2.58**	1.89/**2.47**	1.84/**2.38**	1.80/**2.30**	1.74/**2.21**	1.71/**2.15**	1.67/**2.08**	1.64/**2.04**	1.61/**1.98**	1.59/**1.94**	1.57/**1.91**
36	4.11/**7.39**	3.26/**5.25**	2.86/**4.38**	2.63/**3.89**	2.48/**3.58**	2.36/**3.35**	2.28/**3.18**	2.21/**3.04**	2.15/**2.94**	2.10/**2.86**	2.06/**2.78**	2.03/**2.72**	1.98/**2.62**	1.93/**2.54**	1.87/**2.43**	1.82/**2.35**	1.78/**2.26**	1.72/**2.17**	1.69/**2.12**	1.65/**2.04**	1.62/**2.00**	1.59/**1.94**	1.56/**1.90**	1.55/**1.87**
38	4.10/**7.35**	3.25/**5.21**	2.85/**4.34**	2.62/**3.86**	2.46/**3.54**	2.35/**3.32**	2.26/**3.15**	2.19/**3.02**	2.14/**2.91**	2.09/**2.82**	2.05/**2.75**	2.02/**2.69**	1.96/**2.59**	1.92/**2.51**	1.85/**2.40**	1.80/**2.32**	1.76/**2.22**	1.71/**2.14**	1.67/**2.08**	1.63/**2.00**	1.60/**1.97**	1.57/**1.90**	1.54/**1.86**	1.53/**1.84**
40	4.08/**7.31**	3.23/**5.18**	2.84/**4.31**	2.61/**3.83**	2.45/**3.51**	2.34/**3.29**	2.25/**3.12**	2.18/**2.99**	2.12/**2.88**	2.07/**2.80**	2.04/**2.73**	2.00/**2.66**	1.95/**2.56**	1.90/**2.49**	1.84/**2.37**	1.79/**2.29**	1.74/**2.20**	1.69/**2.11**	1.66/**2.05**	1.61/**1.97**	1.59/**1.94**	1.55/**1.88**	1.53/**1.84**	1.51/**1.81**
42	4.07/**7.27**	3.22/**5.15**	2.83/**4.29**	2.59/**3.80**	2.44/**3.49**	2.32/**3.26**	2.24/**3.10**	2.17/**2.96**	2.11/**2.86**	2.06/**2.77**	2.02/**2.70**	1.99/**2.64**	1.94/**2.54**	1.89/**2.46**	1.82/**2.35**	1.78/**2.26**	1.73/**2.17**	1.68/**2.08**	1.64/**2.02**	1.60/**1.94**	1.57/**1.91**	1.54/**1.85**	1.51/**1.80**	1.49/**1.78**
44	4.06/**7.24**	3.21/**5.12**	2.82/**4.26**	2.58/**3.78**	2.43/**3.46**	2.31/**3.24**	2.23/**3.07**	2.16/**2.94**	2.10/**2.84**	2.05/**2.75**	2.01/**2.68**	1.98/**2.62**	1.92/**2.52**	1.88/**2.44**	1.81/**2.32**	1.76/**2.24**	1.72/**2.15**	1.66/**2.06**	1.63/**2.00**	1.58/**1.92**	1.56/**1.88**	1.52/**1.82**	1.50/**1.78**	1.48/**1.75**
46	4.05/**7.21**	3.20/**5.10**	2.81/**4.24**	2.57/**3.76**	2.42/**3.44**	2.30/**3.22**	2.22/**3.05**	2.14/**2.92**	2.09/**2.82**	2.04/**2.73**	2.00/**2.66**	1.97/**2.60**	1.91/**2.50**	1.87/**2.42**	1.80/**2.30**	1.75/**2.22**	1.71/**2.13**	1.65/**2.04**	1.62/**1.98**	1.57/**1.90**	1.54/**1.86**	1.51/**1.80**	1.48/**1.76**	1.46/**1.72**
48	4.04/**7.19**	3.19/**5.08**	2.80/**4.22**	2.56/**3.74**	2.41/**3.42**	2.30/**3.20**	2.21/**3.04**	2.14/**2.90**	2.08/**2.80**	2.03/**2.71**	1.99/**2.64**	1.96/**2.58**	1.90/**2.48**	1.86/**2.40**	1.79/**2.28**	1.74/**2.20**	1.70/**2.11**	1.64/**2.02**	1.61/**1.96**	1.56/**1.88**	1.53/**1.84**	1.50/**1.78**	1.47/**1.73**	1.45/**1.70**

Reprinted by permission from *Statistical Methods* by G. W. Snedecor and W. G. Cochran, sixth edition © 1967 by Iowa State University Press, Ames, Iowa.

The 5 (Roman Type) and 1 (Boldface Type) Percent Points for the Distribution of F—continued

n_1 degrees of freedom for numerator mean square

n_2	1	2	3	4	5	6	7	8	9	10	11	12	14	16	20	24	30	40	50	75	100	200	500	∞
50	4.03 **7.17**	3.18 **5.06**	2.79 **4.20**	2.56 **3.72**	2.40 **3.41**	2.29 **3.18**	2.20 **3.02**	2.13 **2.88**	2.07 **2.78**	2.02 **2.70**	1.98 **2.62**	1.95 **2.56**	1.90 **2.46**	1.85 **2.39**	1.78 **2.26**	1.74 **2.18**	1.69 **2.10**	1.63 **2.00**	1.60 **1.94**	1.55 **1.86**	1.52 **1.82**	1.48 **1.76**	1.46 **1.71**	1.44 **1.68**
55	4.02 **7.12**	3.17 **5.01**	2.78 **4.16**	2.54 **3.68**	2.38 **3.37**	2.27 **3.15**	2.18 **2.98**	2.11 **2.85**	2.05 **2.75**	2.00 **2.66**	1.97 **2.59**	1.93 **2.53**	1.88 **2.43**	1.83 **2.35**	1.76 **2.23**	1.72 **2.15**	1.67 **2.06**	1.61 **1.96**	1.58 **1.90**	1.52 **1.82**	1.50 **1.78**	1.46 **1.71**	1.43 **1.66**	1.41 **1.64**
60	4.00 **7.08**	3.15 **4.98**	2.76 **4.13**	2.52 **3.65**	2.37 **3.34**	2.25 **3.12**	2.17 **2.95**	2.10 **2.82**	2.04 **2.72**	1.99 **2.63**	1.95 **2.56**	1.92 **2.50**	1.86 **2.40**	1.81 **2.32**	1.75 **2.20**	1.70 **2.12**	1.65 **2.03**	1.59 **1.93**	1.56 **1.87**	1.50 **1.79**	1.48 **1.74**	1.44 **1.68**	1.41 **1.63**	1.39 **1.60**
65	3.99 **7.04**	3.14 **4.95**	2.75 **4.10**	2.51 **3.62**	2.36 **3.31**	2.24 **3.09**	2.15 **2.93**	2.08 **2.79**	2.02 **2.70**	1.98 **2.61**	1.94 **2.54**	1.90 **2.47**	1.85 **2.37**	1.80 **2.30**	1.73 **2.18**	1.68 **2.09**	1.63 **2.00**	1.57 **1.90**	1.54 **1.84**	1.49 **1.76**	1.46 **1.71**	1.42 **1.64**	1.39 **1.60**	1.37 **1.56**
70	3.98 **7.01**	3.13 **4.92**	2.74 **4.08**	2.50 **3.60**	2.35 **3.29**	2.23 **3.07**	2.14 **2.91**	2.07 **2.77**	2.01 **2.67**	1.97 **2.59**	1.93 **2.51**	1.89 **2.45**	1.84 **2.35**	1.79 **2.28**	1.72 **2.15**	1.67 **2.07**	1.62 **1.98**	1.56 **1.88**	1.53 **1.82**	1.47 **1.74**	1.45 **1.69**	1.40 **1.62**	1.37 **1.56**	1.35 **1.53**
80	3.96 **6.96**	3.11 **4.88**	2.72 **4.04**	2.48 **3.56**	2.33 **3.25**	2.21 **3.04**	2.12 **2.87**	2.05 **2.74**	1.99 **2.64**	1.95 **2.55**	1.91 **2.48**	1.88 **2.41**	1.82 **2.32**	1.77 **2.24**	1.70 **2.11**	1.65 **2.03**	1.60 **1.94**	1.54 **1.84**	1.51 **1.78**	1.45 **1.70**	1.42 **1.65**	1.38 **1.57**	1.35 **1.52**	1.32 **1.49**
100	3.94 **6.90**	3.09 **4.82**	2.70 **3.98**	2.46 **3.51**	2.30 **3.20**	2.19 **2.99**	2.10 **2.82**	2.03 **2.69**	1.97 **2.59**	1.92 **2.51**	1.88 **2.43**	1.85 **2.36**	1.79 **2.26**	1.75 **2.19**	1.68 **2.06**	1.63 **1.98**	1.57 **1.89**	1.51 **1.79**	1.48 **1.73**	1.42 **1.64**	1.39 **1.59**	1.34 **1.51**	1.30 **1.46**	1.28 **1.43**
125	3.92 **6.84**	3.07 **4.78**	2.68 **3.94**	2.44 **3.47**	2.29 **3.17**	2.17 **2.95**	2.08 **2.79**	2.01 **2.65**	1.95 **2.56**	1.90 **2.47**	1.86 **2.40**	1.83 **2.33**	1.77 **2.23**	1.72 **2.15**	1.65 **2.03**	1.60 **1.94**	1.55 **1.85**	1.49 **1.75**	1.45 **1.68**	1.39 **1.59**	1.36 **1.54**	1.31 **1.46**	1.27 **1.40**	1.25 **1.37**
150	3.91 **6.81**	3.06 **4.75**	2.67 **3.91**	2.43 **3.44**	2.27 **3.14**	2.16 **2.92**	2.07 **2.76**	2.00 **2.62**	1.94 **2.53**	1.89 **2.44**	1.85 **2.37**	1.82 **2.30**	1.76 **2.20**	1.71 **2.12**	1.64 **2.00**	1.59 **1.91**	1.54 **1.83**	1.47 **1.72**	1.44 **1.66**	1.37 **1.56**	1.34 **1.51**	1.29 **1.43**	1.25 **1.37**	1.22 **1.33**
200	3.89 **6.76**	3.04 **4.71**	2.65 **3.88**	2.41 **3.41**	2.26 **3.11**	2.14 **2.90**	2.05 **2.73**	1.98 **2.60**	1.92 **2.50**	1.87 **2.41**	1.83 **2.34**	1.80 **2.28**	1.74 **2.17**	1.69 **2.09**	1.62 **1.97**	1.57 **1.88**	1.52 **1.79**	1.45 **1.69**	1.42 **1.62**	1.35 **1.53**	1.32 **1.48**	1.26 **1.39**	1.22 **1.33**	1.19 **1.28**
400	3.86 **6.70**	3.02 **4.66**	2.62 **3.83**	2.39 **3.36**	2.23 **3.06**	2.12 **2.85**	2.03 **2.69**	1.96 **2.55**	1.90 **2.46**	1.85 **2.37**	1.81 **2.29**	1.78 **2.23**	1.72 **2.12**	1.67 **2.04**	1.60 **1.92**	1.54 **1.84**	1.49 **1.74**	1.42 **1.64**	1.38 **1.57**	1.32 **1.47**	1.28 **1.42**	1.22 **1.32**	1.16 **1.24**	1.13 **1.19**
1000	3.85 **6.66**	3.00 **4.62**	2.61 **3.80**	2.38 **3.34**	2.22 **3.04**	2.10 **2.82**	2.02 **2.66**	1.95 **2.53**	1.89 **2.43**	1.84 **2.34**	1.80 **2.26**	1.76 **2.20**	1.70 **2.09**	1.65 **2.01**	1.58 **1.89**	1.53 **1.81**	1.47 **1.71**	1.41 **1.61**	1.36 **1.54**	1.30 **1.44**	1.26 **1.38**	1.19 **1.28**	1.13 **1.19**	1.08 **1.11**
∞	3.84 **6.64**	2.99 **4.60**	2.60 **3.78**	2.37 **3.32**	2.21 **3.02**	2.09 **2.80**	2.01 **2.64**	1.94 **2.51**	1.88 **2.41**	1.83 **2.32**	1.79 **2.24**	1.75 **2.18**	1.69 **2.07**	1.64 **1.99**	1.57 **1.87**	1.52 **1.79**	1.46 **1.69**	1.40 **1.59**	1.35 **1.52**	1.28 **1.41**	1.24 **1.36**	1.17 **1.25**	1.11 **1.15**	1.00 **1.00**

Reprinted by permission from *Statistical Methods* by G. W. Snedecor and W. G. Cochran, sixth edition © 1967 by Iowa State University Press, Ames, Iowa.

Glossary

This section lists the most important technical terms in the text. Some of the terms are discussed in detail within the text; others are defined here to distinguish a commonplace meaning from a specific meaning in experimental psychology. Technical terms that arise while describing experiments used to illustrate a particular methodology are not included in this glossary.

Absolute and comparative judgments   In comparative judgment the subject is asked to rate one stimulus relative to another ("Is A larger or smaller than B?"). In absolute judgment the subject is asked to rate a stimulus without a standard for comparison ("Is A large or small?").

Absolute threshold   See **Threshold.**

Abstract   The section of a research report, generally at the beginning between the title and the introduction, that presents a summary of the research question, the background of the problem, the methods of investigation, findings, and interpretations.

Abstracts   See **Literature.**

Analysis   Technical label of procedures, statistical and otherwise, for making sense of the data, for description, and for deciding about the trustworthiness of the patterns of effects.

Between-subjects design   See **Experimental design.**

Between-subjects factor   See **Factor.**

"Blind" procedures   Techniques used to alleviate *experimenter bias* (see **Experimenter expectancy and bias**). In a *single-blind* procedure, the subject may not be fully informed about the nature of a study until the end of the testing. In a *double-blind* procedure, both subject and experimenter may be partly unaware of the nature of the study, the differences between the treatment conditions, the conditions to which individual subjects are assigned, or the expected outcomes.

Boundary conditions   The levels of a factor that correspond to the high and low points of performance; an important consideration in choosing the levels of a factor.

Category rating   See **Psychophysical methods.**

Comparison stimulus   See **Psychophysical methods.**

Condition   A particular level or combination of levels of treatment factors.

Confounding   A flaw in experimental design, in which a set of conditions varies on two or more factors simultaneously. Any observed effects may be due to any combination of the confounded factors.

Constitutive definition   A substantive or "dictionary" description of a construct, and of its relation to other constructs; for instance, intelligence is smartness, the ability to reason and do well on school tasks. In contrast to an **operational definition,** which emphasizes observable techniques for measuring an unobservable construct.

Construct   See **Psychological construct.**

Construct validity   See **Validity.**

Content validity   See **Validity.**

Continuous adjustment   See **Psychophysical methods.**

Control   All procedures used to design, carry out, and analyze an experimental study so that the experimental question can be answered clearly and without ambiguity.

Control group   A group of subjects, similar in all respects to a second "experimental" group, except that the experimental treatment is not administered. See **Experimental design, experimental-vs.-control design.**

Counterbalance   Arrangement of conditions in a within-subjects or mixed design to ensure that time and materials are not confounded with treatment variations. See also **Experimental design, Latin square design.**

Criterion validity   See **Validity.**

Data collection   The process of making observations during an experiment. Included in this process are the activities of observing, measuring, and recording each event.

Debriefing   Procedures at the end of a research session in which the subject is fully informed about the study and is given an opportunity to raise questions and concerns. Can also be useful for discovering the subject's interpretation of the session.

Dependent variable   See **Response measure.**

Descriptive method   See **Method.**

Difference threshold   See **Threshold.**

Double-blind procedures   See **"Blind" procedures.**

Effects   Influence of a factor or group of factors on performance. Typically measured by subtracting average performance under a particular condition from the average over all conditions. See the appendix.

   Floor and ceiling effects   Some response measures have limits so that performance can go only so high or so low; these floor and ceiling limits can lead to interactions that are not of particular interest.

   Interaction effects   Systematic variations in performance due to changes in a factor from one level to another in a second factor. *Low-order interaction effects*, which involve combinations of two or three factors, are generally interpretable. *High-order interaction effects*, which involve four or more factors, are often difficult to understand.

Main effects   Difference in performance from one level to another for a particular factor, averaged over all levels of other factors in a factorial design.

Novelty effect   The positive response of a subject when conditions are changed in any way.

Order effects   Changes in performance over repeated sessions or conditions in a within-subjects or mixed design.

Empirical question   See **Question.**

Equal-interval scale   See **Measurement.**

Ethical principles   Behavioral and social scientists, because they are given authority over other individuals, are responsible for using this authority ethically. Hence these principles place on the individual researcher responsibility for ensuring that the subject is appropriately informed, participates willingly, is not harmed, and is not embarrassed by breach of confidentiality.

Ethnographic method   See **Method.**

Experimental design   Techniques for deciding on the factors to be varied in an experiment, choosing levels for each factor, and arranging combinations of factors.

One-way design   A plan consisting of a single factor with two or more levels.

Factorial design   A plan consisting of combinations of two or more factors.

Experimental-vs.-control design   A plan in which one group is administered a treatment and compared to a control group that is not treated. Simplest version of a one-way design, and often plagued by confounding.

Quasi-experimental design   "Cut and paste" procedures for establishing as much control as possible when random selection and assignment are not possible; a method of control for research in field settings.

Between-subjects design   A research plan in which different groups of subjects are assigned to each of the conditions in the study. Also referred to as a *randomized-groups* design.

Within-subjects design   An experimental plan in which subjects are tested under all combinations of all factors. Also referred to sometimes as a *repeated-measures* design.

Mixed design   The most common experimental plan in present-day research, in which some factors are between-subjects and some are within-subjects.

Latin square design   A plan for counterbalancing for time and materials in within-subjects designs; a subset of treatment sequences is selected equal to the number of sequences and arranged so that each treatment occurs once for each subject and once on each trial. An extension of this principle, the *Graeco-Latin square*, allows for counterbalancing of a fourth factor, typically materials.

Experimental method   See **Method.**

Experimental-vs.-control design   See **Experimental design.**

Experimenter   Technical label for the person or persons who conduct a research study; also used for the individual who conceptualizes and designs a study.

Experimenter expectancy and bias   Effects on subject performance of (usually) unconscious activities of the experimenter. If the experimenter expects results to turn out in a particular way, this expectation may lead to systematic errors in making observations, subtle cues to the subject, and other biased behavior by the experimenter.

External validity   See **Validity.**

Factor   A variation in treatments, subjects, or other dimensions of an investigation. Also referred to as an *independent variable.*

> **Treatment factor**   A variation in environmental conditions, expected to have some influence on performance, and under direct control of the investigator. Treatment factors are usually of primary importance to the researcher in designing an experiment.
>
> **Subject-classification factor**   Preexisting and stable characteristic of subjects used by the experimenter in selecting subjects.
>
> **Nuisance factor**   A variable included in the design of an experiment to control for effects of variables not of direct interest but likely to affect performance (e.g., time, materials, etc.). Also called a *control factor.*
>
> **Between-subjects factor**   Different subjects are assigned to each level of a factor.
>
> **Within-subjects factor**   Each subject is tested on all levels of a factor.

Factorial design   See **Experimental design.**

Floor and ceilng effects   See **Effects.**

Independent variable   See **Factor.**

Individual differences   A technical label for the variations between subjects (and between persons more generally); experimental psychologists wish that individual differences would disappear, whereas educational psychologists spend a lot of time studying them.

Interaction   The extent to which the effects of one factor vary from level to level of a second factor. See also **Effects, interaction effects.**

Interaction effects   See **Effects.**

Internal validity   See **Validity.**

Just noticeable difference (jnd)   See **Threshold.**

Latin square design   See **Experimental design.**

Level   A specific variation in a factor. Qualitative or categorical factors have a (usually) small number of distinct levels (e.g., the subject's gender); quantitative or numerical factors have a (potentially) large number of levels, only a few of which are likely to be of practical interest.

Linear function   A mathematical relation between two variables in which one variable increases proportionately with the other; a straight-line relation.

Literature   The collection of all documents describing previous research on a topic.

> **Abstracts**   Publications of the Abstract section of research reports, usually indexed by major topics and including the citation (author, title, journal, date, and volume).

Research reports Journal articles, book chapters, technical reports, and other primary sources in which original research is presented.

Reviews Articles in which the research reports on a particular question are summarized, critiqued, and interpreted. Reviews are also used to describe and evaluate theoretical positions.

Log scale A mathematical relation between two variables in which one variable increases by a multiplier of the other. Thus, if you are breeding dogs and every pair produces four offspring, then the number of dogs will increase logarithmically with the number of generations.

Magnitude estimation See **Psychophysical methods.**

Main effects See **Effects.**

Materials A technical label for the "stuff" used to present information to subjects during an experiment; also refers to the section of a research report in which the materials are described.

Measurement In science, most often a process for assigning numbers to objects. In the physical sciences, direct measurement is often possible, and indirect measurement is aided by theory. In psychological measurement, direct measurement less often provides a valid index of important concepts, and indirect measurement is guided by intuition.

Unit of measurement A standard that is assigned a value of 1.0 in establishing a measurement scale.

Zero point The point on a measurement scale that is the "beginning" of the scale. Generally chosen, if possible, to correspond to an absence of the quantity being measured (e.g., a stick that is zero inches long has no length) but is sometimes defined in other ways (e.g., the Fahrenheit and Centigrade scales of temperature).

Nominal scale Numbers are assigned to objects as labels, not as true numbers (e.g., numbers on football uniforms).

Ordinal scale Numbers are assigned according to the order of objects, a weak form of measurement (e.g., house numbers).

Equal-interval scale Numbers are assigned so that distances between objects are reflected in distances between numbers (e.g., the Fahrenheit temperature scale or the street addresses in a housing tract).

Ratio scale The kind of measurement with which you are most familiar; equal intervals and a true zero point (e.g., length and weight).

Logarithmic scale Measurement used when relative magnitude is more important than absolute magnitude (e.g., the Richter scale for earthquakes or the decibel scales used to measure light and sound intensity). See also **Log scale.**

Method In science, method refers to the approach and the techniques used to investigate a problem. Most problems in behavioral and social science call for a combination of methods.

Descriptive method In this approach the scientist acts as a naturalist, observing and recording without intruding or intervening.

Ethnographic method A variation on the descriptive method, in which the scientist immerses himself or herself in the situation so as to become a "participant observer."

Experimental method   An experiment is usually a "trying out" in which the scientist actively intervenes to change a situation and then observes the results of the intervention.

Method section   The section of a research report in which the methodology is described.

Mixed design   See **Experimental design.**

Nominal scale   See **Measurement.**

Novelty effect   See **Effects.**

Nuisance factor   See **Factor.**

Observation   A single datum; a measurement taken under a specified set of conditions.

Observational method   Description of behavior by rich description or by more formal methods of rating; generally in contrast to simpler measures like button presses, multiple-choice tests, and the like. Not to be confused with an **observation.**

One-way design   See **Experimental design.**

Operational definition   An unobservable construct is defined by one or more operations; for instance, intelligence is whatever an intelligence test measures. In contrast with a *constitutive definition*, which comes closer to the substance of a construct.

Order effects   See **Effects.**

Ordinal scale   See **Measurement.**

Outlier   An observation that departs markedly from the norm; the subject has to sneeze just when the light flashes in a reaction time experiment, and takes five seconds to press the button instead of the usual half a second.

Placebo effect   The positive (or negative) effect that occurs when a person thinks that something has been done to help (or to hurt) him or her; the "sugar-pill" response.

Power   The power of an experiment is a technical label for the likelihood that the researcher can detect the effects of a factor when these actually exist. The power depends on the size of the effects, the amount of unsystematic variability, the statistical procedures, and the sample size.

Predictive validity   See **Validity, criterion validity.**

Procedures   All of the nondesign decisions that must be arranged once the basic design of a study has been completed.

Psychological construct   A (usually) unobservable entity used as an explanation for observable behavior. Examples include empathy, memory, intelligence, and so on.

Psychophysical methods   A set of procedures for measuring psychological response to variation in physical factors; for example, as a sound becomes more or less intense, what is the change in the perception of loudness?

Continuous adjustment   The physical stimulus is increased or decreased in small steps until the subject detects a change. A special variation is the *staircase method*.

Random presentation   Several fairly distinctive values of the physical are selected and presented in a random sequence; after each presentation the subject makes a judgment. A special variation on this method is the *signal detection* procedure.

Category rating   Psychological measurement procedure in which the subject is given a fixed set of categories, and asked to assign each stimulus to a category.

Magnitude estimation   Psychological measurement procedure in which the subject is asked to assign a number to each stimulus; the number scale is usually *anchored* by presenting a standard stimulus to the subject with an assigned number ("This stimulus is a '10'").

Comparison stimulus   Stimulus value presented to subject to compare with a fixed standard.

Standard stimulus   Fixed stimulus value used as a frame of reference for psychophysical judgments.

Quasi-experimental design   See **Experimental design.**

Question   Research questions or "problems" are more carefully phrased than everyday questions. In general, the question must be answerable by the methods of scientific inquiry.

Empirical question   Some investigations are based primarily on curiosity or practical interest in the effects of one or more factors on behavior. Where there is no underlying theory to guide the framing of the problem, the research is referred to as empirical (based on experience or observation alone).

Theoretical question   Some investigations are designed to evaluate a theoretical model, or to compare two or more theoretical positions. A good theory makes predictions that can be tested against the results of an experiment; a good theory can be disproven!

Random   A decision that is based on chance; unsystematic; indeterminate and unbiased.

Random assignment   Placement of the subjects in a sample into conditions by some procedure that ensures randomness in assignment; pulling names out of a hat.

Random selection   Selection of subjects for a study at random from a larger collection; same as **random sample.**

Random presentation   See **Psychophysical methods.**

Random sample   See **Sample.**

Ratio scale   See **Measurement.**

Reliability   Consistency, stability, accuracy, and dependability of a measurement procedure.

References   Section of a research report listing other literature used in preparing the report.

Representative sample   See **Sample.**

Research reports   See **Literature.**

Response measure   The variable chosen by the researcher to evaluate performance; also called the *dependent variable.* As is true of a factor or independent variable, measures may be qualitative/categorical or quantitative/numerical.

Replicational variability   See **Variability.**

Results   Section of a research paper presenting the analysis of the data.

Reviews   See **Literature.**

Sample   Technical label for the collection of individuals who are selected as participants in a psychological experiment; each individual is referred to as a *subject*.

   Random sample   Selection of a sample of subjects from a larger collection of potential subjects in such a way that every individual in the collection has an equal chance of being selected for the sample.

   Representative sample   A sample of subjects whose characteristics are a good match to the collection from which they were selected. A random sample will be representative if it is large enough.

   Stratified sample   A subject-classification design is used to describe the original collection of subjects, and then subjects are selected at random from the cells of this design, ensuring that the sample will be closely representative of the collection on the factors chosen for the design.

Sample size   The number of subjects selected for each treatment condition (usual definition) or for the experiment as a whole. See **Power**.

Single-blind procedure   See "Blind" procedures.

Standard stimulus   See **Psychophysical methods**.

Stratified sample   See **Sample**.

Subject   Technical name for the individuals who participate in behavioral and social science research studies.

Subject-classification factor   See **Factor**.

Task   The technical label for the subject's "job" during a study.

Theoretical question   See **Question**.

Threshold   A psychological concept that corresponds more or less to the subject's awareness or unawareness of a particular state of the environment.

   Absolute threshold   Intensity of a stimulus that can be just barely detected by a subject.

   Difference threshold   Amount by which a comparison stimulus must differ from a standard stimulus to be just barely detected as different. A difference threshold in which the comparison stimulus is more intense than standard is called the *upper threshold*; when the comparison stimulus is less intense it is called the *lower threshold*.

   Just noticeable difference (jnd)   The gap on the stimulus scale between the upper and lower thresholds around a standard stimulus.

Treatment factor   See **Factor**.

Treatment variability   See **Variability**.

Unit of measurement   See **Measurement**.

Unsystematic variability.   See **Variability**.

Validity   To the degree that a data collection procedure succeeds in measuring what the researcher intends, the procedure is valid.

   Criterion validity   If an independently validated procedure exists for measuring a construct, then a new procedure can be validated by comparing measures under the old and new methods. Also called *predictive validity*.

Content validity A measurement procedure is built around a careful and comprehensive examination of the domain, which is included in the construct; the procedure is then said to have content validity. For many constructs, establishing content validity may be costly and inefficient for practical purposes.

Construct validity Related to content validity. The investigator considers the range of measurement operations that might be relevant, and designs a set of procedures that may point to a single underlying construct. If the measures agree, then the *convergent evidence* supports the validity of the construct and the measurement procedures.

External validity The extent to which a particular set of findings transcends a particular situation or group of people; if the results of a study are limited to the conditions of the study, they lack external validity.

Internal validity If the results of a study are consistent and dependable, if the unsystematic variability is small compared to the treatment effects, then the study is internally valid; if there is a lot of slop in the findings, the study lacks internal validity.

Variability The inherent tendency of biological systems to change somewhat from time to time and situation to situation.

Treatment variability Changes in performance that can be traced to systematic variations in environmental conditions.

Replicational variability Changes in performance when the conditions appear to be stable but the situation differs (time, place, or people).

Unsystematic variability "Error of measurement," unpredictable fluctuations, unexplainable variance—all the sources of variability that remain unaccounted for when treatment variability and replicational variability have been considered.

Warm-up A chance to practice the procedures in an experiment before data are collected. Important in within-subject designs to reduce unwanted variability during the early stages of testing an individual.

Within-subjects design See **Experimental design**.

Within-subjects factor See **Factor**.

Zero point See **Measurement**.

References

Adair, J. G. *The human subject: The social psychology of the psychological experiment.* Boston: Little, Brown, 1973.

Adams, C. K., Hall, D. C., Pennypacker, H. S., Goldstein, M. K., Hench, L. L., Madden, M. C., Stein, G. H., & Cantania, A. C. Lump detection in simulated human breasts. *Perception & Psychophysics,* 1976, 20, 163–167.

American Psychological Association. *Principles for the care and use of animals.* Washington, D.C.: APA, 1971.

American Psychological Association. *Ethical principles in the conduct of research with human participants.* Washington, D.C.: APA, 1973.

American Psychological Association. *Publication manual of the American Psychological Association* (2nd ed.). Washington, D.C.: APA, 1974.

American Psychological Association. *Ethical standards of psychologists.* Washington, D.C.: APA, 1977a.

American Psychological Association. *Guidelines for nonsexist language in APA journals.* Publication Manual Change Sheet 2. Washington, D.C.: APA, 1977b.

American Psychological Association. *Publication manual of the American Psychological Association* (3rd ed.). Washington, D.C.: APA, 1983.

Anderson, J. R., & Bower, G. H. *Human associative memory.* Washington, D.C.: V. H. Winston, 1973.

Anderson, N. H. Application of an additive model to impression formation. *Science,* 1962, 138, 817–818.

Anderson, N. H. Serial position curves in impression formation. *Journal of Experimental Psychology,* 1973, 97, 8–12.

Anderson, N. H. Algebraic rules in psychological measurement. *American Scientist,* 1979, 67, 555–563.

Anderson, N. H. *Methods of information integration theory.* New York: Academic Press, 1982.

APA Task Force on Issues of Sexual Bias in Graduate Education. Guidelines for nonsexist use of language. *American Psychologist,* 1975, 30, 682–684.

Argyris, C. Some unintended consequences of rigorous research. *Psychological Bulletin*, 1968, *70*, 185–197.

Asher, S. R. Children's ability to appraise their own and another person's communication performance. *Developmental Psychology*, 1976, *12*, 24–32.

Atkinson, J. W., & Feather, N. T. (Eds.) *A theory of achievement motivation*. New York: John Wiley, 1965.

Atkinson, R. C., Bower, G. H., & Crothers, E. J. *Introduction to mathematical learning theory*. New York: John Wiley, 1965.

Bandura, A. *Principles of behavior modification*. New York: Holt, Rinehart and Winston, 1969.

Barber, B. The ethics of experimentation with human subjects. *Scientific American*, 1976, *234*, 25–31.

Benson, P. L., & Catt, V. L. Soliciting charity contributions: The parlance of asking for money. *Journal of Applied Social Psychology*, 1978, *8*, 84–95.

Bernstein, B. Social class and linguistic development: A theory of social learning. In A. H. Halsey, J. Floud, & C. A. Anderson (Eds.), *Education, economy and society*. New York: Free Press, 1961.

Biederman, I., Glass, A. L., & Stacy, E. W., Jr. Searching for objects in real-world scenes. *Journal of Experimental Psychology*, 1973, *97*, 22–27.

Binder, A., McConnell, D., & Sjoholm, N. A. Verbal conditioning as a function of experimenter characteristics. *Journal of Abnormal and Social Psychology*, 1957, *55*, 309–314.

Birnbaum, M. H. Comparison of two theories of "ratio" and "difference" judgments. *Journal of Experimental Psychology: General*, 1980, *109*, 304–319.

Birnbaum, M. H., & Veit, C. T. Scale convergence as a criterion for rescaling: Information integration with difference, ratio, and averaging tasks. *Perceptions & Psychophysics*, 1974, *15*, 7–15.

Bjork, R. A. Positive forgetting: The noninterference of items intentionally forgotten. *Journal of Verbal Learning and Verbal Behavior*, 1970, *9*, 225–268.

Bjorkman, M. An exploratory study of predictive judgments in a traffic situation. *Scandinavian Journal of Psychology*, 1963, *4*, 65–76.

Boring, E. G. *A history of experimental psychology*. New York: Appleton-Century-Crofts, 1950.

Bower, G. H. Analysis of a mnemonic device. *American Scientist*, 1970, *58*, 496–510.

Bower, G. H., Clark, M. C., Lesgold, A. M., & Winzenz, D. Hierarchical retrieval schemes in recall of categorized word lists. *Journal of Verbal Learning and Verbal Behavior*, 1969, *8*, 323–343.

Bramel, D., & Friend, R. Hawthorne, the myth of the docile worker, and class bias in psychology. *American Psychologist*, 1981, *36*, 867–878.

Bruner, J. S. Going beyond the information given. In J. S. Bruner (Ed.), *Contemporary approaches to cognition: The Colorado symposium*. Cambridge, MA: Harvard University Press, 1957.

Buckner, D. N., & McGrath, J. J. *Vigilance: A symposium*. New York: McGraw-Hill, 1963.

Calfee, R. C. *Human experimental psychology*. New York: Holt, Rinehart and Winston, 1975.

Calfee, R. C. Assessment of independent reading skills: Basic research and practical applications. In A. S. Reber & D. L. Scarborough (Eds.), *Toward a psychology of reading*. Hillsdale, N.J.: Lawrence Erlbaum Associates, 1977.

Calfee, R. C., Hetherington, E. M., & Waltzer, P. Short-term memory in children as a function of display size. *Psychonomic Science*, 1966, *4*, 153–154.

Campbell, D. Factors relevant to the validity of experiments in social settings. *Psychological Bulletin*, 1957, *54*, 297–312.

Campbell, D. T., & Stanley, J. C. *Experimental and quasi-experimental designs for research*. Chicago: Rand McNally, 1963.

Cannell, C., & Kahn, R. Interviewing. In G. Lindzey & E. Aronson (Eds.), *The handbook of social psychology* (2nd ed.). Reading, MA: Addison-Wesley, 1968.

Carlson, R. Where is the person in personality research? *Psychological Bulletin*, 1971, *75*, 203–219.

Carroll, J. B. Psychometric tests as cognitive tasks: A new "structure of intellect." In L. B. Resnick (Ed.), *The nature of intelligence*. Hillsdale NJ: Lawrence Erlbaum Associates, 1976.

Carterette, E. C., & Friedman, M. P. (Eds.) *Handbook of perception*. New York: Academic Press, 1973–1978.

Clark, H. H. The language-as-fixed effect fallacy: A critique of language statistics in psychological research. *Journal of Verbal Learning and Verbal Behavior*, 1973, *12*, 335–359.

Clark, H. H., & Clark, E. V. *Psychology and language*. New York: Harcourt Brace Jovanovich, Inc., 1977.

Cohen, G. *The psychology of cognition* (2nd ed.). New York: Academic Press, 1983.

Cole, M., Gay, J., Glick, J. A., & Sharp, D. W. *The cultural context of learning and thinking*. New York: Basic Books, Inc., 1971.

Collingwood, V., & Hughes, D. C. Effects of three types of university lecture notes on student achievement. *Journal of Educational Psychology*, 1978, *70*, 175–179.

Cook, T. D., & Campbell, D. T. *Quasi-experimentation: Design and analysis for field settings*. Chicago: Rand McNally, 1979.

Coombs, C. H., Dawes, R. M., & Tversky, A. *Mathematical psychology: An elementary introduction*. Englewood Cliffs, N.J.: Prentice-Hall, 1970.

Cronbach, L. J. Evaluation for course improvement. In R. W. Heath (Ed.), *New curricula*. New York: Harper & Row, 1963.

Dale, P. S. *Language development: Structure and function*. Hinsdale, Illinois: Dryden Press, 1972.

Dillehay, R. C., & Jernigan, L. R. The biased questionnaire as an instrument of opinion change. *Journal of Personality and Social Psychology*, 1970, *15*, 144–150.

Ebbinghaus, H. *Memory, a contribution to experimental psychology* (1885). Ruger, A. A., & Bussenius, C. E. (Trans.), New York: Teachers College Columbia University, 1913. Reprinted New York: Dover, 1964.

Edwards, A. L. *Experimental design in psychological research* (3rd ed.) New York: Holt, Rinehart and Winston, 1968.

Egan, J. P. *Signal detection theory and ROC analysis*. New York: Academic Press, 1975.

Elman, D., & Killebrew, T. J. Incentives and seat belts: Changing a resistant behavior through extrinsic motivation. *Journal of Applied Social Psychology*, 1978, *8*, 72–83.

Engen, T. Psychophysics: I. Discrimination and detection. In L. A. Riggs & J. W. Kling (Eds.), *Experimental psychology*. New York: Holt, Rinehart and Winston, 1971a.

Engen, T. Psychophysics: II. Scaling methods. In L. A. Riggs & J. W. Kling (Eds.), *Experimental psychology*. New York: Holt, Rinehart and Winston, 1971b.

Estes, W. K. (Ed.) *Handbook of learning and cognitive processes*. Hillsdale, NJ: Lawrence Erlbaum Associates, 1975–1978.

Farr, J. L., & Seaver, W. B. Stress and discomfort in psychological research: Subject perceptions of experimental procedures. *American Psychologist*, 1975, *30*, 770–773.

Fechner, G. T. *Elemente der psychophysik*. Leipzig: Breitkopf and Harterl, 1960. English translation of Vol. 1 by H. E. Adler (D. H. Howes and E. G. Boring, Eds.). New York: Holt, Rinehart and Winston, 1966.

Fillenbaum. S. Prior deception and subsequent experimental performance: The "faithful" subject. *Journal of Personality and Social Psychology*, 1966, 4, 532–537.

Fisher, R. A., & Yates, F. *Statistical tables for biological, agricultural and medical research.* Darien, Conn.: Hafner Publishing Co., 1970.

Fraiberg, S. H. *The magic years: Understanding and handling the problems of early childhood.* New York: Scribner, 1959.

Gilinsky, A. S. Perceived size and distance in visual space. *Psychological Review*, 1951, 58, 460–482.

Glucksberg, S., & Krauss, R. M. What do people say after they have learned to talk? Studies of the development of referential communication. *Merrill-Palmer Quarterly*, 1967, 13, 309–316.

Glucksberg, S., Krauss, R. M., & Weisberg, R. Referential communication in nursery school children: Method and some preliminary findings. *Journal of Experimental Child Psychology*, 1966, 3, 333–342.

Goldstein, A., & Foa, E. B. (Eds.) *Handbook of behavioral interventions: A clinical guide.* New York: Wiley, 1980.

Goody, J. *The domestication of the savage mind.* London: Cambridge University Press, 1977.

Gould, S. J. *The mismeasure of man.* New York: Norton, 1981.

Grice, G. R. Dependence of empirical laws upon the source of experimental variation. *Psychological Bulletin*, 1966, 66, 488–498.

Gunter, B., Clifford, B. R., & Berry, C. Release from proactive interference with television news items: Evidence for encoding dimensions within televised news. *Journal of Experimental Psychology: Human Learning and Memory*, 1980, 6, 216–223.

Hall, J. F. *Verbal learning and retention.* Philadelphia: Lippincott, 1971.

Hays, W. L. *Statistics* (3rd ed.). New York: Holt, Rinehart and Winston, 1981.

Hearnshaw, L. S. *Cyril Burt, psychologist.* Ithaca, NY: Cornell University Press, 1979.

Hersey, J. *The wall.* New York: Alfred A. Knopf, 1950.

Holmes, D. S., & Bennett, D. H. Experiments to answer questions raised by the use of deception in psychological research. *Journal of Personality and Social Psychology*, 1974, 29, 358–367.

Homans, G. Group factors in worker productivity. In H. Proshansky and B. Seidenberg (Eds.), *Basic studies in social psychology.* New York: Holt, Rinehart and Winston, 1965.

Hunt, E., & Lansman, M. Cognitive theory applied to individual differences. In W. K. Estes (Ed.), *Handbook of learning and cognitive processes: Introduction to concepts and issues* (Vol. 1). Hillsdale, NJ: Lawrence Erlbaum Associates, 1975.

Inglish, J., & Jackson, J. E. *Research and composition: A guide for the beginning researcher.* Englewood Cliffs, N.J.: Prentice-Hall, Inc., 1977.

Johnson, R. F. Q. The experimenter attributes effect: A methodological analysis. *Psychological Record*, 1976, 26, 67–78.

Jung, J. *The experimenter's dilemma.* New York: Harper & Row, 1971.

Kahneman, D., Slovic, P., & Tversky, A. *Judgment under uncertainty: Heuristics and biases.* Cambridge: Cambridge University Press, 1982.

Kelman, H. C. The rights of the subject in social research: An analysis in terms of relative power and legitimacy. *American Psychologist*, 1972, 27, 989–1016.

Keppel, G., & Underwood, B. J. Proactive inhibition in short-term retention of single items. *Journal of Verbal Learning and Verbal Behavior*, 1962, 1, 153–161.

Kerlinger, F. N. *Foundations of behavioral research* (2nd ed.). New York: Holt, Rinehart and Winston, 1973.

Kirk, R. E. *Experimental design: Procedures for the behavioral sciences* (2nd ed.). Monterey, CA: Brooks/Cole, 1982.

Klatsky, R. L., Martin, G. L., & Kane, R. A. Semantic interpretation effects on memory for faces. *Memory & Cognition, 1982, 10,* 195–206.

Kling, J. W., & Riggs, L. A. (Eds.) *Woodworth & Schlosberg's experimental psychology* (3rd ed.). New York: Holt, Rinehart and Winston, 1971.

Krauss, R. M., & Glucksberg, S. Some characteristics of children's messages. Paper presented for delivery at the meetings of the Society for Research in Child Development, Santa Monica, California, April 1969a.

Krauss, R. M., & Glucksberg, S. The development of communication: Competence as a function of age. *Child Development,* 1969b, *40,* 255–266.

Kryter, K. D. Psychological reactions to aircraft noise. *Science,* 1966, *151,* 1346–1355.

Kulka, R. A., & Kessler, J. B. Is justice really blind?—The influence of litigant physical attractiveness on juridical judgment. *Journal of Applied Social Psychology,* 1978, *8,* 366–381.

Kunnapas, T. Scales for subjective distance. *Scandinavian Journal of Psychology,* 1960, *1,* 187–192.

Lampel, A. K., & Anderson, N. H. Combining visual and verbal information in an impression-formation task. *Journal of Personality & Social Psychology,* 1968, *9,* 1–6.

Lindzey, G., & Aronson, E. (Eds.) *The handbook of social psychology* (2nd ed.). Reading, MA: Addison-Wesley, 1968.

Loftus, E. F. Leading questions and eyewitness reports. *Cognitive Psychology,* 1975, *7,* 560–572.

Loftus, E. F., & Marburger, W. Since the eruption of Mt. St. Helens, has anyone beaten you up? Improving the accuracy of retrospective reports with landmark events. *Memory & Cognition,* 1983, *11,* 114–120.

Mackie, R. R. (Ed.). *Vigilance.* New York: Plenum Press, 1977.

Mandler, J. M., & Johnson, N. S. Remembrance of things parsed: Story structure and recall. *Cognitive Psychology,* 1977, *9,* 111–151.

Marks, L. E. *Sensory processes: the new psychophysics.* New York: Academic Press, 1974.

Masling, J. Role-related behavior of the subject and psychologist and its effects upon psychological data. In D. Levin (Ed.), *Nebraska Symposium on Motivation* (Vol. 14). Lincoln: University of Nebraska Press, 1966.

McGuinness, D. How schools discriminate against boys. *Human Nature,* February 1979, 82–88.

Menges, R. J. Openness and honesty versus coercion and deception in psychological research. *American Psychologist,* 1973, *28,* 1030–1034.

Mills, J. A procedure for explaining experiments involving deception. *Personality and Social Psychology Bulletin,* 1976, *2,* 3–13.

Mussen, P. H. (Ed.) *Carmichael's manual of child psychology* (Vols. 1 & 2). New York: John Wiley, 1970.

Myers, J. L. *Fundamentals of experimental design* (3rd ed.). Boston: Allyn and Bacon, 1979.

Neisser, U. Decision time without reaction time: Experiments in visual scanning. *American Journal of Psychology,* 1963, *76,* 376–385.

Orne, M. T. On the social psychology of the psychological experiment: With particular reference to demand characteristics and their implications. *American Psychologist,* 1962, *17,* 776–783.

Orne, M. T. Demand characteristics and the concept of quasi-controls. In R. Rosenthal & R. L. Rosnow (Eds.), *Artifact and behavioral research*. New York: Academic Press, 1969.

Parducci, A. The relativism of absolute judgments. *Scientific American*, 1968, *219*, 84–90.

Parsons, H. M. What happened at Hawthorne? *Science*, 1974, *183*, 922–932.

Pearson, K. The grammar of science. London: A. & C. Black, 1892.

Pierce, A. H. The subconscious again. *Journal of Philosophy, Psychology, and Scientific Methods*, 1908, *5*, 264–271.

Robinson, F. P. *Effective study* (4th ed.). New York: Harper & Row, 1970.

Rodriguez, R. *Hunger of memory*. Boston: David R. Godine, 1981.

Rosenberg, M. J. The conditions and consequences of evaluation apprehension. In R. Rosenthal & R. L. Rosnow (Eds.), *Artifacts in behavioral research*. New York: Academic Press, 1969.

Rosenthal, R. *Experimenter effects in behavioral research* (Enlarged ed.). New York: Halsted Press, 1976.

Rosenthal, R., & Rosnow, R. L. *The volunteer subject*. New York: Wiley, 1975.

Rubin, Z. Measurement of romantic love. *Journal of Personality and Social Psychology*, 1970, *16*, 265–273.

Runkel, P. J., & McGrath, J. E. *Research on human behavior: A systematic guide to method*. New York: Holt, Rinehart and Winston, 1972.

Schneider, W., & Shiffrin, R. M. Controlled and automatic human information processing: I. Detection, search, and attention. *Psychological Review*, 1977, *84*, 1–66.

Schofield, J. W., & Francis, W. D. An observational study of peer interaction in racially mixed "accelerated" classrooms. *Journal of Educational Psychology*, 1982, *74*, 722–732.

Semb, G. Scaling automobile speed. *Perception & Psychophysics*, 1969, *5*, 97–101.

Shepard, R. N. On subjectively optimum selection among multiattribute alternatives. In M. W. Shelly II & G. L. Bryan (Eds.), *Human judgments and optimality*. New York: Wiley, 1964.

Sherman, J. A. *Sex-related cognitive differences*. Springfield, IL: Charles C Thomas, 1978.

Silverman, I. The experimenter: A (still) neglected stimulus object. *Canadian Psychologist*, 1974, *15*, 258–270.

Smith, E. E. Relative power of various attitude change techniques. Paper presented at the meeting of the American Psychological Association, New York, September 1961.

Spradley, J. P. *The ethnographic interview*. New York: Holt, Rinehart and Winston, 1979.

Spradley, J. P. *Participant observation*. New York: Holt, Rinehart and Winston, 1980.

Stein, N. L., & Glenn, C. G. An analysis of story comprehension in elementary school children. In R. O. Freedle (Ed.), *New directions in discourse processing*. Norwood, NJ: Ablex, 1979.

Sternberg, S. Retrieval from recent memory: Some reaction-time experiments and a search theory. Psychonomic Society, Niagara Falls, August 1963.

Stevens, S. S., & Galanter, E. H. Ratio scales and category scales for a dozen perceptual continua. *Journal of Experimental Psychology*, 1957, *54*, 377–411.

Stevens, S. S., & Guirao, M. Subjective scaling of length and area and the matching of length to loudness and brightness. *Journal of Experimental Psychology*, 1963, *66*, 177–186.

Stevenson, H. W. Social reinforcement with children as a function of CA, sex of E and sex of S. *Journal of Abnormal and Social Psychology*, 1961, *63*, 147–154.

Sullivan, D. S., & Deiker, T. E. Subject-experimenter perceptions of ethical issues in human research. *American Psychologist*, 1973, *28*, 587–591.

Torgerson, W. S. *Theory and methods of scaling.* New York: Wiley, 1958.

Torgerson, W. S. Quantitative judgment scales. In H. Gulliksen & S. Messick (Eds.), *Psychological scaling.* New York: Wiley, 1960.

Tulving, E. Episodic and semantic memory. In E. Tulving & W. Donaldson (Eds.), *Organization of memory.* New York: Academic Press, 1972.

Tversky, A., & Kahneman, D. The belief in the "law of small numbers." *Psychological Bulletin,* 1971, 76, 105–110.

von Restorff, H. Über die Wirkung von Bereichsbildungen im Spurenfeld: Analyse von Vorängen im Spurenfeld. *Psychologische Forschung,* 1933, *18,* 229–342.

Wallace, W. P. Review of the historical, empirical and theoretical status of the von Restorff phenomenon. *Psychological Bulletin,* 1965, 63, 410–424.

Waugh, N. C. Free recall of conspicuous items. *Journal of Verbal Learning and Verbal Behavior,* 1969, 8, 448–456.

Webb, E. J. *Nonreactive measures in the social sciences* (2nd ed.). Boston: Houghton Mifflin, 1981.

Webb, N. M. Peer interaction and learning in cooperative small groups. *Journal of Educational Psychology,* 1982, 74, 642–655.

Weber, S. J., & Cook, T. D. Subject effects in laboratory research: An examination of subject roles, demand characteristics, and valid inference. *Psychological Bulletin,* 1972, 77, 273–295.

Wickens, D. D. Encoding categories of words: An empirical approach to meaning. *Psychological Review,* 1970, 77, 1–15.

Williamson, J. B., Karp, D. A., Dalphin, J. R., & Gray, P. S. *The research craft: An introduction to social research methods.* Boston: Little, Brown and Co., 1982.

Wittlinger, R. P. Phasic arousal in short term memory. Unpublished doctoral dissertation, Ohio State University, 1967.

Woodworth, R. S. *Experimental psychology.* New York: Holt, Rinehart and Winston, Inc., 1938.

Zimbardo, P. G. Transforming experimental research into advocacy for social change. In M. Deutsch & H. A. Hornstein (Eds.), *Applying social psychology: Implications for research, practice, and training.* Hillsdale, NJ: Lawrence Erlbaum Associates, 1975.

NAME INDEX

Adair, J. G., 50
Adams, C. K., 107
Anderson, R. C., 40
Anderson, J. R., 179
Anderson, N. H., 126, 128, 133
Argyris, C., 42
Aronson, E., 26
Asher, S. R., 199
Atkinson, J. W., 42
Atkinson, R. C., 109–111, 179

Bandura, A., 89
Barber, B., 49
Barr, R., 22
Bennett, D. H., 59
Benson, P. L., 201
Bernstein, B., 195
Berry, C., 238, 240
Binder, A., 46
Birnbaum, M. H., 125
Bjork, R. A., 237, 238
Bjorkman, M., 133
Boring, E. G., 45
Bower, G. H., 109–111, 179, 180, 184
Bramel, D., 157
Bruner, J. S., 15, 87
Buckner, D. N., 109
Burt, C., 49

Calfee, R. C., 71, 125, 126
Campbell, D., 99, 155
Campbell, D. T., 140, 155, 158
Cannell, C., 84
Cantania, A. C., 107
Carlson, R., 58
Carroll, J. B., 42
Carterette, E. C., 26
Catt, V. L., 201
Clark, E. V., 77
Clark, H. H., 77, 163
Clark, M. C., 180
Clifford, B. R., 238, 240
Cole, M., 165
Cook, T. D., 42, 43, 140, 168
Coombs, C. H., 110
Cronbach, L. J., 155
Crothers, E. J., 109–111, 179

Dale, P. S., 77
Dalphin, J. R., 81, 82, 84, 165
Dawes, R. M., 110
Deiker, T. E., 61
Dillehay, R. C., 132
Duffy, G., 22

Ebbinghaus, H., 179
Edwards, A. L., 166

Egan, J. P., 115
Elman, D., 185
Engen, T., 102

Farr, J. L., 61
Feather, N. T., 42
Fechner, G., 101
Fillenbaum, S., 42
Fleming, A., 144
Foa, E. B., 89
Fraiberg, S. H., 195
Franchis, W. D., 41
Friedman, M. P., 26
Friend, R. H., 157

Galanter, E. H., 121, 122
Gay, J., 165
Gilinsky, A. S., 135
Glenn, C. G., 79
Glick, J. A., 165
Glucksberg, S., 196–200
Goldstein, A., 89
Goldstein, M. K., 107
Goody, J., 195
Gould, S. J., 49
Gray, P. S., 81, 82, 84, 165
Grice, G. R., 224
Guirao, M., 126
Gunter, B., 238, 240

Hall, D. C., 107
Hall, J. F., 179
Hay, W. L., 178
Hearnshaw, L. S., 49
Hench, L. L., 107
Hersey, J., 129
Holmes, D. S., 59
Homans, G., 157
Hunt, E., 42

Inglish, J., 245

Jackson, J. E., 245
Jernigan, L. R., 132
Johnson, N. S., 79
Johnson, R. F. Q., 46
Jung, J., 43

Kahn, R., 84
Kahneman, D., 51
Karp, D. A., 81, 82, 84, 165
Kelman, H. C., 59
Keppel, G., 237

Kerlinger, F. N., 20, 84, 85, 87, 93–94
Killebrew, T. J., 185
Kling, J. W., 26
Krauss, R. M., 196–200
Kryter, K. D., 2
Kulka, R., 22
Kunnapas, T., 135

Lansman, M., 42
Lesgold, A. M., 180
Lindzey, G., 26
Loftus, E. F., 87, 235

Mackie, R. R., 109
McConnell, D., 46
McGrath, J. E., 58
McGrath, J. J., 109
Madden, M. C., 107
Mandler, J. M., 79
Marburger, W., 235
Marks, L. E., 119
Masling, J., 42
Menges, R. J., 58
Mills, J. A., 59
Mussen, P. H., 26

Neisser, U., 230, 231

Orne, M. T., 42, 50
Osgood, 158

Parducci, A., 130
Parsons, H. M., 157
Pearson, K., 95
Pennypacker, H. S., 107
Pierce, A. H., 43

Reynolds, R. E., 40
Riggs, C. A., 26
Robinson, F. P., 251
Rodriguez, R., 196
Rosenberg, M. J., 43
Rosenthal, R., 42, 46, 48–51
Rosnow, R. L., 42
Rubin, Z., 58
Runkel, P. J., 58

Schneider, W., 232
Schofield, J. W., 41
Seaver, W. B., 61
Semb, G., 135
Sharp, D. W., 165
Shepard, R. N., 133

Shiffrin, R. M., 232
Silverman, I., 50
Sjoholm, N. A., 46
Slovic, P., 51
Smith, E. E., 45
Spradley, J. P., 64–67, 87
Stanley, J. C., 155
Stein, G. H., 107
Stein, N. L., 79
Sternberg, S., 230, 231
Stevenson, H. W., 46
Stevens, S. S., 116, 121–124, 126
Sullivan, D. S., 61

Torgerson, W. S., 89
Tulving, E., 179
Tversky, A., 51, 110, 133

Underwood, B. J., 237

Veit, C. T., 125

Wallace, W. P., 235
Webb, E. J., 87
Webb, N. M., 40
Weber, S. J., 42, 43
Weisberg, R., 196
Wickens, D. D., 157, 237
Williamson, J. B., 81, 82, 84, 165
Winte, D. von, 22
Winzenz, D., 180
Wittlinger, R. P., 237
Woodworth, R. S., 105

Zimbardo, P. G., 59

SUBJECT INDEX

Absolute judgments, 130
Absolute threshold (detection), defined, 101
Abstracts
    described, 21–24
    research report, 248, 275
Assignment
    nonrandom, 167
    random, 164–167
Author(s), research report, 247–248
Attention, judgment and, 133–135
Automation, 51

Between-subjects designs, 173–204
    advantages and disadvantages of, 227–228
    choice of within- or, variation in a factor, 223–228
    enhancing recall through novelty as field study of memory for television news, 236–241
    factorial, see Factorial (many-way) between-subjects designs
    individual differences and, 144–146
    one-way designs as, see One-way designs
Between-subjects variation, defined, 14
Blind procedures, 157
Boundary conditions, defined, 176
"Buckle up," encouraging people to, field study, 184–187

Categorical data, 68–73
Category rating, 119, 120
Category rating task, 120
    compared with magnitude estimation, 120–126
Code of ethics, 52–55
Communication skills, development of, as example of factorial design laboratory study, 195–201
Comparative judgments, 129–130
Comparison stimulus, defined, in continuous adjustment method, 102
Complex data, collecting, 77–88
Concept learning in laboratory, 67
Condition, defined, 10
Confidentiality, 55
Confounding, experimental control of, 151–158
Constancy in experimental control, 143–144
Constitutive definitions, defined, 89
Construct validity, interpreting, 90–93
Content validity, interpreting, 91–92
Context, effects of, on judgment, 129–133
Continuous numerical data, 73–77
Continuous adjustment method of measurement, 102–106
    other methods compared with, 108–109
Control, 16
    factor, 9–10
    see also Experimental control; Measurement

Control group, and confounding, 155–156
Convenience, as advantage of within-subjects method, 223–224
Convergent evidence, 92
Correlation, statistical, 318–323
Counterbalancing, 209–210
  Latin square method of, 211
Courtroom, ethnographic method in, 65–67
Criterion measure, 91
Criterion validity, interpreting, 91

Data collecting, 63–97
  of complex data, 77–88
  ethnographic method of, 64–67
  interpretation after, 88–95
  as procedural matter, 163–164
  of simple data, 68–77
Data set, statistical description of, 300–301
Debriefing, 59–60
Deception, 58–59
Decision, see Measurement
Description in ethnographic method, 64
Design procedures, experimental control of, 162–164
Detection, see Measurement
Detection graph, 111, 112
Dialing study, 214–223
Difference threshold (discrimination), defined, 101
Discrete categorical data, 68–73
Discrimination, see Measurement
Discussion
  research report, 250
  writing, for research report, 268
Double-blind procedures, 157
Double-blind studies, 50–51
Drafts, research report, see Research reports
Driving study, 205–208

Editing, see Research reports
Equal-interval measurement, 117
Equal-interval scale, 117
Essentiality, as advantage of within-subjects method, 224–226
Ethical responsibilities, 51–62
  code of ethics and, 52–55
  at end of experiment, 59–60
  practicing, 55
  and recruiting subjects, 55–56
  in running experiment, 56–59
  subjects' views on, 60–61
Ethnographic method of data collecting, 64–67
Expectancy effects, 48–49

Experimental control, 138–172
  of confounding, 151–158
  of design procedures, 162–164
  of interaction, 158–162
  in subject selection and assignment, 164–170
  of variability, see Variability
  statistical analysis and, 306–312
Experimental designs, 8–15
Experimenters, 45–59
  behavior of, 46
  bias of, 47–51
  ethical responsibilities of, see Ethical responsibilities
  expectations of, 47–51
  interactions between subjects and, 47
Experimental design
  between-subjects variation in, 14
  factorial, 12–14
  factors in, 8–10
  levels in, 8–10
  mixed, 15
  one-way, 11–12
  as research plan, 11
  response measures in, 8, 10–11
  within-subjects variation in, 14–15
External validity, definition, 140–141
Extreme values, in simple data collection, 74–76

F-ratio, 310–311
Factorial (many-way) between-subjects designs, 187–203
  asking for money as example of, 201–203
  basic issues in planning, 188–195
  development of communication skills as example of, 195–200
Factorial designs, definition, 12–14
Factors (independent variables), definition, 8–10
False-positive errors, 177–178
Field notes in ethnographic method, 65
Field research, assignment problems in, 167
Field study, see One-way designs
Floor and ceiling limits, 191

Glossary, 329–337
Graeco-Latin square method, 214–217, 220
Grammar, in research reports, 272–273, 282–283

Handbooks, 26

Indices, described, 21–24
Individual differences, control over, 144–149
Information, integration of, from measurements, 126–135

Information integration theory, 126–129
  see also Measurement
Information-processing approach to thinking, 252–257
Information-processing theory, 6
Informed consent, 53–54
Interactions
  experimental control of, 158–162
  in factorial design, 191–195
Interference, release from proactive
  television news study, 238–241
  and von Restorff effect, 235–238
Internal validity jeopardizing, of experiment, 140–141
Interpretation, of data collected, 88–95
Interpreting findings, in research report, 247
Interval of uncertainty, definition, 104
Interviews, for collecting data, 84–86
Introduction
  research reports, 248–249
  writing, to research paper, 267
Introspection, in ethnographic method, 64
Involuntary constraint, 57

Journals, research publishing, 28

Laboratory, concept learning in, 67
Laboratory study, *see* One-way designs
Language
  nonsexist, in research report, 273–274
  public and private, 195
Language data, collecting, 77–79
Latin Square method, 210–213, 217
Lecture notes, effects of three types of university, on student achievement, sample report, 257–264
Levels, definition, 8, 10
Literature, *see* Research literature
Logarithmic measurement, 118–119
Logarithmic scale, 118–119

Magnitude estimation, 119–120
  category rating task compared with, 120–126
Materials, selection of, as procedural matter, 162–163
Maltreatment, 56–57
Measurement, 98–137
  comparison of methods of, 108–109
  continuous adjustment method of, 102–106
  integration of information from, 126–135
  psychological magnitudes, *see* Psychological magnitudes
  random presentation method of, 106–107

Measurement (*cont.*)
  signal detection theory, 109–115
  zero point and unit of, 99–101
  of zero point and unit of, for the human senses, 101–102
Memory
  enhancing recall through novelty, field study of memory for television news, 235–241
  organizational effects in, 179–184
  visual and, search, 228–235
Memory search time, 230
Methodology
  in research report, 249
  writing, for research report, 267–268
Mixed designs, 217–223
  definition, 15
  enhancing recall through novelty as field study of memory for television news, 235–241
Money, asking for, field study, 201–203

Nominal measurement, in number scales, 116–117
Nominal scale, 116–117
Nonrandom assignment, 167
Novelty, enhancing recall through, as field study of memory for television news, 235–241
Novelty effects, confounding, 156–158
Nuisance factors
  control over, 149–151
  definition, 9–10
Number scales, 116–119
Numbers, human use of, 115–116
  see also Measurement
Numerical data, 73–77

Objects, searching for, in real-world scenes, single report, 252–257
Observation, definition, 63
Observational data collecting, 86–88
One-way (single factor) designs, 173–187
  basic issues in planning, 174–179
  definition, 11–12
  encouraging people to "buckle up" as example of, 184–187
  organizational effects in memory as example of, 179–184
One-way four-level study, statistical analysis of, 311–315
Operational definition, definition, 90
Order effects, controlling for, in within-subjects design, 208–217
Ordinal measurement, 117
Ordinal scale, 117
Outline, research report, 269–270

Paired-associate learning, 139
Participation in ethnographic method, 64
Perceptual state, in Atkinson model, 110–111
Personal responsibility, 53
Placebo effect, confounding and, 156–158
Population and sample, in statistical analysis, 301–303
Power, sample size and, of experiment, 177
Precision, in single data collection, 74
Prediction, statistical, 318–323
Predictive validity, interpreting, 91
Private language, 195
Protection from harm, 54–55
Psychological constucts, interpreting, 88–90
Psychological experiments, 1–18
    experimental designs in, *see* Experimental designs
    meaning of answers gotten through, 15–17
    models in, 6–7
    role of questions in, 2–3, 7–8
    as system to test hypotheses, 3, 5
    variables in, 3–7
Psychological magnitudes, 115–126
    and human use of numbers, 115–116
    number scales, 116–119
    and psychological scaling tasks, 119–126
Psychological research, purposes of, 2
Psychological scaling tasks, 119–126
Psychological theories, 5–7
Public language, 195

Quasi-experimental designs, 168
Questionnaires, for collecting data, 79, 81–84

Random presentation method of measurement, 106–107
    other methods compared with, 108–109
Random sample
    definition, 164
    stratified, 169
Randomized-groups, designs, 173
Randomness, in subject selection and assignment, 164–66
Ratio measurement, 117
Ratio scale, 117
Recruiting subjects, 55–56
References, research report, 250, 275–276
Reliability
    interpreting data, 93–95
    statistical, 318–323
Replicational variability, definition, 140
Representative sampling, 168–170
Research literature, 19–39
    approach to, 19–21

Research literature (*cont.*)
    research reports, *see* Research reports
    varieties of, 21–26
Research reports, 26–38, 244–297
    example of editing and revising, 276–287
    examples for studying, 252–264
    final draft of, 288–296
    first draft of, 270–271
    introduction and reference sections of, 30–38
    for literature review, 27, 29–30
    preparing to write, 267–270
    revising final, 271–276
    strategy for studying, 250–252
    studying contents of, 245–252
Response measures (dependent variables), definition of, 8, 10–11
Results
    research report, 249–250
    writing, for research reports, 268
Reviews, described, 24–26

Sample and population, in statistical analysis, 301–303
Sample size
    in factorial design, 193
    in one-way design, 177–179
Scale of measurement in simple data collection, 76–77
Schneider-Shiffrin experiment, 232–235
Selection, random, 164–167
Signal detection theory, 109–115
Simple data, collecting, 68–77
Single-blind procedures, 157
Single-blind studies, 50
Social situation
    experiment as interaction between experimenter and subject(s) in, 40
    See also Experimenters; Subjects
Split-half index, 321, 323
Standard stimulus, definition, in continuous adjustment method, 102
Statistical analysis, 299–328
Statistical inferences, 304–306
Stratified random sample, 169
Style, research report, 272–273, 282–283
Subject-classification factors, 168–170
    definition of, 9
Subjective equality, point of, 104
Subjects, 40–45
    and code of ethics, *see* Ethical responsibilities
    experimental control of selection and assignment of, 164–170
    and experimenter bias, 48

Subjects (*cont.*)
    interactions between experimenters and, 47
    origins of, 41–42
    recruiting, 55–56
    types of, 42–45
    typical descriptions of, 40–41

t-statistic, 304
Task, experimental, as procedural matter, 163
Technical errors, research report, 282, 284–285
Technical revisions, research report, 273
Television news study, 238, 241
Theoretical papers, described, 24–26
Thesis statement, 245
Threshold, concept of, 101
Title, research report, 247–248, 275
Treatment factors, definition, 9
Treatment variability, definition, 140
Two-by-two factorial design, 188
    statistical analysis of, 315–316

Undergraduates, college as subjects, 42–43
Unit of measurement, *see* Measurement
Unsystematic variability
    controlling, 141–144
    definition, 140–141
    reduction in, with within-subjects method, 223

Validity, interpreting data, 90–93

Variability, 139–151
    controlling unsystematic, 141–144
    individual differences in, controlled, 144–149
    nuisance factors in, controlled, 149–151
Variable, *see* Factors
Visual and memory search, laboratory experiment, 228–235
Voluntary participation, 53–54
Von Restorff effect, 235–238

Within-subjects designs
    advantages of, 223–224
    choice of between- or, variation in as factor, 223–228
    disadvantages of, 226–237
    enhancing recall through novelty as field study of memory for television news, 235–241
    and mixed designs, 217–223
    one-way and factorial, 205–217
    visual and memory search as laboratory experiment of, 228–235
Within-subjects plan, individual differences and, 144–148
Within-subjects variation, definition, 14–15
Writing style, of research literature, 20–21

Yes-no detection task, 110–112

Zero point, *see* Measurement